Black Belt Client/Server Software Development

Practical Techniques from Master Programmers

R&D Books
Lawrence, KS 66406

R&D Books
an imprint of Miller Freeman, Inc.
1601 West 23rd Street, Suite 200
Lawrence, KS 66046
USA

Distributed in the U.S. and Canada by:
Publishers Group West
P.O. Box 8843
Emeryville, CA 94662
ISBN: 0-87930-498-7

 **Miller Freeman**
A United News & Media company

Foreward

Welcome to Black Belt Client/Server Software Development the Software Development Conference Masters Collection. This book is designed for the individual software developer or manager who needs to understand development technology that is changing at an ever increasing rate. As a application developer of some of the breakthrough products for the PC industry in the early 1980s, I was always confronted with the vexing problem of getting to market more quickly than the competition. This competitive pressure of increasingly short development cycles has been, and will probably continue to be, one of the key driving forces for application development projects.

Our collection focuses on technologies and processes that will play a significant role in giving "the advantage to the swiftest" if properly implemented.

The articles gathered here represent an accurate snapshot of the current wisdom of key developers from across the industry, with a variety of important perspectives. We begin with two overview articles on software process improvement and how Object Technology is only part of many solutions, and then delve into the such areas as Architecture driven Intranet applications, Anatomies of Intranets, and Intranet Application Development for the enterprise, all related to designing Client/Server Architectures for the next generations of computer systems.

The section on new tools and techniques for software development focuses on Process and Methodologies such as Model based development and Languages such as Java using distributed Objects across the enterprise. Another key language technology is Multithreading for Client/Server based architectures using C++. Other areas covered are C++ Object Persistence with Client /Server and Relational Databases, Future

Language developments in a Multi tier architecture using MFC DAO vs. MFC ODBC or OLE. We also provide an analysis on how to leverage Object Oriented Technologies such as tools for building distributed databases, Full Life Cycle OO Testing, and a practical approach to OO User Interface Design

Database Development for the Enterprise is a key concern for 90s companies and we offer three topics for your consideration; Building a Highly Scalable Data Warehouse, an analysis of the leading database vendors " Oracle vs Sybase vs Informix" and managing non-relational data. More and more applications developers are facing the task of managing non-relational date, e.g. in health care -- when tracking such objects as Xrays, Sonographs, medical charts, etc. The book ends with a focus on the Building of Open and Distributed Systems, which seems to be an unstoppable paradigm. David Linthicum's paper on "Selecting Distributed Objects" explores the benefits and perils of embracing standards.

As you will see upon closer inspection of this collection, it really does focus on the state of the art technology that is driving application development by the industry leaders today. I hope that this book will stimulate your interest in these technologies enough to get involved to the point that (to paraphrase a Silicon Valley area news commentator, by the name of Scoop Nisker) "If you don't like what's happening in Client/Server Technology today, go out and invent some of your own."

Dave Burleigh
Fall 1997 - San Francisco

Table of Contents

ix

Chapter 17   *A Practical Approach to Object-Oriented*
                  UI Design *269*
                  Dick Berry, Dave Roberts, Scott Isensee, and John Mullaly

Chapter 18   *Building a Highly Scalable Data Warehouse*. *283*
                  Ken Rudin

Chapter 1

Software Process Improvement: 10 Traps to Avoid

Karl E. Wiegers

(This paper was originally published in *Software Development*, May 1996. It is reprinted with permission from *Software Development* magazine.)

Surviving in the increasingly competitive software business requires more than hiring smart, knowledgeable engineers and buying the latest development tools. You also need to use effective software development processes, so those smart engineers can systematically use the best technical and managerial practices to successfully complete their projects. More organizations are looking at software process improvement as a way to improve the quality, productivity, and predictability of their software development, acquisition, and maintenance efforts. However, software process improvement efforts can be derailed in many ways, leaving the members of the organization jaded, frustrated, and more committed than ever to the ways of the past.

Here are 10 common traps that can undermine a software process improvement program. Learning about these process improvement killers — and their symptoms and solutions — will stop them from bringing your initiative to its knees.

Trap #1: Lack of Management Commitment

Symptoms: While individual groups can improve the way they do their work through grass roots efforts, sustainable changes across an organization require management commitment at all levels. Senior managers may claim to support process improvements (how can they say otherwise?), but they may not really be willing to make short-term sacrifices to free up the resources required for the long-term investment. Larger organizations must establish alignment between senior management and one or more layers of mid-managers.

If you're leading the software process improvement effort, you might obtain senior management commitment, but get pushback from middle managers. In this case you'll be forced to spend time and energy debating the importance of software process improvement with people who should only have to be educated, not sold.

Such mixed signals from management make it hard for team leaders and software developers to take the effort seriously. Watch out for lip service and buzzwords masquerading as commitments. Lower-level managers who assign their least capable people (or none at all) to the program are sending a clear sign that the lack of management commitment is about to foil your effort.

Solutions: Managers at all levels need to send consistent signals about software process improvement to their constituencies. Executives must be educated about the costs, benefits, and risks so they will have a common vision and understanding of this complex area of software development. Commitments need to be aligned along the organizational hierarchy, so that managers are not working at cross purposes, and a reluctant manager cannot sabotage the effort through inaction. Make sure that commitments from management translate into resources devoted to software process improvement, realistically defined expectations of the process group and the engineering staff, and accountability for the results.

Management commitment to software process improvement also affects the morale and dedication of people who are working to advance the cause of better processes in the organization. When management objectives change with the wind and the staff devoted to facilitating process improvement is downsized, those affected may be embittered at having months or years of their technical careers sidetracked for nothing. Once burned in such a fashion, they may be reluctant to step forward the next time the organization is looking for people to enable change.

Trap #2: Unrealistic Management Expectations

Symptoms: Excessive enthusiasm by ambitious managers can also pose risks to the improvement program. If the goals, target dates, and results expected by managers are not realistic, the software process improvement effort is ultimately set up for failure.

Managers, particularly those with little software experience, may not appreciate the effort and time involved in a large-scale software process improvement effort, such as one based on the Software Engineering Institute's five-level Capability Maturity Model^{SM} (CMM^{SM}).* These managers may be confused about how process improvement frameworks like the CMM relate to other software engineering approaches, such as a specific object-oriented methodology. They may focus on issues of pressing importance to them that are not realistic outcomes of the process improvement effort. For example, a manager may hope to solve current staff shortages by driving the organization to reach CMM Level 2, which typically leads to higher software productivity and quality. However, since it can take two years or more to reach Level 2, this is not an effective solution to near-term staffing problems.

Management needs to understand that the behavioral changes and organizational infrastructure that are parts of a successful software process improvement program cannot be mandated or purchased. Catchy slogans like "Level 5 by '95" or "Six Sigma by '96" are not constructive. In an unhealthy competitive environment, process improvement can become a contest: Department A sets an objective of achieving CMM Level 3 by the end of 1997, so the head of Department B says that they can do it by the middle of 1997. With rare exceptions, such behavior is neither inspiring nor motivating.

Solutions: Educate your managers to help them to understand the realities of what a serious process improvement initiative will cost and what benefits they might expect. Collect data from the software literature on results that have been achieved by other companies with effective improvement programs and the investments those companies made over a specified time period. Every organization is different, so it is risky to promise an eight-fold return from each dollar invested just because you read that some company actually achieved that level of success. Use data available from the software literature or from other areas of your own company to help your managers develop realistic expectations and set reasonable, even ambitious, goals. Software process improvement is no more of a magic silver bullet than any other single software tool or technology.

Trap #3: Time-Stingy Project Leaders

Symptoms: When a senior manager states that he or she is committed to improving the software processes used in the organization, most project leaders will say that they are, too — whether they mean it or not. However, successful software process improvement initiatives require project leaders to adjust their project schedules to permit team members to devote some time to improvement activities. A project leader

---

* ^{SM} Capability Maturity Model and CMM are service marks of Carnegie Mellon Institute.

who claims to believe in software process improvement but who treats it as a burden added on top of the project activities is sending conflicting signals.

Even if team members are permitted to work on improvement tasks, these tasks often get low priority, and "real work" can easily squeeze process improvement activities out of a busy engineer's schedule. Project leaders may respond to the pressure of delivering the current product by curtailing the effort that should go into upgrading the organization's process capability.

Solutions: You need to have consistent, active commitment at all stages of management; a bottleneck anywhere in the organizational hierarchy can bring the software process program to a screeching halt. One way to achieve consistency is through an interlocking management commitment process as a corporate or organizational policy. Top managers publicly state their goals and priorities (including software process improvement), and people at the lower management levels write their goals and priorities to support those of their superiors.

Senior management must make it clear that project leaders will be evaluated on the effectiveness of their process improvement activities, as well as on the success of the software projects themselves. Software project planning needs to account for the staff resources that are being devoted to design and implement the new software processes. In small organizations with shallow management hierarchies, the first-level manager is the most critical factor in the success of any process improvement effort. If this person doesn't make software process improvement a visible priority, it just isn't going to happen.

One way to keep a program viable is to treat all software process improvement activities as mini-projects, to give them the visibility and legitimacy they need for success. Write an action plan for each mini-project. This plan identifies resources, states timelines, itemizes deliverables, clarifies accountability, and defines techniques to assess the effectiveness of new processes implemented as a result of each mini-project.

The need to treat improvement activities with the respect afforded to technical projects does not require extensive documentation; most action plans can be written in just one or two pages. Don't try to solve every process problem in your group at once. Instead, concentrate on the two or three top priority items, as determined through some process assessment mechanism, then tackle the next three, and so on down the line.

Project leaders can't just assign their least effective people to the software process improvement efforts, either. We all want to keep our best people working on technical projects. However, if good people and respected leaders are not active contributors, the process improvement outputs generated will have less credibility with the rest of the organization.

Trap #4: Stalling on Action Plan Implementation

Symptoms: Action plans might be written after a process assessment, but little progress is made on them because management does not make them a clear priority, assign individuals to work on them, or otherwise take them seriously. Managers may never mention the action plans after they are written, so team members get the message that achieving improved processes by implementing the action plans is really not important. The lack of progress on improvement plans is frustrating to those who actually want to see progress made, and it devalues the investment of time and money made in the process assessment itself.

Solutions: As with Trap #3, a good way to turn action plans into actions is to treat improvement activities as mini-projects. Concentrating on just two or three improvement areas at a time avoids overwhelming the project team. You need to measure progress against the plans and to measure the impact of each action plan on the business results achieved. For example, a plan to improve the effectiveness of unit testing performed by the programmers might include an interim goal to acquire test automation tools and train developers in their use. These interim goals can be tracked easily. The desired business outcome of such an action plan should be a specific quantitative reduction, over some period of time, in the number of defects that slip through the unit testing quality filter.

If your project leaders never seem to make much progress against their action plans, you may need to implement a management oversight function to encourage them to take software process improvement more seriously. For example, in a particular organization I know of, all project leaders must report the status of their action plans every three months to a multilevel management steering committee. When this occurs, no one wants to be embarrassed by reporting little or no progress on his or her plans.

From one perspective, such periodic reporting reflects appropriate management accountability for the commitments that people have made to improve their software processes. From another, this approach represents a "big stick" strategy for enforcing software process improvement, which is best avoided unless action plans simply are not being implemented. Your culture will determine the most effective techniques for driving action plans to completion. The management oversight approach did achieve the desired effect in the aforementioned organization.

Trap #5: Achieving a CMM Level Becomes the Primary Goal

Symptoms: Organizations that adopt the CMM framework for process improvement risk viewing attainment of a specific CMM maturity level as the goal of the process improvement, rather than as one mechanism to help achieve the organization's real business goals. Software process improvement energy may be focused on a race to the Level N rating, when some energy should perhaps be devoted to other problem areas that can contribute quickly to the quality, productivity, people, and management issues facing the organization.

Sometimes, a company is in such a rush to reach the next maturity level that the recently implemented process improvements have not yet become well established and habitual. In such cases, the organization might actually regress back to the previous maturity level, rather than continue to climb the maturity ladder as it is attempting to do. Such regression is a surefire way to demoralize practitioners who are eager to move steadily toward a superior software engineering culture.

Solutions: In addition to aiming at the next CMM level, make sure your software process improvement effort is aligned with corporate business and technical objectives. Mesh the process improvement activities with any other improvement initiatives that are underway, such as ISO 9001 registration, or with an established software development framework already in use. Recognize that advancing to the next CMM maturity level can take one to three years. It is not feasible to leap from an initial ad hoc development process to a super-sophisticated engineering environment in one fell swoop. Your goal is not to be able to chant, "We're Level 5! We're Level 5!" Your goal is to develop improved software processes and more capable development engineers so that your company can prosper by offering higher quality products to your customers more efficiently than before.

Use a combination of measurements to track progress toward the business goals as well as measure the progress of the software process improvement program. Goals can include reducing project cycle times and product defect levels. One way to track software process improvement progress is to perform low-cost interim assessments to check the status of your project teams in various CMM key process areas (such as requirements management, project planning, and software configuration management). Over time, you should observe steady progress toward satisfying both CMM key process area goals and your company's software success factors. This is the outcome of a well-planned and well-executed program.

Trap #6: Inadequate Training Is Provided

Symptoms: A process improvement initiative is at risk if the developers, managers, and process leaders do not have adequate skills and training. Each person involved must understand the general principles of software process improvement, the CMM and other pertinent software process improvement methodologies, change leadership, software measurement, and related areas.

Inadequate knowledge can lead to false starts, well-intentioned but misdirected efforts, and a lack of apparent progress. This can undermine the improvement effort. Without training, the organization's members will not have a common vocabulary and understanding of how to assess the need for change or how to interpret specialized concepts of the improvement model being followed, such as the CMM or ISO 9001. For example, "software quality assurance" means different things to different people; training is needed to achieve a common understanding of such terms among all participants.

Solutions: Training to support established process improvement frameworks can be obtained from various commercial sources (such as process improvement consultants or training vendors), or you can develop such training yourself. Different participants in the software process improvement activities will need different kinds of training. If you are using a CMM-based approach, the process improvement group members should receive two to three days of training on the CMM. However, four hours of training about software process improvement using the CMM will be enough for most participants.

If you become serious about software process improvement, consider acquiring training in other key software improvement domains: setting up a software engineering process group (SEPG), establishing a metrics program, assessing the process capability of a project team, and action planning. Use commercial sources of training wherever possible. This way you avoid having to create all of your own training materials.

Trap #7: Expecting Defined Procedures to Make People Interchangeable

Symptoms: Managers who have an incomplete understanding of the CMM may expect that having repeatable processes available (CMM Level 2) means that every project can expect to achieve the same results with any set of randomly assembled team members. They may think that the existence of a defined process in the organization makes all software engineers equally effective. They might even believe that working on software process improvement means that they can neglect technical training to enhance the skills of their individual software engineers.

Solutions: Individual programmers have been shown to have a 10-to-1, 20-to-1, or even higher range of performance (quality and productivity) on software projects. Process improvements alone can never equalize such a large range of individual capability. You can close the gap quite a bit by expecting people to follow effective defined processes, rather than using whatever methods they are used to. This will enable people at the lower end of the capability scale to achieve consistently better results than they might get otherwise. However, never underestimate the importance of attracting, nurturing, and rewarding the best software engineers and managers you can find. Aim for software success by creating an environment in which all team members share a commitment to quality and are enabled — through superior processes, appropriate tools, and effective team interactions — to reach their peak performance.

As you chart a course to improve your software process capability, be aware of the many minefields lurking below your organization's surface. Your chances of success increase dramatically if you watch for the symptoms that identify these traps as a threat to your software process improvement program and make plans to deal with them right away. Process improvement is succeeding at many companies. Make yours one of them, by controlling these risks — and others — as well as you can.

Trap #8: Failing to Scale Formal Processes to Project Size

Symptoms: A small organization can lose the spirit of the CMM (or any other process model) while attempting to apply the model to the letter, introducing excessive documentation and formality that can actually impede project work. This undermines the credibility of software process improvement, as team members look for ways to bypass the official procedures in an attempt to get their work done efficiently. People are reluctant to perform tasks they perceive as adding little value to their project.

Solutions: To reach a specific CMM maturity level, you must demonstrate that your organization is satisfying all of the goals of each key process area defined at that maturity level and at lower levels. The process definitions your group develops should be no more complicated or elaborate than they need to be to satisfy these goals. Nothing in the CMM says that each procedure must be lengthy or documented in excessive detail. Strive for a practical balance between documenting procedures with enough formality to enable repeatable project successes, and having the flexibility to get project work done with the minimum amount of low-value overhead effort.

This nondogmatic view doesn't mean that smaller organizations and projects cannot benefit from the discipline provided by the CMM. It simply means that the practices recommended by the CMM should be scaled rationally to the size of the project. A 20-hour project should not demand eight hours of project planning just to conform to a CMM-compliant "documented procedure." Your process improvement action teams should provide a set of scalable processes that can be applied to the various sizes and types of projects your group undertakes.

Trap #9: Process Improvement Becomes a Game

Symptoms: Yet another way that software process improvement can falter is when the participants pay only lip service to the real objective of improving their processes. It creates the illusion of change while actually sticking with business as usual for the most part. The focus is on making sure a process audit is passed, rather than on really changing the culture of the organization for the better. Software process improvement looks like the current flavor of the month, so group members just wait for this latest fad to pass so they can get back to working in their old familiar ways. Sometimes, the quest for ever-higher process maturity levels becomes a race. Project teams go through the appropriate motions in an attempt to satisfy some aspect of the CMM, but time is not provided for the group to really internalize the corresponding behaviors before management sets its sights on the next CMM maturity level.

Solutions: To succeed with software process improvement, focus on meeting organizational and company objectives with the help of improved software processes. Do not simply try to conform to the expectations of an established framework like the CMM, ISO 9001, or the Malcolm Baldrige quality award. It is not enough to simply create documented procedures to satisfy the letter of some improvement framework; you must also satisfy the spirit of the framework by actually following those procedures in your daily project work.

The CMM talks about institutionalizing process improvements, making new practices routine across the organization. Organization members must also internalize improved procedures, becoming committed enough to the new processes that they would not consider going back to their old ways of building software. As a process change leader, identify the behaviors you would expect to see throughout the organization in each improvement area if superior processes are successfully internalized and institutionalized. As a manager, your group members need to understand that you are serious about continually striving to improve the way they build software; the old methods are gone for good. Continuous improvement means just that, not a one-shot game we play so that someone's checklist can be filled in properly.

Trap #10: Process Assessments are Ineffective

Symptoms: If process capability assessments (often led by the SEPG) are conducted without adequate participation by the software development staff, they turn into audits. This can lead to a lack of commitment, buy-in, and ownership of the assessment findings by the project team. Assessment methods that depend solely on the responses to a CMM-based questionnaire can overlook important problem areas that should be addressed. Outside "experts" who purport to identify your group's process weaknesses based on insufficient practitioner input will have little credibility with your technical staff.

Solutions: Process change is a cultural change, and the ease of this cultural change depends on the extent of the team's involvement with the process assessment and action planning activities. Include a free-form discussion with a representative group of project team members as part of the assessment process whenever time permits. This discussion can identify problem areas that might relate to CMM practices that were not covered by an assessment questionnaire, but which can still be profitably addressed. For example, software testing is not addressed by Level 2 of the CMM, but if poor testing practices are hurting a project in a Level 1 organization, you should do something about that soon. Similarly, topics may come up in a project team discussion that are not part of the CMM at all, including management or organizational issues, lack of resources for acquiring tools, and so forth.

Use your SEPG to actively facilitate the change efforts of your project teams, not just to audit their current process status and report a long, depressing list of findings. Identify process liaisons or champions in the project teams to augment the assessment activities of the process group. Those process liaisons can also help drive effective changes into the project team's behaviors and technical practices. The project team must understand that the SEPG is doing software process improvement with the members of the project team, not for them or to them.

Bibliography

Carnegie Mellon University/Software Engineering Institute. *The Capability Maturity Model: Guidelines for Improving the Software Process*. Reading, Mass.: Addison-Wesley, 1995.

Tom DeMarco and Timothy Lister. *Peopleware: Productive Projects and Teams*. New York: Dorset House Publishing, 1987.

Steve Maguire. *Debugging the Development Process*. Redmond, Wash.: Microsoft Press, 1994.

Watts S. Humphrey. *Managing the Software Process*. Reading, Mass.: Addison-Wesley, 1989.

Gerald M. Weinberg. *Quality Software Management: Systems Thinking*, Vol. 1. New York: Dorset House Publishing, 1992.

Karl E. Wiegers. *Creating a Software Engineering Culture*. New York: Dorset House Publishing, 1996.

Chapter 2

Requirements Engineering with Use Cases

Cecilia Haskins

While many industries have given special attention to requirements capture as a necessary phase for successful project management, software developers have been slow to grasp the significance of this step. Increased awareness of the value of requirements has opened the question of how to best capture requirements in a manner that integrates them into the lifecycle and ensures their usefulness and use. This author proposes use cases as a technique for requirements engineering for projects using object-oriented techniques.

The Importance Of Creating Requirements

Requirements are, very simply, the expression of what the users need from the system. However, they begin to provide other benefits once they exist. When requirements are well defined they contribute to the collective understanding of what will be delivered in the system. If not actually tied to a formal contract, they still serve as a tacit contract between users and developers.

When requirements have been written down, they can be validated, prioritized, analyzed for completeness and consistency, refined, and tracked. Requirements form a basis for system verification before the user accepts delivery of the product. They provide an appropriate starting point for change management throughout a software application lifecycle. In essence they have a life of their own!

User-Centered Analysis

At the crux of the decision to focus project resources on the task of requirements engineering is the benefits derived from a body of properly defined requirements; namely, building the right solution and building the solution right. Without a requirements baseline, neither of these assessments can be made objectively.

Object oriented techniques have improved the opportunities of practitioners to perform requirements capture from the viewpoint of the user. One of the advantages is the relative simplicity of diagramming notations used for communication. A project team's biggest decision is choosing the development process and forms of communication that will support the process.

Even prior to the OMG initiatives in OAD, there was a growing consensus among OO methodologists that the use case concept is important. And use cases allow the project team to shield the user from the nitty-gritty of object modeling details.

Analysis/Synthesis Methods

Use Cases and Scripts for Requirements Capture

Use cases support the concept of capturing a contract. If you begin by interviewing users, you are interviewing them in the first person which means that most of what you gather are more along the lines of concrete examples — of perhaps how someone actually does their job. The goal at this stage is to not lose that information. Then review the body of accumulated interviews for the possibility of generalizing to an expectation for a use case of this system. Just as you refine the interviews into abstractions from the concrete examples, what you want to do then, is further refine your understanding of the case and work though various conditions and success criteria. As you layer your understanding of the system, you reach a point where you are ready to really look at the interactions. Rather than capturing what some authors call a scenario, this author will use the term "script," with a definition closer to an OBA script than to a scenario.

You have completed this phase when you have a problem definition that establishes the boundaries of the system domains and suggests some categorization for further analysis. It is very important to find some way to begin an initial partitioning, even at the use case level.

Building Use Cases

The focus of the interviewing activity is understanding the expected behavior of your system. What you are looking for is to understand an overview and the basic mission of this system being designed. All your users really can tell you is what their personal

Table 2.1   Purposes of use cases.
Define functional requirements
Communicate with End-users and Customers
Design the User Interface
Derive Objects
Define Test Cases
Estimate project size and resources
Capture and trace requirements
Delimit a system
Determine development increments
Compose user documentation and manuals

Table 2.2   Remember these use case guidelines.
Do
Retain user's language as this is the way they will express changes
Clarify inconsistencies
Simplify the number of interacting actors in a single Use Case
Look for opportunities for abstraction
Don't
Write "War & Peace" in one Use Case
Introduce solutions in the description
Focus solely on data without behavior
Forget to identify possible exceptions in successful exchanges

expectations are on the system. So in fact you are writing use cases that essentially are looking at "What sort of stimulus do I think I need to give to this system to request what I want?" and "What sort of response do I expect to come back?" One note of warning: Often a user's "input" for a request is information provided by the system earlier. Uncover these situations during your validation of the sequences of behaviors or they may have adverse affects on your class definitions during object modeling.

The big challenge with use cases is "How to write them." There are many suggested techniques. If your intention is to eventually manage these as a requirements baseline, then this author suggests that you write your use cases very compactly and as close to one sentence as possible. The concept here is that you are looking for a succinct expression of your understanding at any given level. What you are going to see is a real explosion and propagation of use cases. The implications will be discussed in more detail.

The next step is to analyze these cases and look for opportunities to create abstraction from the concrete cases collected. What you are looking for with abstraction is to understand an overview and the basic mission of the system being designed. Abstraction also contributes to the better management of the use cases. If it does not make sense to abstract, do not. Most people find this analysis and forcing themselves into some discipline up front is an extremely valuable practice.

Generally your set of primary or external actors is limited, and their interactions themselves can be summarized into single use cases. In extremely sophisticated or complex systems, this may be a category of actor. If a single primary actor does a broad range of interactions, you might have that single primary actor as the stimulus or trigger for a number of use cases; again this is a value judgment that must be done by analysis. In fact, these broad categories of interactions start to suggest your high level use cases.

Use Case Hierarchies

With use cases you are looking at the behavior of the system — what is it that the system is achieving. You begin by looking at a high-level set of interactions or behaviors that are implicated by the statement of work to be done to meet this stimulus/response requirement at any particular point. Assume a nontrivial problem. You want to create an environment in which you delegate a body of these nontrivial behaviors to be further described in the next hierarchy of your use cases.

The significance of this hierarchy is the concept of expressing delegations without the overhead of saying "I'm the use case that happens before this other one," etc., and having to embed control behaviors in each use case. It is much too easy to lose a real context of the kind of control mechanisms that are necessary to be built into your systems without a control level of use cases for describing a behavior sequence. At the high level a triggering actor is a primary actor. As you progress down the hierarchy, repeat this process: either where a use case is trivial enough that it is suitable as a stopping point, or where a use case is still not quite trivial enough. The reason to do this is to create use cases that are not too complex for managing. In fact what you really want to have as a potential goal is to define use cases to the point that they are encapsulating single behaviors, not quite interaction, but certainly behavior in terms of perhaps either a unique stimulus/response or a set of very closely related stimulus/responses that involve an actor.

The real issue in analysis is the number of hierarchy levels that you're supporting. The trade-off is that if you do not define your use cases in sufficient detail, you've just delayed the definition explosion to the script. If you delay, the implications are that you will find the building of scenarios, and/or the building of scripts very tedious — much more tedious than the building of use cases. Remember you're still in a natural language view with use cases; you're still talking warm and fuzzy words that end-users use. In scripts you would start defining modes of success and failure within a structure that's still only semiformal, but nonetheless much more precise. Remember, the whole point of scripts is an attempt to reduce ambiguity. This author suggests that some of this discipline be inverted. It becomes a question of what do you want to explode? Do you want to explode script/scenarios or do you want to explode use cases?

As a stopping rule, if you believe that the next use case level would truly be fairly trivial, you are probably at the ending of use case definition and ready to start to talk at the interaction or scripting level. It's a judgment call at what point you think that now you're really much closer to an interaction description than a high-level behavior. One question to ask is "Are you still talking about behaviors in terms of sequences of things that can be done that are fairly important in their own right, or are you talking about things that need done like sending a message."

Building Scripts

At this point, your actors have been defined in use cases as users of system capabilities. Now, you want to capture their related activity in scripts. With scripts you will use a method closer to OBA than scenarios in that it's not completely formal, but it is more structured. The scripting concept is that you start to analyze the interactions that are intended to be understood from the natural language text. In the early analysis phase you have taken the problem and expanded it quite extensively. It is very important to then move into synthesis and look for collaborating actors who themselves begin to suggest additional objects for your design. Collaborating actors are sometimes identifiable during use case diagramming.

The major point of this task is that you want to maximize the very important value-added feature of identifying variations which start to describe exception behaviors, failure modes, reconstruction, etc. Scripting allows you to encapsulate this work for purposes of traceability.

What starts to evolve from the scripting mechanism is much more of an idea about what are the internal mechanisms and internal actors of the system to be designed.

We're now at a set of secondary actors. Their names are still expressed in terms that an end-user might even be able to validate for you, but you begin to get inside the workings of the system itself. Scripting also helps to build up a body of services attributable to the secondary actors. What ends up happening when you're all done is you've got a set of actors now that not only represent primary actors, you also have actors that in fact represent services actually being provided by your system. This is very valuable because this tends to be what you're really trying to understand in moving toward being prepared for design. Scripting is the answer to the "and then a miracle happens" gap between analysis and design.

Partitioning

With the propagation of use cases, it is very valuable to partition your problem domain from an end-user view. If end-users look at a body of use cases that have been accumulated by your arbitrary sorting as belonging to a partition and they say "Why are you talking about this here?" that is a good clue that your partitioning is probably not quite right yet. The advantage of not trying to prepartition your problem domain is that even if the list of use cases gets very long, it gives you a good validation point.

While the quality of the use cases depends on the maturity of your sources of information and your interviewees and IS department personnel who are involved, the use cases at the first level may in fact be a good initial partitioning. As a rule of thumb, your partitioning strategy should align with your work flow assignments.

One possible exception is a system being modeled close enough to the core business so that it implies some BPR. When use cases are used this way, it seems to become a common practice to have "before" (as is) use cases and "after" (to be) use cases, separated either by different partitions or by naming conventions. In some instances, project teams use the use case to actually capture the interviewing results. It is very important to them to know precisely what was said by these various users as they were describing both the work they do and their hypothesis of how they believe computing will help them. They will have a partition that will keep those separate from use cases that are later used to capture requirements.

Validation

Essentially what happens during analysis is that you have this large body of actors and their corresponding services. Up to now you have been dealing in end-user language, and that is very appropriate because you'd like to stay as close to a validation language as you possibly can in working with your end-users; so in all probability you have collected some synonyms. One of the very first things you do with the body of actors is you establish a glossary that says, "This actor is really an alias for some other term that I have captured essentially responsible for an equivalent set of services!" There may be some overlap, there may be some uniqueness, and so you can build a glossary both from the actors and their related services. Actors can be propagated as objects into the object model for traceability.

Theoretically you have what should be a fairly well thought out set of classes available for design. If you are in a corporate culture where there is some sense of a throwing analysis results over a wall, and we do all know that that still exists, the team that takes the hand-off has something to go back to say "why do you think I need a class with this kind of name?" And they can actually go into analysis results and say "Oh, that is because this class name really is this actor participating in this set of use cases" and the use cases with their scripts begin to suggest what type of behaviors and attributes need to be accounted for during object modeling.

Graphical views are supported by use case diagramming. The value of the use case diagram is that there are real visual clues on this diagram. If you choose partitioning schemes for your use cases that are too complex, your actor interactions reflect that complexity. Either one actor is triggering too many use cases, or the same actor is needed in too many locations. There may be something about your initial partitioning to describe behavior that is not practical. The author suggests as a criteria that your primary actors tend to have minimal numbers of interfaces for triggering purposes and if you can accumulate the use case behavior, they'll have a tendency to group very nicely for diagram purposes. Basically, "ugly" is not a guarantee that you're wrong, but it's a good clue that you should look more carefully at the partitions. And "pretty" is not a guarantee that you're right, but it has a better chance.

Summary

In performing requirements engineering you are looking to understand the basic mission of the system being designed. Over time, a complete set of use cases should be expected to capture the definition of the functional requirements of the system. With the added inputs from scripting, a first set of objects emerges for use in design and traceability between the phases. Hence, as the application matures and the users eventually ask for changes, the use case is the starting point for managing the operations and maintenance phases of the software lifecycle.

However, many other valuable features come to light during the development of use cases. Users often provide clear insights into their preferences for human factors issues that can be captured in the use case. The use case becomes the boundary for creating test cases for user acceptance, and if they feel some ownership for the content of the use case, this provides a truly objective criteria for project acceptance. Likewise, user documentation and manuals can be written based on the information provided in use cases.

Communication is generally one of the biggest challenges to a corporate organization. Use cases provide a mechanism that is acceptable to the technical staff, yet understandable by the end-users.

Project managers will find that an evaluation of the use cases will offer a reliable basis for the estimation of project size and resources needed. Partitioning allows the manager to determine reasonable development increments and properly scope deliveries.

One final note: Many requirements of a system are nonfunctional. These are the quantifiable measures of "how often," "how many," "how fast," etc. A mechanism for maintaining and linking these requirements to their functional counterparts should be considered as part of this exercise.

Chapter 3

From Design to Implementation: Facilitating Project Success

William R. Dodson

About 95 percent of information-technology application issues involve power and organization, not technology. Since these issues are largely political, start to work through them now because they're on the 'critical path' for implementation.
—Tom Peters

Organizations are learning that successful projects depend on coordination much more than any other single factor.
—Peter Senge

Now more than ever before in the short history of software development there are more individuals, interests, personalities, agendas, constraints, and directives involved in the success of software product design and implementation efforts. The compressed timetables of projects and the greater expectations for system functionality have forced the definition of project success to a new dimension that dramatically roots projects in the culture, politics, and personalities of the organization.

Key to realizing project success is a facilitator working at every stage of systems development who can orchestrate, focus, and coordinate the often conflicting forces that shape IS efforts: during the design phase of an IS project a facilitator can guide the different visions of managers, staff, and systems engineers to consensus through the Joint Application Design (JAD) process. And during construction and systems integration the facilitator as Implementation Coordinator can be the project manager's ally in overcoming corporate communications barriers, political land mines, and resistance to change.

The Classical Definition of Project Success

The classical definition of project success involves the project being on time, within budget, and per specification. These dimensions of project success also serve as the constraints of a project; that is, a project cannot exceed a predefined budget and still be a success; nor a certain time frame; nor a set of functionality (Figure 3.1).

Combined, these constraints define the classical definition of the scope of the project. The scope of the project is often considered the area within a triangle, wherein each of the edges of the triangle represents in turn the budget, the timetable, and the functionality of the project. This is the domain of the classical project manager. Typically, the project manager was most concerned with keeping the project within its predetermined budget, within the time frame that upper management declared, and with all the functionality the Information Systems (IS) felt was necessary.

Traditionally, most, if not all, of the functionality of a system was approximated, established, and declared solely by IS. An IS department's experience with a particular business process also came from within IS: the project manager would declare that the Human Resources (HR) department would have to hire a systems designer from outside who had experience with the new system IS was developing. The new hire would know the functionality the system required because of his previous experience on another HR systems project. In this way, the project manager could reduce, if not completely eliminate, the need for end-user input. The lack of "confusion" end-user input would cause would help the project manager keep the scope of the project as close to the original vision as possible; hence, project success.

How is it then that a project that meets the strict constraints laid out above could still have been considered a failure?

Project failure arises in this context when technical experts solely define the budget, timetable, and specifications for a project in a vacuum, devoid of the input of the customers who will be using their product or service. The definition of the success of a project must then be extended to include customer satisfaction.

Who Is the Customer?

The greatest advantage of high-structure projects like Payroll and Accounts Receivable for IS was the Great Known: you knew who you had to deal with in the organization and how to deal with him or her. Communications channels were a given. As well, the glass of the glass house in which IS worked was reinforced glass. It was difficult for users to breach the undeniable authority and defenses of IS.

Now, with low-structure client-server projects more the rule than the exception, IS has had to come out of its ramparts and deconstruct those defenses that had so ably kept the masses of end-users at bay. Technologies, business needs, end-user requests are happening too quickly for IS to refer to its departmental oracle to divine (and then to direct) what systems end-users and management need and how those systems should work.

Hence the inevitable drive for IS toward a customer orientation; that is, the customer knows what the customer wants and it is the seller's (i.e., IS's) responsibility to satisfy the customer by finding out what the customer needs. However, IS has more

Figure 3.1

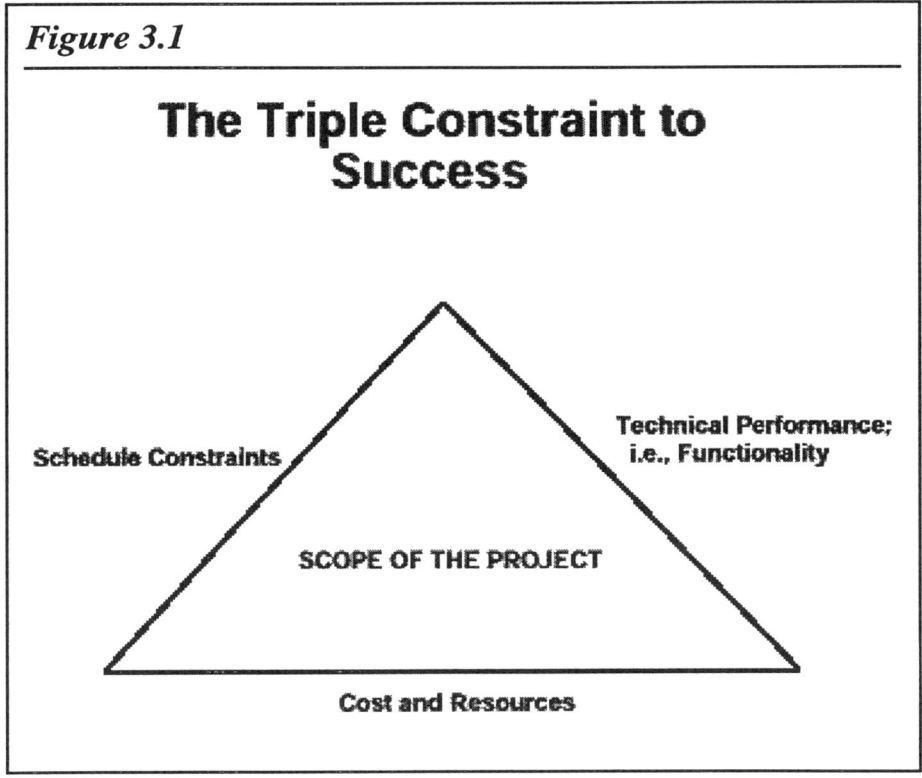

The Triple Constraint to Success

Schedule Constraints

Technical Performance; i.e., Functionality

SCOPE OF THE PROJECT

Cost and Resources

than one customer within an organization, and each of these customers must be included in projects that affect them or their standing within the organization. And IS must identify and include these customers from the outset of the project for the project to be successful. IS's customers, explicit and hidden include:

- The End-User
- The Department or Division Head
- The Controller
- Upper Management

The end-user is an important customer precisely because of the level of detail in which she is immersed. Often, she has actual contact with the organization's final customer, the consumer of the company's product or service. The challenge project managers have with the end-user as customer is that her knowledge and experience is highly internalized. A substantial portion of the project duration must be spent in drawing out and rationalizing the end-user's work.

The department or division head is a very important customer not only for the valuable insights her position lends, but also for her authority. This authority has two levels: the authority to organize and direct her staff — the end-users — and the authority to negotiate system interfaces with other department or division heads. Without this authority, communications structures within low-structure projects cannot be built and maintained.

The Controller or CFO has to be considered a prime customer in the project because she holds the purse strings on the project. Ultimately, if the project does not address the bottom line upon which so many CFO's focus, the project will not be considered a success at best — or will be cancelled at worst. Either way, subsequent funding and backing for future projects will be hard won.

Finally, project facilitators must include upper management as customers from the inception of the project. Without upper management's explicit vision or strategy for the organization rationalized, the project can suffer the fate of losing its focus or original intent. Without upper management's buy-in, the tough decisions that need to be made cannot be made — either because middle management does not have the vantage or the authority to make such decisions.

An Extended Definition of Project Success

Adding customer satisfaction as another constraint to the definition of IS project success literally adds another dimension to the Triple Constraint for Success model. The triangle of the classical definition becomes a three-dimensional pyramid (Figure 3.2). The new edges that arise from the deepening of the constraints model combine with the edges of the classical model to create new facets of customer satisfaction.

One of the new faces of the pyramid is bounded by the classical constraint of Project Duration, while another edge of the face is Customer Satisfaction. The third face extrapolates out to the Project Management ownership role the customer can and should play to ensure project success (Figure 3.3).

Another new face of the constraints pyramid is made up of the edges Customer Satisfaction and the classical edge of Functionality. The third, synergistic edge of this face then reveals the customer also playing the role of Programmer/Analyst, explicitly working with engineers to design and test the software implementation.

The practical basis for the new roles the customer must play to ensure IS project success can be found in the Joint Application Development (JAD) context and, as a project continues, through the Joint Implementation Process (JIP). These facilitated formats make for a viable means of resolving inevitable conflicts between business unit realities and IS expediencies during low-structure projects. During the design and analysis stage of application development, JAD sessions help build consensus between different parties, as well as constructing living documents that reflect an integrated vision of what the system should be and how it should operate.

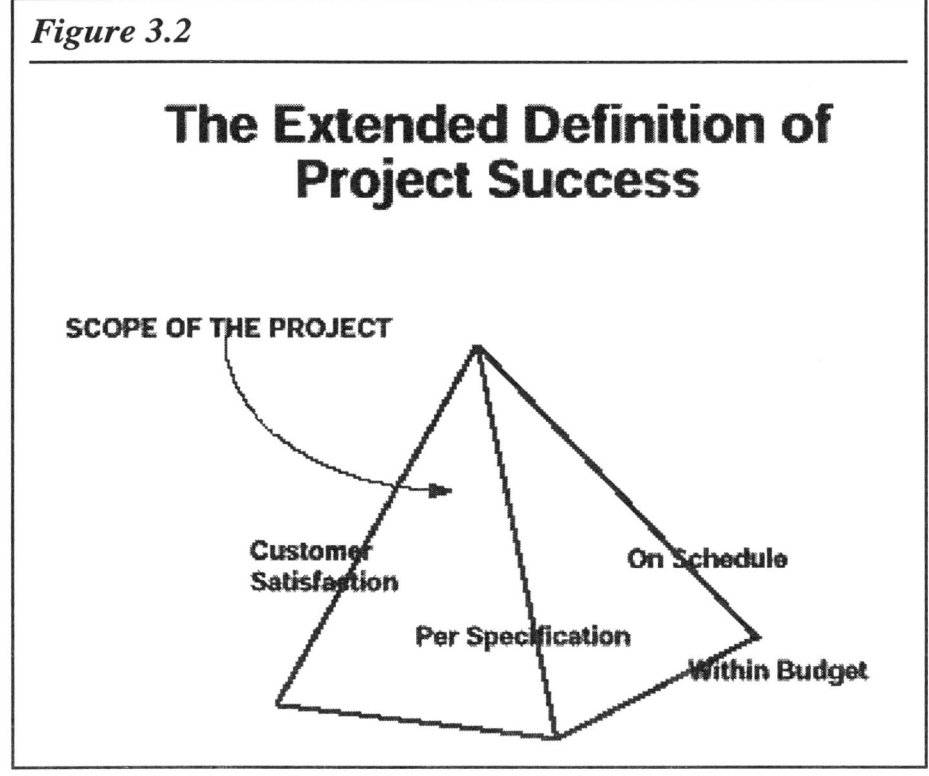

Figure 3.2

The Extended Definition of Project Success

SCOPE OF THE PROJECT

Customer Satisfaction

On Schedule

Per Specification

Within Budget

Once into the programming, testing, and systems integration stage of development, Joint Implementation Process sessions ensure commitment by the faction remains strong and focused and that the risk of failure due to a lack of communication is zero.

Reality of the Systems Development Process

The software development process has often been explained through a simple four-step model (Figure 3.4) that presents the process as a relatively straightforward affair: requirements definition, design, implementation, training, and documentation.

In reality, the software development process is better represented by the diagram in Figure 3.5.

In fact, the number of activities involved in bringing software into production has increased exponentially. The lines between the activities in the diagram represent communications. Those communications might be simple one-on-one meetings,

Figure 3.3

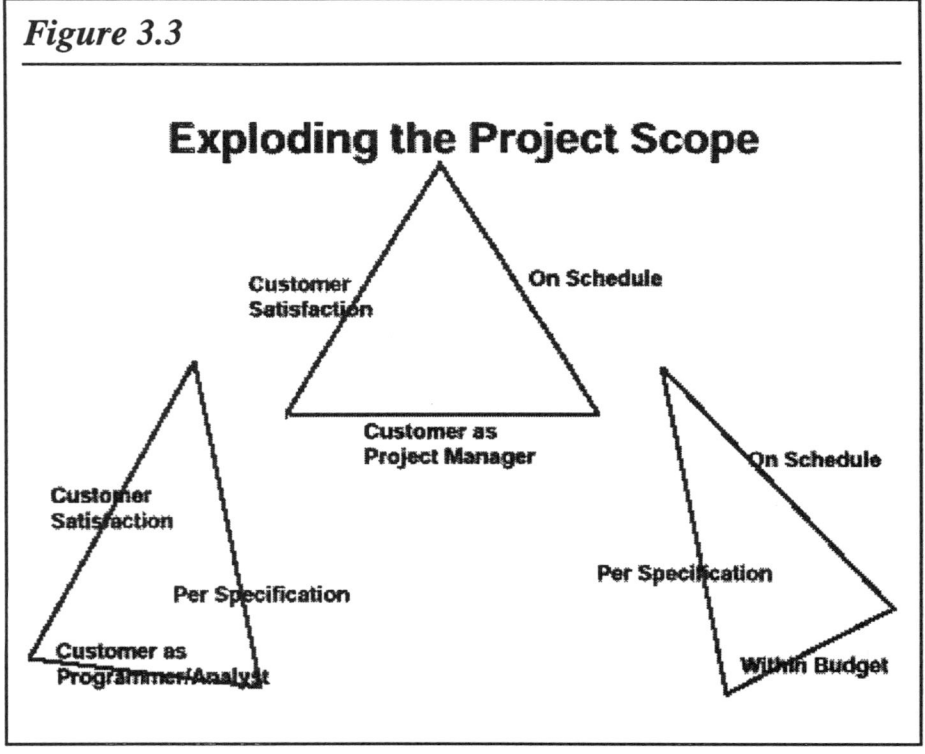

Exploding the Project Scope

Customer Satisfaction

On Schedule

Customer as Project Manager

Customer Satisfaction

Per Specification

Customer as Programmer/Analyst

On Schedule

Per Specification

Within Budget

e-mail correspondences, memos, walk-throughs, etc. Much more so than in development projects in the past, current and future efforts rely on the thoughts, ideas, and actions of a lot of people who, in the past, were unconcerned with the "how" of development. Previously only concerned with the "what" — that is, the end product — of development, managers, line staff, and customers have come to understand that the manner in which the process is pursued affects the quality of the product as well as the degree to which the product will enable the end-user in his or her work.

The challenge in software development had always been putting together the latest and greatest technologies in a vacuum and unveiling the result as a sort of hi-tech second coming. The engineer-as-mind-reader of the technical and human factors trends in society were what counted most. Scoring the big one (whether internal to an organization or as a consumer product) was what mattered.

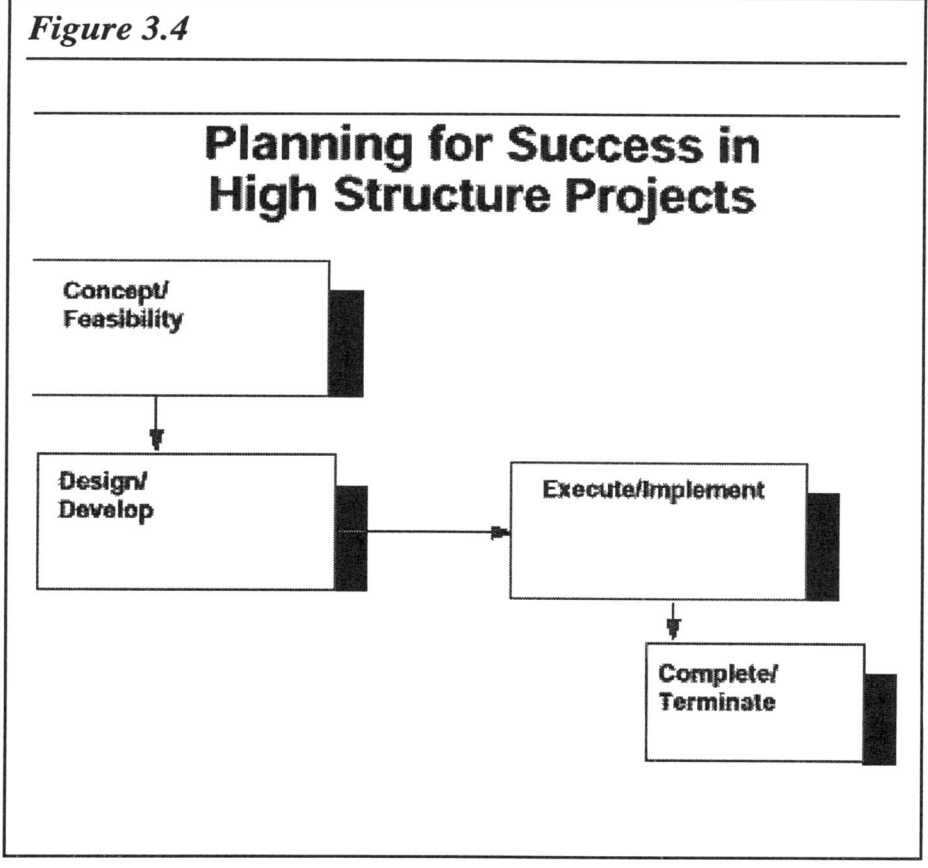

Figure 3.4

The complexity of the technologies, the pace of business, and the greater demands of consumers has refocused the efforts of development more on coordinating the babble of communications that flood the design floor and overwhelm the staff in production. The inevitable conflicts between management, engineers, and consumers have to be normalized; relevant information has to be reduced from the cacophony of demands, mapped to other needs and requests, prioritized, and followed through on.

Enter the project facilitator, whose hybrid role as project manager, referee, troubleshooter, cheerleader, and lead negotiator lends itself to coordinating the efforts of so many.

Who and What Is a Facilitator?

The facilitator in a systems setting is responsible for initiating and moderating meetings that involve individuals from within and without an organization, each with their own interests. Within the organization, the facilitator can be faced with normalizing

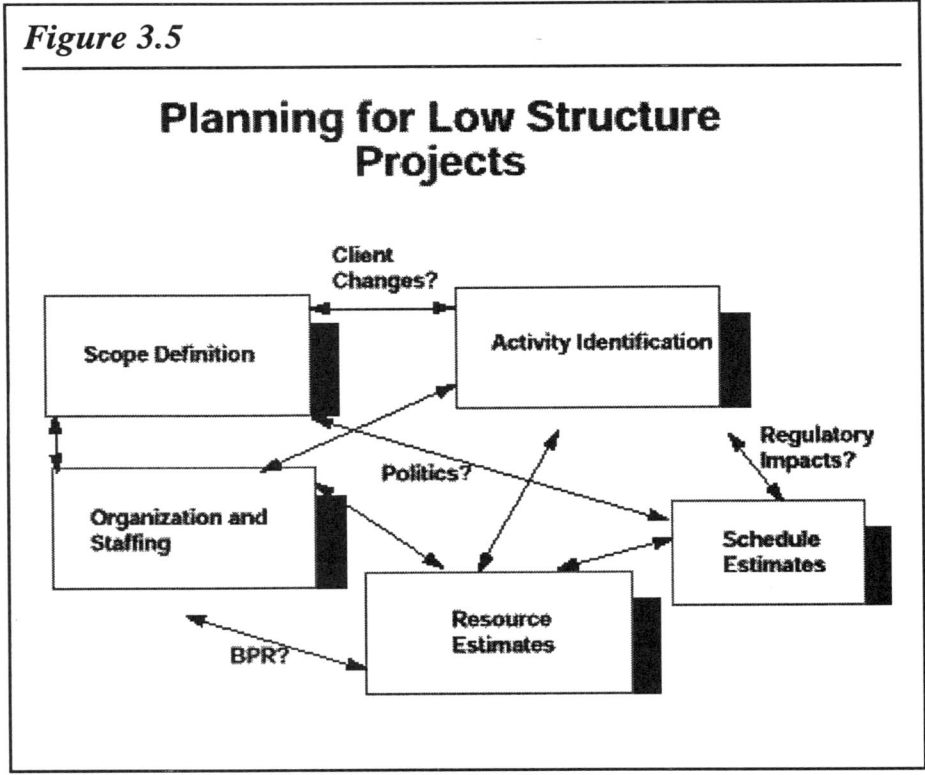

Figure 3.5

Planning for Low Structure Projects

the needs and requests of individuals across departmental borders. The aim of the facilitator is to identify the information or agreements that the group needs to produce in order that the project meets the four constraints to its success: on time, within budget, per specification, and meeting customer satisfaction.

Typically, the facilitator as an outside, impartial agent has no authority within the project or the organization. Instead, the facilitator shares in and leverages off the authority of the management team that hired her and vests in the priority of the project. The facilitator "shares in the aura" of power with managers without actually having any herself and without actually using any. Facilitators must personally feel comfortable with shouldering substantial responsibility without having commensurate authority.

The Project Manager and the Project Facilitator

The line between project manager and project facilitator is one that can be blurred by any number of factors, including: the size of the organization, the size of the project budget, the value upper management places on the project. Within organizations where a project manager is actually in charge of multiple projects, the project facilitator must be a separate individual. In this case, the project manager primarily interfaces with upper management on whether the project is coming in on time and within budget. Meanwhile, the project facilitator works "in the trenches," coordinating the various parties affected by the project, negotiating project conflicts, pushing and pulling team participants toward project completion.

Case in Point

"... an application group with the organization — named GOOS (Got Our Own Schedule) — was so large it was a bureaucracy unto itself.... Since GOOS was the most sought-after group for every implementation, it saw itself as the big dog on the block. When a group is used to being the "big dog," it doesn't like being the tail on the implementation. Or if it does become the tail on a particular implementation, it will try to wag the dog. The IC [facilitator as Implementation Coordinator] had a scheduling problem that was going to be difficult to negotiate. So she called and facilitated a JIP Test Planning Session at which all the other downstream applications presented their business cases for why they needed the GOOS group to get into integration testing earlier. If the IC had taken on the GOOS group alone, it would have been a very tough sell to convince GOOS to change its schedule. However, by resorting to the JIP session and letting all the other applications present their specific reasons for needing the GOOS group to change its schedule, the IC was successful in getting the scheduling conflict resolved to the betterment of the implementation."

— Fallon, pg. 203

More and more though — in step with the corporate trend toward downsizing and outsourcing — the project facilitator can find herself in charge of ensuring all the constraints to project success are met: on time, within budget, per specification, and supported by customer satisfaction. From design through implementation, the project manager as project facilitator will be responsible for reporting both to upper management and for channeling organizational resources and energies toward project end. This scenario dominates in organizations in which large-scale projects are more the exception, rather than the rule, making it prohibitively expensive to maintain a full-time IS project manager.

The Facilitator's Tools of the Trade

The facilitator's tools of the trade are simple indeed: an overhead projector; a box of clear, clean transparencies; different color white board markers; a cleaning solution and a stack of paper towels (to modify the transparencies as the facilitator works through the session), a flip chart, and a role of tape.

Mechanically, the facilitation process is quite simple: during the design phase, the facilitator transforms the words and ideas of participants into graphic and text models while balancing political and personal dynamics of participants to long-term constructive ends in what is called the Joint Application Design (JAD) process. Typically, the facilitator uses the transparencies to draw our data flow diagrams and entity relationship diagrams, and she uses the flip charts for the attribute determination of the entities that arise and to list the business rules as they appear.

In the Joint Implementation Process (JIP) session, which occurs after the development of Functional Specification, the facilitator uses the flip chart to record session discoveries, identify project tasks, and to describe participant agreements. When the

---

Case in Point

"... the IC [facilitator as Implementation Coordinator] scheduled a JIP [Joint Implementation Process] Walk Through of a JIP Interface Specification Document with the approval of the programming group's manager. The JIP Walk Through was attended by the business user who was going to own the system to be implemented, the programmers who produced the JIP Interface Specification Document, the programming group's manager, and the programming group's senior manager. But the JIP Interface Specification Document was incomplete and poorly documented. It had been 'thrown together' by the programmers, had been given a sloppy 'once-over' by the technical writer, and was now being presented without rewrite or consideration. The programming group's senior manager was visibly upset, and after the JIP Walk Through reassigned the programming group's manager to other projects. The IC was delighted. The JIP Walk Through had proven to be a good forum for accountability...."

—Fallon, pg.151

facilitator begins a new list in either the JAD or JIP sessions, she tears off the current page of the flip chart and tapes it to a wall or white board. By the end of the day's session, the walls are covered with taped-up sheets of flip-chart paper so participants can see and understand the development of the consensus items they have established.

The project might require a scribe, if the scope of the project is great. The scribe records the details that pour out of the sessions as rapidly as the group provides them. The scribe is responsible for both documenting the information gathered during the session and providing it back to the team as needed during the session. The scribe relieves the other participants of having to divert their attention from resolving the issues at hand to taking notes.

The scribe can use any outliner to capture the detail of the project, switching quickly from topic to topic as needs evolve. Powerpoint is a good tool which allows the scribe to transform detailed outlines into presentations for future sessions. And then there are any of the standard word processing packages the scribe will need to develop status reports and memos.

All the JAD information the facilitator and scribe process also needs to be consolidated in a CASE (Computer Aided Software Engineering) or workflow mapping tool. Popular CASE tools are ERWin and Popkin's System Architect. Popular workflow tools include Action Technologies Inc.'s Action Workflow line of software, Computron Software Inc.'s Computron Workflow, NCR Corp's Process IT workflow system, and IBM's FlowMark package.

Project facilitators can use any of a multitude of project management tools to coordinate resources and scheduling, including Microsoft Project, Scitor Corporation's Project Scheduler, or Primavera Systems' Primavera Project Planner, to name just a few.

The Facilitator in Software Design

Business often sees the facilitator during the software design phase in a Joint Application Design (JAD) context. The project's most effective and enduring forum for building engineering and business staff relationships is the JAD session.

Within this setting, the entire engineering team (or at least representatives), can come together with staff members to hear and to thrash out differences of intention, vision, and approach. The facilitator's goal, through the JAD process, can be to produce a Systems Requirements document and/or Functional Specification for the corporate information system that incorporates, builds on, and supersedes the parochial priorities and agendas of individuals and island-departments. The process ensures the requirements of the system are well-grounded in the needs and expectations of users, managers, and executives in the organization.

The Facilitator in Software Implementation

After the design phase of software development is complete, and the project moves into the programming and implementation stages of the process, the facilitator changes clothes and becomes the Implementation Coordinator (IC). While JAD tends to be focused on resolving project design issues that happen at the front-end of a project, the IC works in the later stages of the project to address the issues and problems of implementing that information system into the organization.

Still, the facilitator as IC has a great deal of responsibility for project success without the direct authority to make it happen. Instead, the IC must leverage off the knowledge and authority of those she gathers in facilitated sessions to unearth issues that require resolution, make project decisions, and build consensus across the borders that express and obstruct the organization. Howard Fallon, in his book *How to Implement Information Systems and Live to Tell About It* calls these facilitated sessions Joint Implementation Process (JIP) sessions. The JIP sessions work to eliminate one of the major causes for project failure: a lack of consensus-building and accountability for decisions made throughout the lifetime of the project. Only through joint ownership of project results by both the engineers and business staff can projects successfully negotiate the boundaries between departments and across hierarchies.

Case in Point

The facilitator ran a total of 10 half-day JAD sessions, about two per week to determine the requirements for a client/server project that would affect 10 departments throughout a prestigious Medical in New England. There was one session that involved 15 individuals from around the medical school. On average, eight individuals attended each session: six business representatives and two technical personnel. Business representatives consisted of department heads, end-users, and an individual who was the Division financial officer and project patron. The technical personnel consisted of the Division IS representative and the contract systems architect/facilitator. The final technical team consisted of two programmers, the Division IS representative, and a user documentation specialist.

The project was almost derailed twice: The project patron gave one month's notice that he was leaving the organization; this, in the second week of prototyping the application (after the JAD sessions). Upon leaving, project decisions reverted to the Division assistant director, who needed to brought up to speed on the project. The scope of the prototype increased threefold. Then, two months later, the Division IS manager gave notice he was leaving in two months. One month before he left, the Division replaced the financial officer, who, in addition to learning about her new job, needed to be educated about database technology so she could become the project patron.

Building a partnering relationship and sense of ownership with Division staff was key in ensuring that engineers delivered to the Division exactly what it expected from the JAD sessions and the second-generation prototype. Without the relationship, the probability was high that the Division would have faltered.

Joint sessions facilitated by an IC and documented by a scribe build a coherent, focused body of knowledge about the details of a project. The reality of systems implementation is that there are too many details for any one person to retain, and too many decisions that have to be made about too many aspects of the project and the organization for one person — or many persons not working in concert — to make them.

The Facilitator and the Group Memory

In the end, founding a well-rounded team that includes engineers and corporate administrative/management staff involves the evolution of a new knowledge base, new vocabulary, and new relationship dynamic that is proprietary. As well, a new corporate understanding arises: engineers internalize the intricacies of departmental operations; organization representatives internalize development methodology and symbology, as well as gain an intimate sense of the potentials and limitations of technology.

A Group Memory arises, which is as important as any Requirements document the team produces. The Group Memory supports the subsequent stages of development through its innate understanding of organization needs and development realities. Snags always arise after the JAD stage has concluded: system functionality that had inadvertently been overlooked, new business opportunities that suddenly arise that management would like to have the system address, BPR (business process reengineering) decisions that weigh on every enterprise-wide implementation. These are issues that only the Group Memory can quickly and effectively resolve. The Group Memory's continuity of and extreme focus on the project are major assets on which the organization must rely for the positive results it seeks.

Without the facilitator establishing, coordinating, and maintaining a project Group Mind to support decision makers, decision makers find it easier to back down from

---

Case in Point

A gas utility company with a strong union labor component had been unsuccessful for 18 months in pulling together a Requirements document for its enterprise-wide IS project. During this time, the IS department had been conducting sequential interviews of project stakeholders to pull together the Specification, and was unable to gain the organization-wide support the project required to move from conception to design.

The utility company called in a facilitation team from a large consultancy to focus project stakeholders and to gain their buy-in. The facilitation team was made up of a facilitator and a scribe. At the rate of one session per week, the facilitator was able to achieve in six weeks what the entire IS department had been unable to achieve in a year and a half. The consultant in charge of the facilitation cited the several reasons for the quick success: a half-day kick-off introducing project participants to the facilitated approach; a consistent, structured approach to gathering requirements; and the emphasis on documentation.

decisions they had made earlier, or to counter those decisions without basis, or to down right deny such decisions ever having been made — all overt signals of a project gone awry.

The Necessity of Coordination and Communications

The Politics of Projects

Projects can very easily become political footballs in organizations. Projects provide windows of opportunity for individuals and entire departments to advance their agendas within the business. The facilitator from the design phase through implementation must conscientiously guard against the machinations that organizations depend on to sell their products or services to customers.

As Jeffrey Pinto writes in his book *Power and Politics in Project Management* (Project Management Institute, 1996):

> "For better or worse, project managers do not have the luxury of turning their backs on organizational politics. Too much of what they do depends upon their ability to effectively manage not only the technical realms of their job, but the behavioral side as well. Politics constitutes one organiza-

---

Case in Point

A medical center needed to replace its failing 16-year-old legacy system, without which the clinic would not be able function. The information system affected hundreds of administrative staff, practitioners, faculty, and students. Politically, the Center was divided within itself, with department staff aggressively competing against one another for influence and resources. Upper management realized that with the sophistication of the new system it had chosen, and with the divisive nature of the organization, it was not going to be feasible even for the IS department to implement the system with the level of cooperation Management knew was required for a successful effort.

Management contracted a consultancy to facilitate the implementation. After seven months and literally hundreds of facilitated sessions that cut across departments, through levels of authority, and involved coordinating the software vendor and programming team — which resided in another state — the project facilitator was able to achieve a level of consensus and organization-wide buy-in the COO admitted "he wouldn't have been able to do — wouldn't know how to do — himself." The project facilitator gained decisions and agreements that ensured the system went live on time and assured staff that they would not have to bend the way they worked to the idiosyncrasies of the new system, but that, instead, the system was actually working for them.

---

tional process that is ubiquitous; it operates across organization and functional boundaries. Politics is not inherently evil or vicious. Rather, it is only in how it is employed that has earned so much animus. All of us, bearing the scars of past experiences, understand the potential for misuse that comes from organizational politics."

Individuals immersed in the politics of an organization are very much like fish in water: the individuals are used to and depend on the politics to maneuver about organization. Projects can be like huge bubbles of air inserted into the watery environment — they can potentially disempower the political animal; that is, projects can make people feel like the proverbial fish out of water.

As such, to bring partisan individuals and groups into the artificial construct of "the project," an environment not of the same nature as that of the rest of the organization, is to risk a bursting of the bubble. Yet what alternative does the facilitator have if she is to ensure that information and consensus crucial to project success is drawn upon?

The art and craft of facilitation demand that the facilitator above all else maintains and fortifies the integrity of the wall of the project bubble. The project bubble must be resilient to withstand the torques and stresses organizational politics place on the effort. While resilient, the bubble wall must also be permeable, to ensure the project participants remain in communication with the rest of the organizational environment.

The facilitator is key in presenting a model of trust and of flexibility to project participants, to in the least work with them to direct their political influence toward fortifying the constructive results of the project for the organization. To this end, the facilitator must not ignore the realities of organizational politics, and must herself be politically savvy. Without such a perspective, the facilitator can all too quickly become "fish food" and the project atomized to insignificance.

Case in Point

"...[In this case] the IC [the facilitator as Implementation Coordinator] needed to reduce dependency on WUYS [Without Us You're Screwed], and work out a deal with some other group to step forward and accept responsibility for building and maintaining the history file. You can make a business case for just about any group owning a given task. So the IC went politicking! She soon sold the people in the WWDI (We Will Do It) group on the prospect of becoming heroes throughout the corporation by building the history file. And it turned out that WWDI could do it with considerably less effort than the WUYS group said it could. So the WWDI group would look great, not only for building the history file, but for doing it for less than the WUYS budget amount. And that's what happened ... the WWDI group built the file, and its management garnered a lot of acclaim and prestige useful for political advantage. And the IC got her implementation done in a timely manner, owing to the strategy of reducing dependency."
—Fallon, pg. 247

Within the organization, the facilitator — of all project participants — has the best chance of building bridges of trust between politically contrasting factions. The facilitator is typically from outside the organization, or is, in the least, not involved in the more sensitive zones of contention between business groups. The facilitator also serves as a lightning rod for the political lightning bolts that factions sometimes hurl at one another. Indeed, the facilitator is sometimes the target of such maneuvers: typically, the facilitator has gained entree into the project at the request or demand of a group of like-minded managers who, as advocates of the project, likely have political contrarians who would feel they have lost ground to the advocates.

Projects as Cultural Exchange

The first definition of culture that comes to mind when speaking of corporations is that of the corporate culture. It is also important to realize that the various departments within an organization also constitute cultures within their own right. So, for instance, the Information Systems department is often a culture apart from others within a business. For instance, the individuals in IS tend to be more introverted than others in the organization, with a focus that is more centered on computers and software and making the systems themselves work than on dealing with individuals on a political level. The facilitator must take this cultural difference into account when gaining the cooperation and expertise of this group.

The complexion and accent of projects has shifted subtly yet dramatically over the past 10 to 15 years from a predominantly white male domain to one in which decision makers are women and men from a variety of cultural and religious persuasions that contrast or perhaps are even at odds (on the geopolitical level) with Christian Western European values. More and more projects are becoming contexts for negotiating cultural expressions and interpretations that until recently had not been a factor in projects.

The facilitator can be invaluable during projects with a diverse team membership for several reasons, then: the facilitator as an individual aware of the different values

---

Case in Point

At one utilities business in Massachusetts, 80 percent of the Human Resources department were black women from the Caribbean, while the IS department that was putting together the new Human Resources system was 95 percent white male — 60 percent of whom were Irish! Such cultural differences make for a minefield of miscommunications and misunderstandings that contribute to strained relations between groups. Though after two years the IS department was able to present something workable to HR, a project review revealed that IS ultimately did not want to listen to what "the girls" in HR had to say about the way HR worked and what it actually needed.

that other peoples support can help keep the project free of the subtle yet destructive force of prejudice and xenophobia.

The facilitator as an impartial project participant has an advantage in building bridges of trust between other project participants. Indeed, the skill of the facilitator will allow her to become "transparent" to the preconceptions of project members, to help build comfort zones for participants that are inclusive of the others on the team.

Ultimately, the facilitator is responsible for identifying and removing any barriers to communication and action that may hinder project participants in their work together. This could be anything from researching the etiquette and colloquialisms of cultures to making participants feel more secure in their environment through ensuring foods served at a team meeting do not step over the bounds of good taste or sacrilege.

The BPR Factor

The facilitator is key to making Business Process Reengineering (BPR) efforts succeed. BPR as an aspect of systems implementation is a necessary evil if the systems in question are to fit hand-in-glove with the way individuals work. In other words, there is no such thing as an out-of-the-box software application that meets all the quirks of the implicit work habits of staff; and there are no organizations that can work efficiently and "spontaneously" while constrained by the idiosyncrasies of computer systems. There has to be a middle path between the two operational extremes — BPR.

BPR by its very definition is a disruptive and upsetting process. The changes in the work patterns of staff create ripples throughout the organization that affect all levels of the business and reach across the breadth of the company. Reworking business processes demands bringing into the same room together the steady, unflinching authority of upper management, the in-the-trench responsibilities of front-line staff representing diverse departments, and the technical savvy of IS. This volatile mix can be maintained at moderate temperatures only by the expertise of a nonpartisan facilitator.

The responsibility of the facilitator within the context of a BPR effort is to catalyze and maintain the momentum of the alchemy of transformation that the organization will endure. The combination of cross-functional disciplines and entrenched habits with the demands of IS regimen can explode into sparks of anger and frustration and fear. The role of the facilitator is then to rationalize current work processes, to help build the theoretical framework for the reworked process, then to shepherd the team through a practical mock office exercise in which theory and reality are exercised before the final restructuring is realized throughout the organization.

Conclusion

The complexity of software development projects and the increased expectations of project stakeholders have demanded a new hybrid role be added to the classic roster of project manager, executive management, IS, and end-users. The facilitator as an agent of change, focus, continuity, consensus, collaboration, and coordination has become a necessity in IS projects that span departments, power centers, and cultures. Now, organizations are finding that instead of better mousetraps, what they really need is better communications.

References

Deborah Asbrand. "User Satisfaction is Essential to Successful Projects." *Infoworld*, 15 February 1993.

Judy August. *Joint Application Design.*. Englewood Cliffs, NJ: Yourdon Press, 1991.

Richard Barton. "Human Factors in Join Application Design." Software Development Conference East Proceedings, Fall 1991.

William Dodson. "Coordinating Aggregate Systems." *Databased Advisor*, September 1996.

William Dodson. "How to Manage Personnel Changes." *Databased Advisor*, March 1995.

William Dodson. "Secrets of a High-Performing Team." *Databased Advisor*, December 1994.

Howard Fallon. *How to Implement Information Systems and Live to Tell About It.* New York: John Wiley and Sons, 1995,

Jim Geier. "Don't Get Mad, Get JAD!" *Software Development*, March 1996.

Jane Griffin. "Building Bridges, Not Rivalries." *PM Network*, August 1996.

Jaclyn Kostner. *Virtual Leadership*. New York: Warner Books, 1994.

Case in Point

"... the IC [Implementation Coordinator] facilitated several JIP [Joint Implementation Process] BPR Sessions to help the organization model its business work-flow. The model that was developed contained several hundred business processes. Together, the IC and a team of knowledgeable persons in the organization then systematically attacked the credibility of each process. They found that many of the processes supported historical procedures that no longer existed. Although these procedures had been institutionalized into organizational policy, they were no longer relevant because the nature of the business had changed, or they were mandated by legal requirements that were no longer in force and, in some cases, they even supported outdated technologies such as pneumatic tubes and carbon copies. The IC and the JIP session participants were able to reduce the number of business processes in the model by 75 percent! ICs find that these kinds of inefficiencies, which are supported by historical policies, tend to be the rule rather than the exception.

—Fallon, pg. 278

Joy Matthews. "JAD to the Rescue." *ComputerWorld*, 4 December 1995.

Jim McCarthy. "Implementing Feature Teams." *Software Development*, December 1995.

John McMullen. "Developing a Role for End-Users." *Information Week*, 15 June 1992.

Carl Moore et al. "Partnering: Guidelines for Win–Win Project Management." *Project Management Journal*, March 1992.

Jeffrey K. Pinto. *Power and Politics in Project Management*, Project Management Institute, 1996.

Gerard L. Rossy. "Building Commitment in Project Teams." *Project Management Journal*, June 1992.

Jennifer Schmidt. "User Developers Building Sophisticated Business Applications." *Application Development Trends*, July 1995.

Marcia Steele. "Test Your System with a 'Conference Room Pilot." *Databased Advisor*, January 1993.

William Stinnet. "Lone Wolf Teams: Reconciling the Need for Collaboration with the Need for Individual Accomplishment." *PM Network*, May 1992.

Chapter 4

Architecture-driven Intranet Application Development

David S. Linthicum

As more and more users surf the World Wide Web, smaller waves are forming within many corporations for the exclusive use of their employees and customers. Locked behind corporate firewalls, these Web-enabled applications run on a new platform called the intranet. Application development for private intranets is the latest rage.

But what happened to client/server? With the rise of the intranet as a legitimate development platform, there is a paradigm shift away from "traditional" client/server development. Tool vendors that normally keep up with what's best in client/server are quickly retooling for the Web. What's more, developers who once sought C++ and PowerBuilder training are lining up in hordes to learn Java.

The question, therefore, is one of architecture. Where does the intranet fit into the world of client/server and distributed computing? How can the application development community best leverage the intranet to complement the existing client/server paradigm? Where will the intranet take us in the future? The answer to these questions lies in intranet technologies, and what each brings to the application development table. Clearly, the intranet changes the way we think about distributed application development. The most important questions are how much change can we expect and how can we change to meet the new challenge?

Intranet Movement

At first, intranets were easy mechanisms for information dissemination, such as employee manuals, directions to the division meeting, or the latest stock prices and company news. These were generally simple text and graphics, with some multimedia capabilities such as sound and video in the mix as well.

As Web-enabled technology became more sophisticated, intranet developers began to employ new enabling technologies such as Sun's Java, Common Gateway Interface (CGI), and Microsoft's ActiveX, as a means of providing dynamic behavior and content to the once limited Web. Intranet users could now interface with full-blown interactive client/server applications using standard browsers such as Netscape's Navigator and Microsoft's Explorer.

Intranet applications are sprouting up all over corporate America. Take the case of John Deere. John Deere Works' Waterloo Division uses web browsers to integrate corporate data with agricultural information and test site results, and even allows employees to access online documentation as well as a database of tractor parts. Deere uses the intranet to build custom applications that run on any of the many platforms they support, leveraging the multiplatform capabilities of Netscape Navigator.

Deere places its parts database online which allows employees to not only find information and the location of needed parts, but provides an image of the part as well. Test results from new models of tractors and heavy equipment are represented to employees as text, pictures, and sound. The sound capabilities of their intranet lets Deere employees listen to engine noises for diagnostic purposes.

There are, of course, many other examples of intranets at work. Xerox uses its own internal "Web Board" to link more than 15,000 employees to shared documents and product information. AMP Corporation will place its product catalog on their internal web, and Cisco Corporation has an intranet-ready on-line order entry system in the works with links to an EDI subsystem for just-in-time processing. Morgan Stanley distributes their daily trading information summary on their intranet. The list goes on. The amazing thing is, we've only just begun.

The future of the intranet is bright. A study from Zona Research, Inc. states that the intranet will enjoy more growth by the year 2000 than commercial applications deployed over the Internet. And that means web technology will find a larger market share within the firewalls. Zona asserts that corporate users are better able to leverage the power of web technology and have the most to gain from its internal use as a multiplatform information dissemination and application deployment vehicle. Other research organizations agree with Zona. IDC contends that the future demand for intranet applications will be five times that of traditional internet applications by the year 2001.

However, the intranet is still not for every application. The file-oriented character-istics of the intranet can cause performance problems in high volume transaction-oriented applications. As many as 200 users may request the same HTML file at the same time, or invoke the same CGI process. Of course, we can solve some of these performance problems with tricks like proxy servers and higher-end multiprocessing web servers. Java and ActiveX use a "download once, run many times" (DORMAT) which will disconnect the user from the performance limitations of the web server. Unfortunately, true mission-critical applications that use Java or ActiveX are slow to appear. Those who use the intranet for "must run" applications should proceed with caution.

Paradigms of Client/Server

To get a sense of where the intranet fits into modern corporate client/server comput-ing, it's helpful to examine existing client/server paradigms. In many instances, the intranet simply means the use of existing paradigms, redeployed for the Web.

The first paradigm is the file-oriented shared database access paradigm. Although not technically client/server, the idea was to keep the database on a shared file server that allows any connected clients to access the data as if the file was local. The para-digm was simple, it worked, and it met the needs of many smaller workgroup-based applications.

However, the first paradigm has some scaling and performance issues. The archi-tecture depended upon sending the database file to and from the client to process a simple database request.

To solve the limitations of the first paradigm, developers began to use the tradi-tional two-tier client/server architecture. Let's call this the second paradigm. The sec-ond paradigm provides better scaling and performance since developers can partition the processing between two machines; the client and the server. This architecture marked the boom of client/server technology, and still leads the way today as the pre-ferred architecture for small- to medium-sized systems. It's also the architecture of popular specialized client/server tools such as Powersoft's PowerBuilder, Microsoft's Visual Basic, and Borland's Delphi.

Although the second paradigm solves many IT problems, it does not solve them all. The two-tier architecture falls down quickly when one attempts to scale to enter-prise-level applications. Moreover, the tendency to place most of the application pro-cessing at the client (fat client) means slower clients, or more expense for new hardware and software. Second paradigm systems are usually tied to a single client platform.

To resolve the issues with the second paradigm, developers began to add application servers to the client/server mix, creating a three-tiered or multitiered (sometimes called n-tiered) architecture. We'll call this the third paradigm. This highly sophisticated and expensive system architecture places most of the application processing load on single or multiple middle tiers. The end result is an architecture that is significantly more scalable than traditional two-tier client/server computing, and provides central application control as well. Third paradigm tools include application partitioning tools from Forte and Dynasty, as well as TP monitors such as Transarc's Encina and distributed objects such as IBM's SOM/DSOM.

Although systems that use the third paradigm can handle most processing loads, they do so with highly complex technologies and proprietary solutions. All this leads to a high cost per user for application development, as well as significant cost for application deployment and support.

The Fourth Paradigm

The intranet is the fourth paradigm of client/server. In many respects the intranet is retroactive, using bits and pieces from the existing paradigms such as file-oriented application deployment, as well as three-tier and two-tier client server. However, the application integration happens within the confines of the web browser.

When a client pulls a web page, he or she is really downloading an HTML file for display inside a web browser. Same goes for graphics, sound, and video.

When using CGI (or SSI and API for that matter), the user can send information to a process that resides on the web server. That process can then access information on a database server and return the data to the middle tier (the web server) for processing. The middle tier process then returns the information back to the intranet user as a standard HTML document. This is traditional three-tier client/server computing.

The intranet is very much like traditional two-tier client/server computing when factoring in Java. Although Java applets are deployed by downloading them with content from internal web servers, unlike CGI, they really execute within the web browser on the client. If an applet must link to an external resource (e.g., a database server), the applet must create the link by connecting back to the web server or another server it's authorized to access. Like other traditional two-tier client/server tools, applets make simple API calls to the remote resource servers, which returns the information to the applet and thus the user.

If you haven't noticed, we are well into the fourth paradigm. Already the line between traditional client/server development and intranet development is difficult to see. More than any other paradigm shift before, developers, product vendors, and IT managers are scrabbling to align their organizations with what they see as the next wave of distributed computing. Clearly, this is the short-term direction.

Complementing Client/Server

So where does the intranet fit into the world of client/server and distributed computing? It's complementary, not competition. Architecturally, the intranet is just an extension of existing technology and tools. The ease of use of the Web is a natural for internal application development, and application distribution capabilities of the intranet are attractive as well. Developers and architects need to embrace the fourth paradigm as another architecture that may fit future client/server and distributed development application. It's another weapon in our arsenal to build applications.

For example, most of the heavy hitters in the client/server development world are now aligning their products for the intranet. There seem to be several distinct categories of tools emerging: tools that are based on Java, tools that are based on ActiveX, tools that leverage CGI, and tools that leverage web server dependent APIs such as Microsoft's ISAPI and Netscape's NSAPI.

As Java in its post beta form finally hits the streets, there are already Java tools aplenty from traditional client/server tool vendors. The success of the Delphi client/server development tools drives development of the Java-enabled Latte. Latte is written in Delphi and will take on a Delphi look and feel, but will generate Java code. Latte is significant in that developers will have built-in access to databases directly from Latte applications. Symantec has recast its popular C++ compiler for Java as well. Symantec's Café for Windows and Macintosh, like Latte, provides a visual rapid application development (RAD) environment for Java, as well as a just-in-time compiler for speedier local applet execution. JAM 7 from Jyacc, a multiplatform client/server development tool, is now spinning off a Java-enabled version called JAM/WEB. JAM/WEB provides a visual environment that can generate Java code for the creation of database applications. Finally, Rogue Wave Software is taking its C++-ready client/server experience to the Web through their new product called JFactory. JFactory is another Java-enabled visual development environment that drives Java to RAD. These are only a few samples of the available Java tools for intranet application.

The delivery of JDBC (Java Database Connectivity) in the near future promises to ease database connections from Java applications. JDBC is functionally equivalent to ODBC, and can connect to any database that supports ODBC. The significance of JDBC on intranet development is great. Developers can create applications that run inside of a web browser and connect back to corporate database servers.

Client/server tools that are moving to intranet development through ActiveX (formally OCX) are less numerous but have buy-in from the two most popular client/server tool vendors — Powersoft and Microsoft. Microsoft is revamping its premier visual client/server product, Visual Basic, to support the creation of ActiveX web components. Like Java applets, ActiveX components may be downloaded and executed in ActiveX-enabled web browsers such as Microsoft Explorer. Although

ActiveX does not have the momentum of Java for intranet application development, the sheer strength of Microsoft, as well as their ability to buy into the intranet market, could give Java a run for its money. Neither technology has proven its ability to support highly scalable intranet applications, and we may see a few generations of tools before we can rely on the intranet to deliver such applications.

Although CGI, and tools that use CGI, are considered passé in light of Java and ActiveX, CGI provides flexible intranet development today. Developers may hand code CGI directly using a 3GL or a scripting language, or developers can employ tools that leverage CGI such as Parcplace-Digitalk Visual Wave or Web Objects from NeXT Computing. These tools both provide visual development environments, as well as the ability to generate CGI code to access databases when required by an application. As a sign of the times, both tools plan to support Java as well.

The popularity of Netscape Enterprise web server and Microsoft's Internet Information server continues to drive interest in their native APIs — NSAPI and ISAPI. NSAPI, for instance, is accessible through JavaScript applications running in a the Netscape web server using Livewire. Developers simply create intranet applications using the object-oriented JavaScript language, which provides built-in classes for linking to external databases.

In addition to tools, database vendors are becoming intranet aware as well. Oracle, Sybase, and Informix are already planning web-aware versions of their database servers. These products will send HTML to web browsers in response to SQL. Web-aware databases, when ready for prime time, will find the largest market for intranet development.

The application development community can best leverage the intranet to complement the existing client/server paradigm by looking at the intranet as a new platform. A platform that's a good fit for some applications is not a good fit for others. For instance, while the intranet is a natural for information dissemination applications such as distribution of reports and graphs, the intranet in its current incarnation may not yet provide the performance required by the sales department to quickly take orders on the phone. The dynamic capabilities and true application development features of Java and ActiveX are unproven in high volume transaction processing environments. However, as tools begin to saturate the market, the appearance of these sorts of applications is just a matter of time.

The tools that support intranet development need to focus on the ability to support transaction-oriented applications and less on the hype of easy-to-use visual development environments. Java applications will do you no good if they can't connect to a back-end database or read real-time information using standard off-the-shelf APIs. Java needs to move out of the cute animation demos and show a real knack for making client/server happen on the new intranet platform.

Moreover, the file-oriented nature of the Web could leave many of the first intranet applications lacking the performance of their traditional client/server cousins. The new breed of client/server tools for intranet development needs to address these issues before the intranet can become the next generation of client/server.

What's Next

The intranet is here to stay. In the near future we will see a gradual shift from traditional client/server-based development to intranet development, and traditional client/server will absorb the change to the fourth paradigm. Client/server development tools will continue to move toward support for intranet development, and modern tools available in '96 and '97 will produce HTML and Java as easily as they produce Windows applications. In addition, developers can expect better database support with the appearance of connectivity standards such as JDBC.

Aside from a shift in technology, there will be an equal (and equally important) shift in expectations. Users will expect to access corporate information and applications using the easy-to-understand web browser, and distributed access will become the norm. It will not be unusual to deploy applications to thousands of users in just a single hour by distributing URL information rather than disks.

Client/server developers, designers, and architects should not fear the rapid rise of the intranet. They should, however, accept change as an inevitable fact of life and embrace the fourth paradigm of client/server before it embraces them.

Chapter 5

Designing a Client/Server Architecture

Ellen Gottesdiener

Note to readers: Portions of this paper appear in a chapter entitled "Application Development" in the SAMS Publication, Client/Server Unleashed, *ISBN: 0-672-30726-X, 1996. The techniques discussed in this article are fully explored in the workshop "Client/Server Analysis & Design" offered by EBG Consulting, Inc.*

This paper examines client/server logical design strategies. Business events are the driving force for defining and detailing client/server applications. Using multiple application models, iterative prototyping, application usage information, and knowledge of the technical infrastructure, an effective and efficient design architecture can be determined.

Client/server logical design entails deciding which application components should be placed where in the architecture. The principles apply whether the application will have two, three, or more physical tiers. Despite the ability to prototype and design an interface quickly, analysis and design activities are needed more than ever. These activities should encompass using a clean data design with a new model — one that is iterative, event-driven, job/role-oriented. The result is an application architecture that conforms to project and technical constraints while achieving business goals.

Note to object-oriented designers: This paper addresses partitioning issues using more traditional Information Technology logical models (e.g., data, process, event) as opposed to object-oriented models. However, the event model is roughly equivalent to the use case model, and the essential partitioning issues are the same regardless of how the application domain is modeled.

Framework for Application Development

One of the benefits of client/server systems is their ability to mirror how the business responds to real-world events. Therefore, business events are used to define and detail the client/server application. These events, along with definition of the context in which the application will reside, are the basis for the application models. Business events trigger a series of processes which affect data collected about the business, and change the states of that data. These ingredients — process, data, and states — are tightly interwoven within the application and thus make up the key components of an effective application model.

For thousands of years, humans have used models to represent concepts. In the world of information systems, models are best expressed using both visual representations and text. Visual models convey concepts quickly, while text models convey the same concepts with accuracy. This permits both Information Systems and end-user the opportunity to define requirements. The process, data, and state models serve as a focal point for iteratively discovering details about the application and transforming those details into application software.

Figure 5.1 Framework for client/server application development.

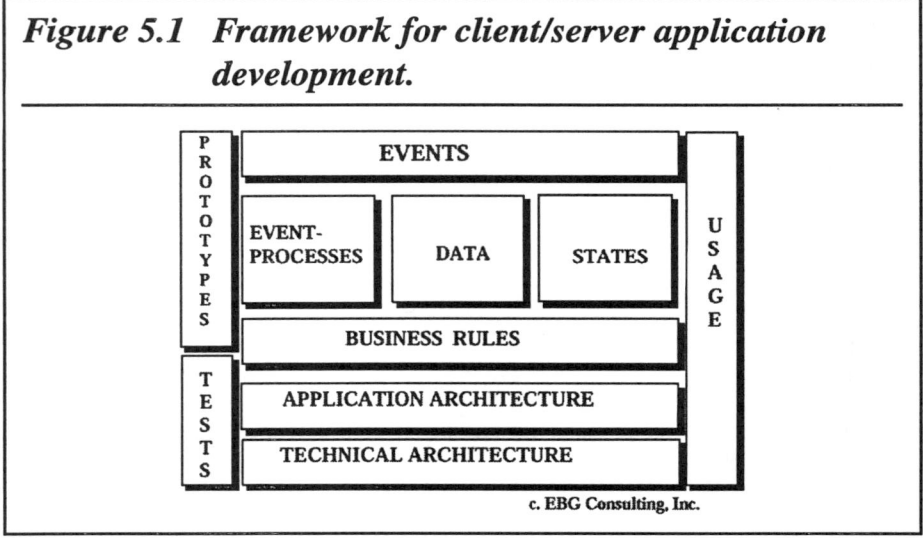

c. EBG Consulting, Inc.

Each singular model, or view, is designed to validate the other possible views, thereby populating the details of the application. Details from each model are added to an event table. The event table is a model which contains information on what events are within the scope of the application (domain) and how the application should handle those events. It is built concurrently with the application models and prototypes. The event table is thus a repository for details about the application's behavior, data, and usage.

Interface prototypes, application code, and data structures are built from the models. Usage characteristics for each model are needed to design an appropriate application and technical architecture. Module, integration, and performance tests can be used to prove the viability of the application (Figure 5.1).

Events

The guiding principles for a client/server application are the real-world events to which the end-user must respond. The term "event-driven" is greatly overused and misunderstood. Events have two different contexts. The first is a business event, such as a customer calling to check the status of an order. The second is a GUI (graphical user interface) event, that is, an action which "drives" the application like a mouse click or a menu selection. Application development starts with determining the business events within the application domain. Through the iterative process of modeling and prototyping, GUI events emerge naturally. Business events are therefore transformed into GUI events when they are brought to their most granular form.

The process of modeling events involves creating a list of events and an accompanying context diagram, which show the events to which the system must respond. The other application models (process, data, and state) are built based on satisfying responses to the events. In this way, events are used to control project scope. The events that must be defined are business events and temporal events. Both business and temporal events cause processes to be triggered within the application (Figure 5.2).

Event List

Application domain, or scope, is defined using a list of business and temporal events. These events drive all requirements definition and design activities. Events from the event list are used to create the Event Table (following). This is supplemented with a visual model called the context diagram. Together they define the project domain. The domain, or subject matter of interest, shows the scope of the business problem and/or opportunity to be addressed by the client/server application.

Event Table

The Event Table shows all external and temporal events within the scope of the project in an easy to read format of columns and rows. It is an analysis and design tool and acts as a central location for showing all event-responses within the application domain. Additional details about how each event is handled in the application are added iteratively as the team is prototyping and modeling the application (Table 5.1). The event table provides a text-based account of how the application handles events: who, what, when, where, how quickly, and how importantly.

Multiple Application Models

A synthesis of three application models is appropriate to manage the complexity of client/server applications. These models, or views, are "orthogonal" (at right angles) to each other and are built in an iterative fashion. They are the: event-processor, data, and state models.

As orthogonal views of the application, each provides an independent axis of understanding (Table 5.2). Yet, when combined together, they provide a complete picture of the application. Each view responds to a well-defined set of events, and is constrained by rules, guidelines, or protocols that govern the process, data, or state (Figure 5.3).

Figure 5.2   Events trigger activities within the application.

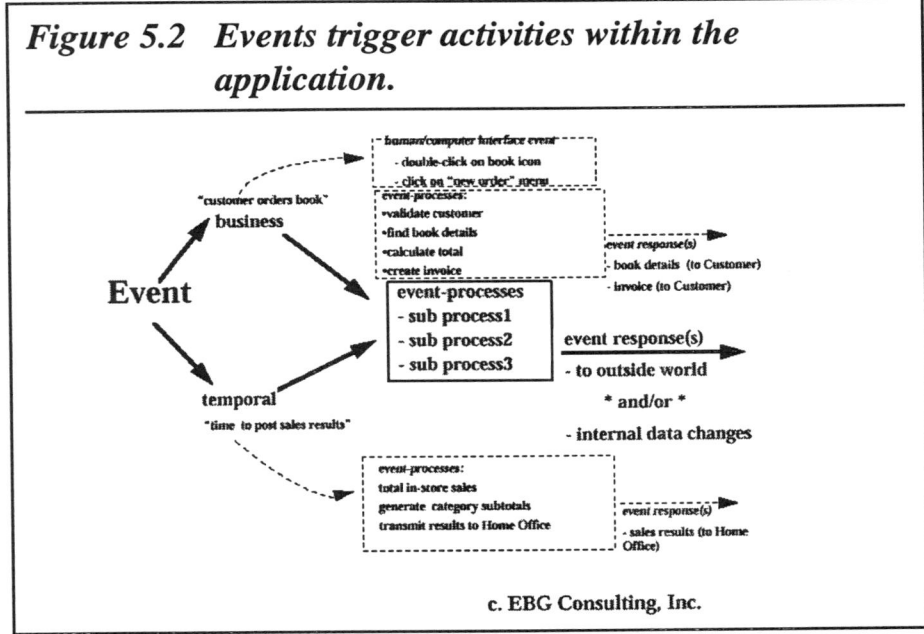

c. EBG Consulting, Inc.

Because all models are defined by the same business events, their order of creation is not important. In fact, they can be developed concurrently. By so doing, the models can be used to validate each other (Figure 5.3), giving the project team the flexibility of not having to determine all the in-scope events at the very start of the development effort. Although an initial list of business events, along with the context diagram, is generated early in the project, new events are likely to be discovered. The team will then add these events to the event list and context diagram. The data, process, and behavior needed to support those event are also modeled.

Table 5.1   Columns used in the Event Table.

Column	Discovery Phase
Event name	Scope/project domain definition
Event category	Scope/project domain definition
System response	Scope/project domain definition
Event-processor	Process modeling
Roles/Users	Process modeling
Location of Roles/Users	Process modeling
Frequency baseline	Process modeling
Frequency of usage	Process modeling
Event-processor dependencies	Process modeling
Response time requirements	Process modeling
Business Priority	Process modeling
Data Entities and CRUD*	Data Modeling
Data Entity Freshness	Data Modeling

Note: Details such as data entity start up volume and growth is stored with the Data Model.
*CRUD = create, read, update, delete; essential actions done to data

Table 5.2   Orthogonal views of the client/server app.

Axis of Emphasis	Visual Model
Data/Information	Entity Relationship Diagram (ERD)
Process/function/action	Event-processors or data-flow diagram (DFD partitioned by business event)
Dynamics/Behavior/Time sensitive	State Transition Diagram (STD)

The data-oriented view defines what data will be stored in the database and the constraints that apply to the data. The process-oriented view defines the actions performed by the system (human and automated) in transforming the data to accomplish the action. The dynamic-oriented view shows how the system undergoes change over time by describing the states that data experiences and the conditions that give rise to the transition from one state to the next. Each view is needed for a comprehensive understanding of the application.

Business Rules

Business rules are constraints, tests, or conditions which describe business policy. They can be expressed in nontechnical natural language (e.g., English) which means that nontechnical business subject matter experts can specify them. As statements of business policy, they are universally enforced by the business regardless of the technology applied to them.

Rules can be found by examining how the business experts discuss the business, within written policy and procedure documentation, and in other forms of business such as graphs, charts, and tables. Since rules are so fundamental, they span the three dimensions of analysis — information, process, and dynamics.

Each application model may represent multiple business rules. The event-processor model will have processing rules such as formulas for derived information and validation logic. The data model will have rules that include entity definition, relationship and attribute derivation, existence, and dependencies. The state model will have rules about the triggers for new states and allowable state transitions. One rule may apply to multiple models. For example, the rule "products must be ordered from approved suppliers" implies:

Figure 5.3   Application models validate each other.

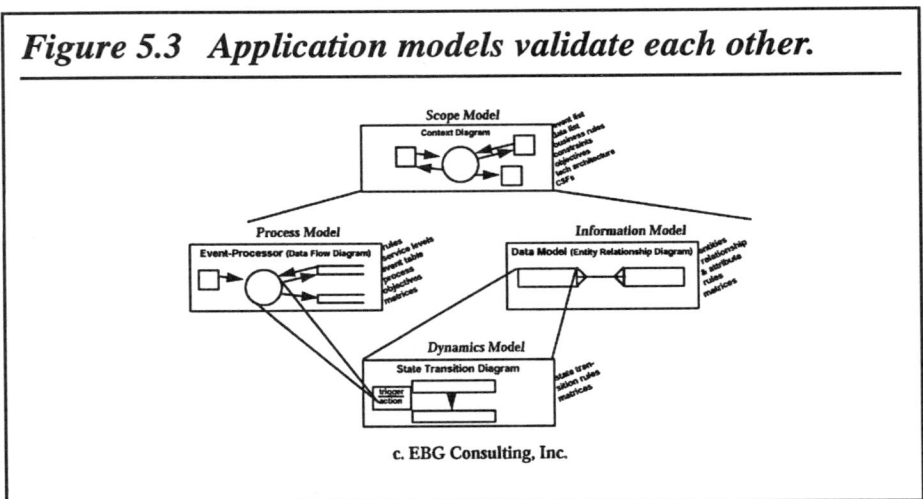

c. EBG Consulting, Inc.

- a data relationship rule (products are related to suppliers)
- a data type rule (suppliers can be approved)
- a processing rule (certain actions are done to approve a supplier)

Eventually, rules will become application code. Those which enforce referential integrity (maintaining relationships between entities) may take the form of code (such as database triggers) or may be handled by the DBMS (e.g., declarative referential integrity). In any case, all rules should be captured and documented along with the model to which they apply.

Design Requires Application Usage Information

Specific characteristics of how the application will be used must be known in order for the project team to determine which architecture, or combination of architectures, is the most efficient. These characteristics include: number of end-users, locations of end-users, event locations, business priority of the event-processors, frequency of each event, response time required for the process, data required to process each event, data currency (how up-to-date the data must be), volume of transactions and/or queries, and type and patterns of data access required by location.

This usage information is gathered as the application models are built (Table 5.3). It is also added as columns to the event table. This is necessary to analyze design scenarios for the application.

Usage information is needed to bridge from the logical to the physical design of the application. Technical choices are made based on the physical requirements of the application. For example, if there is a tolerance for "older" data (and response time delays), data distribution options like replication and fragmentation are possible. Non-instantaneous response time permits using less network bandwidth and devices such as routers. On the other hand, if many high priority event-processors are required at all locations, or if the processing is highly volatile, technical options like stored procedures or TP (transaction processing) monitors should be considered. The distribution of data is an important consideration as well. For example, data used only by a given location should be partitioned only to that location. Highly volatile data might be centralized, as opposed to distributed. This usage information, in conjunction with the models to which it applies, is needed to determine the best application design.

Application Design Challenges

In the end, client/server application development involves the careful management of trade-offs. These trade-offs deal with balancing the application's performance requirements with the end-users' need for security, integrity, and maintainability. It is necessary to understand the capabilities of the technologies that are planned or in place. For example, if the application requires high levels of data currency at all sites, response time may suffer. When transaction processing speed is critical, allowing data to be a little old (e.g., hours, one-half day, day) may be needed. Application design requires balancing the needs of the end-user, the project and technical architectural constraints, and the characteristics of the problem at hand. These are complex issues leading to challenging "techno-business" decisions which should be made together by IS and business.

Table 5.3 Application model usage information.	
Usage Information	*Application Development Discovery Activity*
Locations	Project Domain Definition (Scope) Document
Roles	Project Domain Definition (Scope) Document
Event Location (physical or geographic location that triggers an event)	Event-Processor Model
Business Priority	Event-Processor Model
Response Time (how soon after execution must the output be received)	Event-Processor Model
Volatility (frequency of change)	Event-Processor Model, Data Model
Volume and Growth (initial number of instances and physical sizing information derived from the creation (insertion) and deletion (removal) of entity instances; defined for all locations)	Data Model
Access patterns to data entities (tables) for each location, e.g., constant or bursty	Data Model
Data Sharing (locations requiring the same data entities — rows and columns — and type of access required (C, R, U, and/or D)	Data Model
Retention	Data Model
Currency (how fresh the data must be and still satisfy the business need — lag time tolerance between propagating updates)	Data Model

Data Distribution

In distributing data in a client/server application, it is desirable to

- place the data closest to the end-user
- make it available in multiple locations
- eliminate a single point of failure
- permit efficient data access
- balance network traffic
- meet data currency needs

There are several ways to distribute, or partition, data across clients and servers (or even servers and servers). Data can be distributed using a variety of techniques: manual extract, snapshot, summarization, replication (or mirroring), fragmentation, or two-phase commit (Table 5.4). Knowledge about how the application is to be used and of the technical architecture is needed to determine which data distribution technique is optimal.

Client/Server Architecture

An architecture is a set of definitions and protocols for building a product. A computer architecture, like that of a building, is a broad plan for the overall shape of the system. A client/server architecture encompasses both the technical and the application architecture, defined in the following section.

Technical Architecture

The technical architecture is the infrastructure upon which the application is built. It is a detailed inventory of all the hardware, software, and network elements that reside on the client and server components for all locations in the application. This will include such elements as:

- operating systems
- DBMSs
- memory
- network schemas
- database schema (physical layout of the databases including such DDLs (Data Definition language)
- space allocations
- index definitions

- security and locking
- program packaging
- network protocols
- physical hardware devices (workstations, servers, wiring, bridges, routers)
- network operating systems
- network monitoring and tuning software
- gateways and connectivity software (APIs, ODBC, messaging, ORBs, RPCs, etc.)
- application development tools
- TP monitors
- security software
- configuration management software

Table 5.4 Data distribution techniques.

Data Distribution Technique	Description
Manual Extract	Data is logically centralized and copied from a central location to multiple locations via an extract process; the central site may initiate the extract, which loads the remote tables, or the sites may issue the extract request.
Snapshot	The distributed database management system is capable of issuing extracts of pre-defined data (tables and the necessary columns) at a pre-defined time or frequency.
Summarization	Different levels of summarized data are stored at different locations; "rollups" or consolidations of the data will vary according to site needs.
Replication	Multiple sites have copies of the same data tables and are periodically updated by a central site coordinator. Data is kept consistent via a synchronous process (all sites have the same data at all times) or an asynchronous process (data is not exactly the same for a period of time, such as minutes, hours, or days).

Because of the unpredictability associated with mixing a variety of application components together, the technical infrastructure can make or break a project. "Test early and often" should be the motto of all client/server project team members.

Application Architecture

Client/server technology affords the designer and end-user great flexibility in how to allocate functions and data between client and server. The scope and complexity of the application architecture is determined by the number of locations, size of the databases, volume of data, and amount of concurrent data access.

An application architecture specifies how application components are distributed between clients and servers. These components represent conceptual layers which are allocated (partitioned) to different physical, or hardware, components. Essentially, three layers need to be distributed: presentation, business rules/ logic, and data management (Figure 5.4).

The presentation layer furnishes the user interface for the overall system. It permits end-users to enter and manipulate data, analyze information, and navigate throughout the system. It may also interact with existing applications on the desktop. This layer should mask the complexity of the overall system with an easy to use interface. Validation and verification logic is often needed in this layer to edit input values and selections.

Table 5.4 (continued)	
Data Distribution Technique	*Description*
Fragmentation	Portions of non-overlapping data are stored at different locations and periodically refreshed via snapshots; data can be fragmented vertically (rows) or horizontally (columns).
Two-Phase Commit	A highly synchronous protocol which assures that data is consistent at all locations at all times; a database change is committed or aborted at all sites; the process uses a commit coordinator site to 1) checks all locations for availability to accept the transaction (prepare) and 2) issue the COMMIT command which will be ROLLBACKed if any site did not respond affirmatively (commit).

The business rules/logic layer processes the policies and constraints that the application is responsible for enforcing. This includes: decisions ("can we schedule this course for next Tuesday?"; "can this account be approved?"), policy enforcement ("credit approval is required for orders exceeding $10,000"), and resource management decisions ("the limit of class size for workshop courses is 20 students"). These are collections of business rules ascribed to the data, state, and event-processor models.

The data management layer maintains consistent and secure data through the enforcement of referential integrity and data security. Transactions and queries against the database are managed in this layer, including:

- accessing
- matching
- updating
- inserting
- locking

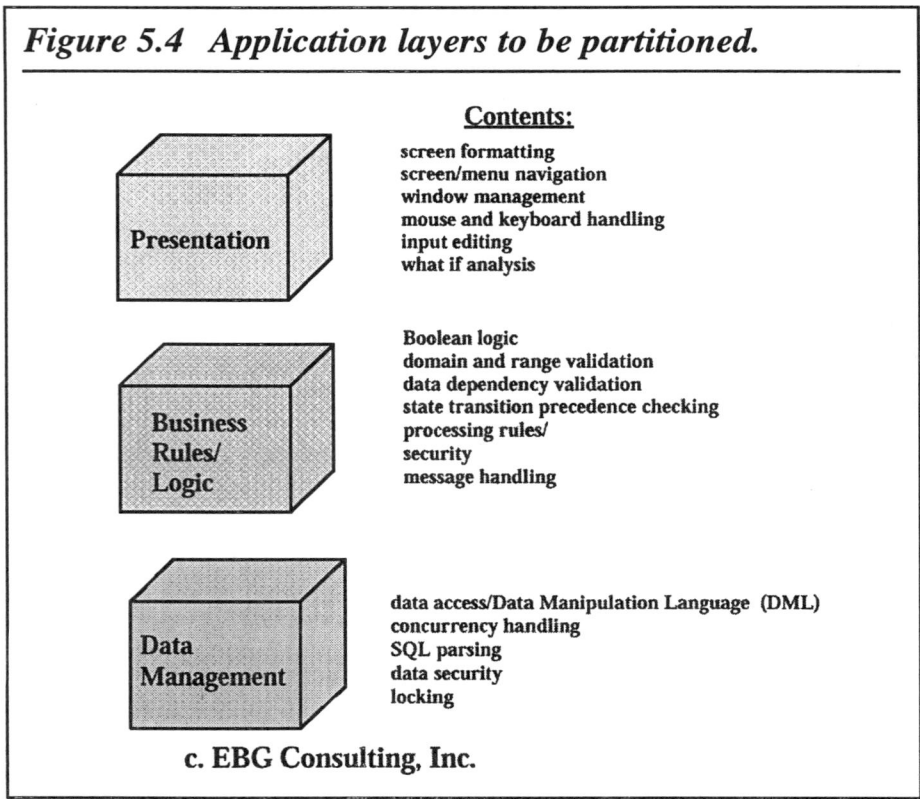

Figure 5.4 Application layers to be partitioned.

Contents:

Presentation
- screen formatting
- screen/menu navigation
- window management
- mouse and keyboard handling
- input editing
- what if analysis

Business Rules/ Logic
- Boolean logic
- domain and range validation
- data dependency validation
- state transition precedence checking
- processing rules/
- security
- message handling

Data Management
- data access/Data Manipulation Language (DML)
- concurrency handling
- SQL parsing
- data security
- locking

c. EBG Consulting, Inc.

- retrieving
- security
- logging
- backup
- recovery

Some of these tasks are performed by the DBMS.

Client/server allows you to implement these layers in a modular fashion for the appropriate physical location. This permits the flexibility to change locations if business need or performance problems so require. The presentation, business rules, and data management layers of the applications can be partitioned in a variety of ways. Some possible applications architectures have been suggested by the Gartner Group (see Figure 5.5). In some cases, portions of a single layer, such as business rules, may be split between multiple physical layers. For example, both the workstation and the application server machine may contain business rules.

Tiers

Tiers are the physical platforms on which client and server application layers reside. A first generation of client/server applications utilizes two collaborating computing platforms. The front-end application, residing on an end-user's workstation, provides the application interface and a large amount of business processing. The back-end application component, residing on one or more hardware processors, provides the database services including data access, management, and integrity services, and some business rule processing in the form of stored procedures and triggers. (Stored procedures are a relational DBMS feature which provides processing capability on the server. They have the advantage of centralizing business rules, enforcing security, and reducing network traffic by allowing access only to the procedure code, as opposed to the data itself. Triggers are a special kind of stored procedures which maintain referential integrity and are executed when the database is updated by an INSERT, UPDATE, or DELETE command.)

In two-tiered applications, application clients invoke the database server using an interface like ODBC or by invoking dynamic SQL. Clients are built using application development tools like Microsoft Visual Basic, Powersoft's PowerBuilder, or Gupta's SQLWindows. They characteristically support small workgroup or departmental applications (up to 20 or perhaps 50, depending on the hardware infrastructure). Because business rules may be executing on the client as application logic, they are known as "fat clients" or clientcentric. For many applications this is a cost-effective and relatively simple architecture.

A more scalable but complex physical architecture uses three or more tiers. Rather than employing server-based application logic which is part of database services, business logic is insulated from the database services by placing them on their own tier (Figure 5.6). In this way, the raw data is separated from the business logic layer. The business logic will operate on its own platform. It will run under the control of its own operating system, TP monitor, or some form of middleware.

In three-tiered architectures, an application server is the new third tier and is used to access multiple heterogeneous databases. It generally executes quicker than stored procedures and removes the need to use a proprietary language (as is stored procedure SQL). It facilitates reuse of application logic and allows application code to reside on a variety of platforms. Maintaining business rules is easier — instead of redeploying application logic to multiple end-user workstations where application logic resides in a two-tiered architecture, the logic is updated only on the server(s) in which it resides.

The three-or-more-tiered application architecture is a more complex environment involving additional hardware, software, and vendors. However, the usage needs for the application may require this "second-generation" client/server architecture.

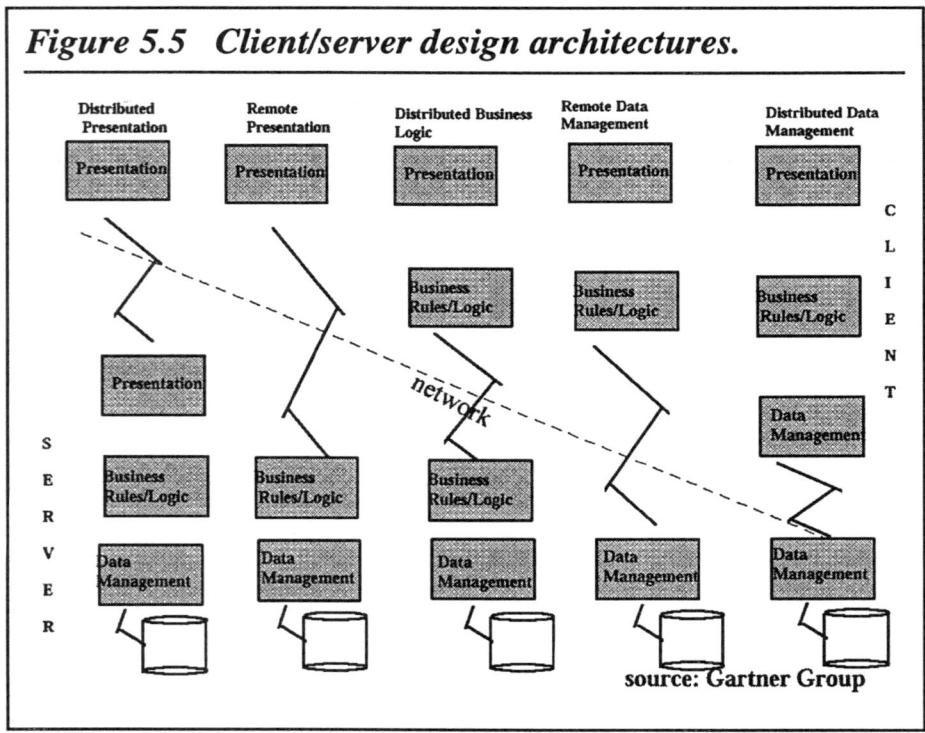

Figure 5.5   Client/server design architectures.

source: Gartner Group

Usage Analysis

In many client/server applications, partitioning is accomplished through guesswork — a slow, expensive, and frustrating process. The best architecture is based on the expected behavior of the user roles and business events to which those user roles must respond. It anticipates the execution environment and expected application workload. It requires detailed examination of information about the locations and characteristics of application processing and data, i.e., usage information (Table 5.4).

Usage analysis is the process of scrutinizing these details with a series of matrices and visual techniques, and is a complex, iterative process. Data distribution guidelines are also used when analyzing data usage information (Table 5.5). Distributed data placement should be based on:

- what needs to be done
- with what data
- where it needs to happen
- how often it will occur
- how accurate the data used in the process must be

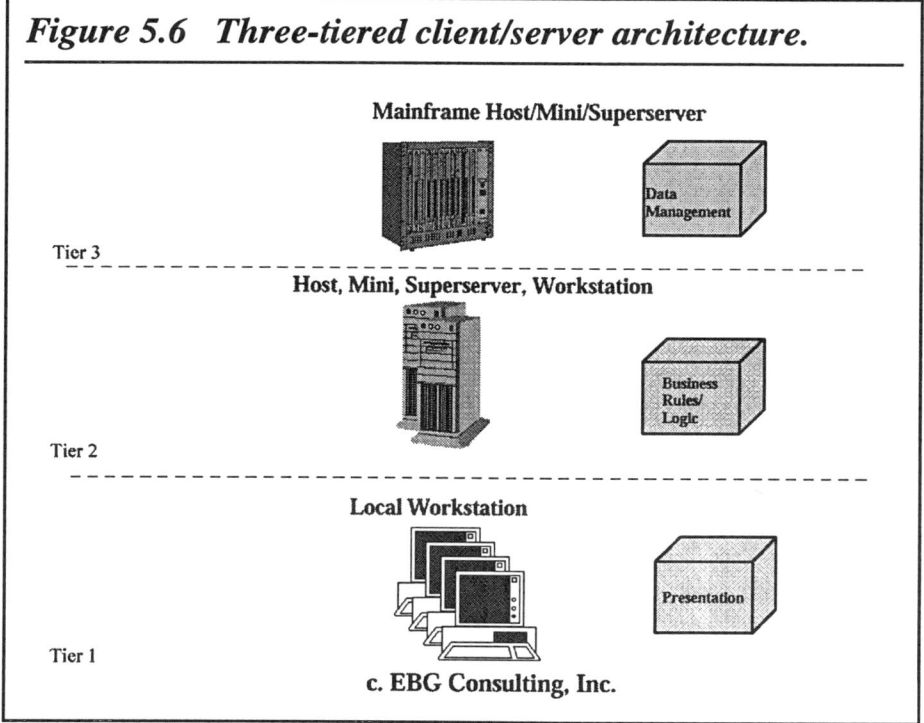

Figure 5.6   Three-tiered client/server architecture.

Performing usage analysis allows the application designer to formulate a best case architecture. The proposed architecture should be tested within the technical environment intended for the application.

Data Distribution Guidelines

High-level recommendations for how data is distributed are based on data currency, volatility, and the source of updates to the data. Other issues such as volume, response time, and retention must be factored into the data distribution strategy (Table 5.6).

Table 5.5 Usage analysis techniques.	
Technique	*Purpose*
Event: Event Coupling matrix	Analyze the percentage of time that events occur together.
Event-Processor: Role Frequency matrix	Understand which business roles (who) perform which activities (what) and how often (when).
Event-Process Distribution matrix	Map where event-processors will be located in the client/server application, e.g., client, stored procedure, trigger, server, or split.
Data Access: Location Partition	Determine which locations need which partition of tables.
Data Placement: Location	Analyze and summarize read and update access needs and traffic patterns for each location and each table.
Data Distribution Network Traffic Scenario Comparison	Analyzes network traffic for various data entity placement scenarios based on access required.
Data Distribution CRUD matrix	Determine what type of access (CRUD) is done to which tables and whether the tables are primary or copy tables.
Data Distribution Guidelines	Provide guidelines for data distribution based on volatility and concurrent usage of data.
Visual Partitioning Scenarios	Analyze trial partitioning strategies using the event-processor models.

Successful Client/Server Development

Client/server development requires IS to marry the best of the PC and mainframe worlds. A balance must be achieved between the benefits of prototyping and the advantages of careful exploration of requirements. The end-user must be at center stage during client/server application development, continually involved in defining and validating models and prototypes and testing the developed system. An event-driven development approach provides a solid foundation for an effective business system and an efficient iterative development methodology. Architectural and design choices must be made using the application models and usage information associated with those models. Techniques must be practiced which promote teamwork, quality, speed, and application integrity and longevity.

Table 5.6 Data distribution guidelines.		
Currency Level — Volatility	*High Currency (Synchronization Required, (e.g., Up to the Second))*	*Low to Medium Currency (e.g., Hours Old)*
Infrequent updates from one source	data distributed to database servers with distributed updates (e.g., two-phase commit or synchronous data replication)	extracts, snapshots, or asynchronous data replication
Infrequent updates from geographically dispersed sources	centralized database or distributed with updates distributed (e.g., extracts or snapshots from central source, two-phase commit, or synchronous replication)	extracts, snapshots, or asynchronous data replication
Frequent updates from one source	same as above	data centralization or distributed with batch updates or asynchronous replication
Frequent updates from multiple geographically dispersed sources	centralized database or transaction server (e.g., CICS, Tuxedo, Top End, Transarc or synchronous replication)	same as above

References and Recommended Reading

Richard Barker. *Case*Method: Entity Relationship Modeling*. England: Addison-Wesley, 1989.

Richard Barker and Cliff Longman. *Case*Method: Function and Process Modelling*. England: Addison-Wesley, 1992.

Alex Berson. *Client/Server Architecture*. McGraw Hill, 1992.

Alan Davis. *Software Requirements: Objects, Functions, and States*, 2nd ed. PTR Prentice Hall, 1993.

Dawna Travis Dewire. *Client/Server Computing*. McGraw Hill, 1993.

Candice Fleming and Barbara Von Halle. *Handbook of Relational Database Design*. Addison Wesley, 1989.

David Hay. *Data Model Patterns: Conventions of Thought*. Dorset House Publishing, 1996.

Neil Jenkins et al. *Client/Server Unleashed*. SAMS Publishing, 1996.

Stephen M McMenamin and John F. Palmer. *Essential Systems Analysis*. Yourdon, Inc., 1984.

Robert Orfali, Dan Harkey, and Jeri Edwards. *Essential Client/Server Survival Guide*. Van Nostrand Reinhold, 1994.

James Robertson and Suzanne Robertson. *Complete Systems Analysis*. Dorset House Publishing, 1994.

Sally Shlaer and Stephen J. Mellor. *Object Lifecycles: Modeling the World in States*. PTR Prentice Hall, 1992.

Graeme C. Simsion. *Data Modeling Essentials: Analysis, Design, and Innovation*. Van Nostrand Reinhold, 1994.

Patrick N. Smith with Steven L. Guengerich. *Client/Server Computing*, 2nd ed. SAMS Publications, 1994.

Phil Sully. *Modeling the World with Objects*. Prentice Hall, 1993.

David Vaskevitch. *Client/Server Strategies: A Survival Guide for Corporate Reengineers*. IDG Books, 1993.

Edward Yourdon. *Modern Structured Analysis*. Yourdon Press, 1989.

Yourdon, Inc. *Yourdon™ Systems Methods: Model Driven System Development*. Yourdon Press Computing Series, 1993.

Chapter 6

An Anatomy of an Intranet

A Case Study — How to Make Your Intranet a Success Story

David F. Carter

This paper and the accompanying charts attempt to transfer what the Department of Defense's Office of Process Improvement went through to begin the process of building our first and subsequent intranets. We knew that we did not know many things about this technology. Much has been written and spoken about intranets since we began. Some of the material has been helpful and some has been discarded. But even in the discarded material there were lessons to be learned to avoid future mistakes. The Office has constructed several inter- and intranets sites with national acclaim. There is yet much to be done and we are about the business of doing it.

The paper and the attached charts are broken into three sections, Obstacles, Killer Applications, and Implementation. In the first section, Obstacles, I have focused on two of the many — people and architecture. I will discuss what we have found in these areas and how we have either overcome or gotten around many obstacles. In the second section, Killer Applications, I will highlight several of the applications that have "sold" the champion of these systems and the positive results these applications have had on their organizations. Finally, the most difficult — Implementation. In this section I go over how have we accomplished the Killer Applications and how we have kept them alive and well.

I will digress from time to time, updating the charts with what we are doing today and the current state of the Killer Applications that are listed in the presentation. Now on with the show. I believe it will be both informative and entertaining.

Obstacles

People

This has been for us the most difficult to deal with in the introduction of anything new. We are in the change management business, therefore, we know that change is trauma. We will address three areas in this section: cost, culture, and incentive.

- Alleviate Cost
  - Use existing data systems where possible
  - Use COTS tools
  - Keep it simple!

Cost is near and dear to most individuals. Our business is providing for the national defense of our country. Our culture wants to know if resources are expended for anything other than the delivery of mission related activity; where is the return on the investment. To alleviate any undue concern, we attempt not to build anything new. We use existing systems wherever possible and/or commercially-off-the-shelf tools and systems. Bottom line, we practice the "KISS" principle. We keep the application as simple as possible. We also practice what we preach — a very important attribute to any success story — we gather cost/benefit data so that we can construct the economic analysis to feed back the return on the investment of precious resources.

- Minimize Culture Shock
  - Everyone can use a browser!
  - Keep it simple!

The culture is where one either succeeds or fails. Sell the culture and you have sold the application. Ignore the culture and you will fail. We involve the providers, developers, and users of the application from the initial point of inception. We keep that group together working as a tightly integrated working group through implementation. Most everyone today has seen or is using a World Wide Web browser from one service or another. The two emerging browsers, Microsoft and Netscape, have very similar constructs to allow virtually universal usage. Both Microsoft and Netscape are extremely intuitive technologies minimizing culture shock both in the introduction and use of inter- and intranet applications. Once again, we try very hard to practice the "KISS" principle. We attempt to keep all aspects of an application as simple as possible.

- Provide Incentive

  - Initiate Management-to-Management Dialogue with Successful Intranet Implementers

  - Time to implementation can be very low

  - Find the Killer App!

Success is based on use. Use is based on incentive. If there is no reason to use an application, guess what, it will not be used. The application must have a champion. This individual must be in a position within the organization to provide the culture with the incentive to use the application. The champion has to be sold on the application or it is finished. Time to develop the application must be short. Develop a prototype — the 60 percent solution. Get it into production. In other words, find the Killer Application that hooks the champion and the culture. Get the application into production quickly with instant payback. Then evolve it, enrich it until the application is institutionalized.

Architecture

- Provide Appropriate Approach

  - Select a Proven Toolset

  - Match Toolset to Your Requirements

We begin with an appropriate approach to building the infrastructure. First is the selection of a proven toolset. This is not the time nor the place to invent one's own building process. There are plenty of toolsets out there. Research the market and select the toolset that meets your requirement. Of course, this belies one of the most important principles: that you know what your requirements are. One of the greatest obstacles to overcome is building an application for which there is no requirement.

- Manage the Implementation

  - Use Appropriate Paradigms

  - Develop a Plan, and Stick To It

We do everything possible to construct a viable and living plan. We develop the plan in a collaborative setting. We bring all of the players together. The champion, providers, developers, and users in a common meeting brainstorm, discuss, and agree on a course of action that has milestones and deliverables. This plan of action is closely monitored by all the players to ensure success. Once again, by keeping everything as simple as possible, we ask our customer what they want and then we deliver.

- Manage the Site

  - Maintain Continuous Dialogue with Players

  - Evolve!

The most important obstacle is to get the customer, not the developer, to manage the application. The customer must take ownership of the application. If this does not happen, the application will fall into disrepair and will cease. We build a continual process improvement component into each application to ensure customer involvement. Once an application is institutionalized, it will evolve into a mature application.

Summary

What I have written in this section is the common sense approach to system life cycle success. Identify a need. Identify a champion for that need. Identify the culture the application will serve to satisfy the need. Make the application affordable with a reasonable return on its investment. Minimize culture shock to new technology. Provide the incentives to both the champion and the culture to use and nurture the application. The result is the overcoming of the most common obstacles in the introduction of new technology and its associated applications.

Killer Applications

We have built four Killer Applications for the United States Atlantic Command. It was these applications that launched us into this business practice. Since then, we have built our own and contributed to several applications for the United States Air Force Air Staff. We practiced many of the precepts that were covered in the Obstacles section of this paper.

The Killer Application that started it all for us was the United States Atlantic Command's Olympic Command and Control Web Site. The commander in chief of the Command was given the responsibility of coordinating the security aspects connected with and surrounding the 1996 Olympic Games in Atlanta, GA. The commander in chief's requirement was to gain "information superiority" in this most critical area. Our first question was, what is information superiority? Working with all of the respective federal, state, and local law enforcement agencies and departments we began the task of weaving together a collection of disparate databases and sources into a single data and information source. In one weeks time using three staff members, a tightly integrated Command and Control information base was constructed and put into place accessible from the police precinct to the National Command Authority level. This effort won high acclaim from the White House to the Atlanta Mayor's Office. The same template has been used in natural disaster response sites (hurricane and wildfires) and is ready for the Command's use upon a moment's notice.

As Figure 6.1 shows, a Killer Application has the following attributes:

- Real-time update from distributed locations over a 24 hour period
- Application deployment primarily web site setup — updates centrally applied (minimal client software distribution)
- Applications were developed in one week (3 staff) using rapid prototyping approach
- Application set available to be stood up during a crisis situation for similar capabilities — slight to moderate customization (example: Hurricane Bertha response site developed in 8 hours by 3 staff)

A current Killer Application is being evolved for the Office of the Secretary of Defense's Functional Process Improvement Office. It is a Business Process Improvement Kiosk, especially emphasizing the development of BPR concepts (Business Process Reengineering). You can view this website at `http://bprkiosk.acom.mil`.

What has to be understood in developing and implementing a Killer Application is that it should knock the entire culture's socks off. The application has to be of immediate use and be perceived as value added. Given these simple attributes you too can have a Killer Application.

Implementation

Here is where the rubber hits the road. You have taken a look at the obstacles that lie before you and hopefully addressed them to your and your customer's satisfaction. You have considered, evaluated, and chosen your Killer Application. Now it is time to get started.

Table 6.1 Killer applications support both static and dynamic information requirements.	
Static Information:	*Dynamic Information:*
Background Information	Incident Reports
Housing and Facility Information	Significant Events
Venue Information	Threat Assessments
Instructions	Weather Updates
Command Relationships	Status Updates
Phone Lists	Personnel Information
Command Post Information	Schedules
Contingency Instructions	Logistics Information

First we must understand just what is an intranet and what makes it different from a World Wide Website. We suggest the following four attributes are discriminating characteristics. 1) Intranets often provide internal and most likely "mission-critical" data. The United States Atlantic Command's Olympic Command and Control intranet certainly handled very mission-critical data. 2) Intranets are normally accessed through very high speed connections not relying on outside sources to determine or

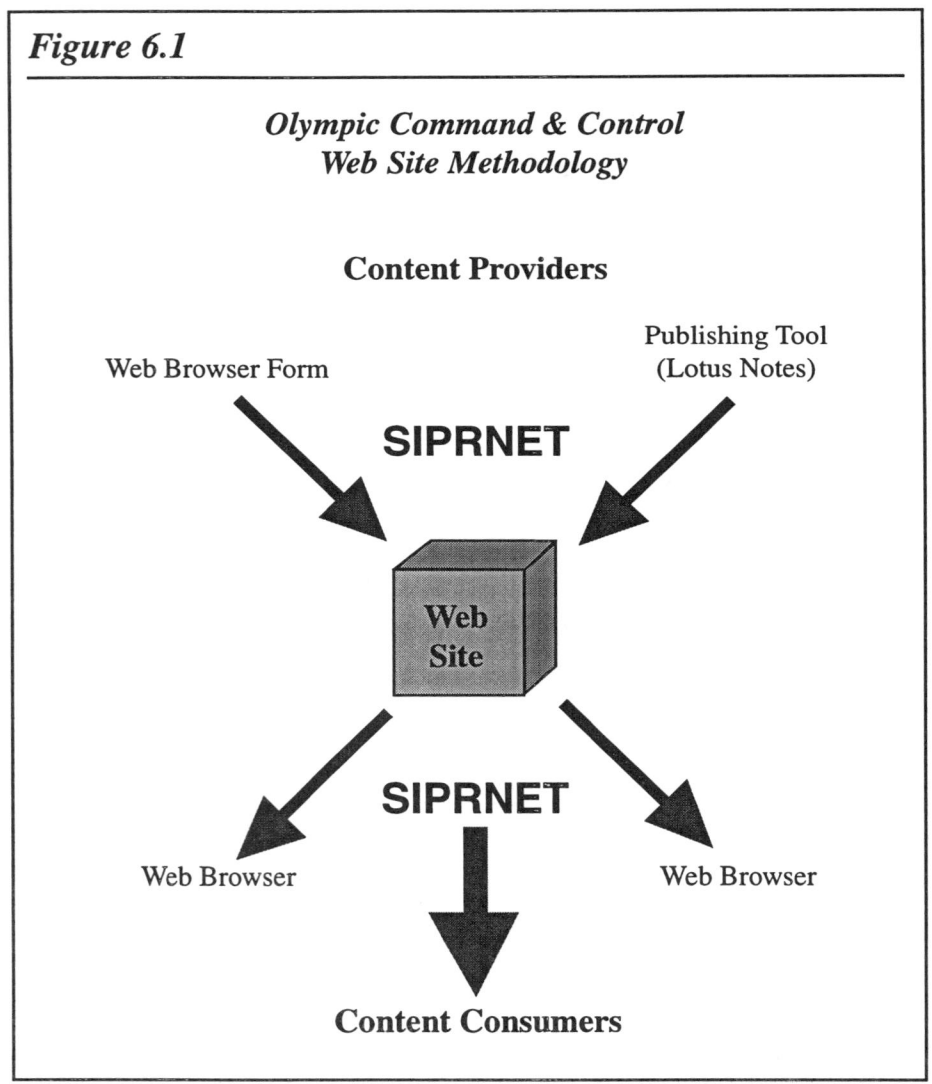

Figure 6.1

Olympic Command & Control
Web Site Methodology

Content Providers

Web Browser Form

Publishing Tool
(Lotus Notes)

SIPRNET

Web
Site

SIPRNET

Web Browser

Web Browser

Content Consumers

regulate input and response times. 3) As was the case with the Olympic Command and Control site, intranets are more likely to hold sensitive data. 4) Finally, the data pushed around an intranet can be more dynamic in nature.

Common Issues

I will offer five common issues to be considered in the implementation phase of an intranet. These are:

1. a need to plan,
2. design and implementation considerations,
3. security,
4. configuration management, and
5. records management.

Need to Plan

We spoke about the need to plan in the obstacles portion of the paper. Without this aspect the project is dead before arrival. The ingredients of any well constructed plan should include, but not be limited to, setting realistic goals; contain the cost to a minimum; acquire a champion and get his/her buy-in; bill the application as a prototype; establish well-defined milestones with deliverables; be certain to build in a generous dose of "casual overtime" during the initial stages of the project. Be ever vigilant that the plan be continual and flexible to allow for change that will always occur.

Design and Implementation

There are a myriad of design and implementations issues. I will go through several of the more interesting ones we encountered thus far. A basic page layout sounds very simple, but can and usually gets quite complex. The basic page must capture the essence of the organization being served. The site design needs to be intuitive. That is, the extensions or page hierarchy must flow and be understandable to the occasional user. We have found the a tasteful use of "special effects" enhances the appearance of the site. This aspect can be overdone and turn off champions and users alike. Always, but always, keep the user in the forefront of the design and implementation considerations. Bottom line, make the site as simple as possible. Once again the "KISS" principle has to be paramount. There are a wide variety of design and implementation tools in the market place. Once again, carefully select the tools to meet your requirements. Do not select the tools because of the glitz and sizzle they portend. Only select the tools that will get your job done in the most economic, effective, and efficient manner.

- Editors
  - Dedicated editors (e.g., Hot Dog) and office automation software add-ons (e.g., Microsoft Internet Assistant for Word)
  - Multimedia editors
- HTML Syntax Checkers
  - Public domain
- Publishing Systems (Super Editors)
  - Lotus Notes/Internotes, Microsoft Frontpage
  - HTML Forms
- Database Connectors
  - Cold Fusion, webDBC, native web server capabilities
- Windows NT Web Servers
  - Microsoft Internet Information Server
  - Purveyor
- UNIX Web Servers
  - Apache
  - Netscape

An important note: Don't expect typical end-users to understand HTML!

Security

Security is of great concern to the Department of Defense. In my presentation we show connectivity through our Secure IP Router Network (SIPRNET) as well as our Non-Secure IP Router Network (NIPRNET). We recommend that security be made a high priority issue. You must understand who are the players in any intranet application. Security policy must be set, implemented, and most of all followed. Decisions must be made concerning who will administer the application. Finally the end-user must be clearly defined. There are a number of ways to "lock down" an applications. One method is to lock down the entire network such as our SIPRNET. If one is designing and developing applications for secure networks the concern is much less. If one is in a nonsecure area, then accessibility to the network is a good place to begin. There are many ways to allow or deny access to a network or to a particular page site. Authentication, encryption, and integrity are just three of many types. Thus far we have used the Department's encryption schemes as well as authentication keys and tables to allow and deny access to our sites and pages. There are an equal number of security tools and techniques. Some of the topics are Address-based, Account-based, encryption, and monitoring. This area of tools and techniques is a whole area unto itself.

Security Tools/Techniques

- Address-Based
  - Firewalls, web server-based
  - Not using DNS
- Account-Based
  - Web server, web server host
- Encryption
  - Secure certificates
  - Hardware
- Monitoring
  - Server logs, operating system audit trails
  - Enhancements via log analyzers
  - Centralized management via proprietary and open (e.g., SNMP) tools

Configuration Management

Configuration management issues strike at the heart of any successful intranet application. There are two major divisions — physical and logical. The physical portion of configuration management deals with the performance management issues of the application and with the integrity of the software components. If we have service levels of agreement with our customers, we are constantly monitoring how are we doing with such tools as NT Performance Monitor. The integrity is concerned with whether an unauthorized attempt has been made to gain access to site or page. In addition we continually watch for instances where an internal breakage occurs. The logical portion deals with link and content management of the site and associated pages. There are tools available, but much is still done by dead reckoning.

Configuration Management Tools

- Performance Management
  - Proprietary tools (e.g., NT Performance Monitor)
- Software Integrity
  - Have I Been Hacked?
  - Did I Break Something?
  - "The Old Noggin" (= none exist)
- Link Management
  - Open (e.g., Frontpage) and proprietary (e.g., Domino) tools
- Content Management
  - Some tool support (e.g., Notes/InterNotes)
  - Mostly "The Old Noggin"

Records Management

Records management issues are central to the development and maintenance of intranet applications. Much like a newspaper, the questions of who, what, when, and where are key to the success of an intranet application. The overall site administrator must determine who publishes, catalogs, updates, and deletes items to and from the application. This should be a daily set of functions. How many time have you gone to a site and found the last update was six months or more old. The confidence level in the quality of information in the application is greatly diminished by the apparent lack of application management. The United States Atlantic Command's Newspaper is updated before the start of business every day. The issues of what, when, and where are purely administrative, but must be accomplished on a scheduled basis. The tools to assist in this issue area are few, and mostly behind the scenes, such as databases. We have found the process to be heavily dependent on manual inspection.

The following is the daily set of functions to be updated:

- Messages (AMHS, e-mail, other message sources)
- News sources (Newswires, WWW, Early Bird, other magazine and newspaper articles)
- Bulletin Boards (Command Directives, Staff news, meeting minutes, flag schedules, other postings)
- Other Internal Information Sources (CDO On-Line, J2 News, departmental Home Pages)

Observations

Bottom line here is that we have not found a 100 percent solution, such as one tool does it all. Further it has been very difficult to define tool categories. We have found, whenever we can, commercial off-the-shelf tools that contain some integration. We find this to be a start in the right direction. There is a need for general programmatic tools to fill the gaps (Figure 6.2). Our development has been done using what tools and languages we could find — Perl, Python, C/C++, TCL, VB Script, Javascript, Java, Winbatch/WebBatch, and APIs such as ISAPI or MAPI. We still rely heavily on the "old noggin" to get the job done.

Futures

We look forward to an exciting near term period as we extend our incremental, rapid prototyping and implementation of a broad range of solutions. As we gain more and more knowledge of the current and emerging technologies we see a lower cost-to-implementation ratio. We also see that the reuse of existing templates will enable near real-time deployment of solutions as problems occur. Deployment of upgrades does not require physical access to a client and platforms and hosts are transparent to the end-users. These facts lead us to the knowledge that we are at the beginning of a very exciting era of reinvention.

The following strengths will soon enable us to better implement Killer Applications:

- Implements incremental, rapid prototyping for a broad range of solutions.
- Lowers cost-to-implementation.
- Enables near-real-time deployment of solutions as problems occur.
- Platform and host are transparent to the end-user.
- Anyone can use a browser.
- Deployment of upgrades does not require physical access to client.
- Use is location-independent.
- Can become an integral component of major systems requiring classical development approaches.

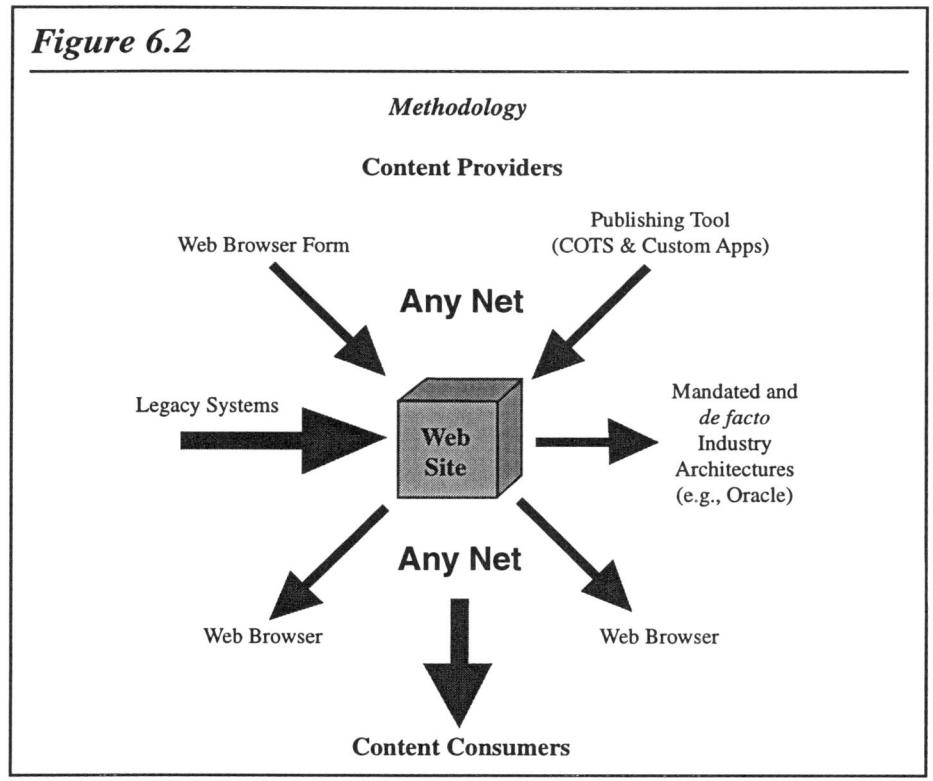

Figure 6.2

Chapter 7

Intranet Application Development for the Enterprise

David S. Linthicum

I'm finding that the web finally provides me with most of the business information I need, including product information, emerging technologies, and industry news. Many corporations understand this as well and are focusing on the Internet as a legitimate corporate resource.

There is a concurrent but less publicized rise of internal web sites, servers, and applications that exist behind the corporate firewalls. These private web sites are known as "intranets," and could be the largest growth area for client/server application development over the next few years. Intranets may also cause a major shift in client/server architectures, paradigms, and tool sets.

Intranet Advantages

Corporate America is just beginning to understand the potential of the intranet. The intranet concept is driven by organizations that want to exploit inexpensive web technology (web browsers and web servers) for in-house applications. Initially, internal web use focuses on corporate information dissemination applications such as online documents, company newsletters, or near-time financial information. By leveraging the application development capabilities of the new Internet tools and technology such as Sun's Java, Netscape's plug-in mechanism, and Microsoft's ISAPI and ActiveX, the intranet also provides a new dynamic client/server application development platform for corporate applications.

A new study from Zona Research Inc. states that the largest opportunity for internet technologies does not lie in supporting commercial applications over the Internet, but the utilization of internet technologies within the enterprise. Zona contends that organizations are better able to quantify the benefits associated with the use of intranet technologies for internal communications and applications. IDC, another internet research organization, estimates that the demand for enterprise applications of web technology will end up being five times greater than external applications in five years.

The intranet offers many advantages over traditional client/server application development platforms including truly open standards, ease of use, simplicity, and lower costs. Web technology uses open standards such as TCP/IP, HTTP, HTML, CGI, and Java, and thus does not lock organizations into proprietary technology with limitations and significant cost. Heterogeneous database connectivity is available as well using open API standards such as ODBC.

The use of point and click hyperlinking technology allows users to easily navigate and locate information using standard web browsers. With the advent of Java and ActiveX-based internet application development tools, users can download and run dynamic applications (or applets) directly from web browsers without having to maintain a server connection. Using web browsers such as the popular Netscape Navigator, a single front-end provides access to all internal and external resources. Therefore, users don't need to learn multiple software interfaces and quickly become proficient with web pages or web applications. In other words, we're bringing applications together using the browser as a single point of integration.

Web applications are significantly less expensive in either internal or external flavors. The software and hardware required to get web servers and clients up and running are cheap, web applications driven from a single browser require less training, and deployment costs are reduced due to the single interface, protocol, and middleware architecture. Large organizations report costs of less than $40 per user to create an intranet infrastructure, compared to approximately $2,000 per user for traditional two-tier client/server application infrastructure (from my own personal experience).

The intranet brings architectural simplicity back to the enterprise. Let's face it folks, the hodgepodge of proprietary client/server development tools, interfaces, platforms, middleware layers, and network protocols, as well as a shortage of standards, have made client/server one of the most complex and frustrating platforms to build and deploy applications on.

The intranet allows users to access a wide assortment of very different applications using a least common denominator approach — the web browsers. When a new corporate application is available, the corporate user simply links to the appropriate web server and runs the new application, either by downloading and executing a Java applet, or by receiving an HTML stream from the server or server-based application layers.

The intranet is portable as well. Popular web browsers such as Netscape and Mosaic are multi-platform, and almost all computer platforms offer some sort of web browser required to run intranet applications. Therefore, intranet applications run on Windows 3.11, Windows 95, Windows NT, most UNIX flavors, and the Macintosh.

Intranet Applications

The intranet is already a part of many corporate infrastructures. For example, more than 15,000 Xerox employees have been given immediate access to a new internal web site called "The Xerox WebBoard," with plans to increase the number of users to 60,000 by year end. The WebBoard contains posting of daily company and market news, as well as a company folklore area, phone directory, and links to other internal and external sites of interest.

Many organizations go beyond the information dissemination capabilities of the intranet to extend corporate applications out to intranet users. GE, for example, is creating its own intranet application called Trading Process Network (TPN). Using TPN, qualified subcontractors can search for GE purchase tenders, receive information, and submit commercial bids via a secure link to GE's intranet web servers. TPN is made up of an Oracle 7.2 database server working with a Netscape Communications commerce server and custom software developed by GE.

Booz, Allen & Hamilton uses Oracle's PowerBrowser in conjunction with Knowledge Online 2.0 to provide a billing, time, expense, and staffing application to intranet users. The application links to an internal Oracle 7 database server for information storage and retrieval. PowerBrowser is a Power Object look-alike with web browsing capabilities as well as the ability to run Java applets and Visual Basic-like programming scripting for application development. PowerBrowser is one of a few tools, including Netscape 2.0 and Microsoft Explorer, that are ready to run dynamic web-based applications, as well as "surf the Net."

Legacy applications now look toward the intranet infrastructure to provide wrappering services for easy application deployment to clients running web browsers. For example, SAP/R3, a popular client/server and mainframe-based financial system, is working with intranet vendors and products such as NeXT Software's WebObjects to provide a mechanism to distribute SAP/R3 application services through the intranet. This will enable anyone running a browser (inside the firewall and with permission) to link to the local SAP/R3 application server. WebObjects translate the application's interface into HTML that's sent to the browsers, and converts the user's response back into a format that the application can understand.

Security Issues

Although the intranet offers many benefits that include scalability, cost, ease of use, and platform portability, there are those who balk at this new architecture due to perceived security risks. Let me set everyone straight on this. When using the intranet, internet security is not an issue since all of the interaction with corporate intranet applications takes place behind the safety of the corporate network firewall. If you don't have a firewall between your corporate servers and the Internet, get one now.

Firewalls allow companies to connect their system to the Internet, or other public networks, and regulate which information is allowed outside the firewall. If firewalls are not secure enough, corporations can simply disconnect themselves from the Internet. The internal intranet applications will still function, but users can't link to external web servers. However, firewalls, for all practical purposes, keep the bad people away from your intranet resources and still allow users to access the vast resources of the Web.

If you do have to extend your intranet to others connected to the Internet, such as a remote sales office or mobile user, there are ways to secure those links as well. Through the use of a Virtual Private Network (VPN), organizations can securely "tunnel" across the Internet using encryption to keep prying eyes away from proprietary data. RSA Data Security is currently working with firewall vendors to come up with VPN standards.

Intranet Development Tools

As the World Wide Web (WWW) moves into mainstream corporate America, innovative software development tool vendors seek new ways to exploit this trend. Thus, many new WWW application development tools quickly made their way into an already crowded tool market. Where intranet development was once a complex process of HTML authoring, convoluted scripting languages, and 3GL object-oriented development, these tools promise to bring rapid application development to the intranet. The first generation of WWW development tools exploit traditional WWW standards such as the Hypertext Markup Language (HTML) and the Common Gateway Interface (CGI). Second generation WWW development tools provide dynamic client-side application development, including tools that use Sun's Java, or Microsoft's ActiveX strategy for the WWW. These tools support existing web browsers directly, or integrate into existing browsers as "plug-ins." Second generation tools are also inclusive of proprietary internet-driven client/server solutions such as internet-aware database servers and database publishing for the intranet. For the third generation of intranet development tools, developers will see the integration of new and existing network application development paradigms, such as messaging middleware, publish and subscribe mechanisms, and the limited use of distributed objects such as Network ActiveX and OpenDoc. Currently, Java-enabled intranet development tools provide the best development environments. In the past six months, the Internet exploded as a popular platform for application development. Most software development tool vendors have either internet-enabled their existing tools, or offer new tools with internet capabilities. The hype that surrounds this new technology confuses developers. The Internet, once a place of rock-solid standards such as TCP/IP, HTTP, and HTML, became another bastion of proprietary tool sets. What's more, the speed with which the vendors bring these tools to market does not allow developers to fully define their internet application development requirements before they select a tool strategy.

Generally speaking, intranet development tools provide an easy-to-build layer between the complexities of intranet development (HTML, CGI, NSAPI, ISAPI, Java, etc.) and the application. True intranet application development requires that the developer learn the details of HTML, including support levels and verification processes. To add input and output services, the developer must also learn CGI, as well as enabling language such as C, C++, or Perl to implement the CGI portions of the application. If the developer wants dynamic functionality with the application, then Java is one of the few places to turn. However, Java development is functionally equivalent to C++, and developers must also learn an elaborate class library. The end result is that a typical intranet application could require the developer to learn three different development environments — HTML, CGI, and Java — to create a single application. For instance, an intranet application with only 1,000 function points could require as much as six man months to build from scratch. Thus, intranet application development to date remains complex, time consuming, and costly. This heavy use of resources limits the capabilities of intranet applications, and so far most organizations have not moved far beyond common text and graphics.

In addition, ongoing maintenance activities add cost to intranet development projects since intranet applications are by nature dynamic environments. The reliance on low level development environments greatly increases this cost and runs the risk of spinning quickly out-of-control as the developer attempts to patch his or her way through day to day application changes. A high level development environment makes ongoing maintenance less of a burden, since most of the low level operations are handled automatically.

The intranet application development tools covered in this presentation can handle the low level programming for the developer, automatically generating the HTML, CGI, and Java applets required to serve the needs of the intranet application. The developer need only define the application at a high level within the domain of the intranet application development tool.

The high level application development layer puts the developer back into an amicable visual application development environment. Intranet application development becomes a familiar process of assembling application components on a form and adding function to those objects through 4GL programming. The intranet development tools generate the application in a form understandable by standard intranet browsers such as Netscape and Mosaic.

Most intranet development environments available today, or in beta, are just extensions of existing client/server development tools. Most tool vendors view intranet application development as no more than a new platform with additional middleware layers to generate that will support applications (e.g., HTML and Java to support the user interface, and CGI to support interaction with external applications). In most cases, this means that today's client/server developers can be intranet developers tomorrow with little additional training. For instance, popular two-tier client/server development tools such as PowerSoft's PowerBuilder, Borland's Delphi, and Microsoft's Visual Basic all provide the ability to generate intranet applications from existing development environments. Unfortunately, they all do it via different deployment mechanisms.

Despite the fact that many of the intranet development tools come from well-known companies, developers should know that these are largely experimental products and thus may not be ready for mission critical application development. Also, many of the tools deploy intranet applications inefficiently, thus performance and stability is compromised for ease of use. In many cases it may make sense for the developer to go to the intranet interfaces directly (HTML, CGI, Java, etc.) rather than use tools to interface with the intranet standards. To date, this is the only way to assure application success. Developers should not take any promised capabilities for granted, and pilot testing should be a part of any intranet development project.

The addition of new intranet development technology has a downside that many organizations do not factor into their intranet development tools decisions. Most of these tools move the developer from intranet standards such as HTML and Java to proprietary technology (e.g., 4GL visual development environments). Although this speeds up the complex intranet application development process, the proprietary nature of these tools allows developers to move away from emerging intranet standards. This creates a dependency on the tool and vendor, and could create a problem if this new industry moves in different directions, or if the vendor or product becomes unstable. The end result could be an application that requires migration from one tool to another or from a proprietary tool back to HTML, CGI, and Java. This was the same dilemma that faced the client/server development world five years ago when proprietary tools began to replace 3GLs for client/server application development. Thus, developers should approach these tools with full knowledge of the tradeoffs they face by going from open to proprietary intranet development technology.

The Changing Vision of Web Application Development

Until recently, HTML and CGI provided intranet developers with a standard method to create and deploy intranet applications. Despite unprecedented explosions in intranet usage based on this technology, there are many shortcomings to this "traditional" approach.

First, HTML restricts user interface capabilities and does not offer the performance of other types of business applications. HTML cannot interact with the user dynamically and can only provide static web pages.

Second, although CGI allows developers to interface with external applications such as links to database services, developers must build CGI applications using a 3GL native to the web server. CGI programs execute in real time, which allows them to output dynamic information back to the web browser. This process carries with it a lot of overhead. When a browser requests a URL, the server must parse the URL to determine how the request should be handled. If the server determines that the URL request is for a file in an executable directory, the URL passes through to the CGI for execution. Building such intranet applications is a complex, time-consuming process of working with web server software, HTML, and a CGI application.

Finally, traditional intranet application development doesn't provide the developer with the ability to scale. Traditional intranet applications run on a single server, and performance and user load is limited by the capacity of the processor, host operating system, and network connection. Unlike the two-tier and n-tier client/server development models, HTML and CGI cannot distribute portions of the processing to the browser, nor are these applications easily partitioned to additional application servers which would allow intranet applications to scale.

Java, COM, and ORBs are natural evolutions of traditional intranet development base technologies, but they provide only a technological foundation for internet application development tool vendors. Java provides good performance on the client's side by allowing the client (browser) to process the application without the need to maintain a connection to the web server.

Java also provides dynamic, real-time capabilities such as the ability to monitor stock market information or keep a running graph on the outside temperature.

Java allows developers to create small programs known as applets. Applets are downloaded into Java-enabled browsers such as Netscape 2.0, Netscape 3.0, and Internet Explorer 3.0, from web servers, usually embedded inside HTML documents. Once downloaded, these applets execute locally within the browser to perform any number of preprogrammed functions. Carefully conceived, Sun took steps to assure that Java applets contain no malicious code.

Java is open technology, in that developers can build Java applets using a variety of tools. Internet application developers can build Java applications using any number of compilers. Or, developers can use any number of intranet development tools that use Java to provide the user interface. Java is a strong contender due to its widespread browser and tool support. Netscape 3.0, currently the most popular browser, supports Java as well as JavaScript.

COM and ActiveX are coming on strong as Java competitors. Driven by Microsoft, and now available with a few innovative intranet development vendors (e.g., OpenScape described later), ActiveX built for the Internet provides the same functionality as Java applets. Initially, Microsoft's Explorer is the only web browser that will support Internet ActiveX as a native component, but Netscape 2.0 and 3.0 can currently use ActiveX-based applications and development tools as plug-ins. As ActiveX controls become more prominent, Netscape will add them as a native control, and allow users to execute Java and ActiveX applets simultaneously.

In the intranet tools race, ActiveX is behind Java in developer acceptance, browser support, and available tools. Despite their late start in the intranet race, Microsoft could quickly surpass Java due to the popularity of their tools, office automation products, and operating systems. ActiveX is able to deliver better on the Windows 95 look and feel.

The popularity of ActiveX as a intranet development technology will drive other OLE-enabled development tools to provide intranet development features. We could also see the extension of DCOM, when available, as Microsoft's next generation intranet strategy. Network ActiveX would allow the distribution of ActiveX automation servers, using the Internet as an RPC or LRPC passing mechanism as well as distributed Internet-enabled ActiveX.

CORBA-based ORB development has not made it to the intranet in large numbers. This reflects ORB's lack of popularity for application development, and the acceptance of lower level technologies such as Java and OLE. Moreover, the popularity of DCOM, when available, will further dilute the popularity of ORBs for intranet applications.

Despite all this, there are a few tool vendors who see the potential of created intranet applications using CORBA compliant ORBs. Digital Equipment Corporation (DEC) offers a technology known as Web Broker (based on ObjectBroker), which runs as a CGI program on a web server. Web Broker, like CGI applications, brokers network services for web clients and internal applications. ANSA (a European software consortium) also offers a similar product. Sunsoft plans to integrate Java with its CORBA-compliant ORBs using Sun's NEO. NeXT software plans to do the same thing with its NeXT Object Model using its WebObjects strategy. Post Modern Computing has a Java-enabled version of their ORBline CORBA 2.0 compliant ORB. However, the best ORB strategy is seen in Visigenic's Visibroker, which will be a part of Netscape 4.0.

The Client/Server Connection

In case you haven't noticed, client/server and web development tools are becoming one in the same. Big client/server tool vendors such as Microsoft, Borland, Symantec, and Powersoft saw the potential of the Web early on, and began to web-enable their existing tool set, as well as create new tools for web-only development.

Borland's new Borland C++ 5.0, for example, not only provides a sophisticated C++ development environment, but can do Java applet development as well. Borland provides the developer with visual development capabilities that augment the cryptic world of low-level Java. Borland C++, like other Java development environments, provides just-in-time-compiler, which allows applet processing to bypass the overhead of the Bytecode interpreter and go directly to the processor. Applet run-time performance is the benefit.

And we've yet to see the best from Borland. Now in the works from Borland is Latte. Latte is basically a Java-enabled version of Delphi that provides the same RAD development capabilities and database connectivity. If Latte lives up to the capabilities of Delphi, it's going to be a sure-fire hit. Latte is due out later this year.

Symantec, unlike Borland, is not web-enabling their existing C++ compiler. Instead, they provide a completely new Java-enabled development tool called Café. Café was one of the first web tools to mix RAD with the 3GL world of Java. Like Borland C++ 5.0, Café provides a just-in-time-compiler, along with the ability to test applications and applets using browser simulators.

PowerBuilder and Optima++, both from Powersoft, plan to provide web-enabled development environments as well. PowerBuilder provides plug-in capabilities today for web development, but plans to move to pure ActiveX development capability in the near future.

PowerBuilder's plug-in capability allows developers to create plug-in applications that take over the functionality of plug-in capable web browsers such as Netscape Navigator. This feature allows developers to create web-enabled applications using the familiar PowerScript scripting language, as well as DataWindows. PowerBuilder supports most Windows controls when creating web plug-in applications.

Powersoft's Optima++, a C++-based client/server development environment, plans to support web application development using Java. When available later this year, Optima++ will provide developers with the ability to build Java applets using Optima++'s visual development environment.

Compuware is web-enabling its Uniface multiplatform client/server development environment using Uniface WebEnabler. WebEnabler allows future and existing Uniface applications to deploy to the Web. Compuware provides this feature without requiring the developer to alter or add code. WebEnabler maintains all the existing business rules and database connections found in the original Uniface application.

WebEnabler simply translates the Uniface application interface into HTML, which is understandable by any web browser. In a sense, Uniface simply added another platform to the long list of platforms they support — this time the Web. WebEnabler also supports multiple interfaces to web servers including CGI, NSAPI, ISAPI, and will allow developers to integrate Java applets into Uniface applications in a future enhancement.

Unify's VISION, another multiplatform tool for client/server development, is also web-enabling itself. Unify VISION/Web can generate Java code even when the Unify VISION/Web developer doesn't understand Java. VISION/Web treats the client as simply another client platform and allows the developer to create a single application that serves many platforms, including the Web.

JAM from Jyacc is still another multiplatform client/server development tool that can deploy to the Web. JAM/WEB (Web Enterprise Builder) is a development tool that creates web applications. JAM/WEB developers use visual form editors to create the look and feel of the application as they would in standard JAM. However, JAM/WEB converts the form directly into HTML for deployment on the Web. In addition, JAM/WEB can process transactions back from the browser using standard application logic, as well as interact with any number of database servers. JAM/WEB can return information back to the web user through standard HTML.

ParcPlace-Digitalk's VisualWave is a web-enabled version of their Smalltalk-based client/server tool. VisualWave offers Smalltalk developers a way to deploy Smalltalk applications to the Web within a graphical development environment that can automatically generate the HTML and CGI code required to deploy your application on a web server.

In addition, VisualWave provides session management capabilities which allow developers to track states within the CGI applications. This is something that has been difficult thus far. Moreover, developers have access to all that constitutes the pure object-oriented development environment including object browsers, inspectors, symbolic debuggers, and resource finder.

Centura, the creator of SQL Windows, plans to web-enable its existing client/server products by providing a Centura Application Server and Web Data Publisher. The Application Server is a repository for Centura client/server applications, as well as Java applets. Centura plans to enable Team Developer to generate applets, which allows developers to deploy applications as native Windows applications or web-enabled Java applets. Web Data Publisher lets organizations publish data from multiple databases on the Web, as well as maintain a repository of metadata about various databases. Web Data Publisher can securely deliver information to Web clients who are authorized to view the data.

WebObjects, from NeXT Software, Inc., is basically a web-enabled version of their Enterprise Object Framework (EOF) client/server development environment. WebObjects allows developers to visually layout the look of a web application, as well as add behavior. Once the application is complete, WebObjects generates the

HTML and CGI code required to support the application, and link to the appropriate databases.

NetCraft, from SourceCraft, Inc., offers a visual Java development environment. NetCraft provides browsers, a menu editor, methods editor, form builder, and Java code generator. NetCraft is based on SourceCraft's ObjectCraft client/server development tool which can generate standard C++ source code and offers ODBC connections to popular databases.

Other Tools

There are several web application development tools that don't have a history with client/server, but still provide a solid path to the Web. JFactory, for example, from Rogue Wave Software, Inc., provides a full-blown Java development environment. JFactory furnishes several subsystems to help developers build their applets including a Project Manager, Window and Dialog Designer, and Menu Design tool. Like both Café and Borland C++ 5.0, JFactory offers a visual development environment that lets developers create interfaces by simply selecting GUI controls from a palette.

Sun's Java Developer's Kit (JDK), the base for most Java development tools, is also a viable Java development tool in its own right. Sun provides an object-oriented development environment, including a Java Applet Viewer for testing applets, as well as a Java Language Runtime interpreter, and Java-enabled Debuggers.

OpenScape, from Business@Web, Inc., provides a component-based development environment for integration as plug-ins. OpenScape employs a distributed component architecture, and comes with a Visual Component Builder for painting and adding behavior to visual components. There is a Component Workbench for storing, naming, and finding components, as well as a Component Engine that can process the communications between the interface and application.

Sapphire/Web, from Bluestone Inc., is a simple web-enabled visual application development environment. Sapphire allows the developer to generate applications as HTML, and interfaces with popular database servers such as Oracle, Informix, and Sybase.

Database-Enable Your Web

Although application development is a key feature for developers, there are a few tools that also specialize in serving enterprise data through the Web. These tools become web application development tools in their own right, since they integrate with standard HTML editors and Java-enabled development environments. Here are just a few:

Spider, from Spider Technologies, provides web application database connectivity. Spider lets developers visually link remote HTML form fields or Java fields to database fields.

Cold Fusion, from Allaire, provides a development platform to build applications with the ability to access information that resides in relational databases. Using Cold Fusion, developers can combine high-level database commands stored in templates with standard HTML.

Other Web/database tools include web.sql from Sybase, and WebDBC from Nomad Development Corp. The web.sql product provides a link between Sybase System 10 databases and HTML, allowing developers to embed SQL directly into HTML documents. WebDBC provides Web developers with an easy link to their favorite database through ISAPI or NSAPI.

LiveWire, from Netscape Communications Corp., offers developers a web application development and database connectivity tool that incorporates the Rouge Wave database libraries for use from the Netscape scripting language. Using LiveWire, developers can link to popular databases such as Sybase, Informix, and Oracle.

Finally, JetConnect, from XDB Systems, Inc., provides database access directly from Java applications. JetConnect is a set of Java class libraries and related drivers that link any Java applet with any database that has ODBC support. JetConnect may have some competition with the upcoming JDBC from Javasoft.

Which Direction Now?

So now that we know where things are, let's explore where things are going in the world of web application development. There are a few predictions that I'm willing to make.

First, the use of CGI and tools that use CGI will drop in favor of better-performing native APIs such as NSAPI and ISAPI. Those that don't need server-side APIs will favor Java or ActiveX as better alternatives for running web clients disconnected from the web server. Java and ActiveX place the processing back on the client end.

Second, the use of plug-ins will subside in favor of nonproprietary standards such as Java and ActiveX. Java, for instance, can better support a large number of browsers and does so using a wide array of tools. A simple check of the number of Java-enabled tools listed below proves this prediction. Those numbers are likely to increase sharply by the end of the year.

Finally, the competition between Java and ActiveX will increase. Unlike the competition between COM and CORBA, Java has a large jump on ActiveX, as well as development tool and browser support. However, with the advent of web-enabled Windows 95, developers will find that the migration to ActiveX is an easier journey for Windows shops, which includes almost everyone. My money is on ActiveX in the long run.

Final Thoughts

This is an extremely tough subject to approach from any angle. The hype and rapid change in the web application development market makes any research effort a daunting task. Just the process of putting this presentation together is a frustrating experience, considering the shift in market forces and the constant bombardment of new tools and technologies.

The key to finding the right web application development tool for your development project is to first define and understand your requirements completely. Then, independent of the hype that surrounds web development, select a few tools that initially look as if they will meet your needs. Then, using the requirements as a guideline, assign weights (e.g., 1–10) as to the tool's ability to live up to a particular requirement. Make sure to include a live evaluation, testing, and a prototype when you make your selection.

It will take time for this relatively new industry to settle down. For now, it's learn as much as you can, and proceed with caution. Attending this presentation was a great start.

Chapter 8

Model-based Development: Buy Your Design

Stephen J. Mellor

Innovative claim:

> "A design can be specified, built, and tested independent of the application it implements. The implementation can be automated."

Software development is proving to be the productivity bottleneck slowing many embedded systems' time-to-market. Over the past 20 years, hardware developers have been improving their productivity dramatically, but software development has lagged significantly.

This situation is analogous to the manufacturing industry of the 1790s. During this time period, a group of workers called "fitters" became the productivity bottleneck. Several different artisans manufactured individual components of the product, creating a pool of raw components. While each of these components looked similar in shape there was wide variation in their actual specifications — the unfortunate result of hand-crafted metalwork. In the final assembly, "fitters" had to assembly the final product by filing and fitting all the components together. The final result was a functional, hand-crafted, one-of-a-kind product.

The challenge came when the product broke in the field. All the components were hand-crafted and the "fitted" together replacement parts had to go through the same "fitting" process. The result was significant downtime whenever equipment broke, as "fitters" were once again on the critical path.

This is much like software development today. "Fitters" in the assembly process are called software developers doing testing and integration. "Fitters" on field products are called software maintenance engineers. Considering the amount of time your team spends in test, integration, and software maintenance, does your organization have a "fitters" bottleneck?

A Traditional Solution

The problem at the time was well understood. Fitters were the bottleneck. A solution was proposed: Give the fitters bigger, better, faster tools. (Does this sound like your software engineers asking for bigger, better, faster compilers, debuggers, or workstations?) The result of this solution was marginal improvements in the problem.

An Innovative Solution

An innovative solution was also proposed: Build the parts with better precision. This solution approach impacts the way components are manufactured to eliminate the need for the fitting task. This is analogous to redefining how software development is done to dramatically impact the test, integration, and maintenance phases of the software life cycle.

An Innovative Solution Applied to Software Development

The claim at the opening of this article tells how this innovative approach can be applied to software engineering:

"A design can be specified, built, and tested independent of the application it implements. The implementation can be automated."

Let's examine critical terms in this claim to better understand it.

Application: An implementation-free statement of the objects and their behavior required to meet the system's functional specification. No assumptions exist about the implementation technologies (e.g., programming language, operating system, communication package, database).

Design: An application-free statement of how specified objects and their behavior are to be realized that uses specific implementation technologies and meets specific performance characteristics. No assumptions exist about the specific application objects and their behavior.

Implementation: An algorithm for mapping the application objects and their behavior into the implementation technologies as specified by the design. No assumptions exist about the specific application objects and their behavior.

Figure 8.1 shows a physical representation of how these three key terms relate to produce working system software code.

Implications of the Innovative Solution

Let's suspend any disbelief of the feasibility of this solution for a bit. Let's pretend it works and discuss some of the implications on software engineering.

Implication #1: Two Separate Assets Are Created

The application and the design become distinct software assets. Changes can be made to the system functionality in the application without impacting the design. Changes in the system performance or implementation technologies are made in the design without impacting the application. Two distinct points of maintenance become available, isolating bugs and problems to one software component or asset (Figure 8.2).

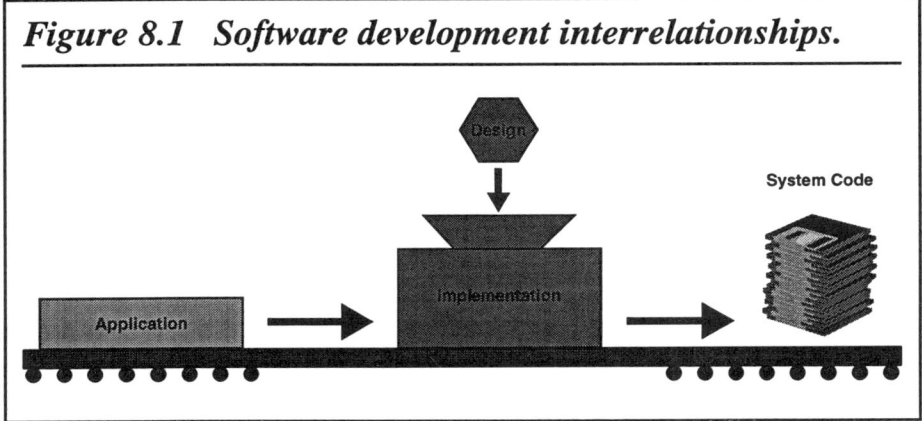

Figure 8.1 Software development interrelationships.

Implication #2: The Design Can Be Reused with Multiple Applications

The same design (performance profile and implementation technologies) can be reused with multiple applications to produce different functioning systems. This allows an organization to leverage one design across many different software products (Figure 8.3).

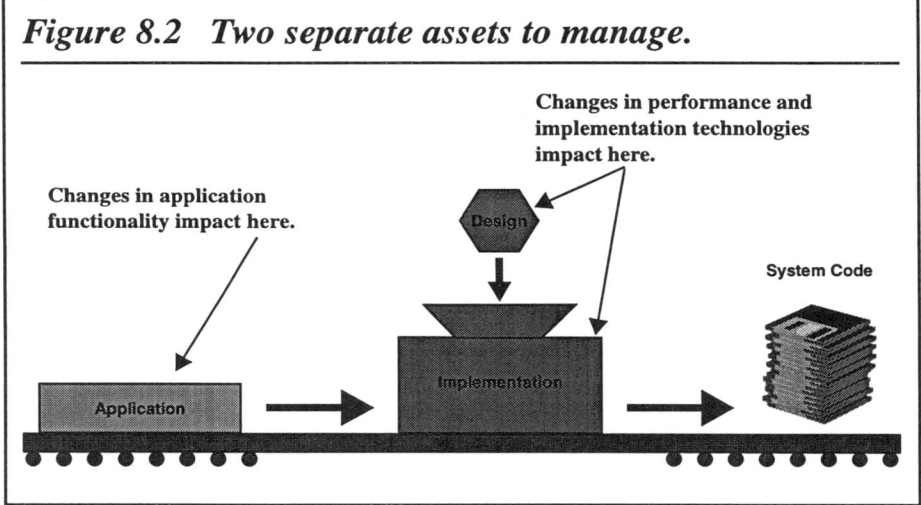

Figure 8.2   Two separate assets to manage.

Changes in performance and implementation technologies impact here.

Changes in application functionality impact here.

Design

System Code

Implementation

Application

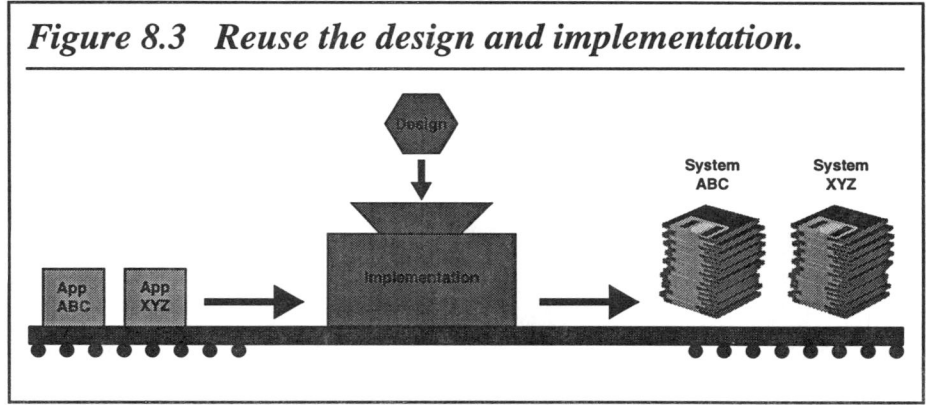

Figure 8.3   Reuse the design and implementation.

Design

System ABC

System XYZ

Implementation

App ABC

App XYZ

Implication #3: The Application Can Be Reused with Different Designs

The same application functionality can be redeployed across several different designs (performance profiles and implementation technologies) to create many different systems. The final systems will have different performance profiles (i.e., speed, memory constraints, power use), but the application functionality will be the same. Imagine designing your software functionality once and then redeploying (or reimplementing) with different designs (Figure 8.4).

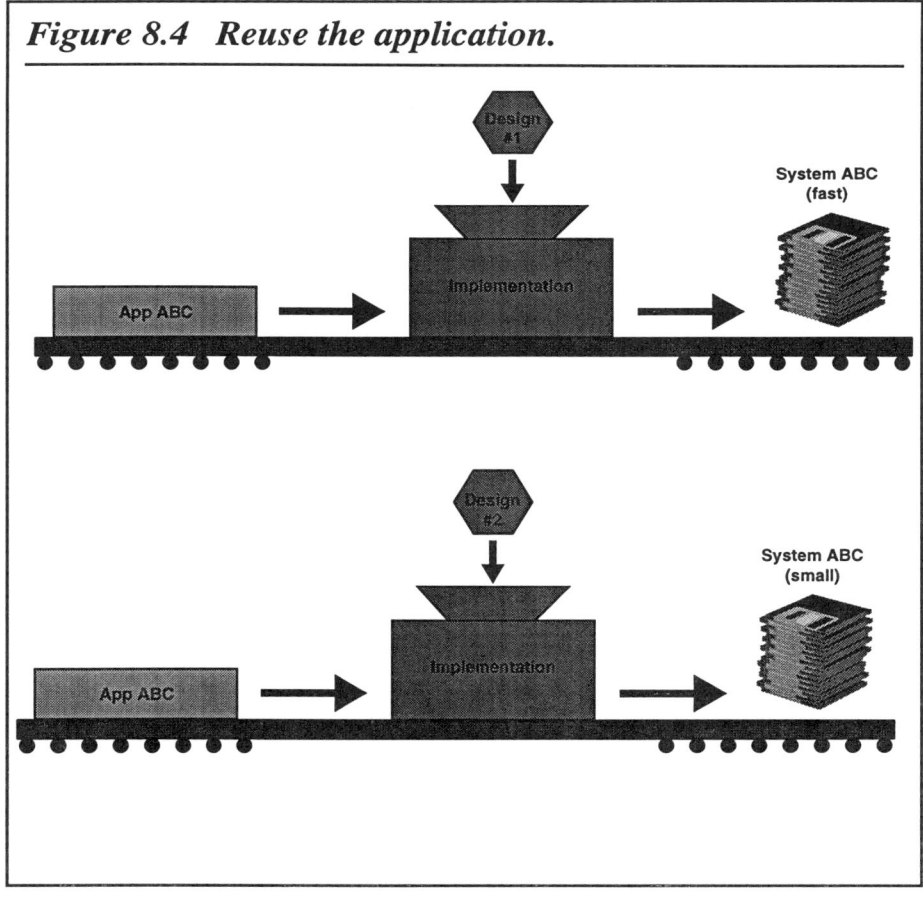

Figure 8.4   Reuse the application.

Implication #4: The New Components Become Corporate Assets

Because these new components can be reused at a high level they become valuable corporate assets. These assets can reused and redeployed over multiple projects across multiple divisions. Or, these assets could even be sold on the open market independent of your organization's final product (Figure 8.5).

Figure 8.5   Components become corporate assets.

**Innovative Software Corp.
Balance Sheet**

. . .

Design #1	$25,000
Design #2	$25,000

. . .

Application ABC	$75,000
Application XYZ	$95,000

. . .

Benefits of the Innovative Solution

Given these four implications of the innovative solution, several benefits can be explained. Figure 8.6 illustrates the different project plans of traditional software development and one with our innovative approach. Several benefits can be illustrated in these project plans.

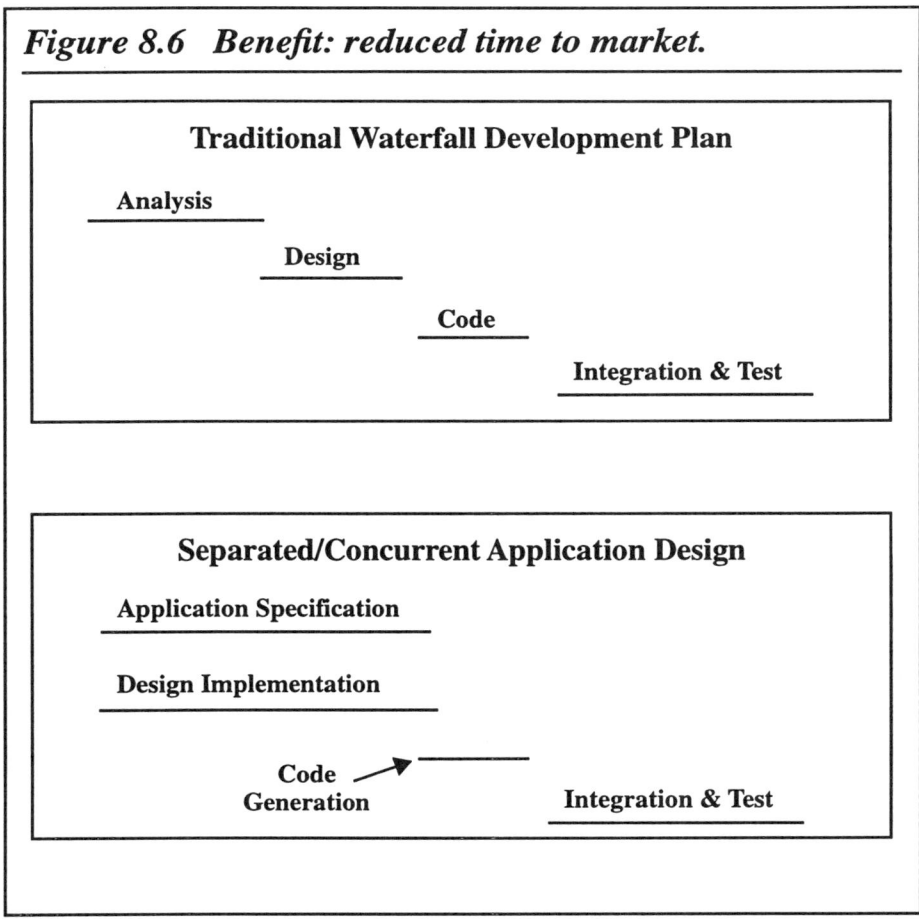

Figure 8.6   Benefit: reduced time to market.

Traditional Waterfall Development Plan

Analysis

Design

Code

Integration & Test

Separated/Concurrent Application Design

Application Specification

Design Implementation

Code Generation

Integration & Test

Benefit #1: Faster Time-to-Market

The much sought after time-to-market reduction is possible. Figure 8.6 illustrates how the components can be developed in parallel with each other. The resulting components are then combined together automatically with system code generation. Then, the final test and integration are performed with significantly less time and effort, because the two components were tested independently.

Benefit #2: Reduced Cost

Significant cost reductions come from the reuse or commercial purchase of individual components. For example, if the design is purchased (remember the title of this article), then the development team only has to produce the application specification and construct the system. A third party provider (or internal corporate tools group) can produce a design and amortize it over multiple projects. The result is a huge cost reduction. Similarly, the application could be redeployed across several designs (or implementations) and similar cost savings can be achieved (Figure 8.7).

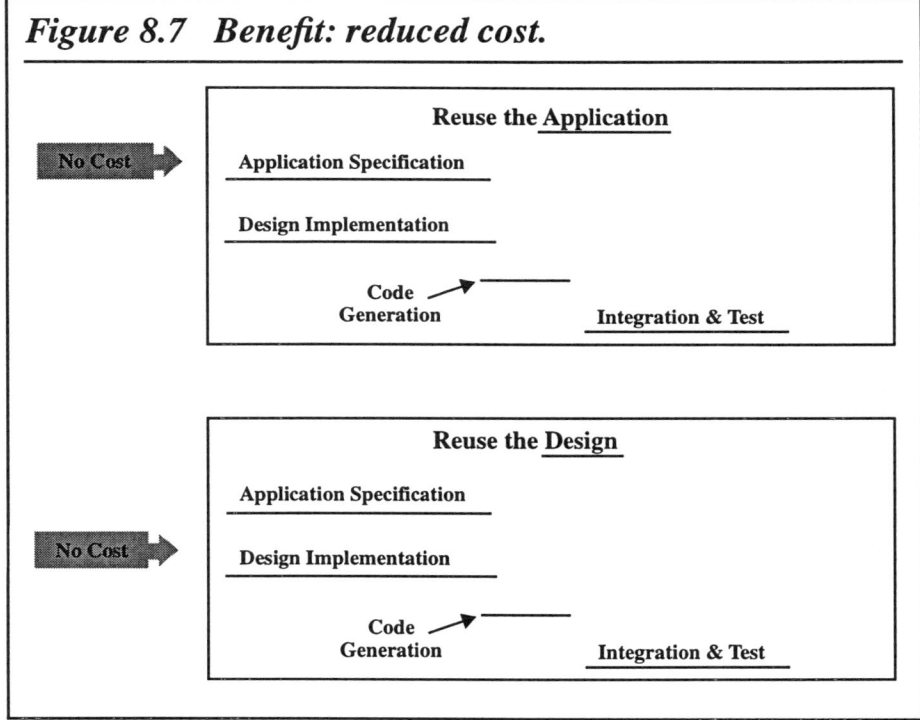

Figure 8.7   Benefit: reduced cost.

Benefit #3: Reduced Risk

By reusing proven components of application specification or design implementations, the risk of bugs and schedule management are reduced. Proven reused components are field tested across multiple projects, significantly reducing the number of potential errors in the component. Also, the schedule risks of using an independent component are significantly reduced, as the component integration is done automatically through code generation (Figure 8.8).

Benefit #4: Improved Maintenance

Most software maintenance activities are of three types: bug fixes, functionality changes, and performance tuning. All three activities become easier with the separation of application from design. Bug fixes are isolated to one component: either the application or the design. The other component remains unchanged, so does not require retesting. Functionality changes are isolated to the application component.

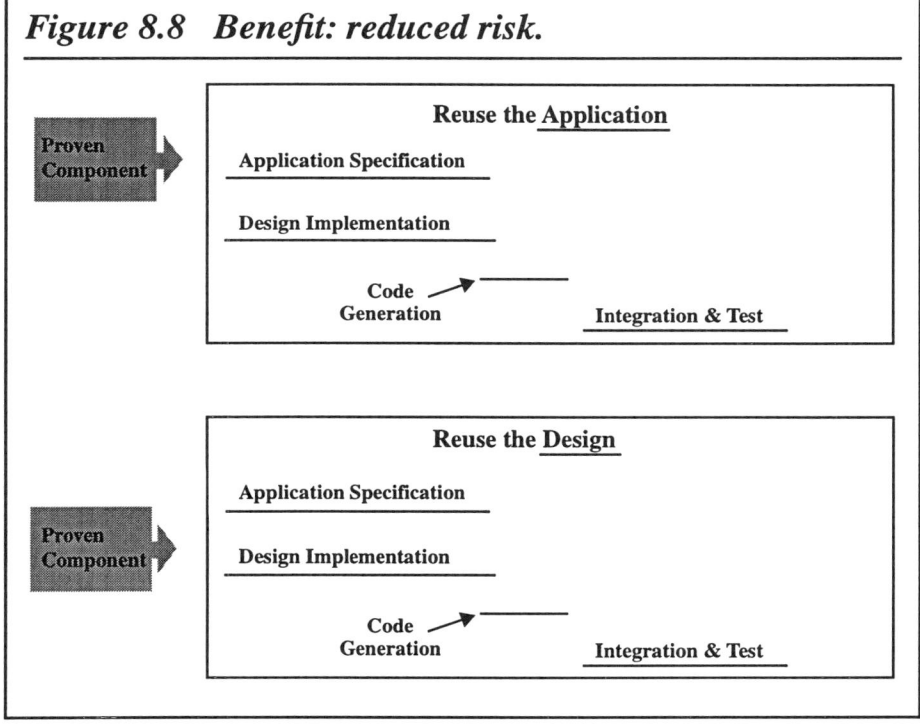

Figure 8.8   Benefit: reduced risk.

Again, this is easier because of reduced test time. Finally, performance tuning is done by modifying the design component. As an added bonus, the performance tune gets applied to the entire application — not just the performance bottleneck. In this way systems achieve dramatic performance changes with relatively minor changes (Figure 8.9).

Premise for this Innovative Solution

The claims and benefits of this innovative solution are quite dramatic. Now let's visit the underlying premise that makes this innovative claim a reality today.

Application functionality and design are separate subject matters. We see this in most of our software development. Application functionality is specified by the end-user — who doesn't have an understanding of implementation technologies. For example, the application specification of ultrasound imaging, cellular communications, or gas chromatography is done by scientists, research doctors, or marketing personnel. On the other hand, design details or implementation trade-offs are determined by software engineering professionals. End-users may provide some performance requirements such as volumes of call connections per hour or average delay times. However, they rarely specify the exact programming language, type of data persistence, or choice of real-time operating systems. These trade-offs are left to the software engineers implementing the software system. Given these are distinct subject matters different professionals can be utilized to specify them — without requiring extensive cross-learning. After all, do research scientists really want to learn programming?

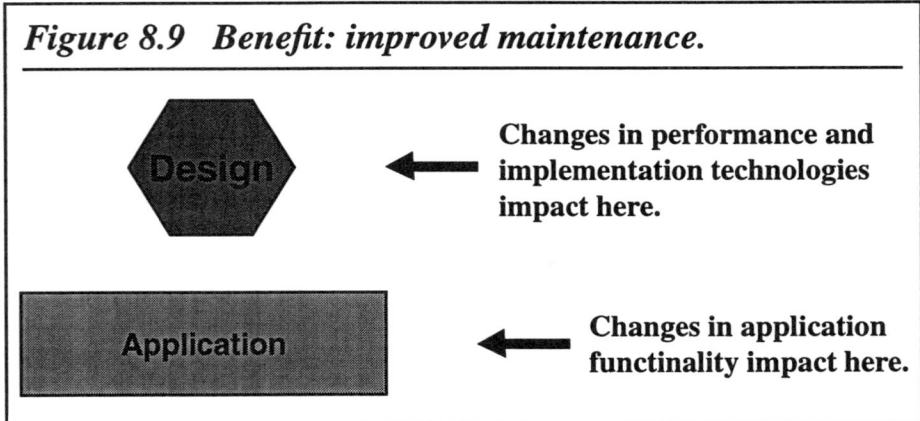

Figure 8.9   Benefit: improved maintenance.

Design

Changes in performance and implementation technologies impact here.

Application

Changes in application functinality impact here.

The subject matters are related, but they can be specified separately. A design must be specified that can successfully realize the final application's performance requirements of speed, size, distribution, and reliability. For the final system, construction trade-offs are made between performance, cost, and time-to-market. These trade-offs, however, are done at a high level early in the project, and the final application and design can be specified separately, according to the issues in the following list:

- Application Subject Matters
    - ATM switching
    - gas chromatography
    - ultrasound imaging
    - cellular communications
- Design Subject Matters
    - task scheduling
    - class structure
    - data persistence
    - memory management

At implementation time the application and design are integrated together. Only the final code has to meet both the functionality requirements of the application and the performance requirements of the design. Implementation is accomplished by a "compilation" of the application OOA models into code that meets the design specification. This approach is available today through model-based development with the Shlaer-Mellor Method (Figure 8.10).

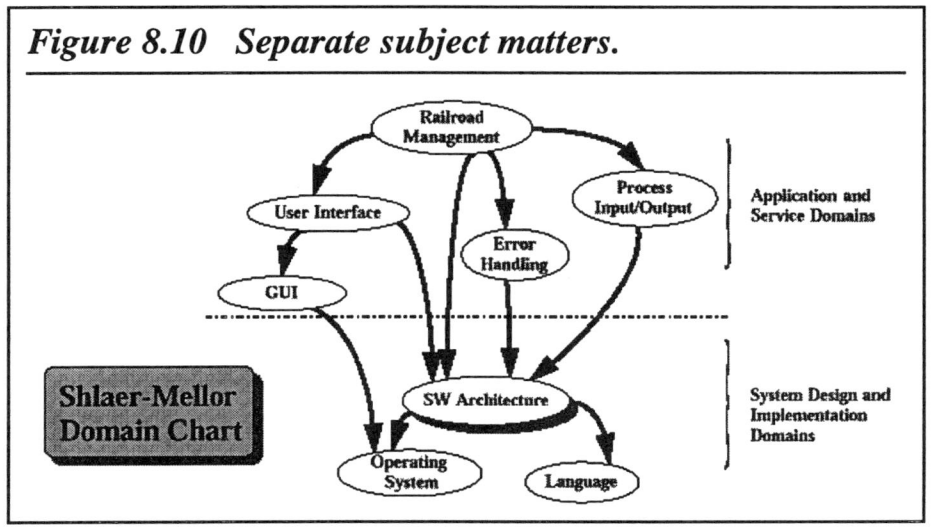

Figure 8.10   Separate subject matters.

Model-Based Development with the Shlaer-Mellor Method

Figure 8.11 illustrates how model-based development, with the Shlaer-Mellor Method, is the next logical step in software abstraction. Object-Oriented Analysis (OOA) models fully specify the application functionality. These are then translated into source code, using a design captured in a model compiler (Figure 8.12). The OOA models become the new programming language, and model compilers become the implementation design (Figure 8.13).

Application specification is done using Shlaer-Mellor OOA, which is a full graphical specification notation. The design specification is done using Shlaer-Mellor Recursive Design. The Shlaer-Mellor Method is a complete specification and design notation that has an underlying formalism allowing for the complete separation of application from design. The formalism ensures that the two components can be combined for final system implementation. For additional information on this notation, the entire Shlaer-Mellor Method is explained in a white paper available from the Project Technology web site (http://www.projtech.com).

Now that application and design can be specified separate from each other, they can also be developed by different teams — even outsourced to different companies. For some systems, preexisting model compilers can be purchased that already met

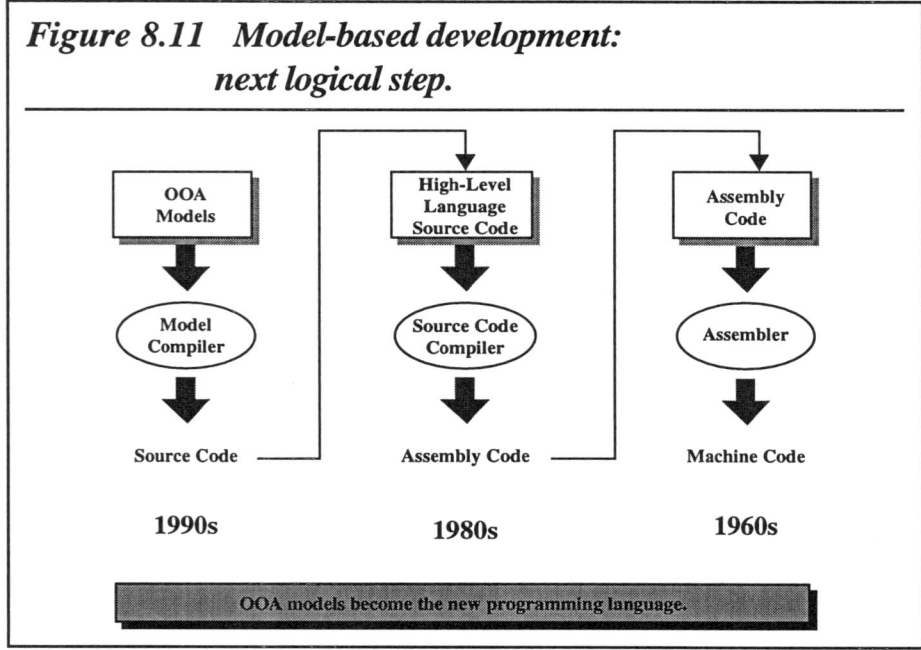

Figure 8.11 Model-based development: next logical step.

performance requirements. Alternatively, these preexisting model compilers can serve as a starting point for modification to specific performance requirements. Either way, the design component of a system software can be substantially purchased, allowing organizations to focus on value-added through the application specification.

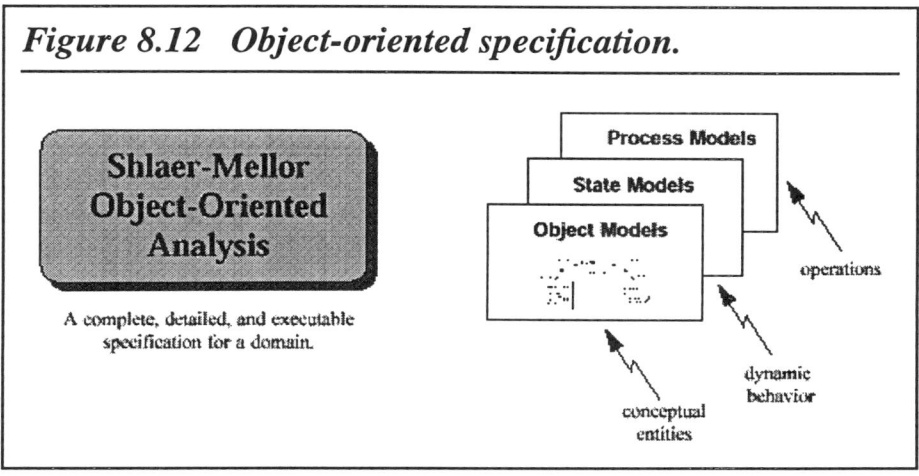

Figure 8.12   Object-oriented specification.

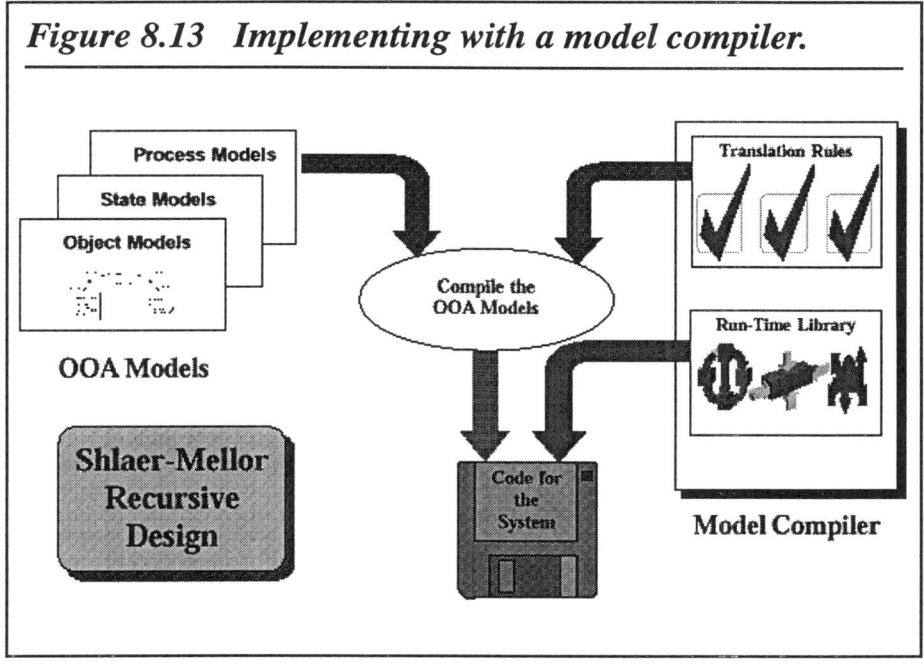

Figure 8.13   Implementing with a model compiler.

But, Does This Work?

Yes, this does work, and it is driving dramatic project successes worldwide. For example, Sybase has developed a multimedia server using the separation of application from design. Their final system contains over 100,000 lines of code, with OOA models being implemented in two different designs (Table 8.1). Some of their application needs high performance, so those models are translated with a high-performance C++ design. Other OOA models have high-data integrity requirements and are translated with a SQL design. This project allowed Sybase to leap to an industry-leadership position in one year. Their system was delivered on-time, with extremely high-quality code, and high performance profiles.

Table 8.1   Project profile: Sybase Multimedia Server.
Product
Multimedia server
Project Statistics
12 Developers
150,000 lines of code
85 percent automatic code generation
Project time was 1 year
2 Custom Software Architectures with CASE tool automation
Software Design C++ source code; and SQL code
Multi-tasking, single processor implementation
Benefits
Leaped to an industry leadership position in one year time frame
Produced extremely high quality software, dramatically reducing testing and integration time
Future Directions
Planning to grow capabilities to Software Architecture to allow full action translation, increasing code generation to 95 percent
Planning to increase OOA model functionality in future releases as multimedia server requirements grow

AT&T has used this approach for a 4ESS adjunct switch development project (Lato and Parks, 1995). Using a small team of developers, they were able to deliver 13,000 lines of real-time C++ code with 100 percent code generation. The resulting software assets (application and design) remained to ease the task of future maintenance (Table 8.2).

Conclusion

Separating software application from it design is an innovative concept — just as building the parts with greater precision was in the 18th century. This innovative solution removes the bottleneck of software development from real-time projects, and it is available today with reusable model compilers and the Shlaer-Mellor Method.

Table 8.2   Project profile: AT&T.
Product
4ESS Adjunct Switch Development
Project Statistics
5 Developers
3 domains
13,000 lines of real-time code
100% automatic code generation
Custom Software Architecture with CASE tool automation
Software Design
C++ code
Single task, single processor implementation
Benefits
Automated code generation
Reduced cycle time in maintenance
Future Direction
Project maintenance and enhancement continued with the C++ software architecture and BridgePoint automation

The results are dramatic reductions in time-to-market, high quality software systems, reduced development costs, and improved maintenance. These benefits all accrue to teams adopting the innovative idea — just as benefits accrued to the manufacturers who first adopted the idea of interchangeable components.

References

Katherine Lato and Tim Parks. "Automatic Code Generation at AT&T." *Object Magazine*, Nov/Dec 1995.

Sally Shlaer and Stephen J. Mellor. *Object-Oriented Systems Analysis: Modeling the World in Data*. Prentice Hall, 1988.

Sally Shlaer and Stephen J. Mellor. "Recursive Design." *Computer Language*, March 1990.

Sally Shlaer and Stephen J. Mellor. *Object Lifecycles: Modeling the World in States*. Prentice Hall, 1992.

Sally Shlaer, Stephen J. Mellor, and Wayne Hywari. "Real-Time Recursive Design." *Course Notes*, Project Technology, Inc.

Chapter 9

Remote Objects

Cay S. Horstmann

Abstract

This class gives an overview of the two principal implementations of distributed objects in Java, namely Remote Method Invocation (RMI) and IDL/CORBA. RMI is a Java-to-Java solution that is simple and natural to the Java programmer. IDL/CORBA is a more complex Java-to-anything solution that allows interfacing Java code with CORBA objects implemented in any language. This class discusses the basic mechanisms, programming examples, and typical application scenarios.

    Portions of this material are taken from Gary Cornell and Cay Horstmann, *Core Java*, 2nd edition, published by SunSoft Press.

Introduction

Periodically, the programming community starts thinking of "objects everywhere" as the solution to all its problems. The idea is to have a happy family of collaborating objects that communicate through a network. Like most bandwagons in programming, this plan contains a fair amount of hype that can obscure the utility of the concept. The purpose of this talk is to

- Explain situations where distributed objects can be useful and where they are not.
- Show you how to use remote objects and the associated remote method invocation (RMI) for communicating between two machines running Java.
- Give a quick introduction into IDL.

The Roles of Client and Server

Suppose you want to collect information locally on a client computer and send the information across the Net to a server. For example, a user on a local machine may fill out an information request form. The form gets sent to the vendor's server, and the server sends back product information that the client can view, as shown in Figure 9.1.

There are a number of simple ways of doing this:

- Use a socket connection to send byte streams between the customer and the vendor computers.
- Use JDBC to make database queries and updates.

Both methods are useful in certain situations. For example, a socket connection is great if you just need to send raw data across the Net. JDBC is useful if the information that you are sending fits into the relational database's table model. But suppose you aren't in one of these two situations?

In a Java program, it is natural to implement the request form and the product information as objects. Using RMI, they can be transported as objects between the client and the server.

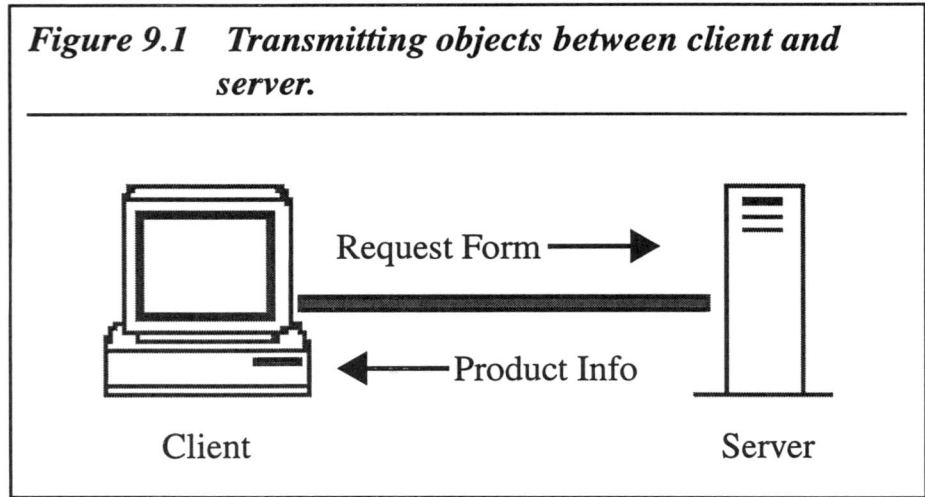

Figure 9.1   Transmitting objects between client and server.

Request Form ⟶

⟵ Product Info

Client   Server

In contrast, if a program uses raw byte streams, there is a significant coding hassle: the programmer has to come up with appropriate ways of coding the data and the transmission protocols for sending the data. Of course, when connecting to a database with JDBC, all the details of communication protocols have been taken care of. But relational databases are not very effective for storing information that doesn't fit into a "rows-and-columns" database structure. In particular, they are not very good at storing collections of objects of different types, such as a mixture of employees, managers, contractors, and other types that may not be known yet. And, as you have seen, these kinds of heterogeneous object collections are very important in object-oriented programming.

How Java implements remote objects falls in between these two extremes. A transport layer handles the data encoding and the transmission and call protocols, so the programmer is not concerned with managing streams of bytes. You can use objects of any type and are not limited to the rigid structure of a database.

There is another major benefit of remote objects. Not only can you transport objects across a network, but you can invoke method calls on objects that sit on another computer without having to move those objects to the machine making the method call. Such method calls are called remote method invocations. For example, the client seeking product information can query a Warehouse object on the server. It calls a remote method find which has one parameter: the request form object. The find method returns an object to the client: the product information object.

The Java designers wanted to make it very transparent that the object executing the remote method call resides on different computers. You will see the details in the coming sections.

Remote Method Invocations

The central concept in the Java remote object implementation is a remote method invocation or RMI. Code on the client computer invokes a method on an object on the server. It is important to realize that the client/server terminology applies to a single method call only. The computer that runs the Java code that calls the remote method is the client for that call, and the computer hosting the object that processes the call is the server for that call. It is entirely possible that the roles are reversed somewhere down the road. The server of a previous call can itself become the client when it invokes a remote method on an object residing on another computer.

Stubs and Skeletons

When client code wants to invoke a remote method on a remote object, it actually calls a regular Java method that is encapsulated in a surrogate object called a stub. The stub resides on the client, not on the server. The stub takes the parameters used in the remote method and packages them up as a block of bytes. This packaging uses a device-independent encoding for each parameter. For example, numbers are always sent in big-endian format. Strings and objects are a little trickier: they must be encoded in a way that uses no object references since object references point to memory locations on the client. These memory locations will not make sense on the server. The process of encoding the parameters into a format that is suitable for transporting them across the Net is called parameter marshalling. This uses the standard Java 1.1 object serialization mechanism for parameter marshalling. The stub method on the client builds an information block that consists of:

- An identifier of the remote object to be used;
- An operation number, describing the method to be called;
- The marshalled parameters.

It then sends this information to the server. On the server side, there is a skeleton object which makes sense out of the information contained in the packet and passes that information to the actual object executing the remote method. Specifically, the skeleton performs five actions for every remote method call:

- It unmarshals the parameters;
- It calls the desired method on the real remote object that lies on the server;
- It captures the return value or exception of the call on the server;
- It marshals that value;
- It sends a package consisting of the value in the marshalled form back to the stub on the client.

The stub unmarshals the return value or exception from the server. This becomes the return value of the remote method call. Or, if the remote method threw an exception, the stub rethrows it in the process space of the caller. Figure 9.2 shows the information flow of a remote method invocation.

This is obviously a complex process, but the good news is that it is completely automatic and, to a large extent, transparent for the Java programmer. Moreover, the designers of the Java remote object architecture tried hard to give remote objects the same "look and feel" as local objects. Nevertheless, there are important differences between local and remote objects, as we will see in this presentation.

Remote objects are garbage collected automatically, just like local objects are. However, the current distributed collector uses reference counting and cannot detect cycles of unreferenced objects. Cycles must be explicitly broken by the programmer.

The syntax for a remote method call is the same as for a local call. If central-Warehouse is a stub object for a central warehouse object on a remote (currently the client) machine and getQuantity is the method you want to invoke remotely, then a typical call looks like this:

```
centralWarehouse.getQuantity("SuperSucker 100 Vacuum Cleaner");
```

The client code always uses object variables whose type is an interface to access remote objects. For example, associated to this call would be an interface:

```
interface Warehouse
{ public int getQuantity(String) throws java.rmi.RemoteException;
    . . .
}
```

and an object declaration for a variable that will implement the interface:

```
Warehouse centralWarehouse;
```

Of course, interfaces are abstract entities that only spell out what methods can be called along with their signatures. Variables whose type is an interface must always be bound to an actual object of some type. In the case of remote objects this is a stub class. The client program does not actually know the type of those objects. The stub classes and the associated objects are created automatically.

While the Java designers did a good job hiding many of the details of remote method invocation from the Java programmer, there are still a number of techniques and caveats that must be mastered. That will be the topic of the rest of this presentation.

Dynamic Class Loading

When you pass a remote object to another Java program, either as a parameter or return value of a remote method, then that program must be able to deal with the associated stub object. That is, it must have the Java code for the stub class. The stub methods don't do a lot of interesting work. They just marshal and unmarshal the parameters and then connect this information with the server. Of course, they do all this work transparently to the programmer.

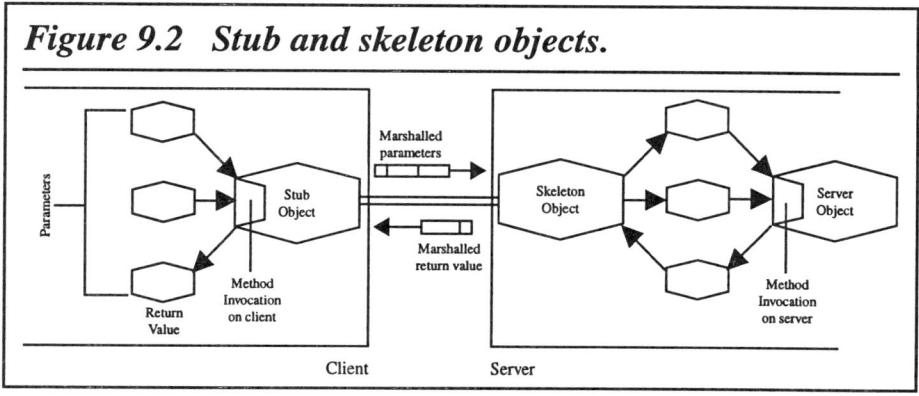

Figure 9.2 Stub and skeleton objects.

Furthermore, the classes for parameters, return values and exception objects may need to be loaded as well. This can be more complex than one might think. For example, a remote method may be declared with a certain return type that is known to the client, but actually return an object of a derived class that is not known to the client. The class loader will then load that derived class.

While unglamorous, the stub classes must be available to the running client program. One obvious way for this to happen is if these classes are available on the local file system. If they aren't, then Java is quite willing to load them from another place. It does this by a process similar to what is used when running applets in a browser.

With an applet, a browser loads the applet class and checks the byte codes for validity. The loading of the applet class from a remote location is the job of a class loader. The applet class loader is quite restrictive. It will only load classes from the same machine that served the web page containing the applet. The stub class loader can be configured to permit more. For example, you can allow it to search for stub code on other network locations. This is particularly useful for distributed Java programs where a number of processors that are cooperating to perform a difficult computation will all want to fetch the same stubs from a central location.

The class loader determines where the classes may be loaded from. The security manager determines what these classes can do when they run. For example the applet security manager won't let classes read and write local files or make socket connection to third parties. The stub security manager is even more restrictive than the applet security manager. Since it only governs the behavior of stub code, the stub security manager prevents all activities except those that stubs must be able to carry out. This is a safety mechanism that protects the program from viruses in stub code. For specialized applications, Java programmers can substitute their own class loaders and security managers, but those provided by the RMI system suffice for normal usage.

Interfaces and Implementations

The client program needs to manipulate server objects, but it doesn't actually have copies of them. The objects themselves reside on the server. The client must still know what it can do with those objects. Their capabilities are expressed in an interface that is shared between the client and server, and so resides simultaneously on both machines.

```
interface Product // shared by client and server
    extends Remote
{ public String getDescription() throws RemoteException
}
```

Just as in this example, all interfaces for remote objects must extend the Remote interface defined in the java.rmi package. All the methods in those interfaces must also declare that they will throw a RemoteException. The reason is that remote method calls are inherently less reliable than local calls — it is always possible that a remote call fails. The server or the network connection may be temporarily unavailable, or there may be a network problem. The client code must be prepared to deal with this. For these reasons, Java forces the programmer to catch the RemoteException with every remote method call, and to specify the appropriate action to take when the call does not succeed.

The client accesses the server object through a stub that implements this interface.

```
Product p = ...;    // see below how the client gets a stub
                    // reference to a remote object
String d = p.getDescription();
System.out.println(d);
```

In the next section, we will see ways the client can obtain such a reference to a remote object.

On the server side, you must implement the class that actually carries out the methods advertised in the remote interface.

```
class ProductImpl // server
    extends UnicastRemoteObject
    implements Product
{ public ProductImpl(String d) throws RemoteException
    { descr = d;
    }
    public String getDescription()
    { return "I am a " + descr + ". Buy me!";
    }
    private String descr;
}
```

This class has a single method, getDescription, that can be called from the remote client. It is a server class, since it extends UnicastRemoteObject which is a concrete Java class that makes objects remotely accessible.

The following table shows the naming convention we will use for client and server classes in this presentation.

Actually, all server classes must extend the class RemoteServer from the java.rmi.server package. But this is an abstract class that only defines the basic mechanisms for the communication between server objects and their remote stubs. The UnicastRemoteObject class that comes with RMI extends the RemoteServer abstract class and is concrete — so it can be used without writing any code. It is the "path of least resistance" for a server class to derive from `UnicastRemoteObject`, and all server classes in this presentation will do so. Figure 9.3 shows the inheritance relationship between these classes.

A `UnicastRemoteObject` object resides on a server. It must be alive when a service is requested. This is the class that we will be extending for all the server classes in this book and is the only server class available in the current version of the RMI package. Sun or third party vendors may, in the future, design other classes for use by servers for RMI. For example, Sun is already talking about a `MulticastRemote-Server` class for objects that are replicated over multiple servers. Other possibilities are for objects that are activated on demand or ones that can use other communications protocols, such as UDP.

Creating Server Objects

For a client to access a remote object that exists on the server, there must be a mechanism to obtain a remote reference that can access the remote object.

There are a number of methods for the client code to gain access to a server object. The most common one is to call a remote method whose return value is a server object. When a server object is returned to the client as a method result, the RMI mechanism automatically sends back a remote reference, not the actual object. There is, however, a chicken-and-egg problem here. The first server object needs to be located some other way. That object typically has plenty of methods to return other objects. The Sun RMI library provides a bootstrap registry service for this purpose.

Table 9.1 Naming conventions for client/server classes.	
no suffix (e.g., Product)	a remote interface
`Impl` suffix (e.g., `ProductImpl`)	a server class implementing that interface
`Server` suffix (e.g., `ProductServer`)	a server program that creates server objects
`Client` suffix (e.g., `ProductClient`)	a client program that calls remote methods
`_Stub` suffix (e.g., `ProductImpl_Stub`)	a stub class that is automatically generated by the rmic program
`_Skel` suffix (e.g., `ProductImpl_Skel`)	a skeleton class that is automatically generated by the rmic program

The server registers objects with the bootstrap registry service, and the client retrieves stubs to those objects. A server object is registered by giving the bootstrap registry service a reference to the object and a name. The name is a string that is (hopefully) unique.

```
// server
ProductImpl p1 = new ProductImpl("Blackwell Toaster");
Naming.bind("toaster", p1);
```

The client code gets a stub to access that server object by specifying the server name and the object name in a URL-style format:

```
// client
String url = "";
    // change to rmi://www.yourserver.com/
    // if server runs remotely on www.yourserver.com
Product c1 = (Product)Naming.lookup(url + "toaster");
```

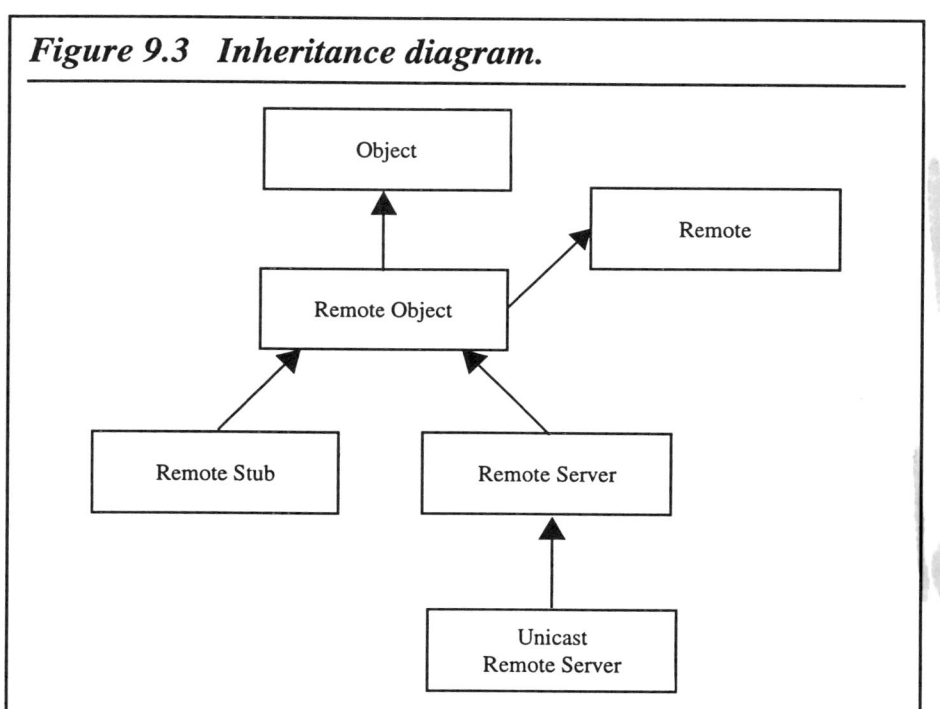

Figure 9.3   Inheritance diagram.

Because it is notoriously difficult to keep names unique in a global registry, you should not use this as the general method for locating objects on the server. Instead, there should be relatively few named server objects registered with the bootstrap service. In our example, we temporarily violate this rule and register relatively trivial objects. The reason is that we need to show you the mechanics for registering and locating objects.

However, we aren't quite ready to register any objects yet. Because the bootstrap registry service must be available, it also must stay active for the duration. Under Windows 95 or NT, you can do this by executing the statement:

```
rmiregistry
```

Next, you need to generate skeletons and stubs for the ProductImpl class. Recall that skeletons and stubs are on the server-level and client-level classes and that these are used by the RMI mechanism in order to marshal (encode and send) the parameters and marshal the results of method calls across the network. The Java programmer never uses these classes directly. Moreover, they need not be written by hand. The rmic tool generates them automatically as in the following example.

```
rmic ProductImpl
```

This call to the rmic tool generates two class files named, ProductImpl_Skel.class and ProductImpl_Stub.class. All server and client programs that use RMI need to install a security manager to control the code of any skeletons and stubs that are dynamically loaded off a network location. Java provides such a security manager, the RMISecurityManager. We install it with the instruction

```
System.setSecurityManager(new RMISecurityManager());
```

Listing 9.1 shows the complete program that registers two Product objects under the names toaster and microwave.

Once you compile this program, you need to run it as a separate process. Under Windows, use the command:

```
start java ProductServer
```

Under Unix, use the command

```
java ProductServer &
```

The Client Side

Now we can write the client program (Listing 9.2) that asks each newly registered product object to print its description.

You run this program on the client, in the usual way:

```
java ProductClient
```

It simply prints

```
I am a Blackwell Toaster. Buy me!
I am a ZapXpress Microwave Oven. Buy me!
```

This doesn't sound all that impressive, but consider what goes on behind the scenes when Java executes the call to the getDescription method. The client program has a reference to a stub object that it obtained from the lookup method. It calls the getDescription method which sends a network message to the skeleton object on the server side. The skeleton object invokes the getDescription method on the ProductImpl object located on the server. That method computes a string. The string

---

Listing 9.1 Register Product objects under toaster and microwave.

```
<<< ProductServer.java >>>
import java.rmi.*;
import java.rmi.server.*;
import sun.applet.*;
public class ProductServer
{  public static void main(String args[])
   {  System.setSecurityManager(new RMISecurityManager());
      try
      {  ProductImpl p1 = new ProductImpl("Blackwell Toaster");
         ProductImpl p2 = new ProductImpl("ZapXpress Microwave Oven");
         Naming.rebind("toaster", p1);
         Naming.rebind("microwave", p2);
      }
      catch(Exception e)
      {  System.out.println("Error: " + e);
      }
   }
}
```

is returned to the skeleton, sent across the network, received by the stub and returned as the result (Figure 9.4).

Cookbook for making an RMI application

Here is a summary of the steps you need to take to get remote method invocation working:

1. Place the interface class extending Remote on the server and the client;
2. Place the implementation class extending RemoteObject on the server;
3. Generate stubs and skeletons on the server by running rmic. Copy the stubs to the client;
4. Start the bootstrap registry service on the server;
5. Start a program that creates and registers objects of the implementation class on the server;
6. Run a program that looks up server objects and invokes remote methods on the client.

Listing 9.2   Client program to print object descriptions.

```
<<< ProductClient.java >>>
import java.rmi.*;
import java.rmi.server.*;
public class ProductClient
{  public static void main(String[] args)
    {  System.setSecurityManager(new RMISecurityManager());
       String url = "rmi:///";
          // change to "rmi://www.yourserver.com/"
          // when server runs on remote machine www.yourserver.com
       try
       {  Product c1 = (Product)Naming.lookup(url + "toaster");
          Product c2 = (Product)Naming.lookup(url + "microwave");
          System.out.println(c1.getDescription());
          System.out.println(c2.getDescription());
       }
       catch(Exception e)
       {  System.out.println("Error " + e);
       }
       System.exit(0);
    }
}
```

Using RMI with Applets

There are a number of special concerns when running RMI with applets. Applets have their own security manager since they run inside a browser. Thus, we do not use the RMISecurityManager on the client side.

We must take care where to place the stub and server files. Consider a browser that opens a Web page with an APPLET tag. The browser loads the class file referenced in that tag and all other class files as they are needed during execution. The class files are loaded from the same host that contains the Web page. Because of applet security restrictions, the applet can make network connections only to its originating host. Therefore, the server objects must reside on the same host as the Web page as well. That is, the same host must store:

- the Web page
- the applet code
- the stub code
- the skeletons and server objects
- the bootstrap registry

Parameter Passing of Nonremote Objects

When Java passes a remote object from the server to the client, the client receives a stub. Using the stub, it can manipulate the server object by invoking remote methods. The object, however, stays on the server. It is also possible to pass and return any objects via a remote method call, not just those that implement the Remote interface.

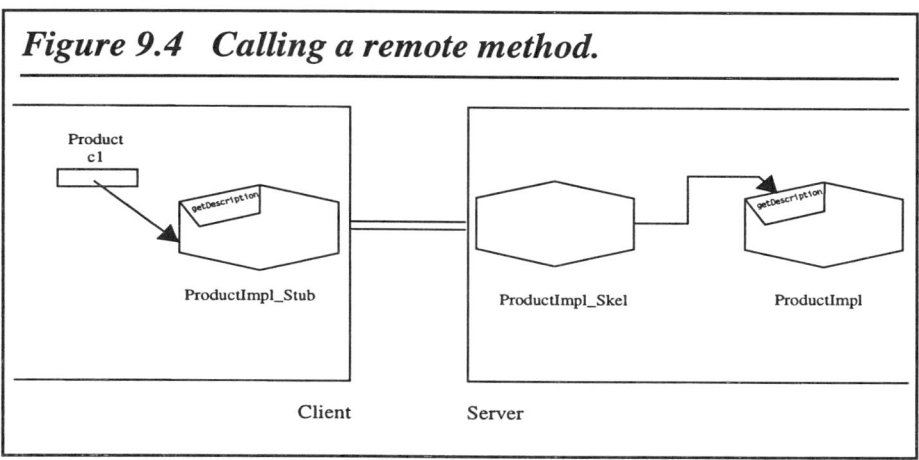

Figure 9.4   Calling a remote method.

Product
c1

getDescription

ProductImpl_Stub

ProductImpl_Skel

getDescription

ProductImpl

Client   Server

For example, the getDescription method of the preceding section returned a String object. That string was created on the server and had to be transported to the client. Since String does not implement the Remote interface, the client cannot return a string stub object. Instead, the client gets a copy of the string. Then, after the call, the client has its own String object to work. This means that there is no need for any further connection to any object on the server to deal with that string.

Whenever an object that is not a remote object needs to be transported from one Java virtual machine to another, the Java virtual machine makes a copy and sends that copy across the network connection. This is very different from parameter passing in a local method. When you pass objects into a local method, or return them as method results, only object references are passed. However, object references are memory addresses of objects in the local Java virtual machine. This information is meaningless to a different Java virtual machine.

It is not difficult to imagine how a copy of a string can be transported across a network. Java can also make copies of objects that instantiate more general classes using the standard Java serialization mechanism. That mechanism automatically translates an object that may itself have pointers to other objects into a linear sequence of bytes and reconstructs an object from such a byte sequence. Whenever an object refers to another object, that object must also be saved. Since object references are meaningless in a disk file, each saved object is given a serial number, and object references are saved as serial numbers. Therefore, the mechanism is called serialization.

The following program shows the copying of parameters and return values in action. This program is a simple application that lets you shop for a gift. The user runs a program on the client that gathers information about the gift recipient, in this case, age, sex, and hobbies.

An object of type Customer is then sent to the server. Since Customer is not a remote object, a copy of the object is made on the server. Note that Customer must implement the Serializable interface to indicate its willingness to be serialized.

The server program sends back a vector of products. The vector contains those products that match the customer profile, and it always contains that one item that will delight anyone, namely a copy of the book *Core Java*. Again, Vector is not a remote class, so the vector is copied from the server back to its client. (The Vector class implements the Serializable interface.) The serialization mechanism makes copies of all objects that are referenced inside a copied object. In our case, it makes a copy of all vector entries as well. We added an extra complexity: The entries are actually remote Product objects. Thus, the recipient gets a copy of the vector, filled with stub objects to the products on the server (see Figure 9.5).

To summarize, remote objects are passed across the network as stubs. Nonremote objects are copied. All of this is automatic and requires no programmer intervention.

Whenever a remote method is called, the stub makes a package that contains copies of all parameter values and sends it to the server, using the object serialization mechanism to marshal the parameters. The server skeleton unmarshals them. Naturally, the process can be quite slow — especially when the parameter objects are large.

Let us now look at the complete program (Listing 9.3). First, we have the interfaces for the product and warehouse services.

Products store a description, an age range, the buyer's appropriate sex (male, female, or both), and the matching hobby. Note that this class implements the getDescription method advertised in the Product interface, and it also implements another method, match, which is not a part of that interface. The match method is an example of a local method, a method that can only be called from the local program, not remotely. Since the match method is local, it need not be prepared to throw a RemoteException (Listing 9.4).

Like the ProductImpl class, the WarehouseImpl class too has remote and local methods. The add method is local. It is used by the server to add products to the warehouse. The find method is remote. It is used to find items in the warehouse.

To show you that the Customer object is actually copied, the find method of the WarehouseImpl class actually clears the customer object it receives. When the remote method returns, the WarehouseClient displays the customer object that it sent to the server. As you will see, that object has not changed. The server only cleared its copy. In this case, the clear operation serves no useful purpose. It only demonstrates that local objects are copied when they are passed as parameters (Listing 9.5).

In general, the methods of server classes such as ProductImpl and WarehouseImpl should be synchronized. Then it is possible for multiple client stubs to make simultaneous calls to a server object, even if some of the methods change the state of the server. We synchronize the methods of the WarehouseImpl class because it is conceivable that the local add and the remote find methods are called simultaneously. We don't synchronize the methods of the ProductImpl class because the product server objects don't change their state.

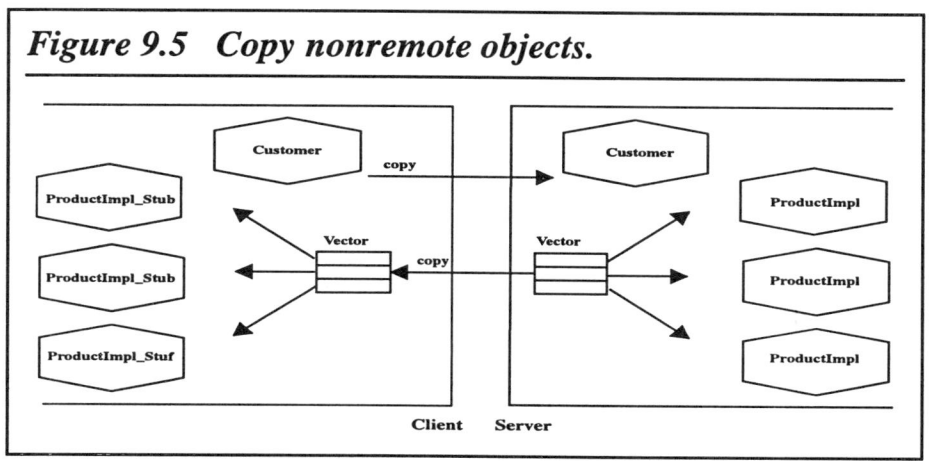

Figure 9.5   Copy nonremote objects.

Listing 9.6 is the server program that creates a warehouse object and registers it with the bootstrap registry service.

Listing 9.7 is the code for the client. When the user clicks the Submit button, a new customer object is generated and passed to the remote find method. Then the customer record is displayed in the text area (to prove that the clear call in the server did not affect it). Finally, the product descriptions of the returned products in the vector are added to the text area. Note that each getDescription call is again a remote method invocation.

Passing Remote Objects

Passing remote objects from the server to the client is simple. The client receives a stub object, then saves it in an object variable whose type is the same as the remote interface. It can now access the actual object on the server through this variable. The client can copy this variable in its own local machine — all those copies are simply references to the same stub.

It is important to note that only the remote interfaces can be accessed through the stub. A remote interface is any interface extending Remote. All local methods are inaccessible through the stub. A local method is any method that is not defined in a remote interface. Local methods can only run on the virtual machine containing the actual object.

Stubs are generated only from classes that implement a remote interface, and only the methods specified in the interfaces are provided in the stub classes. If a derived class doesn't implement a remote interface but a base class does, and an object of the

---

Listing 9.3   Interface for product and warehouse services.

```
<<< Product.java >>>
import java.rmi.*;
public interface Product
    extends Remote
{   String getDescription()
        throws RemoteException;
    static final int MALE = 1;
    static final int FEMALE = 2;
    static final int BOTH = MALE + FEMALE;
<<< Warehouse.java >>>
import java.rmi.*;
import java.util.*;
public interface Warehouse
    extends Remote
{   public Vector find(Customer c)
        throws RemoteException;
}
```

derived class is passed to a remote method, only the base class methods are accessible. To understand this better, consider the following example. We derive a class BookImpl from ProductImpl:

```
class BookImpl extends ProductImpl
{   public BookImpl(String title, String theISBN,
        int sex, int age1, int age2, String hobby)
    {   super(title + " Book", sex, age1, age2, hobby);
        ISBN = theISBN;
    }
    public String getStockCode() { return ISBN; }
    String ISBN;
}
```

Listing 9.4   *Example of remote and local methods.*

```
<<< ProductImpl.java >>>
import java.rmi.*;
import java.rmi.server.*;
public class ProductImpl
    extends UnicastRemoteObject
    implements Product
{   public ProductImpl(String n, int s, int age1, int age2, String h)
        throws RemoteException
    {   name = n;
        ageLow = age1;
        ageHigh = age2;
        sex = s;
        hobby = h;
    }
    public boolean match(Customer c) // local method
    {   if (c.getAge() < ageLow || c.getAge() > ageHigh)
            return false;
        if (!c.hasHobby(hobby)) return false;
        if ((sex & c.getSex()) == 0) return false;
        return true;
    }
    public String getDescription()
        throws RemoteException
    {   return "I am a " + name + ". Buy me!";
    }
    private String name;
    private int ageLow;
    private int ageHigh;
    private int sex;
    private String hobby;
}
```

Now suppose we pass a book object to a remote method, either as a parameter or as a return value. The recipient obtains a stub object. But that stub is not a book stub. Instead, it is a stub to the base class ProductImpl since only that class implements a remote interface (see Figure 9.6).

A remote class can implement multiple interfaces. For example, the BookImpl class can implement a second interface in addition to Product. Here we define a remote interface StockUnit and have the BookImpl class implement it.

```
interface StockUnit extends Remote
{  public String getStockCode() throws RemoteException;
}
class BookImpl extends ProductImpl implements StockUnit
{  public BookImpl(String title, String theISBN,
       int sex, int age1, int age2, String hobby)
       throws RemoteException
```

Listing 9.5 Warehouse *remote and local services.*

```
<<< WarehouseImpl.java >>>
import java.rmi.*;
import java.util.*;
import java.rmi.server.*;
public class WarehouseImpl
    extends UnicastRemoteObject
      implements Warehouse
{  public WarehouseImpl()
       throws RemoteException
    {  products = new Vector();
    }
    public synchronized void add(ProductImpl p) // local method
    {  products.addElement(p);
    }
    public synchronized Vector find(Customer c)
       throws RemoteException
    {  Vector result = new Vector();
       for (int i = 0; i < products.size(); i++)
       {  ProductImpl p = (ProductImpl)products.elementAt(i);
          if (p.match(c)) result.addElement(p);
       }
       result.addElement(new ProductImpl("Core Java Book",
          0, 200, Product.BOTH, ""));
       c.reset();
       return result;
    }
    private Vector products;
}
```

Listing 9.6   The server program.

```
<<< WarehouseServer.java >>>
import java.rmi.*;
import java.rmi.server.*;
public class WarehouseServer
{  public static void main(String args[])
   {  System.setSecurityManager(new RMISecurityManager());
      try
      {  WarehouseImpl w = new WarehouseImpl();
         fillWarehouse(w);
         Naming.rebind("central_warehouse", w);
      }
      catch(Exception e)
      {  System.out.println("Error: " + e);
      }
   }
   public static void fillWarehouse(WarehouseImpl w)
      throws RemoteException
   {  w.add(new ProductImpl("Blackwell Toaster", Product.BOTH,
         18, 200, "Household"));
      w.add(new ProductImpl("ZapXpress Microwave Oven", Product.BOTH,
         18, 200, "Household"));
      w.add(new ProductImpl("Jimbo After Shave", Product.MALE,
         18, 200, "Beauty"));
      w.add(new ProductImpl("Handy Hand Grenade", Product.MALE,
         20, 60, "Gardening"));
      w.add(new ProductImpl("DirtDigger Steam Shovel", Product.MALE,
         20, 60, "Gardening"));
      w.add(new ProductImpl("U238 Weed Killer", Product.BOTH,
         20, 200, "Gardening"));
      w.add(new ProductImpl("Van Hope Cosmetic Set", Product.FEMALE,
         15, 45, "Beauty"));
      w.add(new ProductImpl("Persistent Java Fragrance", Product.FEMALE,
         15, 45, "Beauty"));
      w.add(new ProductImpl("Rabid Rodent Computer Mouse", Product.BOTH,
         6, 40, "Computers"));
      w.add(new ProductImpl("Learn Bad Java Habits in 21 Days Book", Product.BOTH,
         20, 200, "Computers"));
      w.add(new ProductImpl("My first Espresso Maker", Product.FEMALE,
         6, 10, "Household"));
      w.add(new ProductImpl("JavaJungle Eau de Cologne", Product.FEMALE,
         20, 200, "Beauty"));
      w.add(new ProductImpl("Fast/Wide SCSI Coffee Maker", Product.MALE,
         20, 50, "Computers"));
      w.add(new ProductImpl("ClueLess Network Computer", Product.BOTH,
         6, 200, "Computers"));
   }
}
```

```
{  super(title + " Book", sex, age1, age2, hobby);
   ISBN = theISBN;
}
 public String getStockCode() throws RemoteException
{  return ISBN; }
 private String ISBN;
}
```

Listing 9.7   The client program.

```
<<< WarehouseClient.java >>>
import java.awt.*;
import java.rmi.*;
import java.rmi.server.*;
import java.util.*;
import corejava.*;
public class WarehouseClient extends Frame
{  public WarehouseClient()
   {  GridBagLayout gbl = new GridBagLayout();
      setLayout(gbl);
      GridBagConstraints gbc = new GridBagConstraints();
      gbc.fill = GridBagConstraints.NONE;
      gbc.weightx = 100;
      gbc.weighty = 100;
      add(this, new Label("Age:"), gbl, gbc, 0, 0, 1, 1);
      add(this, age = new IntTextField(0, 0, 200, 4), gbl, gbc, 1, 0, 1, 1);
      CheckboxGroup cbg = new CheckboxGroup();
      add(this, male = new Checkbox("Male", cbg, true), gbl, gbc, 0, 1, 1, 1);
      add(this, female = new Checkbox("Female", cbg, true), gbl, gbc, 1, 1, 1,1);
      add(this, new Label("Hobbies"), gbl, gbc, 0, 2, 1, 1);
      hobbies = new List(4, true);
      hobbies.addItem("Gardening");
      hobbies.addItem("Beauty");
      hobbies.addItem("Computers");
      hobbies.addItem("Household");
      hobbies.addItem("Sports");
      add(this, hobbies, gbl, gbc, 1, 2, 1, 1);
      add(this, new Button("Submit"), gbl, gbc, 0, 3, 1, 1);
      result = new TextArea(4, 40);
      result.setEditable(false);
      add(this, result, gbl, gbc, 0, 4, 2, 1);
      System.setSecurityManager(new RMISecurityManager());
      String url = "rmi:///";
         // change to "rmi://www.yourserver.com/"
         // when server runs on remote machine www.yourserver.com
      try
      {  centralWarehouse = (Warehouse)Naming.lookup("central_warehouse");
      }
      catch(Exception e)
      {  System.out.println("Error: Can't connect to warehouse. " + e);
      }
   }
```

Now, when Java passes a book object to a remote method, the recipient obtains a stub that has access to the remote methods in both the `Product` and the `StockUnit` class (Figure 9.7). In fact, you can use the `instanceof` operator to find out whether a particular remote object implements an interface.

Here is a typical situation. Suppose you receive a remote object through a variable of type `Product`.

```
Vector result = centralWarehouse.find(c);
for (int i = 0; i < result.size(); i++)
   Product p = (Product)result.elementAt(i);
   . . .
```

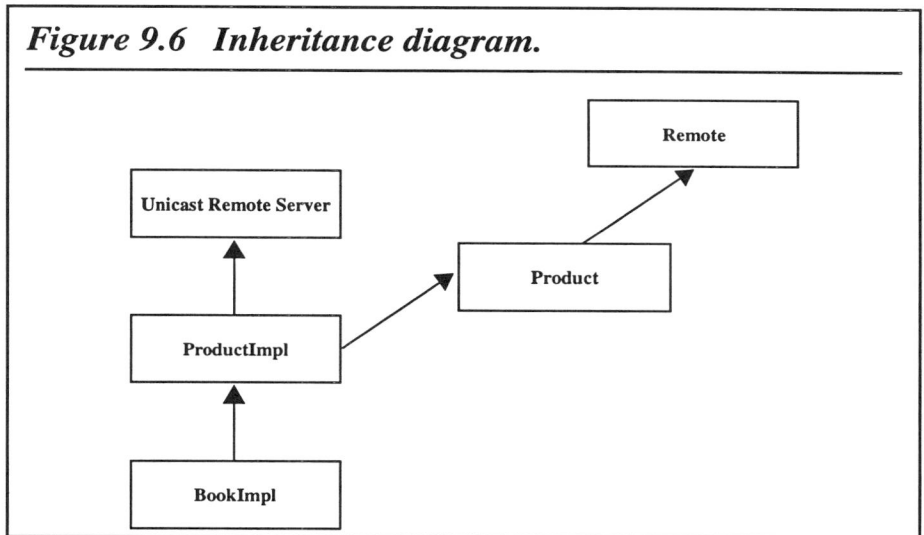

Figure 9.6   Inheritance diagram.

Listing 9.7 (continued)

```
   private void add(Container p, Component c,
     GridBagLayout gbl, GridBagConstraints gbc,
     int x, int y, int w, int h)
{  gbc.gridx = x;
   gbc.gridy = y;
   gbc.gridwidth = w;
   gbc.gridheight = h;
   gbl.setConstraints(c, gbc);
   p.add(c);
}  public boolean action(Event evt, Object arg)
```

Now the remote object may or may not be a book. We'd like to use instanceof to find out whether it is or not. But we can't test

```
if (p instanceof BookImpl) // wrong
    BookImpl b = (BookImpl)p;
    . . .
```

Listing 9.7 (continued)

```
    {  if (arg.equals("Submit"))
       {  if (age.isValid())
          {  Customer c = new Customer(age.getValue(),
                (male.getState() ? Product.MALE : 0)
                + (female.getState() ? Product.FEMALE : 0),
                hobbies.getSelectedItems());
             String t = c + "\n";
             try
             {  Vector result = centralWarehouse.find(c);
                for (int i = 0; i < result.size(); i++)
                {  Product p = (Product)result.elementAt(i);
                   t += p.getDescription() + "\n";
                }
             }
             catch(Exception e)
             {  t = "Error: " + e;
             }
             result.setText(t);
          }
          return true;
       }
       else return false;
    }
     public boolean handleEvent(Event evt)
    {  if (evt.id == Event.WINDOW_DESTROY) System.exit(0);
       return super.handleEvent(evt);
    }
     public static void main(String[] args)
    {  Frame f = new WarehouseClient();
       f.resize(300, 300);
       f.show();
    }
    private Warehouse centralWarehouse;
    private IntTextField age;
    private Checkbox male;
    private Checkbox female;
    private List hobbies;
    private TextArea result;
}
```

The object p refers to a stub object, and BookImpl is the class of the server object. We could cast the stub object to a BookImpl_Stub.

```
if (p instanceof BookImpl_Stub)
   BookImpl_Stub b = (BookImpl_Stub)p; // not useful
   . . .
```

But that would not do us much good. The stubs are generated mechanically by the rmic program for internal use by the RMI mechanism, and clients should not have to think about them. Instead, we cast to the second interface:

```
if (p instanceof StockUnit)
{  StockUnit s = (StockUnit)p;
   String c = s.getStockCode();
   . . .
}
```

This code tests whether the stub object to which p refers implements the Stock-Unit interface. If so, it calls the getStockCode remote method of that interface.

To summarize: If an object that belongs to a class which implements a remote interface is passed to a remote method, the remote method receives a stub object. You can cast that stub object to any of the remote interfaces which the implementation class implements. You can call all remote methods defined in those interfaces but you cannot call any local methods through the stub.

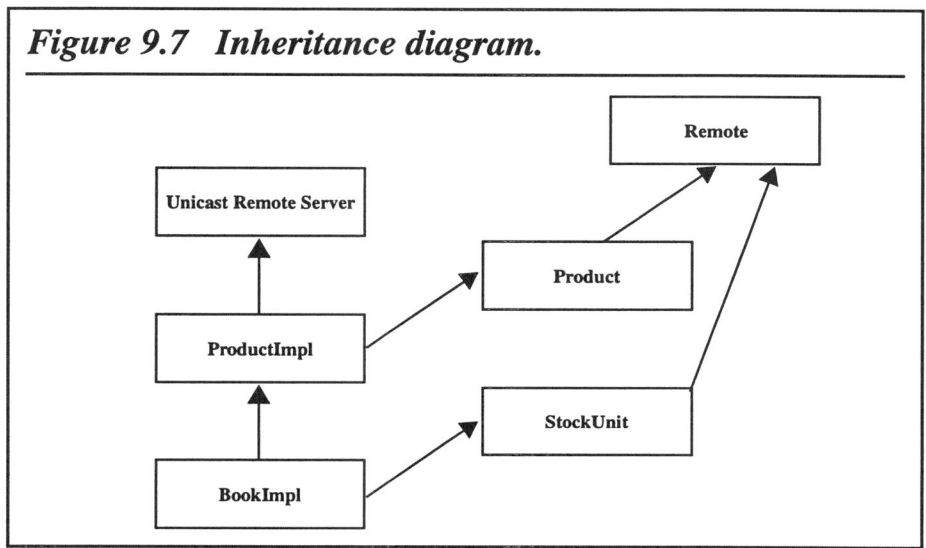

Figure 9.7 Inheritance diagram.

Using Remote Objects in Hash Tables

Objects that are inserted in a hash table need to override the `equals` and `hashCode` methods. Both methods are necessary to find an object in a hash table. First, the hash code is computed to find the appropriate bucket. Then each object in that bucket is compared with the object to be matched, using the `equals` method.

However, there is a problem when trying to do this for remote objects. To find out if two remote objects have the same contents, the call to `equals` would need to contact the servers containing the objects and compare their contents. And that call could fail. But the `equals` method in the class `Object` is not declared to throw a `RemoteException`, whereas all methods in a remote interface must throw that exception. Since a subclass method cannot throw more exceptions than the superclass method that it replaces, you cannot define an `equals` method in a remote interface. The same holds for `hashCode`.

Instead, you must rely on the redefinitions of the `equals` and `hashCode` methods in the `RemoteObject` class that is the base class for all stub and server objects. These methods do not look at the object contents, just at the location of the server objects. Two stubs that refer to the same server object are found to be equal by the `equals` method. Two stubs that refer to different server objects are never equal, even if those objects have identical contents. Similarly, the hash code is only computed from the object identifier. Stubs that refer to different server objects will likely have different hash codes, even if the server objects have identical contents.

This limitation only refers to stubs. You can redefine `equals` or `hashCode` for the server object classes. Those methods are called when inserting server objects in a hash table on the server. But they are never called when comparing or hashing stubs.

To clarify the difference between client and server behavior, look at the inheritance diagram in Figure 9.8.

The `RemoteObject` class is the base for both stub and server classes. On the stub side, you cannot override the `equals` and `hashCode` methods since the stubs are mechanically generated. On the server side, you can override the methods for the implementation classes, but they are only used locally on the server. If you do override these methods, implementation and stub objects are no longer considered identical.

The situation is the same for the `clone` method. Stubs don't define `clone` and, therefore, cannot be cloned. Implementation classes on the server are free to override `clone`, but that method is a local method and can only be used in server code. Actually, this behavior will be improved in the beta version. The `UnicastRemoteObject` class will define `clone` to make and export a clone of the original implementation object.

To summarize: You can use stub objects in hash tables, but you must remember that equality testing and hashing does not take the contents of the remote objects into account.

Inappropriate Remote Parameters

Suppose we enhance our shopping application by having the application show a picture of each gift. Why not simply add a remote method

```
void paint(Graphics g) throws RemoteException
```

to the Product interface? Unfortunately, this code cannot work, and it is important to understand why. The Graphics class does not implement remote interfaces. Therefore, objects of type Graphics are passed by copy. Actually, Graphics is an abstract class. The Graphics objects that are obtained as parameters of the paint method or return values of the getGraphics method of the Component class actually belong to

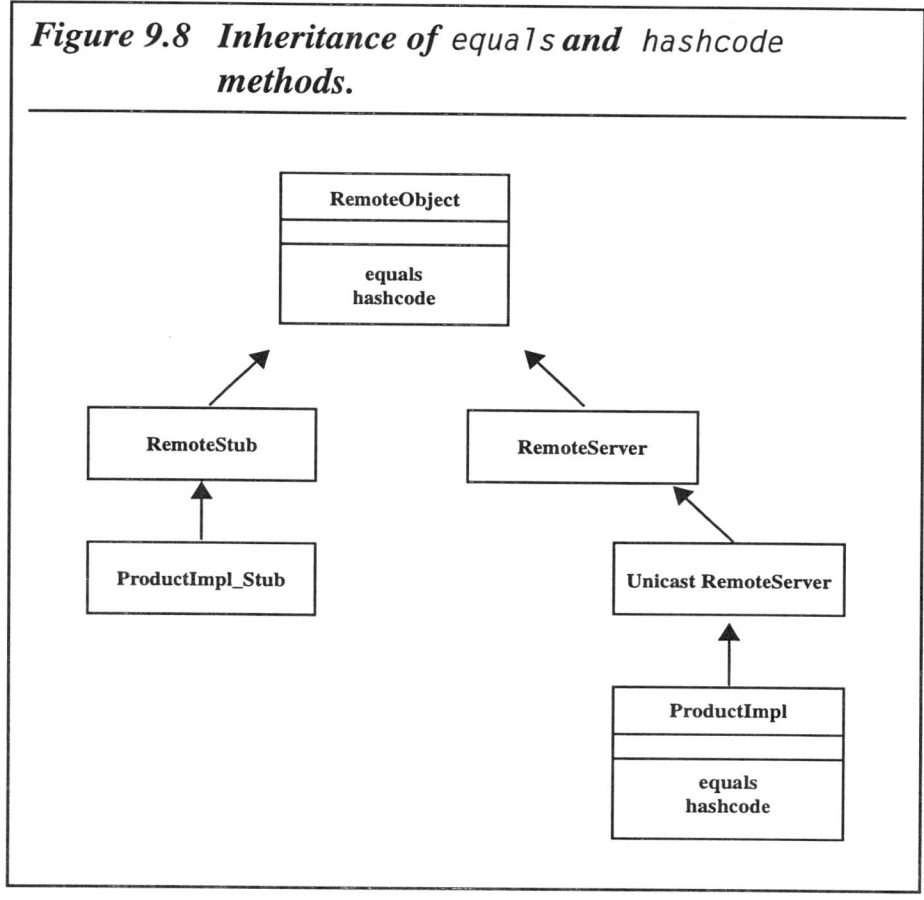

Figure 9.8 Inheritance of *equals and hashcode* methods.

some subclass that implements a graphics context on a particular platform. Those objects, in turn, need to interact with the native graphics code. They store pointers to memory blocks that are needed by the native graphics methods. Java has no pointers, so they are stored as integers in the graphics object and are cast back to pointers in the native methods.

Therefore, it makes no sense to copy a graphics object. First of all, the target machine may be a different platform. For example, if the client runs Windows and the server runs X11, then the server does not have the native methods available to render Windows graphics. But even if the server and the client have the same graphics system, the pointer values would not be valid on the server.

Instead, if the server wants to send an image to the client, it has to come up with some other mechanism for transporting the data across the network. As it turns out, this is actually difficult to do for images. The Image class is just as device-dependent as the Graphics class. We could send the image data as a sequence of bytes in JPEG format, but there is no method in the AWT package to turn a block of JPEG data into an image. (Currently, this can be done only by using unpublished classes in the sun.awt.image package.) However, one can solve this particular problem in a more mundane way, by sending a URL to the client and using a method of the Applet class that can read an image from a URL.

Fortunately, Java does not let you send Graphics or Image objects as RMI parameters or return values. These classes do not implement the Serializable interface. Only classes that implement Serializable can be serialized. Actually, Serializable is a do-nothing interface. Just as with Cloneable, a class implements that interface solely to indicate that it understands the limitations of the serialization process.

Java IDL

The techniques we discussed so far allow Java objects on different machines to communicate with each other through method calls. But what if you want to call a C++ method from a Java object, or write objects in Java that can be called from other languages? Then the RMI mechanism is no longer useful, and you must instead use the Java IDL mechanism.

IDL, the Interface Definition Language, is a language-neutral description of a class interface. The interface of a C++ or Smalltalk class can be described in IDL, as can of course the interface of a Java class. (Here the term "interface" refers to the collection of methods of a class, not to the Java interface concept. However, these concepts are related, as we will see later.) If you want to call a function that is specified in an IDL interface, then you must run an IDL compiler that generates intermediary glue to talk to the actual object on the server, just as in the case of RMI stubs. Similarly, if you write a server object, you must generate skeleton classes. These stubs and skeletons take care of a large amount of the marshalling and network transport between the client and server. However, where RMI gives programmers a near-perfect illusion of making local method calls when in fact they call methods across the network, Java IDL is not nearly as transparent.

Since IDL is a language-independent specification, it has some features that do not have a perfect match in Java. Sometimes, the Java IDL layer can translate automatically between the IDL abstractions and the Java language features. At other times, programmers must use wrapper objects to mimic IDL concepts.

Both RMI and IDL are in the Core API set. But unlike RMI, which will be a part of the Java 1.1 release, IDL will be released at a later time. At this point, the Object Management Group (OMG) is discussing the exact nature of the correspondence between IDL and Java features (the so-called Java binding).

This binding is one aspect of gluing Java together with other so-called CORBA (Common Object Request Broker Architecture) objects. The other aspect is the network protocol. RMI has a fixed network protocol that is transparent to the programmer. IDL sports, at last count, three network protocols: the IIOP protocol that is being standardized by the OMG, the NEO protocol that is proprietary to Sun, and the DOOR protocol, a Java-to-Java protocol that was developed by the designers of Java IDL.

Since IDL is more complex and less convenient than RMI, it should not be considered for homogeneous Java systems. For heterogeneous systems, in particular, communication between C++ and Java objects, it is an attractive solution.

A Simple IDL Example

In this section, we give a few brief examples to show the flavor of the IDL syntax.
Let us write the `Product` interface in IDL:

```
interface Product
{  string getDescription();
};
```

This means that a product is a class whose objects can return a description string. The implementation language and data implementation are not specified — they need not be of any concern to the caller.

Note the return type `string`. IDL specifies a `string` type, and a particular language binding must specify to which language feature that abstract type corresponds. In C, this is tricky — C does not have a string type, and a `struct { char*, size_t }` is used. In Java, the situation is clear — `string` should correspond to `java.lang.String`. Actually, it is not all that clear. The IDL `string` type describes character sequences in the 1-byte ANSI code. Java strings use the 2-byte Unicode. This is not a problem when a remote server returns a string — simply set all high bytes to zero. But it is a problem when a Java string is passed to the remote server. In that case, the binding specifies that an exception is thrown. This is just one of the problems that arises from a less-than-perfect match between the idealized IDL and an actual programming language.

The IDL compiler idlgen translates the IDL interface into six (!) Java files:

- ProductHolder
- ProductOperations
- ProductRef
- ProductServant
- ProductSkeleton
- ProductStub

Only the last two are familiar from RMI. In addition, ProductRef is equivalent to the interface type Product that is used in RMI.

The mechanism to access a server object is similar as in RMI.

```
ProductRef product;
String url = "idl://www.whatnot.com:1234/toaster";
try
{   product = ProductStub.createRef();
    // resolve the name into the holder
    sunw.corba.Orb.resolve(url, product);
} catch (Exception ex) {}
```

Now you can use the ProductRef variable to make method calls:

```
String d = product.getDescription();
```

After creation, you no longer need to use the stub type — always use the reference type.

Now suppose you implement the Product object on the server side. You need to implement the ProductServant interface that was automatically generated by idl-gen, and implement the method that was advertised in the interface.

```
class ProductImpl implements Product Servant
{   public ProductImpl(String descr) { name = descr; }
    public String getDescription() { return name; }
    private String name;
}
```

Finally, some server code must make product objects available.

```
try
{  ProductImpl t = new ProductImpl("Blackwell Toaster");
   ProductRef rt = ProductSkeleton.createRef(toaster);
   sunw.door.Orb.publish("toaster", t);} catch (Exception ex) {
}
```

Again, this is similar as in RMI.

Here we just looked at a very basic examples. You will find a complete discussion of the current proposal of the Java/IDL binding on `http://splash.java-soft.com/JavaIDL/pages/IDLtoJava.html`.

Conclusion

Using the Java Remote Method invocation (RMI), you can call methods on objects that reside elsewhere on the network, pass parameters, and obtain return values. The details of sending the parameters to the remote object and receiving the return value from it are essentially transparent to the Java programmer.

A similar effect, though not always quite as transparent, can be obtained by using IDL, the Java/CORBA interface. IDL is not as transparent as RMI, but it can interface with objects that are written in any language with a CORBA interface.

Chapter 10

Multithreading in C++

Gregory A. Bumgardner

Abstract

Writing multithreaded applications can be quite difficult. While C++ can be used to simplify this task by allowing for the creation and use of abstract, object-oriented, representations of common thread management and synchronization mechanisms, some features of C++ may also introduce new difficulties that must be addressed and overcome. In addition, the procedural nature and requirements of the underlying thread API provided by most systems is often at odds with the object-oriented approach favored under C++.

This paper gives a brief overview of multithreading, identifies some of the commonly-used multithreading APIs, identifies several areas that require special consideration when developing multithreaded applications using C++, and finally, establishes a set of guidelines or rules for dealing with these special situations.

Introduction

Many applications can benefit from the use of concurrency in their implementation. In a concurrent model of execution, an application is divided into two or more threads each executing its own sequence of statements or instructions. The active threads within an application may be distributed across processes, processors, network nodes, and network boundaries.

These separately executing threads must generally compete for shared resources and must cooperate and communicate in order to accomplish their assigned tasks.

Concurrent application development can be difficult and complicated. Some of the significant design decisions to be made include the identification of the number of threads or processes required, their particular responsibilities, and the methods by which they will interact. Also key to this development is the identification of good, legal, or invariant program states in contrast to bad or illegal program states. The critical problem is to find and implement a solution that maintains or guarantees good program states while prohibiting bad ones, even in those situations where there may be two or more threads simultaneously manipulating the same resource or data.

In a concurrent execution environment, maintaining desirable program states is accomplished by limiting or negotiating access to shared resources through the use of synchronization. The principal role of synchronization is to prevent undesirable or unanticipated interference between concurrently executing instruction sequences.

To support concurrent application development, many of today's operating systems provide some level of support for thread creation and synchronization. However, this support is typically supplied as a low-level, procedural API comprised of 'C' language functions. The use of such an API raises several issues:

- The independent nature and loose typing of these low-level functions provide developers with abundant opportunities for implementation errors that may appear only at run time.
- The procedural-style of usage for these functions is often at odds with the object-oriented approach favored by today's C++ programmer.
- The functionality and capabilities of each multithreading API and its mechanisms tend to vary significantly from platform to platform.

While these issues may be partially alleviated by encapsulating the various threading API mechanisms with appropriate C++ classes, the C++ language itself poses some additional problems and concerns that must be addressed, including:

- Exception-safe synchronization and locking.
- Program initialization and termination in the presence of multiple threads.
- Static object construction and destruction in the presence of multiple threads.
- Exception handling within and between threads.

The intent of this paper is to identify and describe some of the critical issues related to implementation of multithreaded application in C++.

The remainder of this paper is organized as follows:

- "Overview of Multithreading" briefly covers multithreading concepts and terminology.
- "Libraries for Multithreading" identifies some of the common multithreading programming interfaces and class libraries used to develop multithreaded C++ applications.

- "Implementation Issues Related to the Development of Multithreaded Applications in C" is divided into subsections that identify and describe some of the important issues that must be considered by anyone developing multithreaded C++ applications and provides some rules or guidelines for dealing with these issues.

- The chapter is summarized in "Conclusion."

Overview of Multithreading

This section introduces some basic definitions and concepts that will be used throughout the remainder of this paper.

Concurrency and Threads

A thread, or thread-of-control, is a sequence of instructions that can be executed on a processor. A thread is associated with, or possesses, an execution context, typically consisting of a program counter and a private stack.

A process is a program that is loaded into memory and prepared for execution. Each process has its own private address space, and starts with a single thread. Many system resources, such as file handles, network connections, etc., are allocated and bound on a per process basis. All threads within a process share the private address space and system resources of that process.

Concurrency exists when two or more threads in one or more processes are in progress at the same time. A single processor system can support concurrency by switching execution between two or more threads. A multiprocessor system can support parallel concurrency by executing a separate thread on each processor.

A multithreaded object, library, or application will use two or more threads in one or more processes for some period during its execution.

An object, library, or application is said to be multithread-hot, or MT-hot, if it creates additional threads to accomplish its task. Labeling something MT-hot is a warning that inclusion of such an object or library in a product may require that the user provide multithread protection or synchronization within other portions of the application.

Threads and Memory

All threads within the same process share the address-space of that process. Globally-named and static variables are implicitly shared among all threads within a process. Object instances dynamically created on the heap, or automatically created on the stack, may be explicitly shared by passing references or addresses between threads.

Each thread possesses its own stack within the process address space. Non-static, function-scope variables, or object instances, are automatically allocated and constructed on a thread's stack as each definition is encountered, and are destroyed and de-allocated when the thread's execution flow exits the block that defines the variable's scope. Automatic variables are generally considered local to the thread, although they may still be accessed by other threads if shared by reference or address.

Since the life span and accessibility of a local variable on a thread's stack is limited by its scope (it only exists within the scope of the function where it was declared, for example), and since global instances are always shared between all threads, another kind of storage is required when threads need to maintain a thread-local instance of some object but also need to share this instance between the functions being executed by the thread. This capability is provided by thread-local storage, also called thread-specific storage, an alternative form of storage that is maintained and accessed on a per-thread basis but has a life-span independent of normal stack scope.

Thread Synchronization

Synchronization describes the use of mechanisms or processes whereby undesirable interleaving of operations or interference between concurrent threads is prevented. Synchronization is generally accomplished using one of two techniques, mutual exclusion or condition synchronization.

Mutual exclusion involves combining fine-grained atomic actions into coarse-grained actions, and arranging to make these composite actions atomic.

Condition synchronization describes a process or mechanism that delays the execution of a thread until the program state satisfies some predicate, or condition.

A thread that is no longer executing because it is delayed or waiting on some synchronization mechanism is considered blocked. Once a thread is unblocked, awakened, or signaled, it becomes runnable and eligible for further execution.

There are two basic uses for thread synchronization: to protect the integrity of shared data, and to efficiently communicate changes in program state between cooperating threads.

Thread Safety

An unsafe routine, class, or library should not be used in a multithreaded application unless the application allows only one thread at a time to access or execute within that routine, class, or library. Unsafe routines, classes, or libraries often contain global and static data that is not protected. Unsafe libraries or classes may contain some routines that are safe, but the library or class as a whole has been deemed unsafe.

A safe routine, class, or library may be accessed or executed from within a multithreaded application. Safe objects are reentrant and protect their internal global or static data from multithreaded corruption. A safe class or library implies that individual operations may be performed safely without user locking and unlocking, but may still may require external synchronization or locking in situations where several individual operations must be combined and treated as a single atomic operation (testing for, and reading the contents of a queue, for example). Labeling an object as "safe" does not necessarily mean that it can support true concurrent access, only that individual operations have been serialized as required to protect the internal state of the object. This level of thread safety is sometimes referred to as MT-safe: Level 1.

An MT-safe routine, class, or library is fully prepared for multithreaded access and execution. MT-safe objects are reentrant, protect their internal global or static data, and provide for a reasonable level of concurrency. This level of thread safety is sometimes referred to as MT-safe: Level 2.

To illustrate the differences between these safety levels, consider a hypothetical linked-list class:

- An unsafe linked-list class would provide no locking or synchronization between threads.

- A safe linked-list would use a single lock to control access to the list. Only one thread at a time would be able to read or write an entry in the list.

- An MT-safe linked-list would associate a lock with each element in the list, allowing for multiple threads to simultaneously read or write within different elements in the list.

Libraries for Multithreading

There are almost as many libraries for multithreading as there are platforms that support multithreading. Nearly all of the major systems vendors now provide some form of support for multithreading. Most often this support is supplied by a procedural library of 'C' language functions. Some systems and third-party vendors also provide C++ classes or libraries for creating multithreaded applications.

Procedural Libraries for Multithreading

The list below identifies some of the procedural-style multithreading APIs that are in common use today, and also lists some of the platform(s) on which each API is supported:

- OSF/DCE Threads (POSIX 1003.1c Draft 4)
  HP-UX — Hewlett Packard Encina/DCE (various platforms) — Transarc

- POSIX 1003.1c Threads
  AIX — IBM
  IRIX — Silicon Graphics, Inc.
  OSF/1 — Digital Equipment Corp.
  Solaris — Sun Microsystems

- DOS Control Program Threads
  OS/2 — IBM

- UNIX International Threads (Solaris)
  Solaris — Sun Microsystems
- Win32 Threads
  Windows NT — Microsoft
  Windows 95 — Microsoft

Class Libraries for Multithreading

There are also several C++ class libraries that provide varying levels of support for object-oriented multithreading:

- Threads.h++ — Rogue Wave Software, Inc.
- Adaptive Communications Environment (ACE) — Doug Schmidt, et al., Washington University
- Microsoft Foundation Classes (MFC) — Microsoft
- Borland C++ Class Library — Borland International
- Visual Age C++ Class Library — IBM

  Each of these libraries relies on, and encapsulates one or more of the procedural APIs listed in "Procedural Libraries for Multithreading."

Implementation Issues Related to the Development of Multithreaded Applications in C++

This section identifies several aspects of the C++ language that are of special concern when developing multithreaded applications using this language. Each subsection identifies and describes a different aspect or issue and suggests guidelines for dealing with that issue.

Exception-Safe Synchronization

The C++ exception model can have significant, and perhaps unforeseen, consequences with respect to the proper implementation of multithread synchronization.

To prevent undesirable interference between two concurrently executing threads, some form of cooperation, or synchronization is often required.

A mutex implements a form of synchronization called mutual exclusion. Mutexes are used when only one thread at a time is to be allowed to enter one or more protected, or critical sections of code.

A thread must acquire ownership of a mutex prior to entering any section of code protected by the mutex. Once a thread is granted ownership of the mutex, it is allowed to proceed into the protected section of code. If other threads attempt to acquire the mutex during that time, they are forced to wait until the current owner releases ownership of the mutex.

A typical object-oriented, C++ implementation of a mutex will provide an interface similar to the following:

```
class Mutex {
    public:
        Mutex();
        ~Mutex();
        void acquire();
        bool tryAcquire();
        void release();
};
```

The constructor of this class is used to initialize the mutex object. The destructor is used to free any resources allocated in creating the mutex. The acquire() function is used to acquire ownership of the mutex for the calling thread, and will block the caller until sole ownership of the mutex can be granted. The release() function is used by the current mutex owner to release ownership of the mutex freeing it for acquisition by another thread. The tryAcquire() function is used to acquire ownership of the mutex only if no other thread currently owns it, returning a Boolean value of true if ownership was granted, and false if another thread already holds the mutex.

A common situation that requires mutual exclusion occurs when some number of threads share an IO stream for output. If, for example, the various threads within an application used a single function for writing some sort of trace or debug records to the cout IO stream, that function would want to synchronize access to the stream to prevent the individual stream output operations from the various threads from becoming interleaved in the final output:

```
void trace(char* message) {
    // Use mutex to make the record output atomic
    // (Keep the end-of-line with the message!)
    static Mutex mutex;
    mutex.acquire();
    cout << message << endl;
    mutex.release();
}
```

There exists a potential problem with this style of implementation; if one of the stream operations produces an exception, the mutex.release() statement will not get executed, essentially leaving the mutex locked forever.

One way to fix this problem is to add a try-catch block around the operation using an explicit mutex release in the catch block:

```
void trace(char* message) {
    // Use mutex to make the record output atomic
    // (Keep the end-of-line with the message!)
    static Mutex mutex;
    mutex.acquire();
    try {
        cout << message << endl;
    }
    catch(...) {
        // Catch all exceptions
        // Make sure to release the mutex!
        mutex.release();
        // Rethrow the exception
        throw;
    }
    mutex.release();
}
```

This approach guarantees that the mutex will be released, even if an exception is thrown by one of the stream operations (barring failure within the mutex itself!).

This solution does provide a greater level of exception-safety, but can become quite cumbersome since it requires the developer to code exception handlers wherever synchronization mechanisms were being used to lock code that might produce exceptions. This is made more difficult when the developer may have no idea whether or not any exceptions can be expected from the code.

Guard classes are "helper" classes can be used to simplify the acquisition and release of various synchronization resources, and to insure exception-safe synchronization.

A guard class uses the "resource acquisition is initialization"[1] idiom where a constructor is used to acquire a resource, and the destructor is used to release the acquired resource.

A "lock guard" class uses this idiom to automatically acquire and release ownership of mutexes and other synchronization mechanisms.

A simple lock guard class might be implemented as follows:

```
template <class Resource> LockGuard {
    private:
        bool acquired_;
        Resource& resource_;
    public:
        LockGuard(Resource& resource) :
            resource_(resource),
            acquired_(FALSE)
        {
            resource_.acquire()
            acquired_=TRUE;
        }
```

```
    ~LockGuard(Resource& resource) {
        if (acquired_)
            resource_.release();
    }
    void acquire() {
        if (!acquired_) {
            resource_.acquire();
            acquired_=TRUE;
        }
    }
    void release() {
        if (acquired_) {
            resource_.release();
            acquired_=FALSE;
        }
    }
    bool isAcquired() const {
        return acquired_;
    }
protected:
    // Disallow copy construction and assignment
    LockGuard(const LockGuard<Resource>&);
    // Disallow assignment
    LockGuard<Resource>&
    operator=(const LockGuard<Resource>&);
};
```

To use this `LockGuard` template class, simply declare and initialize a named instance of the class within the code block that is to be protected by the mutex:

```
void trace(char* message) {
    // Use mutex to make the record output atomic
    // (Keep the end-of-line with the message!)
    static Mutex mutex;
    LockGuard<Mutex> lock(mutex);
    cout << message << endl;
}
```

This version of `trace()` is functionally equivalent to our previous implementation, but is obviously easier to write and easier to understand than the previous version that used the try-catch block. The guard instance will automatically be destroyed when the thread of execution exits the block in which the guard was defined, thus releasing the mutex even if an exception causes the block exit.

To release and reacquire a guarded lock, you should use the `release()` and `acquire()` members of the guard object. These member functions update the internal state of the guard so that the guard's destructor will not attempt to release a resource that is no longer held.

```
{
   LockGuard<Mutex> lock(mutex); // Acquired
   // Exception here will release mutex
   lock.release(); // Released
   // Exception here will not affect mutex
   lock.acquire(); // Acquired
   // Exception here will release mutex
}
// Mutex released by current thread
```

The lock guard implementation described above can easily be modified to produce "try-lock" and "unlock" guard class implementations.

An unlock guard is used to release then reacquire a synchronization resource. The unlock guard is used in the same way as the lock guard class, except that it releases the resource in the constructor and reacquires it in the destructor:

```
// Mutex already owned by current thread
{
   UnlockGuard<Mutex> unlock(mutex); // Released
   // Exception here will acquire mutex
   unlock.acquire(); // Acquired
   // Exception here will not affect mutex
   unlock.release(); // Released
   // Exception here will acquire mutex
}
// Mutex still owned by current thread
```

A try-lock guard defines a constructor that uses a resource method such as `tryAc-quire()` to conditionally acquire a resource. The try-lock guard destructor will automatically release the resource, but only if it was and still is acquired. The guard member `isAcquired()` can be used to test to see whether or not the initial acquisition attempt was successful:

```
// Mutex not owned by current thread
{
   TryLockGuard<Mutex> tryLock(mutex);
   if (tryLock.isAcquired()) {
      // Mutex acquired!
   }
   else {
      // Mutex not acquired!
   }
}
// Mutex not owned by current thread
```

Most existing C++ class libraries that provide synchronization mechanisms also provide versions of some or all of these guard object types.

Rule 1   Use guard objects for exception-safe synchronization.

Global Static Initialization in the Presence of Multiple Threads

The classic "static initialization problem" is often exacerbated when additional threads of execution are introduced.

The static initialization problem[2] is widely recognized by developers of C++ libraries and application. This problem primarily arises from the lack of a predictable initialization order between global static objects defined in different translation units; a static object in one translation unit may accidentally, yet legally, attempt to access an uninitialized static object in another translation unit.

The static initialization problem can typically be solved by:

- Delaying access to static objects until they are initialized.
- Initializing static objects when they are first accessed.

The first approach generally prohibits global static objects in one translation unit from directly or indirectly accessing global static objects in other translation units. This restriction is often unacceptable for general-purpose libraries that maintain internal static data, since it prohibits a library user from calling any library functions that might manipulate internal static data, from within any code that is executed as a result of global static initialization.

The second approach requires an object to test itself for initialization each time it is accessed. While these internal initialization checks add some processing overhead to each object method, they do allow a static object to be accessed and initialized prior to actual construction.

Typically, an object using initialization checks defines a per-instance data member that can be tested to determine whether the instance has been initialized. This member is often implemented as a Boolean or pointer type where a value of zero is used to indicate that no initialization has occurred.

The zero value is significant because the memory where a static object is allocated is initialized to zero when the translation unit that defines the object is first loaded. Any data members within a static object are thus guaranteed to be zeroes before the first access or construction occurs.

Consider the implementation provided by the following hypothetical class:

```
class Object {
  private:
    bool isInitialized_;
    void init() {
      // Initialize Object
      isInitialized_=true;
    }
```

```
  public:
    enum StaticEnum {Static};
    // Constructor for instances created using
    // automatic or dynamic allocation
    Object() {
      init();
    }
    // Constructor for static instances
    Object(StaticEnum) {
      if (!isInitialized_) init();
    }
    void objectMethod() {
      if (!isInitialized_) init();
      // Do something useful...
    }
};
```

While this implementation will work in a single-threaded environment, it is not safe for use in the presence of multiple threads. The test for initialization and the initialization need to be combined and treated as a single, atomic operation.

This change may be accomplished by adding using a mutex to serialize access to the critical-section of code involved in initializing an instance.

One such technique for synchronizing initialization, called the Double-Check Pattern,[3] is demonstrated in the modified version of the Object class, shown below:

```
class Object {
  private:
    bool isInitialized_;
    static Mutex mutex_;
    void init() {
      // Initialize Object
      isInitialized_=true;
    }
  public:
    enum StaticEnum {Static};
    // Constructor for instances created using
    // automatic or dynamic allocation
    Object() {
      init();
    }

    // Constructor for static instances
    Object(StaticEnum) {
      if (!isInitialized_) {
        LockGuard<Mutex> lock(mutex_);
        if (!isInitialized_) init();
      }
    }
```

```
    void objectMethod() {
        if (!isInitialized_) {
            LockGuard<Mutex> lock(mutex_);
            if (!isInitialized_) init();
            // Do something useful...
        }
    }
};
```

This latest implementation has eliminated the possible race-condition that existed in the previous version of the class, but has not completely solved the problem; it has simply transferred the static initialization problem to the static Mutex member of the class!

The problem may yet be solved depending on the style of mutex implementation provided by the host environment. On some platforms, a mutex is defined and represented by a structure in memory, and that structure may be safely used when initialized with zero or a compile-time constant. On other platforms, a mutex must be allocated and managed by the operating system, and cannot be initialized without a function call.

If simple, static initialization cannot be used to initialize a mutex, then the task of providing thread-safe, global-static initialization becomes much more difficult, if not impossible, thus giving rise to the following simple rule:

Rule 2 Avoid creating threads during global static initialization.

Program Exit and Termination in the Presence of Multiple Threads

The process of C++ program termination can pose significant problems if initiated in the presence of multiple active threads.

A C++ program may be terminated by any one of several methods:

By using a return statement to exit main() (or its equivalent*). Only the initial or main thread of a program can return from main(). Executing a return from main() causes static objects to be destroyed in the reverse order of their construction, and causes functions registered using atexit() to be executed in the reverse order of their registration. Many systems will retain the relative ordering of interleaved atexit() registrations and static object constructions (this is often the case when a compiler generates code that uses atexit() to register a separate, compiler-generated function, to call the destructor for each static object constructed).

---

* In some environments or frameworks, such as in Microsoft Windows, the main() function is not directly accessible nor visible to the developer and is implemented by the framework.

- By calling the exit() function (or its equivalent). This function may be called by any thread. Calling the exit() function produces the same termination behavior as is produced by executing a return from main().

- By calling the abort() function (or its equivalent). This function may be called directly by any thread, or may be called indirectly by the default terminate() handler when a thread fails to handle an exception. The abort() function terminates a program immediately without calling the destructors of static objects and without executing functions registered using atexit().

- On some systems, by returning from, or exiting the thread function of the last active, non-daemon, thread. Most systems will always start program termination if the initial thread executes a return from main(). However, some platforms will allow the initial thread to explicitly terminate without initiating program termination. This independent termination of the initial or main thread can only be accomplished by calling a thread-exit function (an activity that, for reasons that are discussed later in this paper, may be inappropriate for C++ programs).

The mechanisms of program termination are relatively easy to use and understand when applied to single-threaded, 'C' language programs but unfortunately become quite troublesome when introduced into multithreaded, C++ programs.

The primary difficulties arise from the fact that C++ program initialization and termination appears to have been designed with single-threaded programs in mind.

The following issues are of most concern when considering the affect of program termination within a multithreaded application:

- Any thread may initiate program termination by calling exit() or abort(). Developers who wish to avoid such behavior may be surprised to find that a third-party library or function will sometimes make its own decision to exit or abort.

- C++ provides no mechanism that allows other threads to reliably detect the start of program termination. One thread may trigger program termination while the remaining threads will blindly continue processing until some static object they rely upon is destroyed, or until the thread is forcibly terminated at process exit.

The most important side effect of program termination is the destruction of local and global static objects. If program termination is to start while other threads are running, then these other threads must somehow avoid accessing static objects, since accessing a static object that has been destroyed might cause the program to fail and abort before it can complete normal termination.

Unfortunately, there is no general way to guarantee that running threads are notified of program termination before any local static objects are destroyed (especially since local-static objects may be constructed at any time, as their definitions are encountered).

How can these problems be avoided? The easiest method is described by the following:

Rule 3   Avoid or delay the initiation of program termination until all threads but one have exited.

Adherence to this rule ensures that only one thread will be active during program termination, thus eliminating the possibility that static object destruction might disrupt other threads causing complete program failure.

Local Static Object Initialization in the Presence of Multiple Threads

The underlying mechanisms that a compiler uses to control the initialization of local, function-scope, static objects may not be thread-safe.

The ANSI/ISO C++ language standard currently guarantees that static object instances declared within a function will be constructed when the flow of control first passes through the static object's definition.

To provide this behavior, a typical compiler will statically allocate a separate, internal, initialization-state flag for each local static object defined within a translation unit. Each flag is initially cleared to zero when its translation-unit is loaded into memory. A cleared flag indicates that the corresponding local-static instance has not yet been initialized. When a thread encounters a local-static object definition, the internal initialization flag for that static object is tested to see whether or not the object needs to be constructed. If the flag is found to be clear, the static instance is constructed, registered for future destruction during program termination, and then its initialization flag is set. The next time a thread encounters the same definition, the initialization flag test will indicate that the object has already been initialized and that the code that constructs the static instance should be skipped.

In a single-threaded environment, this underlying implementation is generally of little concern, but suddenly becomes important when there exists a possibility that two or more threads may simultaneously enter a block containing an, as yet uninitialized, local-static object.

In such a scenario, the compiler must use some form of mutual exclusion to protect the initialization flag, otherwise there arises the possibility for a race-condition. This race condition occurs when two or more threads manage to test the initialization flag and find it clear before any one thread can set the flag to block further attempts at initialization.

Unfortunately, most compilers do not attempt to synchronize threads to prevent this race condition (perhaps, in part, for performance reasons). Without suitable synchronization, local-static initialization cannot be considered multithread-safe!

To demonstrate this problem, consider the following example:

```
#include <iostream.h>
class Object {
  public:
```

```
        Object() { cout << "Constructing" << endl; }
        ~Object() { cout << "Destructing" << endl; }
};
void func() {
    static Object object;
}
```

If this code is compiled using the Microsoft Visual C++ compiler, and disassembled using the Visual Debugger, the underlying implementation may be examined. The follow assembly code listing was produced in this manner; statements of interest have been annotated using bold text:

```
9:      void func() {
  00401050    push     ebp
  00401051    mov      ebp,esp
  00401053    push     ebx
  00401054    push     esi
  00401055    push     edi
10:       static Object object;
  ;Clear the EAX (and AL) register
  00401056    xor      eax,eax
  ;Move the initialization flag value into AL
  00401058    mov      al,byte ptr [(00418d64)]
  ;Is the flag clear?
  0040105d    test     al,01
  ;No, then jump past the initialization code
  0040105f    jne      func+0000003a (0040108a)
  ;Yes, then set the flag and construct the object
  00401065    xor      eax,eax
  ;Move the initialization flag value into AL
  00401067    mov      al,byte ptr [(00418d64)]
  ;Change the flag value to "set"
  0040106c    or       al,01
  ;Store the value in the initialization flag
  0040106e    mov      byte ptr [(00418d64)],al
  ;Call the Object class constructor
  00401073    mov      ecx,00418d60
  00401078    call     @ILT+30(0040101e)
  ;Push the address of a compiler-generated
  ;routine that calls the destructor for the
  ;static instance, onto the atexit stack
  ;(so it can be executed when the program exits).
  0040107d    push     00401094
  00401082    call     atexit (00401300)
  00401087    add      esp,00000004
```

```
11: }
  ;Exit the function...
0040108a   jmp      func+0000003f (0040108f)
0040108f   pop      edi
00401090   pop      esi
00401091   pop      ebx
00401092   leave
00401093   ret
  ;Compiler-generated routine that calls the
  ;destructor for the local static object.
00401094   push     ebp
00401095   mov      ebp,esp
00401097   push     ebx
00401098   push     esi
00401099   push     edi
0040109a   mov      ecx,00418d60
  ;Call the Object class destructor
0040109f   call     @ILT+10(0040100a)
004010a4   jmp      $E12+00000015 (004010a9)
004010a9   pop      edi
004010aa   pop      esi
004010ab   pop      ebx
004010ac   leave
004010ad   ret
```

The disassembled code shows that the compiler did not attempt to synchronize access to the code that tests and sets the local-static initialization flag. Since the test-and-set operation is performed over several machine instructions, the operation is not atomic and therefore, is not thread-safe.

Based on these observations, any one of the following rules may apply:

Rule 4a   Avoid declaring local static object instances that may be simultaneously encountered for the first time by multiple threads.

or

Rule 4b   Ensure that a single thread will pass through all blocks containing local static object instances before any other threads will enter those same blocks.

or

Rule 4c   Use a global lock to serialize access to blocks containing local static object instance definitions. The developer must guarantee that the global lock will be initialized before any thread can enter the block containing the local static definition.

Starting Threads within Constructors

The concept of a "thread-hot" or "active" object[4] is a powerful tool for object-oriented, concurrent programming. It is often tempting to implement such objects by launching threads within the object's constructor, but the sequence of construction used by C++ can often cause problems when using this approach.

Launching a thread within the constructor of an object may seem to be an obvious way to create a thread-hot or active object, but this technique must be used with care if the developer wants the object implementation to behave correctly each and every time such an object is constructed.

The danger with this approach is that many developers will launch threads within a constructor, while forgetting that the object may not be fully constructed and initialized. A developer will often forget that in many situations it may be possible for the new thread to immediately begin functions within the object before the original thread can complete construction of the object.

This oversight will result in problems if there exists the possibility that the object class may be subclassed and if the object defines any virtual functions that may be accessed by the newly created thread and overridden within a subclass.

This scenario can pose problems because the v-table for an object instance will not be fully initialized until the constructor of the most derived class begins execution. This observation suggests the following rules...

Rule 5a Do not start a thread in a class constructor if the newly-created thread may attempt to call a virtual function of that class and that virtual function may be overridden by a subclass. If the internal thread must access virtual functions of the object, then use a member function instead of the constructor to "start" the thread or threads contained within the object.

or

Rule 5b Do not call any virtual function defined by a class from a thread created during construction of an instance of that class unless, of course, the virtual function is called on another instance of the class.

or

Rule 5c Prohibit subclassing of a class that starts threads within a constructor by declaring all class constructors as `private` and using `public`, `static` member functions to create instances of the class.

Exception Handling

Consistent exception handling is key to the creation of reliable multithreaded applications.

In most environments, if the code executing within a thread's entry-point function fails to handle an exception, the program is automatically terminated with a call to terminate(), a function whose default behavior produces a call to abort(). When a program is aborted, the process is terminated without unwinding the call-stacks of other threads, and without calling the destructors of any static or global object instances that were previously constructed.

This behavior is generally unacceptable since it does not allow other threads within the process the chance to continue operating or to cleanup and release resources as part of a deliberate, methodical shutdown process.

This leads to the following conclusion...

Rule 6   Handle all exceptions produced within a thread to prevent premature process termination.

Exiting Threads

The 'C' style functions commonly provided for thread and program termination are inappropriate for use in C++ programs.

Nearly all of the procedural APIs for multithreading provide a function that can be used to explicitly terminate the calling thread. In addition to these thread-exit functions, most compilers also provide a run-time library function(s) for terminating the current program.

Because these functions do not roll-back the call-stack and destroy function-scope objects that were created on the stack, they are often inappropriate for use in a C++ implementation.

If there arises a situation where it becomes necessary to abort the processing of a thread, a better solution is to use an exception to force a roll-back into the thread's entry-point function. This exit strategy gives C++ the opportunity to destroy any objects created on the stack, thereby recovering their resources.

Rule 7   Do not use any thread-exit function provided by a native API to exit a thread; always allow the thread to exit by returning from the thread entry-point function.

Conclusion

Multithreaded application development is a complicated task. Opportunities abound for producing code that will compile without failure, appear to execute successfully, and yet will mysteriously fail at some point in the future, usually because of some hidden implementation flaw that allowed a race or deadlock condition.

The key method for anticipating and avoiding these unexpected failures is to develop a thorough understanding of the techniques and mechanisms required for multithreaded application development, and to recognize that there are specific consequences for implementation that are introduced by C++ language itself.

It is the author's intent that the issues and guidelines established within this paper represent a first step in developing this understanding.

References

1. Bjarne Stroustrup. *The C++ Programming Language,* 2nd ed. Addison-Wesley, 1994, pp. 308–314.
2. Martin D. Carrol and Margaret A. Ellis. *Designing and Coding Reusable C++.* Addison-Wesley, 1995, pp. 263–275.
3. Tim Harrison and Douglas C. Schmidt. "Patterns for Reducing Locking Overhead in Multi-threaded Programs." In *Proceedings of the 3rd Annual Conference on the Pattern Languages of Programs.* Allerton Park, Illinois, September 1996.
4. R.G. Lavender and Douglas C. Schmidt. "Active Object: An Object Behavioral Pattern for Concurrent Programming." In *Proceedings of the 2nd Annual Conference on the Pattern Languages of Programs*, Monticello, Illinois, September 1995.

Chapter 11

Applying the Delphi Model to C++

Marco Cantù

Disclaimer   The text of this paper has been prepared using a public beta version of Borland C++ Builder, with very limited documentation. I've tried to be accurate, but some of the information provided here might actually be incorrect. In the presentation at the conference I'll be able to offer more details and eventual corrections.

Introduction: Visual Programming

The aim of this presentation is to study the C++ language extensions introduced in Borland C++ Builder. This is a new development environment, very similar to Borland Delphi, which extends the C++ language to include several Object Pascal language features. In fact, C++ Builder and Delphi share the same component library and programming model, beside sharing the development environment.

Borland made these language extensions to apply to the C++ Delphi Model and to let C++ programmers enter the realm of visual programming. This basically means that you can create objects by simply dragging an icon over a form (or window) and set their initial values using the Object Inspector. All this is possible simply thanks to the language extensions, which allow design-time manipulation of objects and classes, as we'll see in a while.

During this presentation I'll try to focus on the theory, but I'll certainly make frequent references to both Delphi and Object Pascal, and C++ Builder.

What is a Property?

One of the key elements of visual programming is the idea of object properties. But what is a property? A property is a name with a type, related to some data or data access member functions of a class.

One of the basic ideas of OOP is that data members should always be private. Then you'll often write public member functions to get and set that private value. If you later modify the implementation, you can easily change the code of these access functions, and avoid any change in the code which uses the class. Here is a basic example (written following the standard naming conventions for properties, fields, and access functions):

```
private:
      int fTotal;
protected:
      void __fastcall SetTotal (int Value);
      int __fastcall GetTotal ();
```

The code of these two member functions simply sets or returns the value of the private data. You can use them in the following way:

```
int x = Form1->GetTotal();
Form1->SetTotal (x + 5);
```

Now we can define a property wrapping these access functions:

```
__property int Total = {
     read = GetTotal,
     write = SetTotal };
```

This means we can now access to this value in a more uniform way, since we use the same notation both for reading or writing the property:

```
int x = Form1->Total;
Form1->Total = x + 5;
```

Depending on its role in a statement, the expression Form1->Total is translated by the compiler in a call to the read or the write function. Actually the compiler can translate a similar expression also into a direct data access. Look at the following property declaration:

```
private:
     int fValue;
public:
    __property int Value = {
     read = fValue,
     write = fValue };
```

Although this code seems strange at first, it fully demonstrates the power of properties as an encapsulation mechanism. In fact, we can later change the declaration of this property introducing one of two functions instead of direct data access. In this event, we'll need to recompile the code of the classes which use this property, but we won't need to modify it.

Obviously access functions are not restricted to read and write private data, but can do anything. One of the typical effects of write functions is to update the user interface. Here is a new version of the Value property, followed by the code of its write function (written following the standard style):

```
__property int Value = {
     read = fValue,
     write = SetValue };
 void __fastcall TForm1::SetValue (int Value)
{
     if (fValue != Value)
    {
       fValue = Value;
       Label2->Caption = "Value = " + IntToStr (Value);
    };
};
```

Now if we write the following event response function:

```
void __fastcall TForm1::Button4Click(TObject *Sender)
{
  Value = Value + 2;
}
```

the effect of the change in the data will reflect automatically in the user interface. I really think properties are a sound OOP encapsulation mechanism!

Language Rules for Properties

- Properties have a data type, but are limited to a given set of data types (including most of the basic types and classes).

- Properties can be read-only, this means you cannot assign them a new value. To define a read-only property simply skip the write declaration.

- Component properties generally have a default value. The default value relates to the streaming mechanism. The same streaming mechanism uses also the stored directive, used to indicate if a property must be saved to file along with the object.

- You can also define read-only and read–write properties (and in theory even write-only properties), and use them to specify the public and published interfaces of a class.

- Properties can be declared using any of the access specifiers, including the new __published and __automated specifiers, as we'll see in the next section. Read-only properties cannot be published.

- The visibility of a property can be extended in derived classes. A protected property, for example, can be redeclared as a published property. To accomplish this you don't need to redefine the property, and only to redeclare it (Borland use the term "hoisted properties" to indicate this behavior). When redeclaring a property you can also change it, for example modifying its default value.

- It is possible to declare array properties, that is properties with an index. In this case the required read and write functions have an extra parameter, the index itself. These indexes must also be used to access to the values, since you cannot access to the array as a whole (since it must not exist as an actual field).

- In C++ Builder (but not in Delphi) it is also possible to declare array properties with multiple indexes.

- When properties are of a "pointer to a member function" data type (also known as a closure, as we'll see later on) they are called events!

Access Visibility (Including Published)

A class defines its interface using several access specifiers. Along with the public, protected, and private specifiers, you can use a fourth one, called __published. A published field or method is not only available at run time, but also at design time, because the compiler generates Delphi-style run time type Identification (RTTI) for it. Only classes derived from TObject can have a published section.

The published keyword is generally used for properties (or events) but also forms generally have a published interface. The published interface of a class is available to programmers, although it is generally used only to write tools such as the Object Inspector.

In C++ Builder the published interface of a component is used by the Object Inspector to show and edit property values at design time. The published interface of a property is used by the Object Inspector to find components compatible with a given data type and member functions compatible with a given event. For this reason, the environment automatically adds components and methods to the published section of a form.

There is a fifth access specifier, automated, which is used to define a public interface with corresponding OLE automation type information, making it possible to create OLE Automation Servers. The __automated keyword is used in TAutoObject subclasses.

Closures and Events

Another addition to the C++ language is the idea of a closure. A closure is a sort of member function pointer. Actually it associates a pointer to a member function with a pointer to a class instance, an object. The pointer to the class instance is used as the this pointer when calling the associated member function. This is the definition of a closure:

```
typedef void (__closure *TCounterEvent)(TCounter *Sender);
```

Since in C++ member function pointers are available as well, but seldom used, you might wonder what do we need this awkward stuff for? Closures really matter in the Delphi model. In fact events are closures, holding the value of a member function of the form hosting the related component. For example, a button has a closure, named OnClick, and you can assign a member function of the form to it. When a user clicks on the button, this member function is executed, even if you have defined it inside another class (typically, in the form). Here is what you can write (and C++ Builder usually writes for you):

```
BtnBeep->OnClick = BtnHelloClick;
BtnHello->OnClick = BtnBeepClick;
```

You can also explicitly declare a variable of a closure type, as the common TNotifyEvent type, and use it to exchange the handlers of two events:

```
TNotifyEvent event = BtnBeep->OnClick;
BtnBeep->OnClick = BtnHello->OnClick;
BtnHello->OnClick = event;
```

This means you can assign a member function (as BtnHelloClick) to a closure or event both at design time and at run time.

Inheritance

As in Delphi, all the classes of the component library inherit from the TObject class. Different from Delphi, however, deriving from TObject is not compulsory. This is the list of the most relevant member functions of the TObject class (which provide most of the RTTI capabilities).

// public member function

TObject	~TObject	Free	ClassType
FieldAddress	ClassName	ClassNameIs	ClassParent
ClassInfo	InstanceSize	InheritsFrom	MethodAddress
MethodName	Dispatch	DefaultHandler	

// static member function (public)

InitInstance	ClassName	ClassNameIs	ClassParent
ClassInfo	InstanceSize	InheritsFrom	MethodAddress
MethodName			

Metaclasses and Virtual Constructors

Delphi introduced the concept of class reference, a pointer to the type information of a class. In C++ Builder this has been mapped into the idea of a metaclass, and the TClass type (available also in Delphi) is nothing but a pointer to this metaclass.

```
class TMetaClass;
typedef TMetaClass* TClass;
```

The methods available for a metaclass correspond exactly to the static methods of the TObject class (in fact, there is no TMetaClass in Delphi, but class reference, which can use the static methods directly).

Once you have a TClass variable, you can assign to it a class, extracted from the object (with the ClassType function) or obtained from the class itself by using the __classid keyword. Here is an example:

```
TClass myclass = __classid (TEdit);
```

Objects Persistency

The VCL has a TPersistent class. The published properties of TPersistent-derived classes can be streamed to a file. This always happens for TComponent-derived classes, which are stores in Windows resource files.

The corresponding objects can later be automatically rebuilt loading them from the file. Streaming objects is fundamental for Delphi architecture: you create and set attributes of objects at design time, and these objects are loaded when the form is displayed. Notice that the language has been extended with some properties specifiers (such as default and stored) to support persistency.

*RTTI (*dynamic_cast *and more)*

In short, each object knows its class and base class, and we can ask for this information using some TObject class methods. To check if a class is of a given type, you can use the ClassType method. This is quite common with the Sender parameter of an event handler. This parameter refers to the object which has generated the event, but is of the generic TObject type. Here is a possible way to write the code of an event handler connected with multiple components:

```
if (Sender->ClassType() == __classid(TButton))
    Beep();
```

The alternative (not always valid) is to use the Sender parameter of an event handler and cast it to a given data type, using the standard C++ dynamic_cast technique. This makes sense if we know the data type or that of a common ancestor class, as in this case:

```
TWinControl* wc = dynamic_cast<TWinControl*> (Sender);
wc->Left = wc->Left + 2;
```

Beside these RTTI capabilities, Delphi and C++ Builder share extensive type information, available at run time for every object of a class derived from TObject and having published fields, properties, or methods. For example, you can access to a property dynamically, by name; you can get the list of the names of the properties of a class; you can get the list of parameters of a closure. This allows programmers to build very powerful add-on tools to the environment, and is used by the system itself as a basis of the visual development tools, starting with the Object Inspector (I've actually built a run time clone of the Object Inspector).

Handling Exceptions

Object Pascal exceptions borrowed several ideas from C++, but added a new feature, the finally block. The `finally` block is always executed.

```
dlg = new TDlg(Application);
try {
      dlg->Init(...);
      dlg->ShowModal;
}
finally
      dlg->Free;
```

Finally blocks make sense in languages which use the reference model, as Object Pascal and Java. In C++ Builder it has been added because objects are often dynamically allocated.

Notice that C++ Builder can handle both Delphi-like exceptions and standard C++ exceptions.

Conclusion

As we have seen, Borland added many news features to the C++ language in C++ Builder to make this language compatible with Object Pascal and tailored for component-based programming.

Extending C++ this way may seem a little awkward, since we are trying to map the constructs of a language into another language. However, the ease of use of the environment and the visual development are probably worth this extra complexity, which most of the time remains behind the scenes.

At the same time C++ Builder retains full compatibility with the ANSI C++ standard, including templates and the STL (to name two features not available to Delphi programmers).

Chapter 12

MFC DAO vs. MFC ODBC Classes: Which One to Use and When?

Jocelyn Garner

More Flexible Than Ever

Ever since the MFC DAO database classes were released in October of 1995, the question of which set of classes to use has been on the mind of MFC database developers. This paper does not attempt to answer the question in general terms. Instead the emphasis here is on examining the options so you, the developer, can decide which set of MFC database classes is best for each situation.

Most MFC developers are familiar with the ODBC database classes — they've been around for two-and-a-half years. With MFC 4.2, there are some significant improvements in those classes.

As C++ developers you may not be familiar with DAO because to date it has been available only with Access and Visual Basic. If you are familiar with DAO, you need to know that MFC's implementation of DAO is different, but still comprehensive.

Developers who know the MFC ODBC classes need to know that the MFC DAO classes have more functionality than the ODBC classes, but that the DAO classes do not supplant them.

The MFC Database Strategy

For those of you who are not familiar with MFC in general, let me remind you that MFC has a design philosophy that pervades the database classes as well.

MFC encapsulates the Windows API as a thin wrapper, providing the C++ capabilities you want along with the abstraction you need. We add value to the underlying API when it makes sense. Most of the time though, MFC tries to stay out of the way.

Just as MFC encapsulates a more complex API, so the database classes encapsulate more complicated technologies. Because of MFC's portability across Intel, Macintosh, MIPS, and Alpha, database application solutions can be portable.

We use the same recordset model that Access and Visual Basic use, so developers who already use those products don't have to learn a new paradigm. In addition, because the architecture of the two sets of classes is essentially the same, developers using one set of classes can easily switch and use the other.

The MFC Database Classes

The ODBC database classes have been available in MFC since Version 1.5. Visual C++ 2.0 offered 32-bit versions of the same classes. These classes are widely in use, are based on an industry-accepted standard, and are favored over other database development options because of the portability of ODBC — the ability to use applications created with these classes with a variety of ODBC data sources. Recent performance improvements make the ODBC database classes an attractive option.

The new DAO database classes in MFC 4.0 give you direct access to desktop data sources without the use of ODBC in most cases. The ability to have more than one database type open at a time, to address a wide variety of data sources, and the Data Definition Language capabilities make the DAO database classes a serious development option.

By now you're ready to ask which set of database classes you should use. The answer to this question is difficult to determine without a lot of information from you regarding your project. The first thing to consider, however, is what data sources you're using. If you're using mostly desktop data, we encourage you to consider the MFC DAO database classes, because you'll find them to be efficient and powerful. If you primarily use ODBC server-based data, your project may function more efficiently with the ODBC-based classes.

Other considerations include the kind of network you have, the scalability requirements, and whether speed is more important than anything else. The best thing to do is to prototype applications using the set of database classes you think will work best. Do some benchmarking to determine your best performance options.

The decision is really up to you.

A Continuum of Choices

The set of choices you have for creating database applications is vast. It turns out to be a continuum of choices, with desktop database applications at one end and strict client/server database applications at the other. Probably the only two choices which might seem obvious are to use the MFC DAO database classes with Microsoft Access 95 .MDB data, and to use the MFC ODBC database classes with Microsoft SQL Server 6.0. These two pairings were pretty much designed to work with each other, and both are very efficient — but you probably already knew about those choices. What about everything else?

Briefly, here is the process by which you can make a decision:

Determine Data Source Needs

How large a database do you need? Does more than one person need to get to the data at a time? Sometimes the data source you select can determine most of the rest of these steps.

Determine Interface Needs

If you need to have an interface with lots of user input (such as being able to design their own queries), you have to tune and distribute your database(s) carefully. For example if you need to populate list boxes with data that doesn't change much, and you've selected a server-based data source, it makes sense to store the typically unchanging data locally rather than on the server.

Determine Connectivity Needs

There are a number of network protocols in use today, and each one has its impact on data moving across the network. A discussion of networks is outside the scope of this paper, but you need to know how to optimize your database application to avoid encountering your network's data pitfalls.

Select the Appropriate Tool(s)

Microsoft has a variety of options for the database developer (Access, Visual Basic, Visual Basic Enterprise, and Visual C++/MFC, and SQL Server), and in some cases the functionality overlaps a bit. The scope of this paper is to discuss the Visual C++/MFC options specifically, but if you haven't also considered these other options, you should have a look at them too.

Prototype Before Implementation

You'll see this statement several times in this paper because it's important. You may have selected well, but unless your solution actually works, the job isn't finished!

Again, for this paper, we're assuming that you want to know about MFC's database classes. Let's examine as many of the options as possible so that you will recognize the direction you want to take for your first prototype.

The MFC ODBC database classes use recordset model found in Microsoft Access and Visual Basic. You can filter, sort, scroll through, and otherwise manipulate the records using the member functions built into the classes. The functionality of a particular application is affected by the underlying ODBC driver, so to be more portable, your applications have to be more general or rely on a lower level of ODBC functionality. You can call ODBC directly, if necessary, to accomplish a particular task. Now let's examine the individual classes in this set.

MFC's ODBC Database Classes

As always with MFC, you can make calls to the underlying API (in this case ODBC) as necessary.

A CDatabase object represents a connection to a data source, through which you can operate on the data source. A data source is a specific instance of data hosted by some database management system (DBMS). Examples include Microsoft SQL Server, Microsoft Access, Borland® dBASE®, and xBASE. You can have one or more CDatabase objects active at a time in your application, and you can have multiple connections to a database object.

A CRecordset object represents a set of records selected from a data source. Known as "recordsets," CRecordset objects are available in two forms: dynasets and snapshots. A dynaset is a dynamic recordset that stays synchronized with updates by other users. A snapshot is a static recordset that reflects the state of the database at the time of the snapshot. Each form represents a set of records fixed at the time the recordset is opened, but when you scroll to a record in a dynaset, it reflects changes subsequently made to the record, either by other users or by other recordsets in your application.

MFC 4.2 adds new navigation functionality to the `CRecordset` class in the form of bookmarks, and an ability to identify the `AbsolutePosition` of a record and navigate to it. Bookmarks are unique identifiers that allow you to return to a specific record by calling that identifier.

Class `CRecordView` is an MFC construct — a form for displaying data. Because `CRecordView` is based on `CFormView`, it has all of the inherited functionality of that base class. Essentially, a form view stretches a dialog template over the client area of a window. This makes adding controls and displaying field data very easy to do.

When you use AppWizard and ClassWizard to create an ODBC-based database application, the columns of the recordset are automatically bound (statically) to member variables, which can then be added to the dialog template.

A `CDBException` object represents an exception condition arising from the database classes. The class includes two public data members you can use to determine the cause of the exception or to display a text message describing the exception. `CDBException` objects are constructed and thrown by member functions of the database classes.

The `CFieldExchange` class supports the record field exchange (RFX) routines used by the database classes. Use this class if you are writing data exchange routines for custom data types; otherwise, you will not directly use this class. RFX exchanges data between the field data members of your recordset object and the corresponding fields of the current record on the data source. RFX manages the exchange in both directions, from the data source and to the data source.

Data Access Objects

In its native format, DAO consists of 21 objects and 20 collections. DAO then provides individual objects like tables and fields, as well as collections to which they belong. This clear hierarchy of objects makes it easy to apply object-oriented principles to database development.

DAO has been around for a while. DAO 1.0 appeared in Microsoft Access 1.0, providing only an interface to table and query structures, and objects to represent tables, dynasets, and snapshots with a limited number of properties. Data Access Objects 1.0 in Visual Basic 3.0 added `TableDef`, `QueryDef`, and `Field` objects to programmatically expose structures.

DAO 2.0 in Microsoft Access 2.0 had the first vestiges of OLE Automation and full programmatic access to almost all Microsoft Jet functionality. It had a full object model with robust set of objects and properties.

DAO 2.5 consisted of ODBC Desktop Database Drivers that were created for 16-bit platforms for use with ODBC Desktop Database Drivers 2.0. The 16-bit version was shipped for use with the 16-bit version of Visual Basic 4.0.

DAO 3.0 shipped with Microsoft Access for Windows 95, Visual Basic 4.0 (32-bit), Microsoft Excel 7.0, and Visual C++ 4.0 DAO was enhanced to support a stand-alone interface for any compatible host.

Most importantly, the DAO interfaces are based on OLE COM, which positions DAO well for the future technologies and operating systems.

Figure 12.1 shows the DAO hierarchy chart. At the top, you see the DBEngine object, which contains all of the other objects. This is the only object without a collection, because you can have only one engine. You can have multiple workspaces, databases, and so on, which is why the remaining objects have collections to which they belong.

In a workspace, you can have more than one database, either a base table (.MDB) or an attached/linked table. In each database will be one or more tables, queries, and recordsets, and in each of those will be fields and/or indexes, as well as other types of objects.

Also connected with the workspace are the user and group objects which constitute the security model for DAO.

Off by itself, and connected to the engine object, is the Errors object.

Objects in the Errors collection are appended in a manner different from the other DAO collections. The most detailed errors are placed at the end of the collection, and the most general errors are placed at the beginning.

MFC and DAO

Now let's talk about how MFC implements DAO. Because we don't individually wrap each DAO object, MFC essentially flattens the DAO hierarchy. We offer you 8 objects instead of 21.

We encapsulate all of the DAO functionality with the exception of the Security objects — Users and Groups. We did this deliberately. In looking at these objects, we

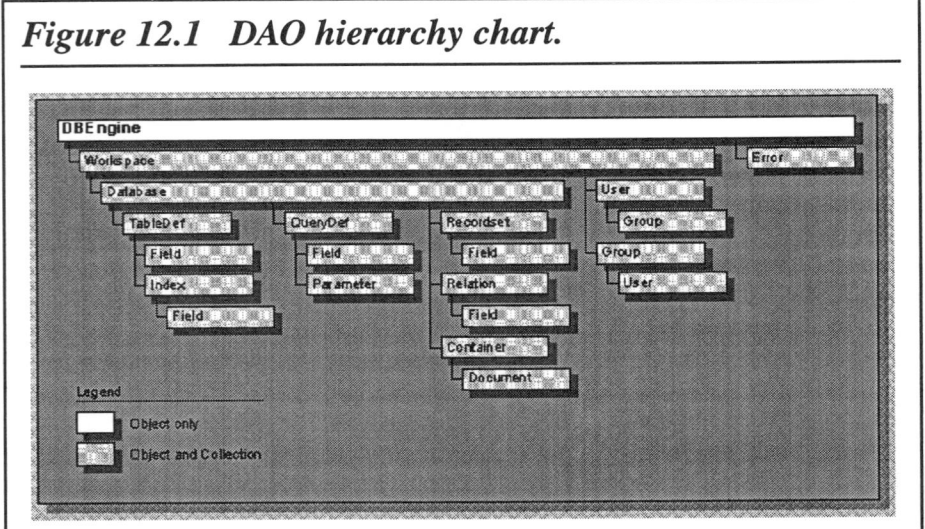

Figure 12.1 DAO hierarchy chart.

felt that creating classes around them would not add any value to the use of DAO, so we just let you make direct calls to DAO to handle those objects. This is in keeping also with the MFC philosophy: Create classes where it makes sense from a value-added standpoint. We do, however, provide instructions on how to implement the security model in MFC Technical Note 54.

We also manage the DAO requirements for adding objects to collections. In DAO, one creates an object then appends it to a collection. With one exception, we do this automatically; for that one case, it made sense to have the developer be able to Append the object or not, as a separate step.

While dynamic binding is possible with the ODBC database classes, functionality for doing so is not built into the MFC classes. It IS built into the DAO database classes, and you can do dynamic binding rather easily.

DAO offers the Data Definition Language from SQL that lets you create databases, tables, recordsets, etc. DDL is not available in the ODBC classes.

Finally, you can always make direct calls to the underlying DAO OLE objects as you need to.

MFC DAO Database Class Hierarchy

The 5 MFC DAO classes that derive from CObject (CDaoWorkspace, CDaoDatabase, CDaoTableDef, CDaoQueryDef, and CDaoRecordset) have all of that base class's functionality (Figure 12.2).

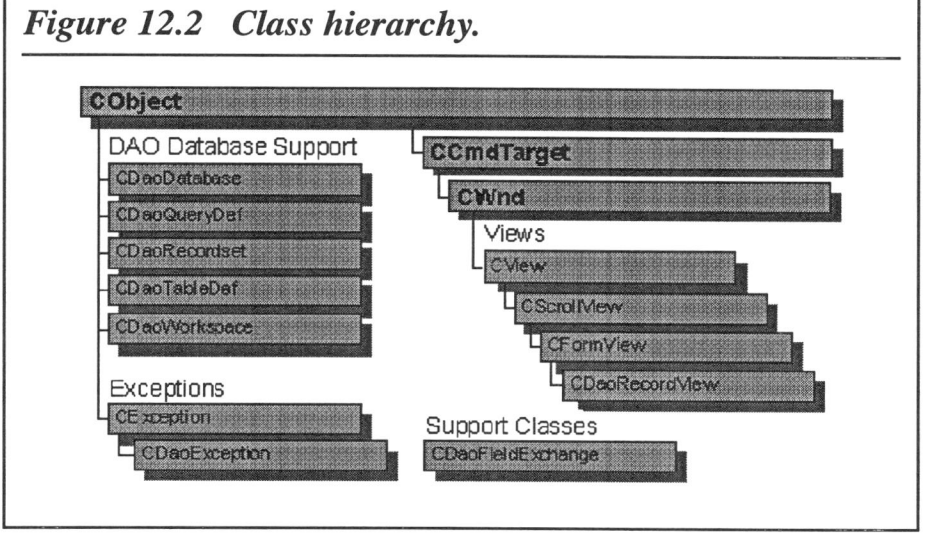

Figure 12.2 Class hierarchy.

CDaoException derives from CException, and has that class's advantages, including the ability to display the error messages from the underlying DAO Errors object.

CDaoRecordView, as I mentioned earlier, derives from CFormView, which derives from CScrollView, etc. You can see all the advantages a CDaoRecordView class has for making form-based display of data quick and easy to implement. In addition, there is Wizard support for CDaoRecordView. The functionality in this class is virtually identical to the CRecordView class.

The CDaoFieldExchange class supports the DAO record field exchange (DFX) routines used by the DAO database classes. You only call this object directly if you are creating custom DFX routines.

The MFC DAO Database Classes

CDaoWorkspace encapsulates both the DBEngine object and the Workspace object. The fact that the MFC DAO classes offer a workspace is very important. The ODBC database classes do not support having more than one database connection at a time.

Transactions are done at the Workspace level in the DAO database classes instead of the Recordset level as in the ODBC classes. One transaction can affect all open databases and recordsets, or you can isolate transactions so that they affect only specific databases, and so on.

Most of the time you don't have to worry about creating a workspace object. MFC will open one for you if you don't. The DAO database classes support having multiple workspaces if you need them.

Finally, you don't have to worry about a workspace object going out of scope or closing before the database session is through. You can use a workspace pointer to access the Workspaces collection, access the Databases collection, access properties of the database engine, and so on.

CDaoDatabase

CDaoDatabase is similar in architecture to the ODBC-based CDatabase class. CDaoDatabase also encapsulates the database connection. Because you don't have to always use ODBC, the location of the data source is expressed as a path for most desktop data sources. CDaoDatabase can store tabledef and querydef objects, a great convenience for you as a developer. CDaoDatabase works with both local and remote data sources. We'll see a list of the data sources you can use a little later in this paper. The database object also persists for the duration of the session. You can explicitly close the database connection as necessary. Just for purposes of comparison, the CDatabase class has 21 member functions, and CDaoDatabase has 26 member functions. The member functions themselves are very similar, with a few more available in CDaoDatabase.

There is no class that corresponds to CDaoTableDef among the ODBC database classes. TableDef objects let you examine the schema (structure) of a database, regardless of whether the table is a native Microsoft Access table (base table) or the table is attached. You can add fields and indexes to external data sources if you open them directly with DAO. If you attach the table, you can examine the structure but you cannot change it. You can base a recordset on a table. Doing so gives you several advantages, including the use of a high speed search member function called Seek. You use CDaoTableDef to determine whether data in a table can be edited by calling CDaoTableDef::CanUpdate. MFC takes care of managing the DAO Fields and Indexes collections for you. With CDaoTableDef, you have the option of appending a table to the TableDefs collection or not — with all other objects, appending is done automatically.

The SQL you use to retrieve records is stored in a CDaoQueryDef object. This object lets you store the "questions" you ask of your data, such as "How many customers did X dollars of business last month?". You can retrieve and reuse stored queries, and they can be used in one of three ways:

- To create a recordset, by passing a pointer to the CDaoQueryDef object.

- Directly execute action queries — a query that moves or changes data. Action queries include append, delete, make-table, and update queries. Delete and update queries change existing data; append and make-table queries move existing data.

- To execute SQLPASSTHROUGH queries. SQL pass-through queries are SQL statements that are sent directly to the database server without interpretation by the Microsoft Jet database engine. SQL pass-through queries provide your application with the ability to directly manipulate the features of your database server.

CDaoRecordset is also very similar to the ODBC-based CRecordset class. Recordsets can be based on tables as well as dynasets and snapshots. Remember, the recordset represent both the records you've retrieved and a way to move through the data. Options for moving through the data include Seek (for table-type recordsets only), Find and Move operations, AbsolutePosition, and if your data source supports them, bookmarks. Bookmarks are unique identifiers that allow you to return to a specific record by calling that identifier. The bulk of the functionality in the MFC DAO database classes is found in CDaoRecordset. CRecordset has only 44 member functions compared to 91 member functions for CDaoRecordset. This additional functionality is found in the navigation, caching, setting, and retrieving of field values, and in setting and retrieving recordset attributes.

The CDaoRecordView and CRecordView classes have functionality that is nearly identical. They both also have the advantages that come with being based on CFormView. Remember, a form view is like a dialog template stretched across the client area of a window, and that makes it easy to add controls and to display field data. The form-based display of data is supported by AppWizard and ClassWizard. If you use AppWizard to create your initial application, the columns of your database are automatically bound to member variables for you.

Exception handling is slightly different for the DAO database classes. Class CDaoException will return the error messages of the underlying DAO OLE object. Most of the time, you can retrieve more information about errors than is typically available with the ODBC-based classes. In MFC, all DAO errors are expressed as exceptions, of type CDaoException. When you catch an exception of this type, you can use CDaoException member functions to retrieve information from any DAO error objects stored in the database engine's Errors collection. As each error occurs, one or more error objects are placed in the Errors collection. When another DAO operation generates an error, the Errors collection is cleared, and the new error object is placed in the Errors collection.

The CDaoFieldExchange class supports the DAO record field exchange (DFX) routines used by the DAO database classes. Use this class if you are writing data exchange routines for custom data types; otherwise, you will not directly use this

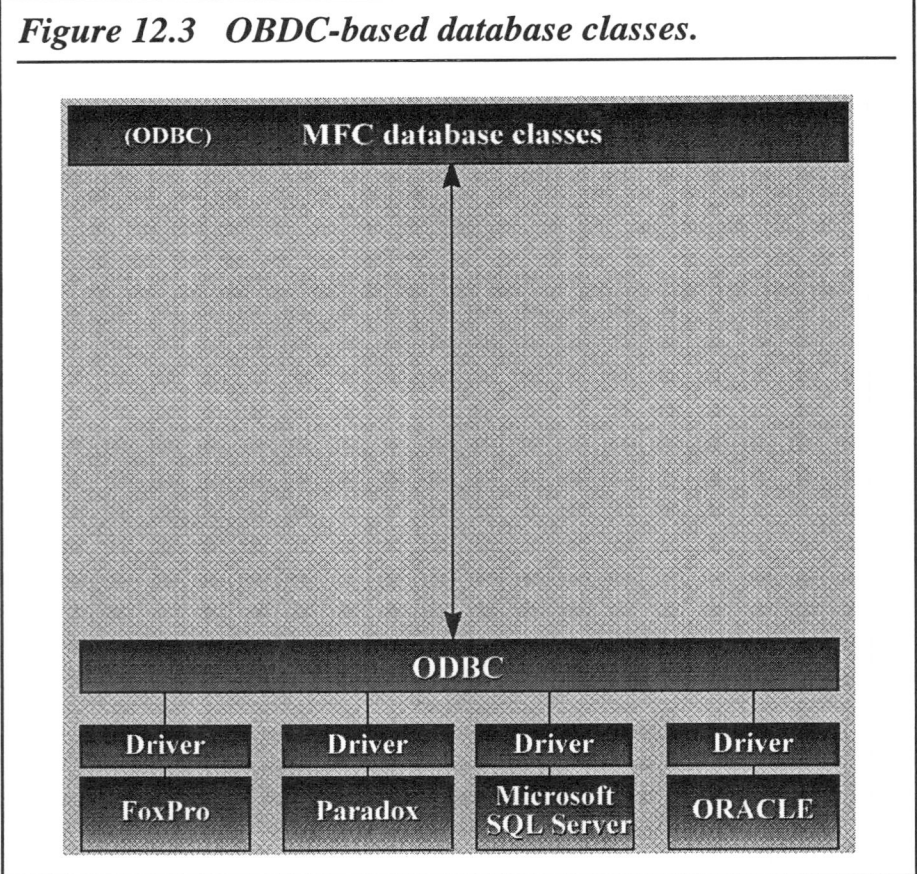

Figure 12.3   OBDC-based database classes.

class. DFX exchanges data between the field data members of your CDaoRecordset object and the corresponding fields of the current record on the data source. DFX manages the exchange in both directions, from the data source and to the data source. See Technical Note 53, available under MFC in Books Online, for information about writing custom DFX routines. A CDaoFieldExchange object provides the context information needed for DAO record field exchange to take place. CDaoFieldExchange objects support a number of operations, including binding parameters and field data members and setting various flags on the fields of the current record. DFX operations are performed on recordset-class data members of types defined by the enum FieldType in CDaoFieldExchange. Possible FieldType values are:

- CDaoFieldExchange::outputColumn for field data members.
- CDaoFieldExchange::param for parameter data members.

Figure 12.3 is a picture of the ODBC-based database classes as you've known them. The bar at the top represents the ODBC-based MFC classes that talk to ODBC. The ODBC drivers for each database interpret the SQL calls and translate them for each data source. I've shown a variety of data sources with their corresponding drivers along the bottom of the diagram to remind you of the flexibility of ODBC.

Figure 12.4 is a picture of the DAO database classes. They communicate via OLE with DAO, and DAO talks to the Jet database engine. The Jet database engine has separate DLLs that are used to communicate with various desktop data sources.

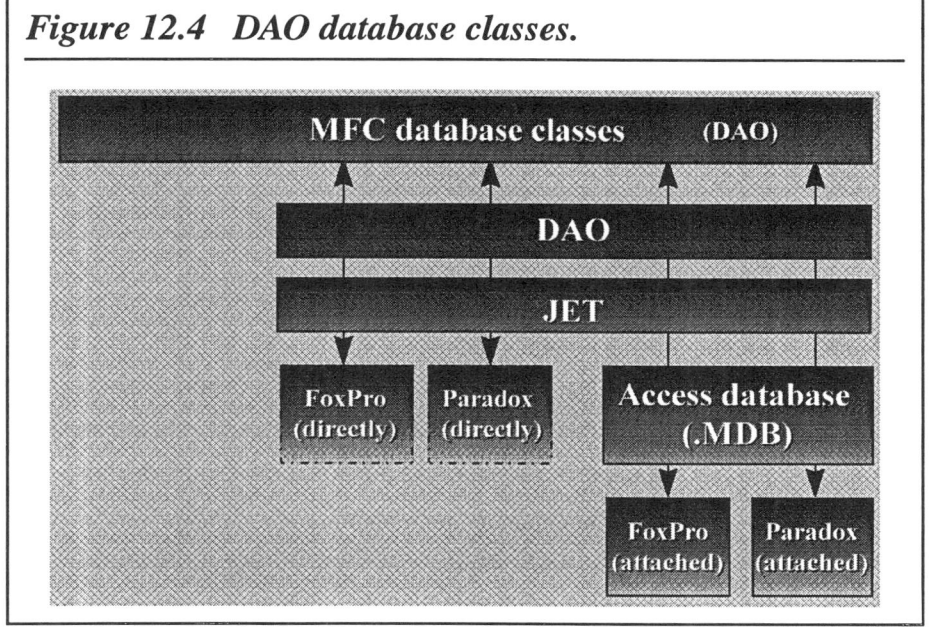

Figure 12.4 DAO database classes.

The Microsoft Jet database engine can open data sources like FoxPro and Paradox directly, but unless you need to change the schema of these data sources, it is actually more efficient to attach these tables to a Microsoft Access database. This is why the FoxPro and Paradox tables (which are just examples) are shown in two places. The dotted line is meant to imply that while it is possible to open the data sources directly, it is less efficient.

A linked table appears and behaves just like any other table in your Microsoft Jet database (although there are slight performance differences associated with connecting to and retrieving remote data). Information necessary to establish and maintain a connection to the remote data source is stored within the table definition.

In contrast, when you open a table directly, you must supply the connection information at the beginning of each session to establish a connection to the data source. None of the information needed to establish a connection to the remote data source is stored in your Microsoft Jet database. To open a table directly, you must use the CDaoTableDef::Create, and you must supply connection information (such as the data source, user name, password, and database name).

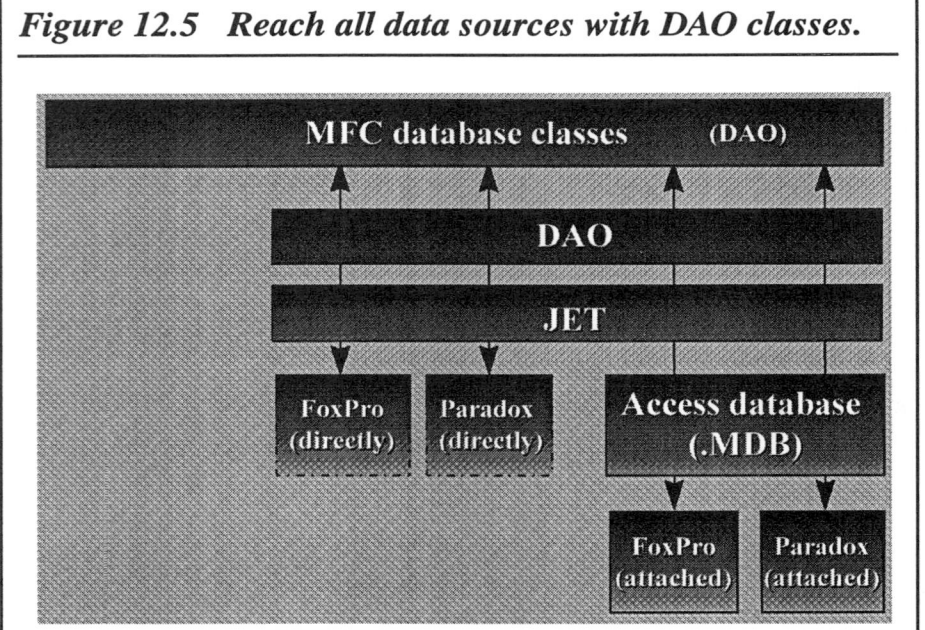

Figure 12.5   Reach all data sources with DAO classes.

With the DAO database classes, you can reach server-type databases such as Microsoft SQL server and Oracle by way of ODBC. Figure 12.5 completes the picture as far as reaching all types of data sources.

Finally, Figure 12.6 is the complete picture of the MFC database classes. Please understand that the vertical line on the MFC bar and the ODBC bar indicates that the two sets of MFC database classes are designed to be used as an either/or decision. You have options for reaching all types of data sources, but you cannot mix MFC database classes from both sets.

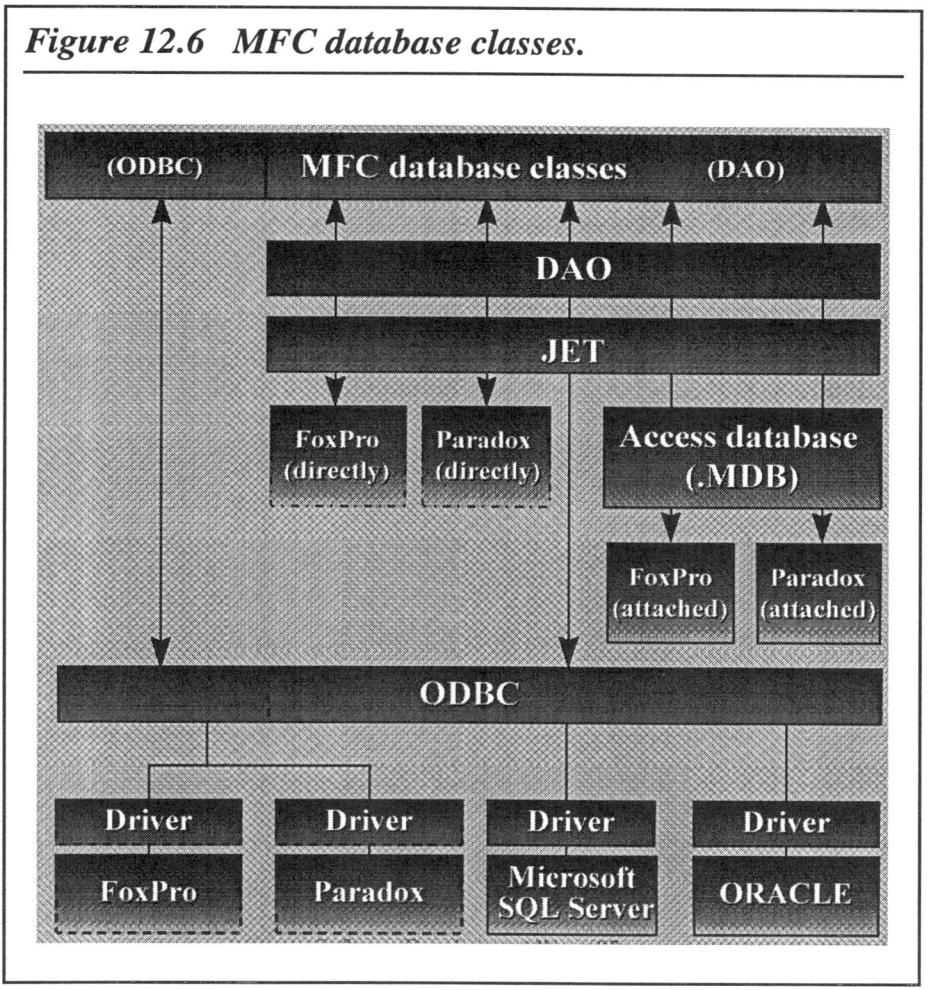

Figure 12.6   MFC database classes.

Data Source Options for the ODBC Database Classes

When you write applications using the MFC ODBC classes, you can connect to any data source for which you have an ODBC driver. The operation of ODBC Driver Manager and ODBC drivers is transparent in applications you write with these classes, but the individual driver capabilities affect the functionality of an application.

Generally, MFC dynasets (but not forward-only recordsets) require an ODBC driver with level 2 API conformance. If the driver for your data source conforms to the level 1 API set, you can still use both updatable and read-only snapshots and forward-only recordsets, but not dynasets. However, a level 1 driver can support dynasets if it supports extended fetching and keyset-driven cursors.

The ODBC Desktop Driver Pack 3.0 supports the level 2 ODBC API call SQLExtendedFetch.

AppWizard and ClassWizard will automatically bind columns of a data source statically to member variables in your application. This is the easiest way to establish a connection between your application and a data source, but not the most flexible. You can add custom Record Field Exchange (RFX) calls to your application by using class CFieldExchange. See Technical Note 43: RFX Routines for more information.

You might also consider binding the database columns dynamically. At the most general level, you follow these steps:

1. Construct your main recordset object. Optionally, pass a pointer to an open CDatabase object, or be able to supply connection information to the column recordset in some other way.

2. Take steps to add columns dynamically.

3. Open your main recordset.

The recordset selects records and uses record field exchange (RFX) to bind both the "static" columns (those mapped to recordset field data members) and the dynamic columns (mapped to extra storage that you allocate).

Data Source Options for the DAO Database Classes

Now let's talk about the data sources you can connect to with the DAO database classes, binding columns statically, binding them dynamically, and the double-buffering of records.

You'll get the fastest access to Microsoft Access databases, naturally, since they are native to Jet. Microsoft Access version 7.0 for Windows 95 has the database format that is native to DAO 3.0. You'll get the fastest performance if you use an Access 95 database.

Jet uses a separate DLL to provide access to Microsoft Jet 1.x and 2.0 databases. The storage engine and format were completely revised with Microsoft Jet 3.0. Given the large number of structural changes, Microsoft Jet 3.0 treats version 2.0 databases as external ISAMs. This has an impact on performance, so if you have not already considered upgrading your Access database, this is a good reason to do so.

You can also access installable ISAM databases and ODBC data sources. ISAMs (indexed sequential access method) databases like FoxPro and dBASE can be opened directly or attached to Access databases for best performance.

Here is a list of the data sources DAO can access:

- Microsoft FoxPro® versions 2.0, 2.5, and 2.6. Can import and export data to and from version 3.0 but can't create objects.

- dBASE III®, dBASE IV®, and dBASE 5.0®

- Paradox, versions 3.x, 4.x, and 5.x

- Btrieve® versions 5.1x and 6.0

- Microsoft Excel version 3.0, 4.0, 5.0, and 7.0 worksheets

- Lotus® WKS, WK1, WK3, WK4 spreadsheets

- Text files

Remember that Microsoft Access 1.x and 2.0 databases fall into this category.

You can reach ODBC Data sources like SQL Server and Oracle through ODBC, so you have the option to use DAO for those data sources. An ODBC data source is any DBMS for which you have the appropriate ODBC driver. For Visual C++ versions 2.0 and later, you need 32-bit ODBC drivers (except on Win32s, where you need 16-bit ODBC drivers). Here is a list of ODBC drivers included in this version of Visual C++.

- SQL Server

- Microsoft Access

- Microsoft FoxPro

- Microsoft Excel

- dBASE

- Paradox

- Text file

The Microsoft Desktop Database Drivers 3.0 (which cover the last six items in the list) offer the best performance for those data sources. These are 32-bit drivers only.

Attaching external data sources such as SQL Server to a Microsoft Access table is the most efficient way to handle the data access. Before you can connect your application to a remote data source, you must make sure that the remote data is accessible to your application's users and that your application is properly designed to handle remote data source security challenges. You must also make sure that your application interacts correctly with case-sensitive data sources and that the installable ISAM is correctly initialized for the data source you want to access. Finally, you must check to see that your code doesn't use objects or calls that are specific to Microsoft Jet data sources when accessing non-Jet data sources.

The easiest way to set up an attachment is to go into Microsoft Access and use the File/Attach Table command in Access 2.0 or the File/Get External Data/Link Tables command in Access 95.

Connection information is stored in the base table (.MDB) you are using. If you move the location of the external data, you must reestablish the link from within Access, or by calling CDaoTableDef::RefreshLink from within your code.

The DAO Record field exchange mechanism works the same way RFX works in the ODBC-based database classes. The recordset object's field data members, taken together, constitute an "edit buffer" that holds the selected columns of one record. When the recordset is first opened and is about to read the first record, DFX binds (associates) each selected column to the address of the appropriate field data member. When the recordset updates a record, DFX calls DAO to send the appropriate commands to the database engine. DFX uses its knowledge of the field data members to specify the columns (fields) in the data source to write.

Binding columns statically is supported by the Wizards. You can add your own DFX calls as you can with the ODBC-based classes. First, members must be added to the CDaoRecordset derived class for each bound field and parameter. Following this CDaoRecordset::DoFieldExchange should be overridden. Note that the data type of the member is important. It should match the data from the field in the database or at least be convertible to that type. MFC Technical #53 describes the process in greater detail.

The CDaoFieldExchange class supports the DAO record field exchange (DFX) routines used by the DAO database classes. Use this class if you are writing data exchange routines for custom data types. A CDaoFieldExchange object provides the context information needed for DAO record field exchange to take place. CDaoFieldExchange objects support a number of operations, including binding parameters and field data members and setting various flags on the fields of the current record.

Dynamic Binding in the DAO Database Classes

While it is possible to bind columns dynamically using the ODBC-based classes, the support for doing so is not built into the MFC classes. Dynamic binding IS built into the DAO database classes, and it is fairly easy to do.

There are other things you can do to optimize performance such as retrieving a part of a record instead of an entire record. We'll cover ways to optimize your application a little later in this presentation.

DFX and dynamic binding are not mutually exclusive options. With the DAO database classes, you can mix static and dynamic binding calls for maximum efficiency.

Double-Buffering in the DAO Database Classes

In MFC's CDaoRecordset class, double-buffering is a mechanism that simplifies detecting when the current record in a recordset has changed. Using double buffering with your DAO recordsets reduces the amount of work you have to do when adding new records and editing existing records. By default, your MFC DAO recordsets keep a second copy of the edit buffer (the field data members of the recordset class, taken collectively; DAO Help calls the corresponding buffer a "copy buffer"). As you make changes to the data members, MFC compares them to the copy (the "double buffer") to detect the changes.

The alternative to double buffering — not keeping a copy of the data — requires you to make additional function calls when you edit a field of the current record.

Double-buffering has been a part of the ODBC-based database classes all along. With the DAO database classes, you can turn that mechanism off if you need to, for improved efficiency.

The master switch for this mechanism is called m_bCheckCacheForDirtyFields, dirty meaning "changed." When you turn this switch ON, you can turn off double-buffering for all or part of the fields. If this master switch is OFF, the entire double-buffering mechanism is disabled.

The fields for which you're most likely to turn off double-buffering include memo fields, picture fields, and other BLOBs (binary large objects).

DAO SDK Classes

The DAO SDK includes some C++ database classes which are separate and distinct from the MFC DAO Database classes. These C++ classes encapsulate the individual objects in the DAO hierarchy. While you can mix the DAO SDK C++ classes with the MFC DAO database classes, the DAO SDK C++ classes do not follow the MFC guidelines for operator overloading, and you must exercise caution when using these classes together. For more information, see the article "The DAO of Databases: Using Data Access Objects and the Jet Engine in C++" in the Microsoft Systems Journal, January 1996.

Table 12.1 compares features of the DAO SDK classes and the MFC DAO database classes.

Using the DAO SDK classes is an easier transition for those accustomed to Visual Basic, but it doesn't conform to MFC. Those developers who already use the MFC ODBC database classes will find the MFC DAO classes to be more familiar in architecture and usage.

Comparing the MFC Database Classes

Let's focus first on the common database functionality in both sets of classes.

- Both support scrolling through recordsets.
  - ODBC classes rely on the underlying driver.
  - DAO classes have better support for MDB, good for installable ISAMs and the same support as the ODBC database classes for server-based data.
- Both support transactions.
  - ODBC classes at Database level.
  - DAO classes at Workspace level.

Table 12.1   DAO SDK vs. MFC DAO classes.

DAO SDK Database Classes	MFC DAO Database Classes
Simple migration from Visual Basic	Simple migration from MFC ODBC database classes
Direct mappings to DAO's OLE automation objects	Conforms to MFC standard two-phase construction
More Jet/DAO functionality	AppWizard and ClassWizard support
Doesn't conform to MFC standard two-phase construction	Hides more difficult DAO functionality

- The Recordset update functions are almost identical.
- Both support locking records during updates.
- Both sets of classes support detection of field data changes.
- Both have Move operations.
- Both `CDatabase` and `CDaoDatabase` can detect whether a data source accepts transactions. Transactions requirements have been considerably relaxed in the ODBC database classes as of MFC 4.2.
- Both database objects allow you to set a predetermined query time-out period.
- Both can execute direct SQL statements.

Additional ODBC Database Class Functionality

- The ODBC database classes are multithreaded as of MFC 4.2. To take advantage of this capability, you must use a multithreaded ODBC driver. DAO is looking into becoming apartment-model threaded, but no dates have been given for its availability.
- The bulk row fetching functionality is new in MFC 4.2. Special navigation capabilities have been added.
- In answer to many requests, we have added better support for console database applications. The new options in `CDatabase::OpenEx` are:

  `CDatabase::noOdbcDialog` Do not display the ODBC connection dialog box, regardless of whether enough connection information is supplied.

  `CDatabase::forceOdbcDialog` Always display the ODBC connection dialog box.

Additional DAO Database Class Functionality

- The `Workspace`, `TableDef`, and `QueryDef` objects are unique to the DAO Database classes. There is no direct equivalent for these objects in the ODBC database classes.
- `CDaoTableDef` and `CDaoQueryDef` functionality can generally be reproduced with direct ODBC calls, as found in the `CATALOG2` sample.
- `CDaoDatabase` supports creation of `TableDefs`, `QueryDefs`, and `Relations`.
- `CDaoRecordset` has greater navigation functionality.
  - `Find` operations
  - Percent position

- Seek
- Bulk record fetching functionality and related caching is built-in.
- The ability to create fields and indexes at run time using a CDaoTableDef object is a wonderful advantage, as is the validation for data sources that support it.
- CDaoQueryDefs can be created using fields and indexes, and stored for repeated use.
- CDaoQueryDefs can also control ODBC time-outs.

Optimizing Your MFC Database Application

There are some obvious but often overlooked ways to improve performance for an application. For example, find out what your network might do to enhance or deter data retrieval (for example, asynchronous queries).

The type of ODBC driver you have may also affect performance across the network.

- Single-tier drivers are intended for non–SQL-based databases. The database file is processed directly by the driver. The driver processes SQL statements and retrieves information from the database. SQL statements, once parsed and translated, are passed to the database as basic file operations. A driver that manipulates an xBASE file is an example of a single-tier implementation.

  A single-tier driver may limit the set of SQL statements that may be submitted. The minimum set of SQL statements that must be supported by a single-tier driver is defined in the ODBC SDK Programmer's Reference in Appendix C, "SQL Grammar."

  Single-tier drivers are generally slower than using the native DBMS tools such as Microsoft FoxPro® because they parse and translate the SQL statements into basic file operations. The degree to which they are slower depends on how optimized this process is. Difference in speed between two different single-tier drivers is usually attributed to the method of optimization.

- In a multiple-tier configuration, the driver sends requests to a server that processes these requests. The requests may be SQL or a DBMS-specific format. Although the entire installation may reside on a single system, it is more often divided across platforms. Typically, the application, driver, and Driver Manager reside on one system, called the client. The database and the software that controls access to the database reside on another system, called the server. There are two types of multiple-tier drivers: two-tier and three-tier (or gateway). For more information, see Colleen Lambert's article "ODBC: Architecture, Performance, and Tuning," found on the Microsoft Developer Network CD.

Optimizing the ODBC Database and Recordset Objects

When you open a CDatabase object you can supply a data source name or NULL to present the user with a selection dialog. MFC ODBC database classes do not support exclusive access to a database, so connections are always shared. You can, however, open a database as read-only. Remember that if you do, all recordsets derived from this CDatabase object will also be read-only. The following options make writing console applications easier. These new options were among the most requested by customers.

> CDatabase::noOdbcDialog   Do not display the ODBC connection dialog box, regardless of whether enough connection information is supplied.

> CDatabase::forceOdbcDialog   Always display the ODBC connection dialog box.

You have the option of loading the ODBC Cursor Library with your application. Depending on the capabilities of the underlying driver, you may not need it. The Cursor Library masks some functionality of the underlying ODBC driver, effectively preventing the use of dynasets (if the driver supports them). The only cursors supported if the Cursor Library is loaded are static snapshots and forwardOnly cursors.

The type of CRecordset object you open greatly affects the performance of your application. If you want to have a dynamic recordset with bidirectional scrolling, choose the CRecordset::dynaset type. For a static recordset with bidirectional scrolling, choose CRecordset::snapshot type. If you don't need to scroll around in the data, choose CRecordset::forwardOnly type which creates a read-only recordset with only forward scrolling. The new CRecordset::dynamic type recordset is a recordset with bidirectional scrolling. Changes made by other users to the membership, ordering, and data values are visible following a fetch operation. Note, however, that many ODBC drivers do not support this type of recordset.

Additional Options for CRecordset *Include*

CRecordset::none   No options set. By default, the recordset can be updated with Edit or Delete and allows appending new records with AddNew. Updatability depends on the data source as well as on the option you specify.

CRecordset::appendOnly   Do not allow Edit or Delete on the recordset. Allow AddNew only.

CRecordset::readOnly   Open the recordset as read-only.

`CRecordset::optimizeBulkAdd` Use a prepared SQL statement to optimize adding many records at one time. This option is mutually exclusive with `CRecordset::use-MultiRowFetch`.

`CRecordset::useMultiRowFetch` Implement bulk row fetching to allow multiple rows to be retrieved in a single fetch operation. This option is mutually exclusive with `CRecordset::optimizeBulkAdd`. Note that if you specify `CRecordset::useMulti-RowFetch`, then the option `CRecordset::noDirtyFieldCheck` will be turned on automatically (double buffering will not be available); on forward-only recordsets, the option `CRecordset::useExtendedFetch` will be turned on automatically.

`CRecordset::skipDeletedRecords` Skip deleted records when navigating through the recordset. This will slow performance in certain relative fetches. This option is not valid on forward-only recordsets. Note that `CRecordset::skipDeletedRecords` is similar to driver packing, which means that deleted rows are removed from the recordset.

`CRecordset::useBookmarks` May use bookmarks on the recordset, if supported. Bookmarks slow data retrieval but improve performance for data navigation. Not valid on forward-only recordsets.

`CRecordset::noDirtyFieldCheck` Turn off automatic dirty field checking (double buffering). This will improve performance; however, you must manually mark fields as dirty by calling the `SetFieldDirty` and `SetFieldNull` member functions.

`CRecordset::executeDirect` Do not use a prepared SQL statement. For improved performance, specify this option if the `Requery` member function will never be called.

`CRecordset::useExtendedFetch` Implement `SQLExtendedFetch` instead of `SQLFetch`. This is designed for implementing bulk row fetching on forward-only recordsets. If you specify the option `CRecordset::useMultiRowFetch` on a forward-only recordset, then `CRecordset::useExtendedFetch` will be turned on automatically.

`CRecordset::userAllocMultiRowBuffers` The user will allocate storage buffers for the data. Use this option in conjunction with `CRecordset::useMultiRowFetch` if you want to allocate your own storage; otherwise, the framework will automatically allocate the necessary storage.

If you want, you can use bulk row fetching to improve performance. Before opening your recordset object, you can define a rowset size with the SetRowsetSize member function. The rowset size specifies how many records should be retrieved during a single fetch. When bulk row fetching is implemented, the default rowset size is 25. Note that if bulk row fetching is not implemented, the rowset size remains fixed at 1.

After you have initialized the rowset size, call the `Open` member function. Here you must specify the `CRecordset::useMultiRowFetch` option of the `dwOptions` parameter in order to implement bulk row fetching. You can additionally set the

CRecordset::userAllocMultiRowBuffers option. The bulk record field exchange mechanism uses arrays to store the multiple rows of data retrieved during a fetch. These storage buffers can be allocated automatically by the framework, or you can allocate them manually. Specifying the CRecordset::userAllocMultiRowBuffers option means that you will do the allocation.

Optimizing the DAO Database and Recordset Objects

When you use a CDaoDatabase object, you use a string expression that is the name of an existing Microsoft Jet (.MDB) database file. If the filename has an extension, it is required. If your network supports the uniform naming convention (UNC), you can also specify a network path, such as "\\\\MYSERVER\\MYSHARE\\MYDIR\\MYDB.MDB". (Double backslashes are required in string literals because \ is the C++ escape character.) Some considerations apply when using the database this way.

If a database is already open for exclusive access by another user, MFC throws an exception. Use that exception to let your user know that the database is unavailable.

If you open the database with an empty string ("") and you're connecting to an ODBC data source, a dialog box listing all registered ODBC data source names is displayed so the user can select a database. You should avoid direct connections to ODBC data sources; use an attached table instead.

CDaoDatabase object can be opened for exclusive access. By default, it is opened for shared access. You can open it as a read-only data source, or for read/write access. All recordsets derived from a CDaoDatabase object inherit the read capabilities of the database object.

As with the CRecordset object, a CDaoRecordset has more than one type. If you select dbOpenDynaset, you have a dynaset-type recordset with bidirectional scrolling. This is the default. A dbOpenSnapshot selection gives you a snapshot-type recordset with bidirectional scrolling. Finally, you can open a table-type recordset with bidirectional scrolling using dbOpenTable. The MFC ODBC database classes do not allow you to open a recordset based on a table.

A CDaoRecordset object has options similar to that of a CRecordset object.

dbAppendOnly   You can only append new records (dynaset-type recordset only). This option means literally that records may only be appended. The MFC ODBC database classes have an append-only option that allows records to be retrieved and appended.

dbForwardOnly   The recordset is a forward-only scrolling snapshot.

dbSeeChanges   Generate an exception if another user is changing data you are editing.

dbDenyWrite   Other users cannot modify or add records.

dbDenyRead   Other users cannot view records (table-type recordset only).

dbReadOnly   You can only view records; other users can modify them.

dbInconsistent   Inconsistent updates are allowed (dynaset-type recordset only).

dbConsistent   Only consistent updates are allowed (dynaset-type recordset only).

Note: The constants dbConsistent and dbInconsistent are mutually exclusive. You can use one or the other, but not both in a given instance of Open.

Optimizing ODBC-based Database Interactions

The following recommendations apply to any interaction that involves ODBC. This applies to the ODBC database classes, but also to the DAO database classes used with server-based data where DAO uses ODBC to communicate with the data source. Many of these recommendations come from Colleen Lambert's article "ODBC: Architecture, Performance, and Tuning," found on the Microsoft Developer Network CD.

- Use as much of a drivers capabilities as possible by querying driver conformance levels. If you do not need to port an application to another platform, you can maximize your application's capabilities by focusing on the abilities of a particular driver.

- Avoid calling data source catalog routines. These can be very time-consuming. Try calling the routine once and cache the information locally.

- Keep scalability in mind, and put data locally and remotely as appropriate. Try to avoid filling combo boxes with data from remote data sources.

- Use SQLExtendedFetch for scrolling. If your driver supports it, this is the fastest way to scroll around your ODBC data source.

- Prepared SQL statements run faster. Take the time to prepare your SQL calls so that they attach to an HSTMT, which won't be freed until that handle is freed.

- Use SQLBindCol rather than SQLGetData. SQLBindCol takes care of the storage and the data type for a column so that you don't have to reacquire it for a result set.

- Cache SQLTypeInfo locally. Some data sources handle this call as a stored procedure, which can be very expensive to execute.

- Use as few connections as possible, and avoid disconnecting and reconnecting repeatedly. Remember that the ODBC driver manager makes calls to prepare a connection in addition to calls made by the driver. All that overhead adds up, and can slow an application considerably.

- Use block fetches for multiple-tier drivers. Multiple-tier drivers often use the network capabilities as part of their own work, and relying on SQLFetch instead of SQLExtendedFetch exposes your application to the vagaries of network operation.

- Optimize your queries by knowing your SQL thoroughly. This may seem obvious, but many programmers get by on a limited set of SQL commands, when more study and refining of SQL statements could mean the difference between a fast application and an even faster one.

- Use high-performance DBMSs. We talked about this at the beginning of the paper — a good data source is fundamental to the abilities and operation of an application. Get the best one your client can afford.

The following recommendations are specifically applicable to the DAO database classes. The starred items in this list refer primarily to interactions with ODBC (server-based) data sources.

- Use attached tables instead of directly opened tables whenever possible. See the article DAO External: Working with External Data Sources and the topic Accessing External Databases with DAO in DAO Help. This recommendation has the most significant impact on performance of all the recommendations in this list.

- Don't use dynaset-type recordsets if you're not updating the data. Use forward-scrolling snapshot-type recordsets if you're only scrolling forward. Don't scroll through records unnecessarily, and avoid jumping to the last record of a large table.

- Retrieve and view only the data you need. Use restricted queries to limit the number of records you retrieve, and select only the columns you need. This requires transferring less data across the network.

- Use caching. In class CDaoRecordset, MFC supports caching a specified number of records. Doing so takes longer initially, when the data is retrieved into the cache, but moving through the records in the cache is faster than retrieving each record as it is scrolled to.

- Turn off the double-buffering option in MFC CDaoRecordset objects. This is a general way to improve performance that applies as well to working with external data sources.

- For bulk operations, such as adding records in bulk, use an SQL pass-through query. When you use a SQL pass-through query, you only need to set the connection information once, as long as you are always performing your SQL pass-through queries through the same connection.

- Avoid using queries that cause processing to be done locally. Don't use user-defined functions with remote column arguments. Use heterogeneous joins (joins on tables in two databases) only on indexed columns, and realize if you do this that some processing is done locally. When accessing external data, the Microsoft

Jet database engine processes data locally only when the operation can't be performed by the external database. Query operations performed locally include:

- WHERE clause restrictions on top of a query with a DISTINCT predicate. Often, you can rearrange your queries to calculate totals or DISTINCT queries after all other operations.

- WHERE clauses containing operations that can't be processed remotely, such as user-defined functions that involve remote columns. (Note that in this case only the parts of the WHERE clause that can't be processed remotely will be processed locally.)

- Joins between tables from different data sources. Simply having joins between tables from different data sources doesn't mean that all of the processing occurs locally. If restrictions are sent to the server, only relevant rows are processed locally.

- Joins over aggregation or the DISTINCT predicate. Doing joins properly is an art anyway, and adding aggregation functions such as AVG, MAX, and MIN, or a predicate containing DISTINCT will only slowdown your queries.

- Outer joins containing syntax not supported by the ODBC driver. The Desktop Database Drivers support left and right outer joins, as well as inner joins. The right table in a left outer join, or the left table in a right outer join, can be used in an inner join. Full and nested outer joins are not supported.

The next three items apply specifically to data you're trying to access from a remote data source.

- DISTINCT predicates containing operations that can't be processed remotely.

- ORDER BY arguments (if the remote data source doesn't support them).

- ORDER BY or GROUP BY arguments containing operations that can't be processed remotely.

    A nonremoteable expression is one that cannot be evaluated by your server. Nonremoteable output expressions (those in the SELECT clause) don't force local evaluation of your query unless they occur in a totals query, a DISTINCT query, or a UNION query. Nonremoteable expressions in other clauses (WHERE, ORDER BY, GROUP BY, HAVING, and so on) force at least part of your query to be evaluated locally.

- GROUP BY arguments on top of a query with a DISTINCT option. Use SELECT DISTINCTROW followed by the GROUP BY clause.

The following features are unsupported on all known ODBC-accessible servers — usually operations that are Microsoft Jet – specific extensions to SQL such as:

- Multiple-level GROUP BY arguments, such as those used in reports with multiple grouping levels.

- TOP or TOP PERCENT predicate.

- Cross-tab queries that have more than one aggregate or that have an ORDER BY clause that matches the GROUP BY clause. Simple crosstab queries can be sent to the server.

General Results

Again, because of the wide range of implementation details required to reach a conclusion, there are no hard and fast rules. However, performance testing of the MFC database classes reveals:

- There is usually not a "clear winner" in these comparisons; ODBC faster in some cases, DAO faster in others, especially for desktop data.
- Attaching tables to Access (for DAO) gives generally better performance than opening tables directly:
  - Dramatically faster for server-based data.
  - Slightly faster for desktop data.
- ODBC gives generally better performance for working with server-based databases.

  As always, we encourage you to prototype your own applications before accepting these conclusions.

Other Resources for Optimizing Your Applications

The documentation that ships with Visual C++ should be your first source of information about MFC's implementation of DAO. Be sure to look over the MFC DAO samples and MFC Technical notes as well as the Class Library Reference and Programming with MFC.

For additional information on how DAO works, consult the "Microsoft Jet Database Engine Programmer's Guide," published by Microsoft Press.

Two additional articles found on the Microsoft Developer Network CD are recommended:

- Neil Black and Stephen Hecht. "Jet Database Engine ODBC Connectivity." This describes in great detail how Microsoft Jet uses ODBC to retrieve server data. Required reading for anyone using DAO to write significant server applications.
- Colleen Lambert. "ODBC: Architecture, Performance, and Tuning." This paper provides a good overview of how ODBC works and addresses performance issues in a realistic and useful fashion.

In Conclusion

MFC's fundamental concept of providing high-level abstractions to more complicated technologies is true in these database classes. You have choices — ODBC or DAO — to give you your best route to success with your clients.

We've taken quite a bit of time to examine ways to improve performance, seen some numbers on how the classes perform on a variety of data sources, and given you lots of things to think about. Whatever you do, prototype before you decide. I hope that today's session will help narrow your options and make your decision easier to reach.

Chapter 13

Debugging ActiveX Applications

George Shepherd

Our industry has arrived at the point where you can't ignore Microsoft's object technology, ActiveX. It's beginning to permeate every nook and cranny of Windows software. If you want to write Windows 95 shell extensions, you've gotta understand ActiveX and the Component Object (COM) Model. Extended MAPI relies on COM, too. And ActiveX controls are ActiveX through and through!

ActiveX (at a higher level) and COM (at a lower level) are just ways of packaging software. ActiveX and COM components are just software. To use Matt Pietrek's phrase, it's just code. Unfortunately, one fact of life is that where there's software, there are often bugs. Since ActiveX components are just software, you're bound to encounter bugs from time to time.

Here we'll focus on some of the issues concerning creating ActiveX components and some techniques for diagnosing bugs and getting rid of them. Since many bugs can be traced to misconceptions about how COM is supposed to work, we'll take a look at what makes COM different from the software development practices we've been used to for the past several years. Then we'll focus on specific issues related to debugging ActiveX applications.

What's Different about ActiveX?

So just what's different about debugging ActiveX applications? COM and ActiveX are formal ways of decoupling the components in your applications. In fact, COM more or less forces you to decouple clients from the services they use. Because of this, using COM and ActiveX helps get rid of some bugs by localizing data and functionality so that bugs are easier to track down and remove from existence.

However, COM programming introduces some new kinds of bugs and challenges. You need to become aware of some of these issues and develop some new debugging techniques.

There's nothing really special about COM objects — they're just pieces of software that conform to a specific binary layout defined by the Component Object Model. At the very core, A COM Object is a piece of code that controls its own lifetime, exposes function tables (interfaces) to clients, and provides the client with a way to navigate between interfaces.

Keep in mind that COM is trying to accomplish an object-oriented way of sharing software at the binary level — that is, at run time. In addition, COM tries to be language and compiler independent. It shouldn't matter what language you use or what compiler you use, COM defines a way that you can write COM objects and client code that can use those objects.

And that's just COM. There's the whole next layer of binary specifications known as ActiveX. This layer includes features like Automation, data transfers, ActiveX Documents, and ActiveX Controls.

As you can imagine, this scenario puts a different spin on the kinds of issues you'll face as you develop and ultimately debug COM software components.

Let's start by looking specifically at some of the rules of COM programming and what can happen if you break them.

Understanding COM

Because COM is only now entering mainstream programming circles, one of the primary debugging issue for COM-based development is to make sure that both the client and the object are following some specific rules. COM-based development is based on certain principles to which the client and the object must adhere or things may start to break. When you have problems with some COM code, one of the first thing to do is check to make sure everybody's following the rules. Let's start with one of the most fundamental aspects of COM — how clients talk to a COM object.

The Way to a COM Object's Heart Is Through Its Interface

One primary rule of COM programming is that the only way for client code to talk to a COM object is through one of its interfaces. An interface is really nothing more than a function table. In fact, most C++ objects implement one interface. However, whereas in C++, that interface may also include data members, COM allows only functions to be exposed. By restricting access to a COM object to only a well-defined interface, COM eliminates layout dependencies between COM objects and their clients.

The point is that you should make sure that clients aren't trying to do anything funny with the objects they're hosting. That is, make sure clients are not doing anything like treating interface pointers as though they were data pointers (I've actually seen this happen!). COM clients should code to an interface spec, not a regular C++ class. It's important to keep the client code decoupled from the object code and to make sure the client code makes no assumptions about the object code. For example, if someone gave you some information about how a specific COM class was laid out, you could conceivably start poking around beyond the bounds of an object's interface pointer. (Of course this works only when the occasion is in-proc). However, by doing things like this, you start making assumptions about the object code causing the object and client to become tightly coupled. This will cause bugs and crashes if you ever try to move the COM object out of proc. In addition, you'll probably see bugs crop up if the object code decides to change its implementation because the client has coded to a specific layout (that may change) rather than the well-known interface spec (which doesn't change).

The next fundamental COMism is to make sure that the client is using `AddRef()` and `Release()` properly.

Pay Attention to the Reference Counting Rules

The second major aspect to monitor when doing COM-based programming is to watch the reference counting being performed on objects. Because COM is a binary standard, there's no more operator `new` and `delete`. COM objects are usually created via a well-known API function, at which point they hand one of their interface pointers to the client. The client uses that interface (possibly to get other interfaces to the same object). The COM object has to remain in memory for as long as it has outstanding interface pointers. COM objects accomplish this using reference counting.

COM objects maintain a data member representing the number of references made to the object. That number is bumped up every time the object hands out an interface. Clients also have the option of incrementing the object's reference count (for example, if the client wants to make a copy of the interface pointer).

Once a COM client gets a copy of an object's interface pointer, the client is on the hook to release the interface pointer when it's done. Once the client releases the interface pointer, the COM object decrements the reference counter by one. When the reference count drops to 0, the COM object deletes itself.

Of course, if you see a problem with memory leaks or unexpected program crashes, there might just be a reference counting problem. If a client doesn't release all its interface pointers, you'll see a memory leak. If a client releases an interface one to many times, you'll see a program crash (in the in-proc case) or an RPC error (in the out of proc case).

The first item to check is to make sure both parties are following the reference counting rules. In short, calls to an object's AddRef() must be balanced by a matching call to Release(). Here's a summary of the reference counting rules:

- Functions that return a pointer value must AddRef() through that pointer before returning. QueryInterface() is a great example of this rule.

- Functions that accept pointer values should only AddRef() pointers when assigning to global or instance variables.

- Functions that overwrite a pointer passed to them and return another pointer in the same reference parameter must Release() the in pointer and AddRef() the out pointer.

Code that doesn't follow these rules is subject to problems like memory leaks, program crashes, or RPC errors. Just keep in mind that the reference counting mechanism determines the life of the object behind the interface. Balancing AddRef()s and Release()s is imperative.

Sometimes you can't figure out if the reference counting is being done properly by just looking at the source code. Once in a while you need to actually step through a debugger to watch the reference counting. This leads to another interesting aspect of debugging ActiveX applications — how to track the reference counting. Choosing whether you want to track how your object's reference count is being manipulated plays a major role in how you implement your COM class. Let's see what those implications are.

Tracking the Reference Count

There are two common ways of implementing COM classes: using multiple inheritance and using nested classes. One way makes tracking the reference count virtually impossible while the other way makes it easy to track reference counts. Let's start by using multiple inheritance to implement a COM class and see why you can't track reference counting if you use this method.

Multiple Inheritance

To use multiple inheritance to implement a COM class, start by deriving the COM class from one or more interfaces that you want to implement. For example, imagine you want to write a COM class named CoSomeObject that implements two interfaces ICaramba and ILoveLucy. The interfaces look like this

```
// IFACES.H
interface ICaramba : IUnknown {
    HRESULT QueryInterface(RIID riid, LPVOID * ppvoid);
    ULONG AddRef();
    ULONG Release();
    HRESULT BartSays();
};
interface ILoveLucy : IUnknown {
    HRESULT QueryInterface(RIID riid, LPVOID * ppvoid);
    ULONG AddRef();
    ULONG Release();
    HRESULT OhRicky();
};
```

Then you'd define the class like so

```
// SOMEOBJ.H
class CoSomeObject: public ICaramba, public ILoveLucy {
public:
// IUnknown functions (shared by both interfaces)
    HRESULT QueryInterface(RIID riid, LPVOID * ppvoid);
    ULONG AddRef();
    ULONG Release();
// ICaramba Interface functions
    HRESULT BartSays();
// ILoveLucy Interface functions
    HRESULT OhRicky();
private:
    ULONG m_cRef;
};
```

Then you'd implement the class like this

```
// SOMEOBJ.CPP
CoSomeObj::CoSomeObj() {
    m_cRef = 0;
}
ULONG CoSomeObj::AddRef() {
    // We'll never know whether this was called through
    // ICaramba or through ILoveLucy
    return m_cRef++;
}
```

```
ULONG CoSomeObj::Release() {
    // We'll never know whether this was called through
    // ICaramba or through ILoveLucy
    return m_cRef++;
    m_cRef--;
    if(m_cRef==0) {
        delete this;
        return 0
    } else
    return m_cRef;
}
HRESULT CoSomeObj::QueryInterface(RIID riid, LPVOID* ppvoid) {
    // Search for requested interface ID, return the correct vtbl,
    // calling AddRef() on the way out.
    ...
}
HRESULT CoSomeObject::BartSays() {
    return NOERROR;
}
HRESULT CoSomeObject::OhRicky() {
    return NOERROR;
}
```

The important thing to notice here that CoSomeObject implements two interfaces, and that those two interfaces share a single implementation of IUnknown. You're never able to tell which interface is manipulating the reference count. Take a look at Figure 13.1, which illustrates how this works.

As you can see, the multiple inheritance path does not lend itself to tracking the reference counting on a per-interface basis. You can see the counter going up and down, but you'll never be able to tell which interface is causing the change. However, there's another way to implement COM classes that let you track reference counting. Now let's take a look at how the nested classes work.

Using Nested Classes

To use the nested class approach to COM class development, derive a single class from IUnknown. Then add nested classes to your COM class — one for each interface you want to implement. Here's how you might define CoSomeObject using nested classes

```
// SOMEOBJ.H
class CoSomeObject : public IUnknown {
    class CarambaObj : public ICaramba {
        CoSomeObject * const m_object;
        CarambaObj(CoSomeObject * obj);

        // declare ICaramba members
        HRESULT QueryInterface(REFIID, LPVOID *);
        ULONG AddRef();
```

```
        ULONG Release();
        HRESULT BartSays();
    } m_carambaobj;
    class LoveLucyObj : public ILoveLucy{
        CoFoo * const m_object;
        LoveLucyObj(CoSomeObject * obj);
    // declare ILoveLucy members
        HRESULT QueryInterface(REFIID, LPVOID *);
        ULONG AddRef();
        ULONG Release();
        HRESULT OhRicky()
    } m_lovelucyobj;
    ULONG m_cRef;
    CoSomeObject() ;
    HRESULT QueryInterface(REFIID, void**);
    ULONG AddRef(void);
    ULONG Release(void);
};
```

Notice how `CoSomeObject` still has a single `IUnknown` implementation. However, since each interface has its own body you have a way to hook into the reference counting and see what's going on. Here's how `CoSomeObject` is actually implemented

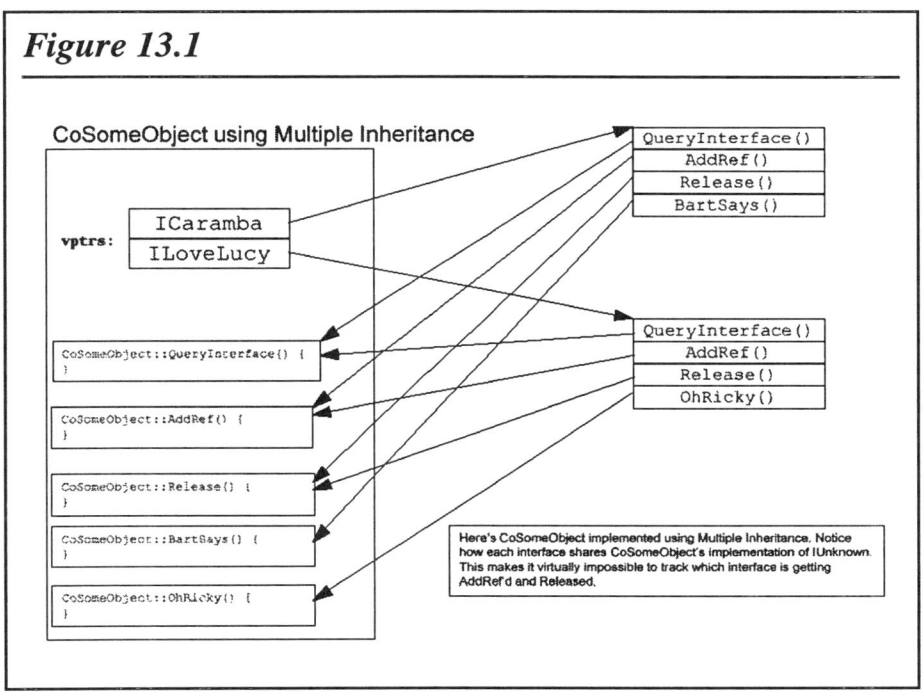

Figure 13.1

CoSomeObject using Multiple Inheritance

Here's CoSomeObject implemented using Multiple Inheritance. Notice how each interface shares CoSomeObject's implementation of IUnknown. This makes it virtually impossible to track which interface is getting AddRef'd and Released.

```
// SOMEOBJ.CPP
CoSomeObject::CoSomeObj() {
    m_cRef = 0;
}
ULONG CoSomeObject::AddRef() {
    return m_cRef++;
}
 ULONG CoSomeObject::Release() {
    m_cRef--;
    if(m_cRef==0) {
        delete this;
        return 0
    } else
    return m_cRef;
}
 HRESULT CoSomeObject::QueryInterface(RIID riid, LPVOID* ppvoid) {
    // Search for requested interface ID, return the correct vtbl
    ...
}
 CoSomeObject::CarambaObj::CarambaObj(CoSomeObject * obj) {
    // CarambaObj constructor
    m_object = obj;
}
 HRESULT CoSomeObject::CarambaObj::QueryInterface(REFIID riid, LPVOID FAR
*ppv) {
    return m_object->QueryInterface(riid, ppv);
}
 ULONG CoSomeObject::CarambaObj::AddRef() {
    // This definitely came from ICaramba.
    // Chalk this AddRef up for ICaramba
    return m_object->AddRef();
}
 ULONG CoSomeObject::CarambaObj::Release() {
    // This definitely came from ICaramba
    // Chalk this Release up for ICaramba
    return m_object->Release();
}
CoSomeObject::::LoveLucyObj::LoveLucyObj(CoSomeObject * obj) {
    // LoveLucyObj constructor
    m_object = obj;
}
 HRESULT CoSomeObject::LoveLucyObj::QueryInterface(REFIID riid, LPVOID FAR
*ppv){
    return m_object->QueryInterface(riid, ppv);
}


ULONG CoSomeObject::LoveLucyObj::AddRef(void) {
    // This definitely came from ILoveLucy
    // Chalk this AddRef up for ILoveLucy
```

```
    return m_object->AddRef();
}
ULONG CoSomeObject::LoveLucyObj::Release(void)
{
    // This definitely came from ILoveLucy
    // Chalk this Release up for ILoveLucy
    return m_object->Release();
}
```

Figure 13.2 illustrates how the nested class method of writing COM classes gives you a hook into examining when and which interface is manipulating the reference count.

Because the nested class approach to COM classes yields separate implementations for AddRef() and Release() (one for ICaramba and one for ILoveLucy), you're free to place trace statements into the code and watch that reference counter go up and down on a per-interface basis.

Figure 13.2

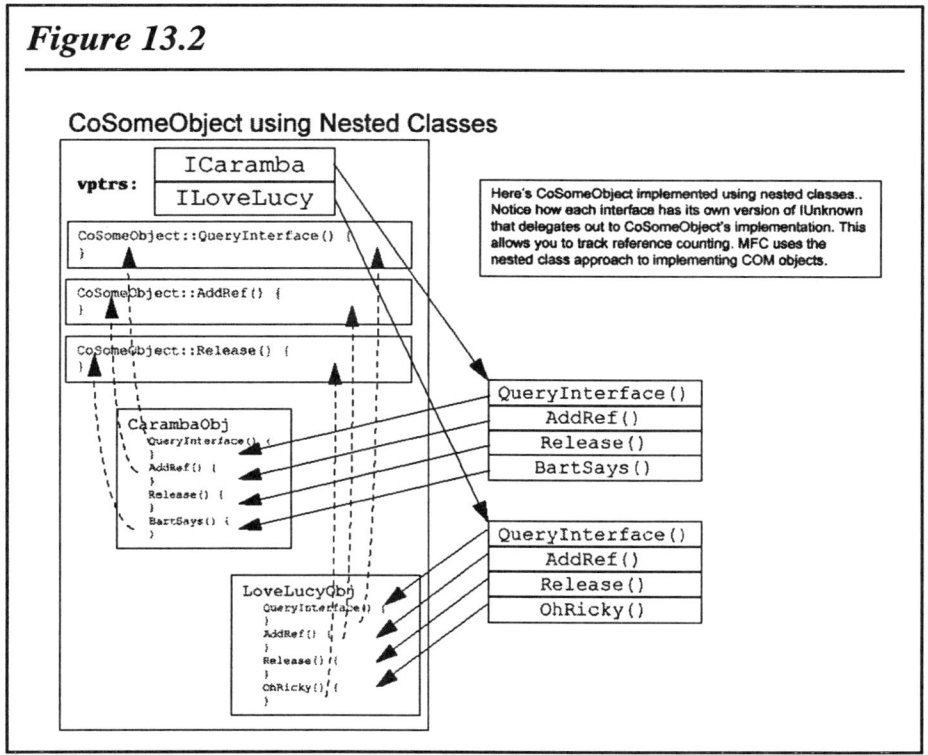

MFC and Reference Counting

If you program using MFC, you may run into the need to implement a COM class using the MFC method. Contrary to popular belief, MFC doesn't stand for Microsoft Foundation Classes, MFC stands for Macro Foundation Classes. As with nearly every other feature implemented through boilerplate code, MFC uses macros to implement its version of COM. MFC's version is really just a variation on the nested class theme. That means you can trace calls to an interface's AddRef() and Release() calls.

Here's how you'd implement CoSomeObject using MFC's COM support: The header file includes the macros that add the nested classes.

```
// SOMEOBJ.h
class CoSomeObject: public CCmdTarget {
    BEGIN_INTERFACE_PART(CarambaObj, ICaramba)
        HRESULT BartSays();
    END_INTERFACE_PART(CarambaObj)
    BEGIN_INTERFACE_PART(LoveLucyObj, ILoveLucy)
        HRESULT OhRicky();
    END_INTERFACE_PART(LoveLucyObj)
};
 // SOMEOBJ.CPP
ULONG CoSomeObject::XCarambaObj::AddRef(void) {
    // This definitely came through ICaramba
    METHOD_PROLOGUE(CoSomeObject, CarambaObj)
    return pThis->ExternalAddRef();
}
 ULONG CoSomeObject::XCarambaObj::Release(void) {
    // This definitely came through ICaramba
    METHOD_PROLOGUE(CoSomeObject, CarambaObj)
    return pThis->ExternalRelease();
}
 ULONG CoSomeObject::XLoveLucyObj::AddRef(void) {
    // This definitely came through ILoveLucy
    METHOD_PROLOGUE(CoSomeObject, LoveLucyObj)
    return pThis->ExternalAddRef();
}
 ULONG CoSomeObject::XLoveLucyObj::Release(void) {'
    // This definitely came through ILoveLucy
    METHOD_PROLOGUE(CoSomeObject, LoveLucyObj)
    return pThis->ExternalRelease();
}
```

Since MFC implements COM classes using nested classes, you're free to add all the trace statements you'd like to the AddRef() and Release() functions of each nested class.

On a final note about MFC, MFC has another hook into the reference counting scheme. CCmdTarget::OnRelease() is a virtual function that is called right before the object deletes itself. You can use OnFinalRelease() to track when the COM object is deleted. The framework calls OnFinalRelease() right before the COM object self-destructs. For example, if you override OnFinalRelease() to display a trace statement and the program crashes right after you see the trace statement, the client code might be releasing one of the object's interface pointers one too many times.

At any rate, using AddRef() and Release() correctly is important because together they control a COM object's lifecycle. If the client calls an object's AddRef() function more than it calls Release(), you'll probably see memory leaks. If you call Release() more than you call AddRef(), you'll see either a program crash (in-proc) or an RPC error (out-of-proc).

Let's swing our attention to ActiveX error codes — that funny HRESULT type that keeps popping up.

Pay Attention to HRESULTs

At this point in time, ActiveX doesn't support exceptions. Instead, status information and errors are passed around using an HRESULT. In fact, about $99^{44}/_{100}$ of all ActiveX API and Interface functions return HRESULTs. So what are these HRESULTs?

An HRESULT is defined as a 32-bit DWORD. It serves a rich error code that gives you well-organized, standard information about the result of calling an ActiveX API or ActiveX interface function. Figure 13.3 shows the layout of the HRESULT type.

In most cases, it's not really necessary to know the exact details of how HRESULTs are laid out. However, it's often useful to know about the various components of the HRESULT. Thankfully, Microsoft has macros to crack open an HRESULT.

- To find out if the function succeeded or flat-out failed, use the SUCCEEDED() macro. SUCCEEDED() takes an HRESULT and returns a BOOL telling you whether the function succeeded or failed.

Figure 13.3 Layout of the HRESULT *type.*

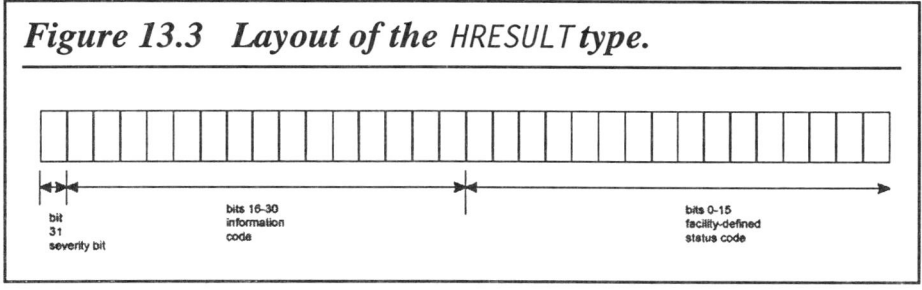

- To get information about what actually happened, use HRESULT_CODE. HRESULT_CODE( ) takes an HRESULT and gives you back bits 16–30 of the HRESULT.
- To get the facility code, use HRESULT_FACILITY. HRESULT_FACILITY( ) takes an HRESULT and tells you the general type of error. This may include such error types as RPC errors, dispatch errors (i.e., automation problems), and WIN32 problems.

So how do you get these error codes? You can usually look at the return values as you debug your application. Hopefully, the client saves the return value in a variable so you can look at it. However, if the client code doesn't save the HRESULT, you can still examine it. For example, imagine running across code that looks like this:

```
void CreateSomeObject(
    LPUNKNOWN punk;
    if(SUCCEEDED(CoCreateInstance(CLSID_CoSomeObject,
                                  NULL,
                                  CLSCTX_INPROC_SERVER,
                                  IID_IUnknown,
                                  (VOID FAR **)&punk)) {
        UseTheInterface(punk);
    } else
        return;
}
```

Unfortunately, the developer hasn't saved the return value of CoCreateInstance( ). However, you can still look at it. HRESULTs are returned in the EAX register. After CoCreateInstance( ) executes, just pull up the registers window. You'll see the HRESULT in the EAX register.

Once you have the HRESULT in all its glory, just look it up in the file WINERROR.H. For example, if you are debugging an ActiveX client and CoCreateInstance( ) fails returning the number 0x80040154, you can look the error up in WINERROR.H and see that for some reason or other the class isn't registered.

Before finishing, let's look at a couple of techniques you can use while using the VC++ debugger while stepping through a COM-based app.

Debugger Hints

Dealing with ActiveX interfaces enforces a new paradigm. With the client code existing in one module and the object coding in a separate module, you have to be able go between modules. COM objects may exist in one of two types of servers: in process servers (DLLs), and out of process servers (another executable on the local machine or on the network). Here's a couple of ways you can seamlessly debug both modules (provided you have the source code to both). Let's start with in-proc ActiveX objects.

Debugging ActiveX In-proc Objects

Here's how to debug an in-proc server. Imagine you've just written the coolest ActiveX Control. Unfortunately, there's a problem with it — it crashes for some unknown reason. You need to be able to step through the source code and see what's going on. The steps to take are as follows

- Load the ActiveX Control project in the IDE.

- Pull down the "Build|Settings" menu and select the Debug tab. The dialog box should look something like the one shown in Figure 13.4.

- Type the name of the host executable into the "Executable for debug session" field.

Once you've set up the host EXE for the debug session, you can set your breakpoints. Press the F5 key and let the fireworks begin!

Debugging a COM object that resides in an EXE requires a similar setup.

Figure 13.4   Debugging an in-proc server.

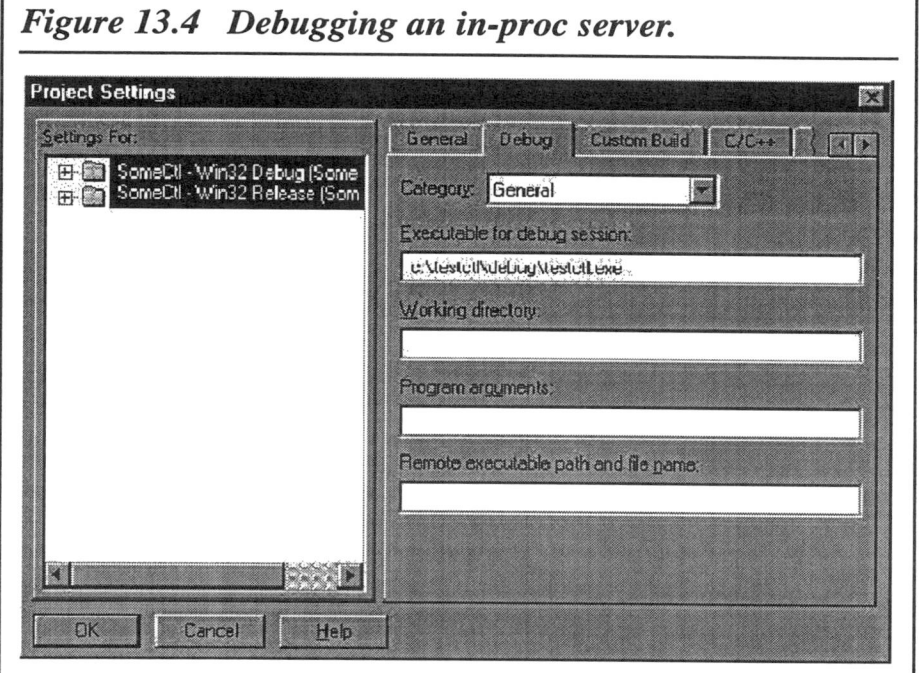

Debugging ActiveX Out-of-proc Objects — Method One

Here's how to go about debugging a COM object that resides in another process space.

- Load the project with the offending COM object in the IDE.
- Pull down the "Build|Settings" menu and select the Debug tab. The dialog box should look something like this one shown in Figure 13.5:
- Type either `/Automation` or `/Embedding` in the Program arguments field. If the out-of-proc server is in a well-behaved server, it will check the command line for either of those command line switches. If one of the switches is present, the application should just start up and run its regular message loop without displaying a window.
- Set your breakpoints and hit F5 in the object server.
- Load the client application in another session of VC++ and run it. The debugger will stop at the offending line of code inside the out-of-proc server and you'll be able to effectively debug the COM object.

Figure 13.5   Debugging a COM object.

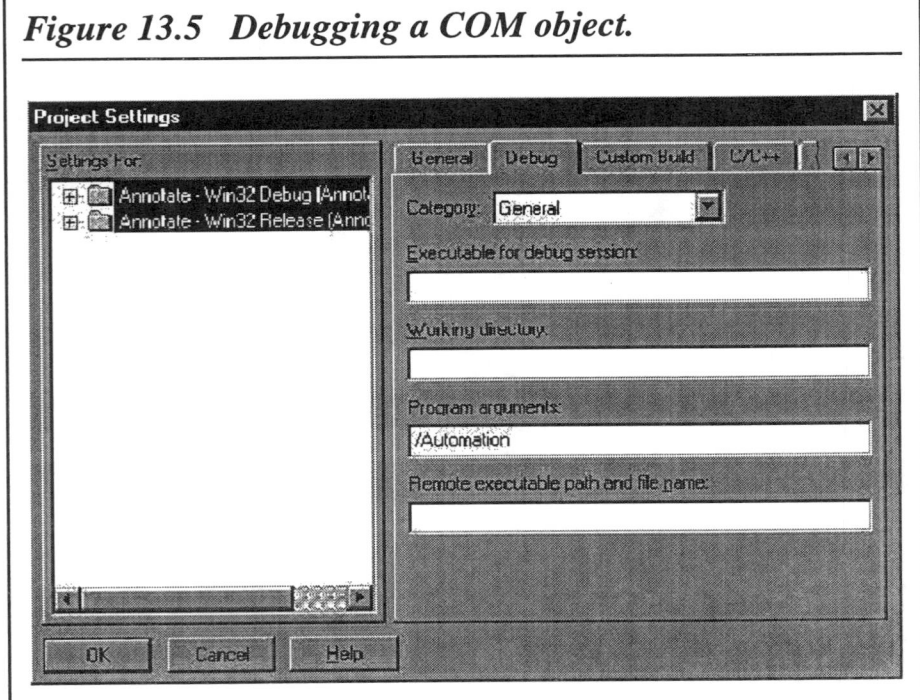

By doing this, you set the object server to just sit around waiting for things to happen. If there's a problem, the debugger running the object code will stop and you'll be able to see the offending code. Of course, this works only for applications that check the command line.

Debugging ActiveX Out-of-proc Objects — Method Two

The other way to debug out-of-proc objects is to simply step into the code. Here's what you do. Fire up the client application in the debugger. When you get to an ActiveX interface call, press the F11 key. Another copy of Visual C++ will come up and land on the corresponding line in the object code. This method is useful for apps that don't check the command line.

Conclusion

Debugging COM-based application isn't really a whole lot more difficult than debugging regular applications. However, there are a few differences involved. For example, the clear separation of client and object code enforces a binary firewall between the two. You've gotta follow the rule of accessing an object strictly through one of its interfaces. In addition, COM's reference-counting mechanism leaves an opportunity for various bugs to crop in. However, now you know that if you use the nested class approach to writing COM classes, you can find out exactly which interfaces are manipulating the COM object's reference counter. Finally, there are a couple of techniques you can use with the debugger to switch between the client module and the object module. Once you get past these barriers, debugging is pretty standard. Do the regular things like checking your pointers before accessing them. The error codes returned by an object are there for a reason. Use them. And happy debugging — keep those programs running smoothly!

Chapter 14

Caterpillar's Fate

*A Pattern Language for Transformation
from Analysis to Design*

Norman L. Kerth

Abstract

Caterpillar's Fate is a pattern language used to support the transformation from fine analysis documents to an initial software design. Just as the concept metamorphosis is used to explain the magical emergence of butterflies, Caterpillar's Fate explores the magic of constructing a system of objects from an object-free analysis.

Introduction

Caterpillar's Fate is an odd name for a software engineering activity. Nevertheless, the name is a most accurate description of the role that this pattern language plays in the software lifecycle. A caterpillar's fate is metamorphosis — the seemingly magical transformation from a sedentary creature to an aerial one. The Caterpillar's Fate pattern language is used to guide the transformation of a system from the analysis stage into the design stage — which has also been viewed by many as a magical transformation.

The structured methodologies of the past suffered during this metamorphosis between analysis and design, I believe in part due to the lack of such a pattern language. I have watched several methodologists try to teach what they can do so easily, as they transition from analysis to design. To the uninitiated, it appears as if the methodologist is making it up on the spot. The reality is that the methodologist is using a great deal of acquired wisdom to aid in their transformation.

A pattern language approach provides an ideal solution to this transformation problem, as it is acquired wisdom that is contained within a pattern language.

Many of the popular object-oriented methodologies have skirted the transformation problem by introducing design issues into the analysis phase (e.g., identification of objects, class definition, and the recording of inheritance). This has put many large projects at risk because of the complexities involved with making design decisions while one is not sure of what the system-to-be-built actually does.

To avoid the risk of failure and the cost of rework, a pattern language like Caterpillar's Fate needed to be developed as part of a comprehensive methodology. This methodology consists of an analysis phase and a design phase. The analysis phase is free of any object bias, leaving the questions of where or how to use objects as a design question. The design phase takes on different design strategies (e.g., object-oriented, object-based, structured, filter-tools, algorithmic, or various hybrids) depending on a number of technical or nontechnical factors.

The object-free analysis phase consists of modeling activities that produce answers to the questions in Table 14.1. This methodology is discussed further in Kerth[1] and Kerth et al.[2]

The Caterpillar's Fate Pattern Language

Caterpillar's Fate captures acquired wisdom, mine and my clients', around developing design solutions from fine analysis models. It documents what I do during the transition. It addresses the popular question, "How do I find the objects?"

The format of Caterpillar's Fate is intentionally taken directly from Christopher Alexander's work.[3,4] Two deviations have been made: I have included a section on "Suggestions" to the designer and not every pattern has a "Sketch."

The suggestions seemed too important to ignore just to emulate Alexander.

Sketches do exist for each of these patterns, and I believe they are important. They were left out of an earlier version of this paper for page count reasons. I am in the process of adding the sketches; the timing is such that this version of the paper has only the most necessary sketches. An explanation of the sketch notation can be found in "The MOOD Notation" at the end of this chapter.

Alexander's sketches were never abstract, they always demonstrated the solution to some real problem. There are times I kept with that philosophy; at other times I moved into an abstract form. I'm still experimenting, and feedback is welcome.

So to begin with Caterpillar's Fate, I begin in the same manner as Alexander — at the top with the first three design decisions to be addressed:

When starting an architectural design from analysis documents, the issues of concurrency seem to be the ones to address first. The patterns addressing these issues are:

1. Concurrent Threads of Execution
2. Synchronization of Concurrent Threads
3. Collaborative Work Packets

Concurrent Threads of Execution

When a system contains processes that run either simultaneously or pseudo-simultaneously (a la operating-system-supported task switching), then careful planning is necessary (Figure 14.1).

The requirements documents often discuss function but rarely do the documents discuss exactly what functions will be available from which concurrent process. In fact such documents shouldn't mention how the functions are deployed, as it is a design decision.

Therefore: Identify the threads-of-execution that have the ability to exist independently from other threads that might exist in the system. In some cases, these threads will reside upon different machines, in other cases they will represent different "user's" each with their own agenda working upon the same machine. In this pattern the word "user" means "an entity, external from the system, requiring service of the system." In some cases a user may be a human, in other cases it may be a device or simply the passing of time.

Table 14.1   The object-free analysis stage.

Analysis Question Modeling	Technique
What information is important in the problem domain?	Information Modeling
How does this information change over time and what incidents cause it to change?	Entity State Modeling
Who are the users and what tasks do they turn to the system to get accomplished?	User Task List
For each user task what is the data flow?	User-Task-Partitioned Data Flow Diagrams
Exactly how does the human interface work?	Four Dimensional Human Interface Perspective

Suggestions: Name each thread, and write the purpose of each thread within a system of threads.

When the concurrent threads of execution have been identified, you can address the issues of *Synchronization of Concurrent Threads* (pattern 2) and *Collaborative Work Packets* (3) If your design has only one concurrent thread of execution, then you are ready to address *Shape of Program* (9).

Synchronization of Concurrent Threads

When the concurrent threads of execution have been identified, you are ready to identify the synchronization that needs to occur between concurrent threads.

Often in the execution of a concurrent thread, there are situations where a thread needs to stop processing or remain in a certain form of processing until another concurrent thread arrives at some well-understood state.

Figure 14.1   Concurrent threads of execution and synchronization.

Sketch:

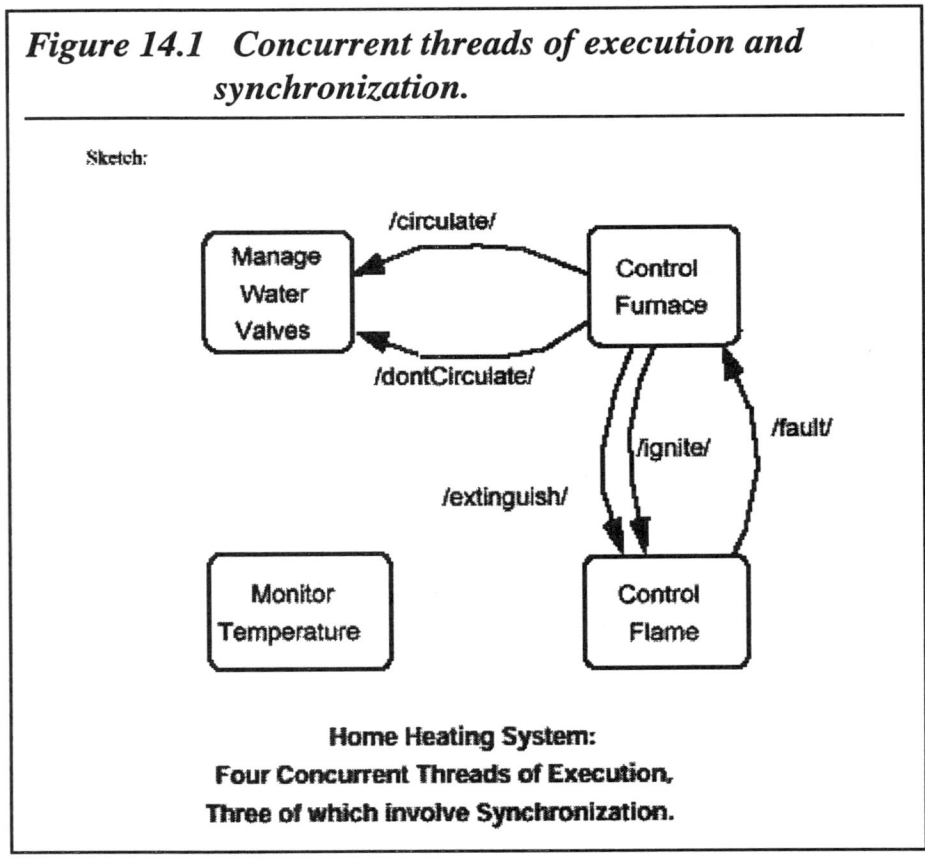

Home Heating System:
Four Concurrent Threads of Execution,
Three of which involve Synchronization.

Therefore: Review each concurrent thread of execution, throughout the life-cycle of its execution and identify those points where a signal is either to be sent to or received from another concurrent thread. Name the signal for the situation it represents, identifying both the sender and the receiver. In this pattern a signal carries no information; it either has arrived or it has not arrived.

Suggestions: If your system seems to have a great deal of synchronization, it demonstrates that the various threads have a great deal of interdependency. A great deal is determined by noting the amount of concentration needed to understand the purpose and interaction of each signal as part of the whole system. If the level of concentration begins to exceed some reviewers' patience, then the probability of creating defects increases as does the cost of enhancement. In such cases, return to the *Concurrent Threads of Execution* pattern (1) and change either the number of threads and/or their purpose in such a way that design decisions from the *Synchronization of Concurrent Treads* (2) pattern become easy to understand.

Now with a clear understanding about how concurrent threads synchronize with each other, you are ready to look at the *Shape of Program* (9) and *Critical Region Protection* (17).

Collaborative Work Packets

When you have a clear idea of what concurrent threads exist within your system, you are ready to look at the work packets that move between them.

Many systems contain the need for the processing of work to be split across processors, or defined and scheduled at one point in time to be accomplished at another point in time. An example of this is the transaction processing systems found in many business applications. In this pattern language, producers and consumers of work packets are the concurrent threads of execution. Over time, the producers and consumers may change. The nature of the work to be accomplished may change. As a result, it is important to design clear separation between the concurrent-threads-of-execution and the work passed between them.

Therefore: For each pair of concurrent threads, review the life-cycle of each thread and identify specific work to be initiated by one thread and continued by the second thread. Name the work packet for the information and work unit it manages or hides. For each work packet, identify the possible producer and consumer concurrent threads.

Suggestions: For each work packet you should be able to easily state what the work packet is responsible for. Usually the responsibility would read: "All that is known about a <fill in the blank>".

Once you have designed the work packets passed among the concurrent threads of execution, you are ready to design the *Work Packet Contents* (4), and also start the design of the *Shape of Program* (9).

Work packets, in some environments called "transactions" require some careful design. This design-like concurrency needs to be thought through early in the design as it represents a "big picture" perspective of how concurrent subsystems or concurrent-threads-of-execution will collaborate. Work packets have many details that need to be addressed early to avoid rework as the system design becomes apparent. The patterns in this section are:

4. Work Packet Contents
5. Work Packet Status Report
6. Work Packet Completion Report
7. Work Packet Priority
8. Work Packet Security

Work Packet Contents

Once a *Collaborative Work Packet* (3) has been discovered, named, responsibility recorded and each of the producing and consuming *Concurrent Threads of Execution* (1) have been identified, you are ready to design the internal contents of a work packet.

Work packets contain information and directions for a number of uses within a system. The internal design of a work packet is likely to become a mess if not conscientiously designed.

Therefore: For each work packet, develop a design which contains all the information necessary for the work to be accomplished. Such information includes: data, state, statement-of-need, and history. Data is used for specific processing. State contains information related to the present situation or condition that the work packet is in. A statement-of-need asks the consumer thread to help with some particular goal to be accomplished. History includes information related to the past experiences of the work packet, often including references to the concurrent threads that it has visited in the past (see "Data Knows Its Roots").

If *Work Packet Status Report* (5) or *Work Packet Completion Report* (6) are patterns of value to this design, then the work packet will also need to contain an identifier or name. As the patterns *Work Packet Priority* (7) and *Work Packet Security* (8) are addressed, they may have an impact on the contents as well.

To assure minimum impact to a work packet when either a producer or consumer changes, the work packet must never contain information related to its future — i.e., it never tells the consumer how to go about processing. A consumer needs to be able to determine the kind of processing by querying about data, state, need, and history. For example, an SQL phrase is a statement-of-need. The actual processing is left up to the consumer. On the other hand, directions to perform a particular function and then pass the work packet on to yet another consumer is an attempt at controlling the future.

Suggestions: Work packet design follows from the analysis documents. The data within a work packet can be determined by inspecting the information model developed in the analysis phase. State information can be deduced by looking at the entity state model. History is not likely to be found in the analysis documents, as it is dependent on the design decisions such as concurrent threads.

If a work packet begins to seem large, study the work packet for variation. If there are a number of kinds of a work packet, consider a design using subtypes of work packets if that would reduce the amount of data, state, or history that needs to be included.

Where several different kinds of work packets are likely to travel to the same consumer for processing, where the processing is different depending upon the packet, develop a design where the differences in processing are contained within the work packet. A good test for such situations is to note if a work packet must answer questions about what type it is — if so, consider a different design.

As work packets become defined, several other design decisions need to be addressed:*Work Packet Status Report* (5),*Work Packet Completion Report* (6), *Work Packet Priority* (7), *Work Packet Security* (8), and *Data Knows Its Roots* (21). With the identification of specific work packets along with their producers and consumers, you are ready to address the *Shape of Program* (9).

Work Packet Status Report

When you have made your design decisions around *Collaborative Work Packets* (3), and *Work Packet Contents* (4), you have enough knowledge to know if some report on the status of the work packet needs to be generated for the benefit of the producer.

In some designs, a producer concurrent-thread-of-execution generates work packets, ships them to the consumer thread and no longer has any interest in that work packet. For such situations this pattern has no value.

In other designs, the producer, often at the request of the user will want to monitor the status of the work packet. So the questions of what status information needs to be returned to the producer, what stimuli causes the report to be returned, what role does the work packet play, and what role does the consumer concurrent-thread-of-execution play. These are the design decisions that need to be addressed at this point in the design.

Therefore: Assess the needs identified in your analysis and make the design decisions on the following questions:

1. When is the report sent? Here are some possibilities:

   • only upon request by the producer;

   • every time the status within the work packet changes;

   • when processing within the consumer achieves a particular goal; or

   • with the elapse of some unit of time.

2. What information should be in the report? Does the work packet require an identifier? Does the identifier need to be unique? Does a combination of pieces of information make a unique work packet identifier (such as user name and time sent)?

What status information is part of the report? What data information? What history information? Is the report tailorable?

3. Is the desire for the report known at the time the work packet is passed to the consumer? If so, then design the work packet to be responsible for producing the report back to the producer, as it contains the knowledge of its producer.

    If the desire for the report occurs some time after transmission of the work packet, then choose a design where the consumer is responsible for producing the report. Such a report is not on one particular work packet but is a summary of all work packets within its control and knowledge.

4. Determine the needs for security around status reporting. Can a concurrent-thread-of-execution request or automatically receive a status report on work packets generated by some other concurrent-thread? Is this request available on a privileged basis? Is it password protected? Does the status report need to be encrypted?

Decide whether the work packet or the consumer has the prime responsibility to produce and send the report. Then determine what support is required from the other. Design a mechanism for communicating between concurrent-threads-of-execution to support your answers to these design questions.

Suggestions: Keep the work packet status report design as simple as possible! Do not put any extra "bells and whistles" in this part of your design. Your system needs to produce status reports, but its prime goal is not about producing these reports, it is about processing work packets in some way. Focus your design creativity there!

When these design decision have been made, you have a clear idea around the design of work packets. Assure that the specific *Shape of Program* (9) addresses the receipt of every status report identified.

Work Packet Completion Report

When you have made your design decisions around *Collaborative Work Packets* (3), *Work Packet Contents* (4), *Synchronization of Concurrent Threads* (2), you are ready to make the design decisions around what happens when a work packet completes its processing within the consumer concurrent-thread-of-execution.

Upon completion of the processing of a work packet, there are many different possible design responses. These responses need to be considered now.

Therefore: Assess the needs identified in your analysis and make the design decisions on the following questions:

1. What gets returned? Is it a success/fail message? Is it an answer to the question contained within the work packet? Is it the work packet itself where data, state and/or history has changed?

2. If a failure report is returned, how much is communicated about the failure? In some situations, you will want to communicate:

   • What the nature of the error was, and

   • suggestions of what should be done differently.

   However, there are some systems that have a security requirement that will be breached if details of the nature of the failure are shared with the producer thread.

3. For purposes of security, does the response need to be encrypted? Does it need password protection?

4. Design the policy on how to deal with responses if the producer concurrent-thread-of-execution is not available at the point in time that the response is ready to be sent. This may occur in distributed systems because the network goes down, or the producing computer goes off-line, or for a number of other reasons. It is possible that the producer, requesting a response, will leave the system forever. How will this situation be handled?

Suggestions: The suggestions offered in *Work Packet Status Report* (5) apply here too. Keep the completion report simple and concise.

When these design decision have been made, you have a clear idea around the design of work packets. Assure that the specific *Shape of Program* (9) addresses the receipt of every completion report identified.

Work Packet Priority

Once you develop the design for *Collaborative Work Packets* (3) and while transforming the general *Shape of Program* (9) to a specific one, you need to make decisions about the order in which work packets are consumed.

In some systems, work packets are queued for processing, either at a later time, when a consumer's processing resource is available or cheaper, or because there are peak times when work packet arrival exceeds the processing capacity. When there is more than one work packet waiting for processing, there are design decisions to be made around which work packet to select.

Therefore: Select a policy on how the next work packet is selected. In most analysis documents this is something that has been overlooked. In such cases, "first-come-first-served" might be all that is needed. However, there may be requirements hidden in the form of general performance statements that may not be easy to find. Review the documents with the following options for selection in mind:

1. First-come-first-served.

2. Assigned priority. Work packet type may contain a priority or it might be a privilege priority associated with the producer that created the work packet.

3. Deadline oriented. Each work packet has a deadline for completion and work is accepted in a manner that the fewest deadlines are missed.

4. Cost–penalty analysis. Each work packet has not only a deadline but also an associated cost for missing the deadline. Selection is based on minimizing the penalties.

These are basic design issues. It is possible that your system may need a combination of these approaches or may create a different selection policy. What is important that the policy for selection is consciously made and designed into the consumer's specific *Shape of Program* (9). Depending on the policy selected, *Work Packet Contents* (4) may need to be revisited to support the selection policy (i.e., it may contain a priority, or deadline).

Suggestions: Keep the selection system as simple as possible. Be prepared for any kind of change that may be suggested by adding no "hooks" into the system now for possible future expansion and do not accept any assumptions or short cuts that will prevent future growth.

"No hooks" is important because the future may not play out in the manner that you visualize it at this point in time. On the other hand, if it does come to pass, the hooks are not likely to be as well-tested as today's working code, leading to suspicion; plus any maintenance that may have occurred is not likely to have respected the unused hooks.

This "no-hooks" suggestion does not only apply to this pattern but throughout the design process. This was the first place the advice was likely to be important. It will not be repeated throughout the this pattern language, though it is tempting.

When these design decisions have been made, you have a clear idea around the design of work packets. Assure that the consumer's specific *Shape of Program* (9) addresses selection design decision and that the producer's *Shape of Program* (9) and/or *Work Packet Contents* (4) are refined as needed.

Work Packet Security

Once *Work Packet Contents* (4) and *Collaborative Work Packets* (3) have been addressed, you are ready to look at questions of security related to work packets.

When work packets can be constructed upon one machine and sent through a network to another machine, and the work packet contains sensitive information or work directives, then there are several security issues that need to be designed into work packets as well as the producer and consumer.

Therefore: Consider the following design issues:

- Does the information within the packet need to be encrypted? The answer is based upon the question of "would someone benefit from accessing the work packet being passed?", not "is it possible to access that information, given our hardware and configuration?". While you may believe that you have a secure network there is no assurance that is true now and in the future, as your configuration changes.

- In systems where some producers of work packets have privileges that others don't, either in information access or functionally permitted, design the prevention of inappropriate function or information access into the producer, for human interface reasons, and design the security checks to occur within the consumer. The work packet will need to carry the information necessary for the consumer to perform the security check.

- In some systems, aspects of security are performed by the regular review of the work packets consumed looking for anomalies. In other forms of security, an audit trail is used to understand what has happened. If either of these needs appear in the requirements, then develop a design for logging the necessary information and activity.

Suggestions: Security is usually left unaddressed or at best vaguely mentioned in most requirement and analysis documents. Most likely, you will find high security wishful thinking with little understanding of the depth of the issues or the cost. If this is the case and security is crucial, then stop all design activities, return to analysis, and develop effective security models.

At this point, you have addressed a few security-related issues; encryption, passwording, and logging are issues that have surfaced. As this pattern language matures, there are many more patterns that need to be discussed.

In this section we begin to look at the early design issues that occur around one program. This includes the early decisions you need to make in regards to the shape of the program, how stimuli will be acquired and responded to, and how a human interface is added to this program shape in such a way that the human interface may be replaced without impact to the rest of the system. This section also includes a pattern that revisits the concurrency questions to discover critical regions. The patterns in this section are:

9. Shape of Program
10. Systems Citizen Role
11. Decision Makers Role
12. Workers Role
13. Interface Role
14. Informational Role
15. Small Family Systems
16. Work Accomplished Through Dialogs
17. Critical Region Protection
18. Event Acquisition
19. Event Routing
20. Human Interface Role is a Special Interface Role

Shape of Program

Once you have a clear idea of the *Concurrent Threads of Execution* (1) within your system, the *Synchronization of Concurrent Threads* (2) across your system, and have itemized the *Collaborative Work Packets* (3), you are ready to apply specific form to a general shape of a program. For systems with only one *Concurrent Thread of Execution* (1) this will be the first pattern considered.

At the early stages of transforming requirements documents into a software design, we have many issues to consider — usually too many to keep in our heads at one time. As a result, it is easy to focus on optimizing design issues for the small part of the system that we have in focus at the moment to the peril of the "big picture" design.

Therefore: Accept a "typical big picture design" until it does not serve you (see "Small Family Systems" and "Work Accomplished Through Dialogs"). This pattern offers a typical shape of a program. While there are many possible shapes, this one seems to work well as a starting point on all the systems with which I have been involved.

The shape of this program is best described as tiered. On each tier, the objects have the ability to call for service upon design components on lower tiers or on the same tier but not on higher tiers.

The first tier contains objects whose responsibility it is to assure that this *Concurrent Thread of Execution* (1) is a good citizen within a community of concurrent threads each working towards their own agenda (see "Systems Citizen Role").

The second tier contains objects that are responsible for the decision making aspects of the system to be built (see "Decision Makers Role").

The third tier contains objects that perform work needed by the system (see "Workers Role").

The fourth tier contains objects that are responsible for hiding the interface to some external entity (see "Interface Role").

For this tiered system to work, there is a type of object that moves through the tiered systems, visiting the other objects. This moving object has the responsibility of providing the appropriate information as well as tailored functionality. Those familiar with object-oriented thinking will refer to these objects as polymorphic; it is the object that is passed as a parameter (see "Informational Role").

The design decisions made during the use of this pattern transform the general shape of program to a specific one that supports the findings in the analysis documents. To accomplish this transformation, you will find it useful to consider the following patterns while accepting the tiered shape of programs: *Systems Citizen Role* (10), *Decision Makers Role* (11), *Workers Role* (12), *Interface Role* (13), and the *Informational Role* (14). When the tiered shape begins to fail, consider *Small Family Systems* (15) and *Work Accomplished Through Dialogs* (16). As you begin to consider the issues around how mouse clicks, key strokes, and the like are handled, you will find *Event Acquisition* (18) and *Event Routing* (19) useful.

Suggestions: Within a tier, services between objects might be called upon, but this should be kept to a minimum. The reason varies depending on the tier. Generally, as the interactions between tier peers grow, the reuse of either without the other decreases. This is particularly true for interface objects and worker objects.

Decision-making objects contain knowledge of a particular application so they are not likely to be reused, so reuse is not an explanation. Interaction between decision makers requires maintenance engineers to master the operations of both decision makers before either one can be changed. Within limits this works, but taken to an extreme causes real problems. When confronted with such situations, revisit the analysis and design decisions that defined the boundaries and responsibilities of these two kinds of objects.

Four tiers may not seem sufficient for large systems. In some cases, I have seen a shape of program structure used recursively within one of the object roles described here, most often for decision maker objects and worker objects. I have also seen the internal working of some of these objects take on the form of a *Small Family System* (15).

When the general shape of program has been transformed into a specific shape for your system, assure that every signal identified in *Synchronization of Concurrent Threads* (2) and every work packet identified in *Collaborative Work Packets* (3) is accounted for.

With the general tier shape transformed to a specific one reflecting the findings of the analysis documents, you are ready to refine the system for various measures of goodness, performance, and other factors beyond the scope of this early architectural pattern language.

Systems Citizen Role

When there is a clear idea of a *Concurrent Thread of Execution* (1) and the *Shape of Program* (9) begins to take shape from the general to the specific, you are ready to look creating a single systems citizen object.

Most programs reside on platforms where there are likely to be several applications running at the same time (e.g., Mac OS 7.X, OS/2, Windows 3.X, etc.). In these environments there are expectations that the operating environment has for each application running. Each of these environments have their own way of operating. There are likely business reasons to design an application that can be moved from platform to platform with ease.

Therefore: Design a single object that is responsible for knowing the protocol that applications must follow to be "good citizens" within a community of applications. As you consider how the particular operating environment handles issues around mouse clicks, key strokes and the like, you will find *Event Acquisition* (18) and *Event Routing* (19) useful.

Suggestions: The information about the responsibilities of a systems citizen are not found in the analysis documents. They are usually found in a programmer's reference manual or tutorial manual for the operating environment chosen.

Some reviewers have commented that a "single object" with all this knowledge might be quite large. I picture the system citizen object's internal design composed of many objects. The design goal is to localize knowledge of a platform's expectation of application behavior hidden within a single unit.

With this pattern mastered, you are in a good position to understand how *Decision Makers Role* (11) and *Human Interface Role is a Special kind of Interface Role* (20).

Decision Makers Role

When the *Shape of Program* (9) begins to take shape from the general to the specific, and the *Systems Citizen Role* (10) becomes defined, you are ready to design the high level policy making aspects of your application.

Most "real life" systems have some interesting design issues around controlling the overall operation of an application. These issues include the fundamental behavior of your application — the work flow, the control, the highest level decision making about the behavior of your application. Often it is these decisions that your customers will use to differentiate your application from your competitors.

If these controlling issues are not respected as interesting in their own right, then the policy/decision-making activities are likely to be distributed across a number of objects. This creates significant difficulties for the maintenance activities. Distributed policy/decision making requires a maintenance engineer to master the workings of a large number of objects before any changes to policy/decision making can occur.

Therefore: Create an object or a number of objects whose prime role is to be responsible for the decision-making activities of your application. In other words, separate the policy-making activities from the mechanisms that carry out the policy.

Suggestions: Decision-making objects look funny. They often have only one external method — doIt. Nevertheless they are key to building systems that are maintainable and reusable. The reusable component comes from placing all that is not likely to be reused (i.e., the policy/decision-making aspects of this application) in one or a number of objects that are not likely to be reused. Decision-making objects are not reused because they are application-specific, unless the application reused involves porting the same application to another environment.

Input for the policy/decision-making object is usually found in the process specification and is what remains when all the lower-level operations can be allocated to worker objects (12), informational objects (14), and interface objects (13).

At this point you have a clear idea of how your application will control the work to be accomplished. You are ready to connect the *Workers Role* (12) objects, the *Interface Role* (13) objects, and the *Human Interface Role is a Special Interface Role* (20) object. It is quite likely that the decision maker will handle a number of *Informational Role* (14) objects, as they are passed among the worker objects and interface objects.

Workers Role

When the *Shape of Program* (9) begins to take shape from the general to the specific, you are ready to design the objects that do work towards helping the application move closer to its goal.

Within many programs there are design decisions that can be combined together to provide a number of related services that help an application move closer to its goal.

Therefore: Build specific objects with the responsibility to do work that the decision makers would find useful in exercising the policy/decision-making responsibilities. Collections are a common kind of worker object.

Suggestions: The number one goal of a worker object is to off-load any work from decision makers that is not directly involved with controlling the application. A secondary goal is to build worker objects that are likely to be reused in similar but different applications.

Worker objects are usually easy to find from an Event-Partitioned Data Flow Diagram. They are often data stores, or are hidden within data stores. The process specifications are used to confirm that they are worker objects and to identify the methods.

When you have identified the worker objects, you are ready to look to the internal design of these objects, comfortable that the big picture will fit with the small picture that now becomes of interest to the designers.

Interface Role

When the *Shape of Program* (9) begins to take shape from the general to the specific, you are ready to design the objects that hide the specific behavior of entities that are not part of your system.

Systems are not built in isolation, they interface with something else — it might be hardware devices, or software not under the control of the designers. Regardless, since it is not under the control of this system design, these external entities may change their behavior.

Therefore: To protect your system-to-be-built, hide the external entity's behavior within an object whose responsibility it is to provide high-level abstract services to the rest of your system.

Suggestions: Interface objects can be found from the Event-Partitioned Data Flow Diagrams; they are usually the external entities. The abstract services can be determined by looking at the process specifications.

When you have identified the interface objects, you are ready to look to the internal design of these objects, comfortable that the big picture will fit with the small picture that now becomes of interest to the designers. There is a special kind of interface object that hides the human interface from the decision-maker objects (see "Human Interface Role is a Special Interface Role").

Informational Role

When the *Shape of Program* (9) begins to take shape from the general to the specific, you are ready to design the objects that move through the system, visiting the interface objects and worker objects at the direction of the decision-making objects.

We have seen a great deal of value from the use of polymorphism. The *Shape of Program* (9) structures a number of objects into a rigid tiered system, similar to the old structured design style of thinking. There were some advantages to such a structure, but polymorphism was not possible. The closest the structured methods could come was to pass complex data structures known as 'tramp data'. This was considered not the best of designs, as the knowledge of the structure of the data was spread across an application. Object-oriented thinking gave us a way to solve this problem by passing objects.

Therefore: Create objects whose responsibility is to deliver specific information at the appropriate places within an application, without letting the structure of the information become known. These are known as informational objects.

Suggestions: Wherever you discover the design needs to ask an informational object what its type is to resolve a number of IF statements, SWITCH statement, etc., stop and look for a way to put the type-related work within the informational object.

Informational objects are found by noting how information flows on an Event-Partitioned Data Flow Diagram. Solid meaningful pieces of information that flow from or to *Interface Role* (13) objects and that have some interesting processing associated noted in the process specifications suggest informational objects. This is especially true if you discover that the data dictionary suggests that there are a number of types or variations on this information.

Smalltalk experts will recognize the similarities between informational objects and the model component of the model-view-controller triad. This is discussed further in *Human Interface Role is a Special Interface Role* (20).

When you have identified the informational objects, you are ready to look to the internal design of these objects, comfortable that the big picture will fit with the small picture that now becomes of interest to the designers.

Small Family Systems

When the *Shape of Program* (9) begins to take shape from the general to the specific, you will encounter times when a tiered system creates awkward designs. In such cases, you do not discard *Shape of Program* (9) but just augment it with another 'mini-shape' for the portions of the system that you are considering. Often the internal design that comes from *Human Interface Role is a Special Interface Role* (20) is benefited by this pattern.

In particular, you will find that there are design segments that are well served by building a small number of objects that work well together as a team. The key feature that makes this design segment unique is that in this 'small family' of objects, no one object takes on the control responsibilities for the others (Figure 14.2).

Therefore: Design the small family as a family but make sure it is a 'healthy family'. In a healthy family, each object has a distinct responsibility, easily differentiated from any of the other family members. For each service provided by this family to the system, there is one object that takes the control responsibility and calls on the other objects for help in accomplishing this goal. The classic Model-View-Controller is an example of a small family system.

Assure that the boundaries of responsibilities among a family are never violated. When a boundary of responsibility is violated, it creates a situation where it is not clear which object is responsible for accomplishing a given activity. In such cases, a maintenance effort is likely to get it wrong, causing some activity to be performed twice or causing an activity to not be performed at all.

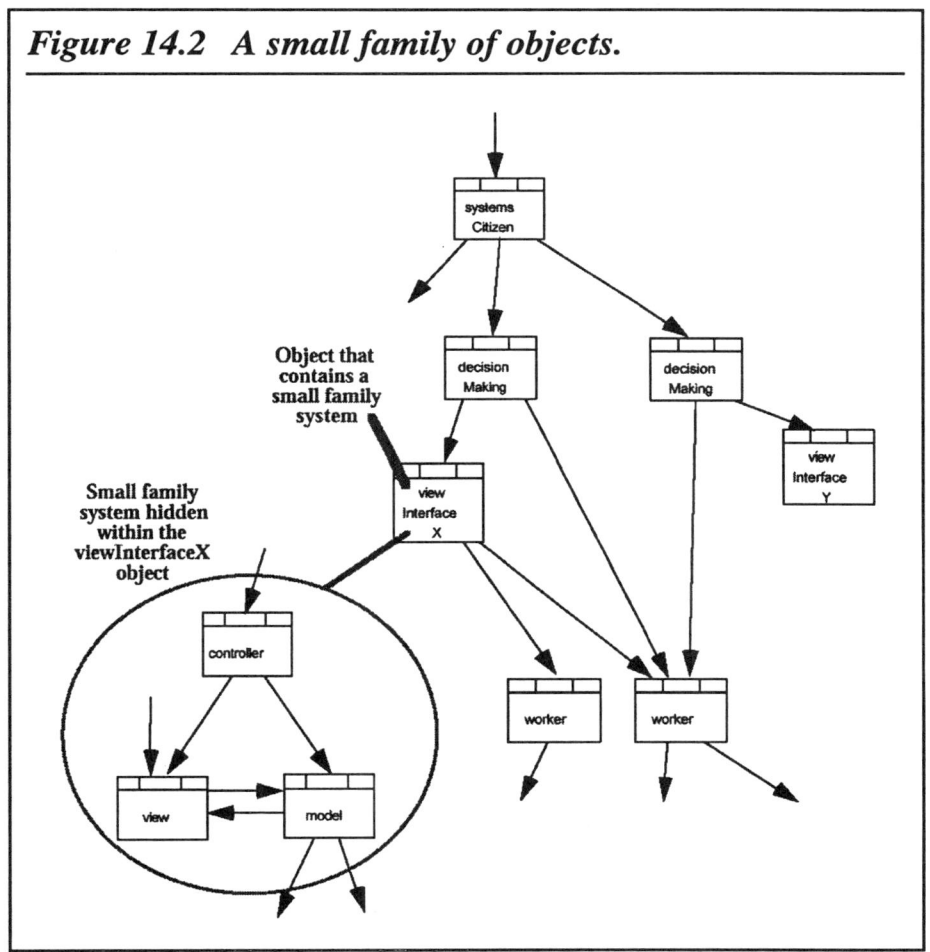

Figure 14.2   A small family of objects.

Depending on your language and operating environment, you may not be able to implement it in this manner. From a design perspective, think of the small family of objects as a single object when placed within the tiered structure of *Shape of Program* (9).

Suggestions: Small family systems are composed of a few kinds of objects — two, three, or rarely four kinds objects — is a good guideline. I have never seen more than four kinds of objects work well as a small family.

Small families are usually not identifiable from the analysis documents; they are usually created to solve a situation that either supports simultaneously a number of design goals or to simplify an awkward structure developing in the tiered structure. They are clever inventions often adapted from one's previous experiences.

Small family systems were chosen as a secondary design strategy after tiered systems because of the amount of effort a maintenance engineer needs to apply to master how the family works. Use this 'effort to master' measure to guide your design decisions and documentation plans.

When you have identified the need for a small family system, you may be ready to look to the internal design of these objects, comfortable that the big picture will fit with the small picture that now becomes of interest to the designers.

Work Accomplished Through Dialogs

As the *Shape of Program* (9) evolves from the general to the specific, you will encounter times when two objects need to invoke methods in each other to get their job done (Figure 14.3). In such cases, you do not discard the *Shape of Program* (9) tier structure, but just augment it with a design decision to allow some objects to call methods in each other.

There are situations where the required work to be accomplished by the system involves the blending of two objects' responsibilities. Neither object contains all of the information or processing ability to achieve the requirements. Combining the two objects does not seem to be a wise idea, each of the responsibilities seems to be well-formulated, and there does not seem to be an undiscovered decision-maker object to control the interactions between these objects.

Therefore: Choose a design where the two objects carry on a dialog with each other. The first object invokes a method in the second object that in processing, calls a method in the first. It is this second object that initiates a dialog with the first object, otherwise we just have a tier connection.

Suggestions: A dialog between two objects is easily understood in moderation.

Between two objects, if the method that is invoked on the dialog (i.e., when the second object calls the first) is one of a questioning nature, then it will be easily understood. Questioning nature is a kind of method whose sole purpose is to provide information or answers that help the second object further its work.

The counter to questioning nature is controlling nature. A method with controlling nature changes the state of the first object and, in the worst case, causes the first object to interact with still more objects in a controlling manner. The deep implications of a controlling nature dialog is hard to comprehend. Reviewers and maintenance engineers are likely to miss subtle implications. Avoid controlling nature dialogs!

A dialog that involves more than two objects is called a chain-letter dialog and is to be avoided at all costs. Picture a design where the first object sends a message to a second object. The second object calls a method in the third and eventually the Nth object asks the first object for some information. In such a case, there is a dependency involving all N objects. No maintenance change can be made to any one object until all N objects have been considered. This violates all that we have learned about information hiding and separation of concerns. Never carry on a chain-letter dialog.

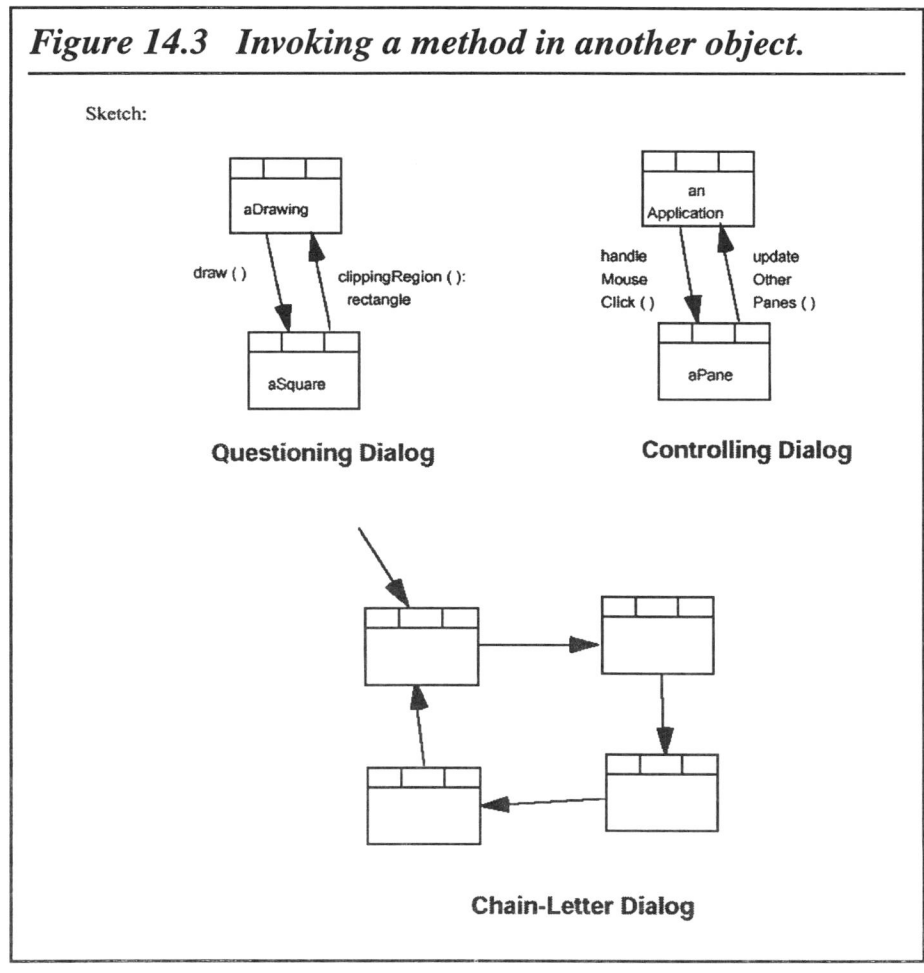

Figure 14.3   Invoking a method in another object.

With the judicious use of questioning nature dialogs to refine the *Shape of Program* (9) design, you can return to the transformation of the shape from general to specific.

Critical Region Protection

When *Concurrent Threads of Execution* (1) have been identified and, for each of those threads, the *Shape of Program* (9) has moved from general to specific, you are ready to look for the potential critical region problems.

Concurrent systems often use the same resources (Figure 14.4), usually in the form of interface objects (13), informational objects (14), or worker objects (15). Occasionally they will share decision-making objects (11). If two concurrent-threads-of-execution access the same object at the same point in time there is the possibility that they will cause harm. This harm might affect the shared object, the work being performed for the other concurrent-thread, or in rare cases the invoking concurrent-thread's own work.

Therefore: For each concurrent thread, review the specific shape of program and identify the shared objects. For each shared object determine if protection from simultaneous access is needed. If so, develop a protection mechanism that assures safe use.

Suggestions: There are several design solutions to this problem and they can be reviewed in any operating systems text. Some solutions include: blocking the second thread upon entry to the critical region; requiring each thread to get permission before entering the critical region; aborting a low priority thread's work when a high priority thread enters the critical region; or removing the critical region by giving each thread its own data memory space.

When this pattern has been addressed, you can be sure that the most difficult defects to discover have been prevented.

Event Acquisition

When the *Shape of Program* (9) begins to take shape from the general to the specific, and the *Systems Citizen Role* (10) is being considered, this pattern will help resolve some design options.

Every platform deals with events in their own unique way. An event being the signal that indicates a mouse click, a keystroke, or the like has occurred. Some operating environments provide a great deal of support, where others leave the responsibility more heavily to the system designer. Nevertheless, the shape of program needs to be tailored to accommodate a consistent design well thought through.

Therefore: Review the event acquisition capabilities provided to designers. Choose capabilities that makes sense for your application and refine the shape of program. Key design questions to consider include:

- Exactly how is an event acquired? Does the operating environment notice the event, acquire it, and decode it? Or is some or all of that activity left for your design? Are any events treated as unique or handled in a different manner? Are there options where event acquisition provided by the operating environment can be overridden? When would you want to do this?

- What operating environment capabilities do you want to accept? How does that impact the shape of program (9)? Are these capabilities able to be contained within the systems citizen object (10)? If not, what consequences does that imply for movement of the application to a different platform?

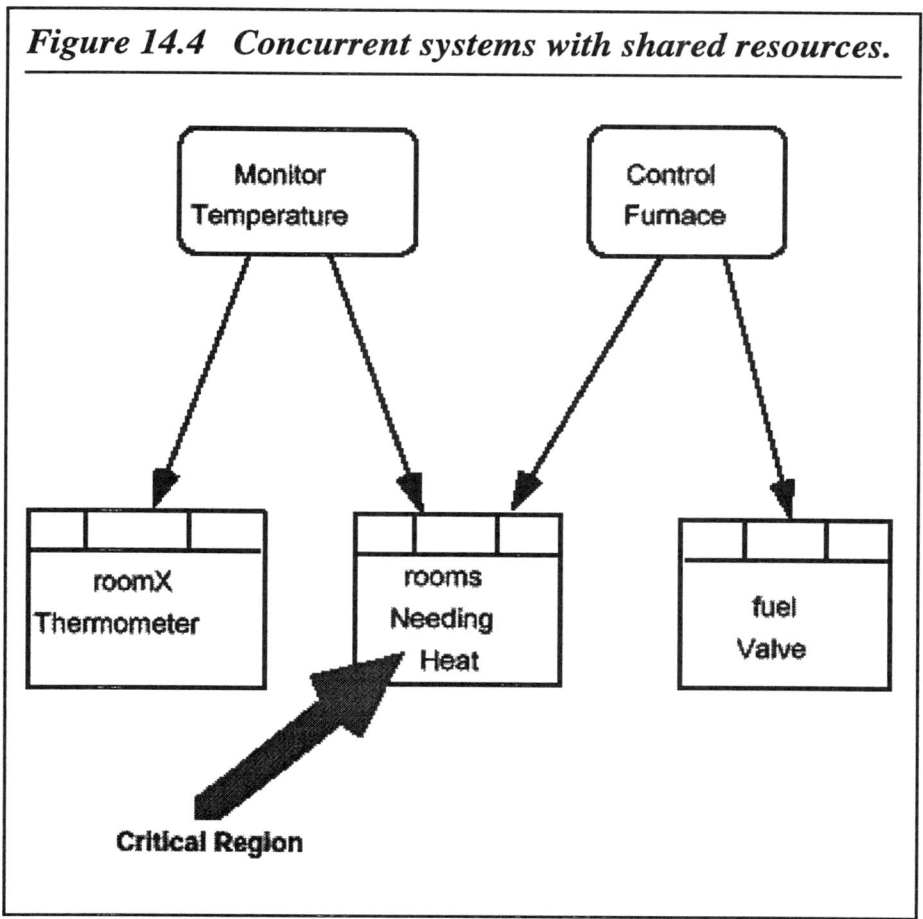

Figure 14.4 Concurrent systems with shared resources.

- When do you provide your own event acquisition design? How does that impact the shape of program (9)? An example might be when the silhouette of a graphic is being dragged across a canvas. For what reasons will you accept not using the platform's supported event acquisition mechanism (e.g., performance, or function not supported).

- Are hardware interrupts supported by the operating environment? Is there a particular design that the operating environment expects from your 'hardware driver'? How does shape of program need to be modified to support these design decisions?

- Does the operating environment support the notion of an 'event consuming object' registering for particular events? If so, then how does shape of program change to take advantage of such a powerful capability? Document when will you not use the registration capability?

Suggestions: If this is the first time you have designed an application for this particular operating environment then sketch a number of variations on shape of program, have them reviewed by a team, and build a number of prototypes. Evaluate each prototype for its advantages and disadvantages. Document your findings for others to follow and for you to review as you work beyond your learning curve.

When you have addressed this pattern, you will have refined *Shape of Program* (9) to better meet your design needs. Return to *Shape of Program* (9) and continue to transform the general shape to a specific one. In the future, patterns that address how systems can be tailored during initialization will be referenced from here.

Event Routing

When the *Shape of Program* (9) begins to take shape from the general to the specific, and the *Systems Citizen Role* (10) is being considered, this pattern along with *Event Acquisition* (18) will help resolve some design options.

Every platform deals with events in their own unique way — an event being the signal that a mouse click, a keystroke, or the like has occurred. When these events occur, there are a number of different approaches to assuring that the event is received and acted upon by all objects that should respond.

Therefore: Refine the shape of program to show how events will be consumed. You have several design decisions to consider:

- Is each event to be routed to only one object or are there likely to be a number objects that want to be informed when the same event occurs?

- How is the routing handled? Is it hardwired as we might find in an interrupt handler? Is there a negotiation activity where event consuming objects (usually decision makers or human interface objects) will answer if they recognize/are interested in a particular event when it arrives? Is registration the right design for your application? (Registration is a design idea where objects register for events with a dispatcher. When the event arrives, the dispatcher routes it to the object that registered for it.)

- Under what situations will you consider circumventing the operating environment's way of routing events?

Suggestions: Keep event routing as simple as possible. Dynamic registration of events, that is, registration that occurs continuously throughout the life of a system, yields a system that is impossible to understand by reading the code. A maintenance engineer will have to watch how events are continually registered and removed from a debugger. In such situations you never know if you have seen all the possible combinations.

When you have addressed this pattern, you will have refined *Shape of Program* (9) to better meet your design needs. Return to *Shape of Program* (9) and continue to transform the general shape to a specific one. In the future, patterns that address how systems can be tailored during initialization will be referenced from here.

Human Interface Role is a Special Interface Role

As you transition *Shape of Program* (9) from a general form to a specific design, you will be putting care into how the decision maker objects (11) get direction from humans. At that point, this pattern should be considered.

The human interface is key to providing information and direction to an application. It is found in numerous places throughout an application (Figure 14.5, page 233). Another factor to consider is how difficult it is to port a system from one platform to another if the human interface has been allowed to pervade the system in an unplanned fashion. As a result, the shape of program needs to be refined to include a human interface component that is isolated from significant portions of the system-to-be-built.

Therefore: Create a special kind of interface object (13) that hides the human interface specific design decisions. The decision-maker (11) objects are the most likely to need input from the human. Refine the shape of program to include human interface objects accessed by the decision-maker objects. The human interface objects deals with the human interface/platform specific issues and leaves the more abstract decision making and control of processing up to the decision-maker object.

Worker objects and interface objects may also need the same kind of special human interface object to support their lower-level work. This would appear in the form of dialog boxes and the like. Informational objects may also carry around a number of special human interface objects, each providing a unique view on the data in the informational object.

Suggestions: The behavior of human interface objects can be found in the details of the Four Dimensional Human Interface Perspective model. Deciding what is the responsibility of the human interface role object and what is the responsibility of the decision maker can be tricky. Develop several alternative designs and discuss them with a peer. Select between the designs by using the guiding principle "simplicity in explaining to someone else."

This pattern has helped you add human interface capabilities to your shape of program. You can return to *Shape of Program* (9) to further refine the general shape into a specific one.

You can also look at the internal design of the human interface object. You will discover that the *Small Family Systems* (15) pattern is quite applicable for the internal design. You will also discover that model-view-controller is a perfect small family system, and that the decision maker object will be passing the model as an informational object (14) into this human interface object. The actual behavior of the controller and view will be hidden within this human interface object. You will be able to follow the design decisions made about *Event Acquisition* (18) and *Event Routing* (19).

In this section we look to the patterns intended to handle the design of data. As this is a pattern language that is best described as "work in progress," this section has only one pattern at this moment. It needs to be expanded, but I did not want to leave this one pattern out given its importance. The pattern is:

21. Data Knows Its Roots

Data Knows Its Roots

When you have identified Collaborative Work Packets, Informational Role-oriented objects, or any other "entity" that contains information, you are ready to determine if "roots need to be known."

Good systems live for quite some time and over time change. Upgrades, added functionality, and addressing new markets are some of the reasons systems change. As new versions are released, it is crucial that "work-in-progress," no matter in what state, be as accommodated by the new version, assuring a transparent transition from the older version. At the same time, with expanded functionality, work packets, informational objects, and the like must be free to improve as new versions are designed.

Therefore: For any "entity" that contains information (work packets, informational objects, etc.) and either

- has a possibility of persisting beyond the lifetime of the program that created it, or
- may move between concurrent-threads-of-execution,

design the information to know the following attributes:

- record the type and a version identification for this informational entity,
- record the version of the program that created it, also include the date of creation and any information on the environment that can be accessed (machine type, machine configuration, OS version, file system version, etc.).
- record the date-of-last-access and date-of-last-change,

- for every concurrent-thread-of-execution visited, record the thread's version and date-last-visited,
- for every application that accesses this information, record the application's version and date-last-visited, and
- embed within this information knowledge about its stored data structure format.

Suggestions: For large entities, this additional "roots" information adds little to the overhead in terms of time and space. For very small entities, the overhead may be significant, but in low quantities it still remains valuable. For high volume, small entities, get creative before you discard the design idea. Consider the design of a transaction log which will record this information and, during slack times, works at condensing the information at the cost of processing time.

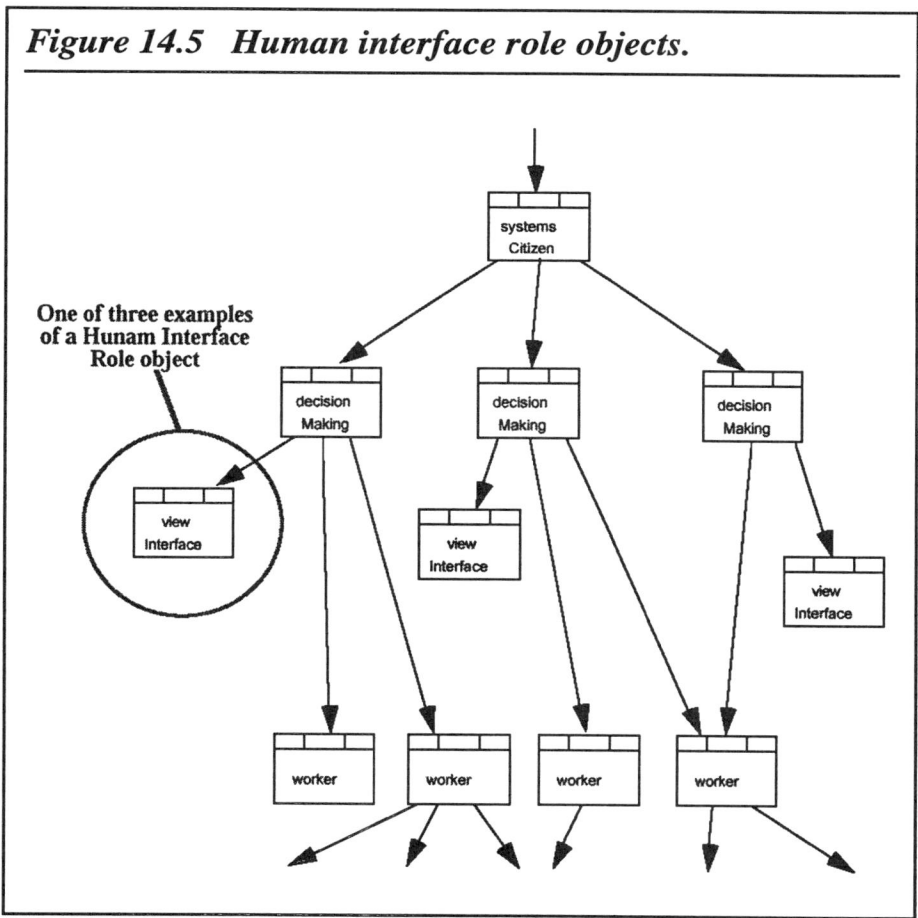

Figure 14.5 Human interface role objects.

Upon completion of this pattern you have assured that your persistent objects will have the information necessary for future versions of your system to grow, and at the same time assure work in progress at any stage can be accommodated.

This is the end of the Caterpillar's Fate programming language. In the next sections, the use of this pattern language is discussed.

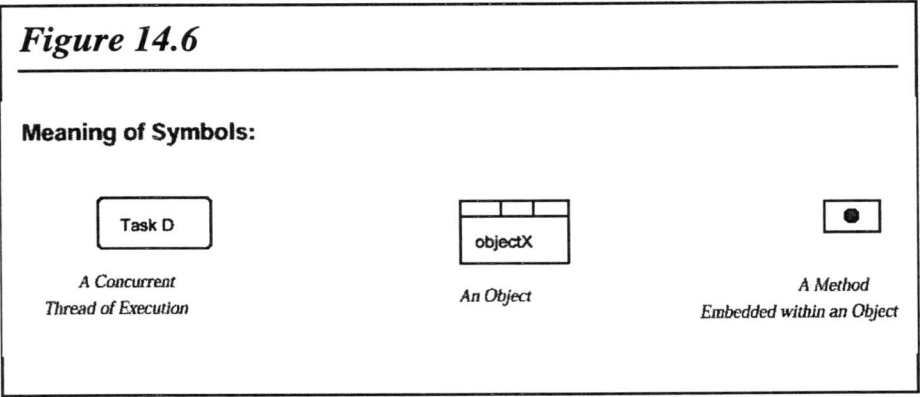

Figure 14.6

Meaning of Symbols:

Task D

A Concurrent
Thread of Execution

objectX

An Object

A Method
Embedded within an Object

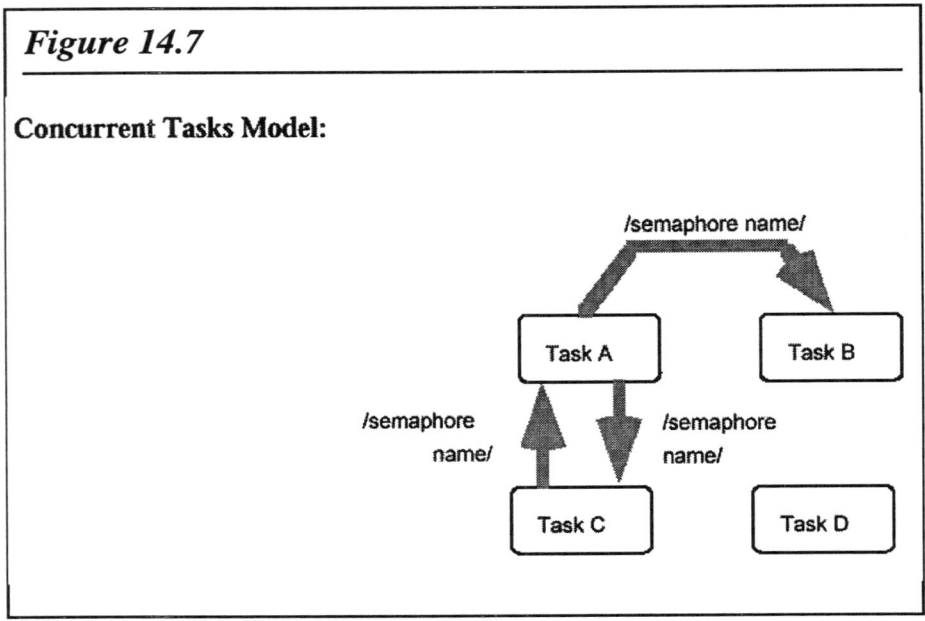

Figure 14.7

Concurrent Tasks Model:

/semaphore name/

Task A   Task B

/semaphore name/   /semaphore name/

Task C   Task D

Use of Caterpillar's Fate

A reader might assume that one can traverse through Caterpillar's Fate without any kinds of iteration or rework. This is not the case. In some cases, the transition from analysis into design points out significant wholes or conflicts in the analysis documents. In other cases, as the design begins to emerge, it becomes clear that certain design issues were not considered. Users of Caterpillar's Fate do experience iterations of many sorts. That is not necessarily a flaw in the methodology, the pattern language, or the project. Building large systems is an activity of learning what the system does. Learning often occurs through iteration. What is a flaw is to know that you need to iterate and to not reanalyze or redesign.

Status of Caterpillar's Fate

This document contains about one third of all the patterns that I have become aware of using. The rest of the patterns were left out for page limitation reasons. I use the

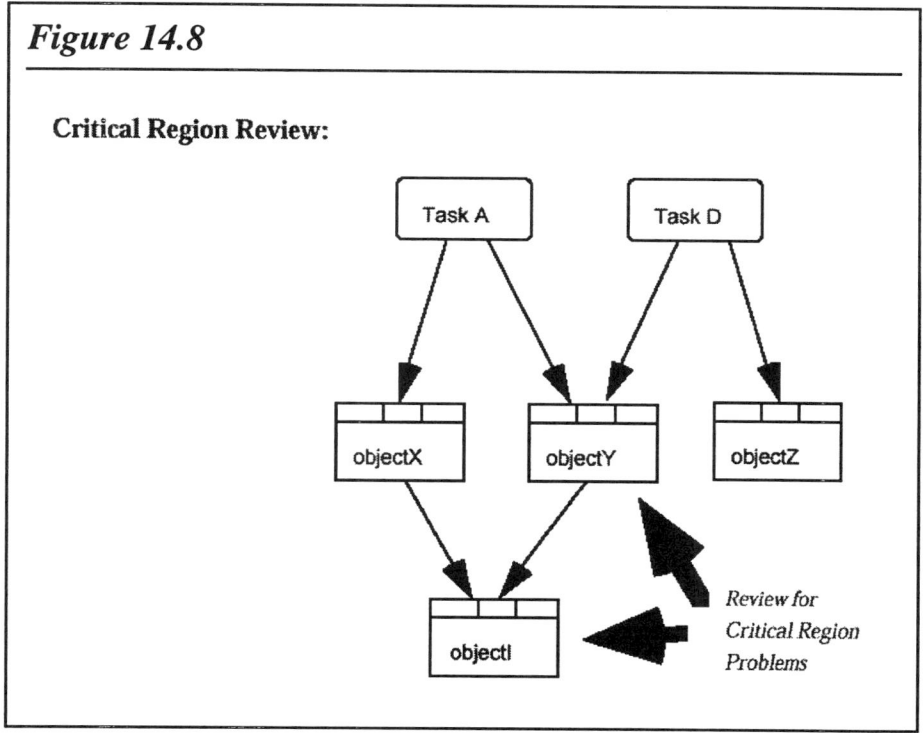

Figure 14.8

Critical Region Review:

Review for Critical Region Problems

phrase "have become aware" because I discover more common design wisdom every time my clients and I use Caterpillar's Fate. Furthermore, there are occasions where insight through use causes me to rework the patterns I have already documented, thus Caterpillar's Fate is to be seen as work-in-progress.

Nevertheless, this work has a high degree of maturity. Caterpillar's Fate has been used by my clients, since 1992, to construct several real-life systems: an investment banking system, an interactive voice-response system, a hand-held computer application, and the control of electricity. Teams ranged from three to twenty people. In all cases, the pattern language was communicated within a methodology course followed by personal coaching as necessary. This paper is an experiment to communicate these concepts solely in a written form. Thus, feedback is welcome and encouraged.

Issues

As I developed the text for this pattern language, I was shocked at how rapidly I consider these patterns while transforming a system analysis into a first design. This leads to a concern of mine about the amount of effort that another person might have to put into mastering this language before he/she can use the wisdom that I have acquired. This is part of the new experiment exploring pattern languages for developing programs. Can pattern languages be used by someone other than the author, and without

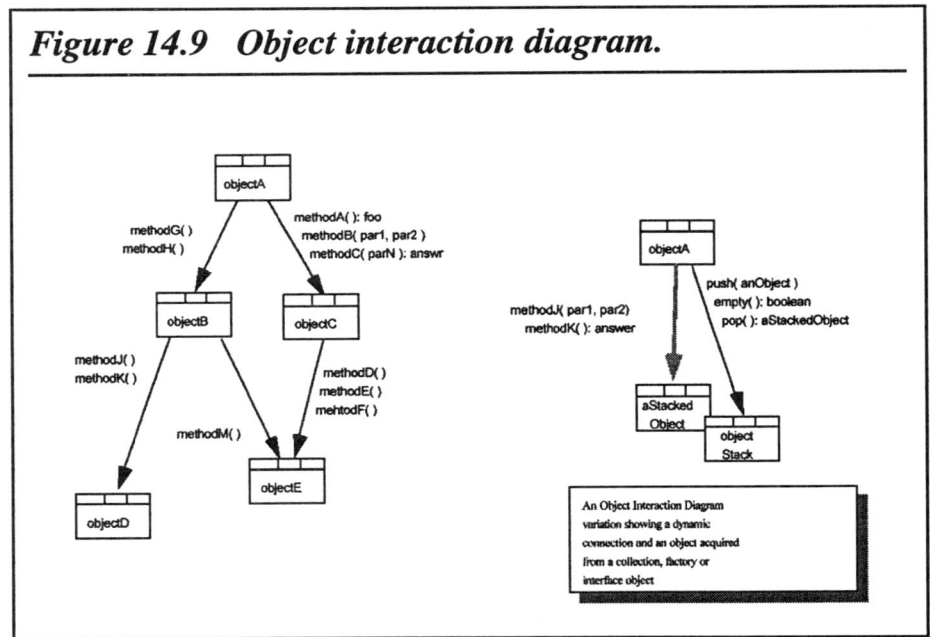

Figure 14.9 Object interaction diagram.

the aid of a masterful teacher? For us to know if that is possible, written pattern languages need to exist.

This is why I have written this paper. It serves as the test bed to see if pattern languages such as Caterpillar's Fate can be distributed widely.

A second concern I have with Caterpillar's Fate is the dependence on objects as the design paradigm. This is not in keeping with Alexander's view that a pattern language is implementation material free. Following his lead, I would like to see the transformation from an object-free analysis be able to metamorphose into any of a number of design strategies. Some of the patterns in Caterpillar's Fate were presented in a non–object-bias manner, such as *Concurrent Threads of Execution* (1), but others, such as *Work Accomplished through Dialogs* (16), have a most definite object-bias. The bias-free presentation of this acquired wisdom remains a puzzle to me.

Another issue to be resolved, not only for Caterpillar's Fate but for all pattern language authors, is how to incorporate the work of other pattern language authors and honor their work. There is at least one other pattern language that I'd like to disassemble and incorporate parts of within Caterpillar's Fate. Can I do this and still respect the original author's work? I may want to rewrite every part except the idea, and I may not even present the author's idea as he/she originally intended. As a community we need to discuss this and related issues.

A final issue has to do with the fear of public attack. Caterpillar's Fate describes details of how I generally design programs. It is risky to say, "this is what I do." I am certain there are programs that, if built following the wisdom of Caterpillar's Fate, would yield something that I would be embarrassed to show my colleagues. I claim the right to not follow any of my wisdom when I believe that it will not serve me well.

Also this is how I design today; I claim the right to learn new and different ways to design and as a result to create a new version of Caterpillar's Fate.

The MOOD Notation

MOOD (Multiview Object-Oriented Design) is a little-known notation for documenting software designs. It includes Structured Design notations and adds important concepts in object-oriented design (Figures 14.6–14.10). It is little-known because it remains unpublished. This should be remedied soon. Here is a brief introduction.

The multiview nature exists because I found one view of all the aspects of an object-oriented design producing a diagram too complex to comprehend. Furthermore, I discovered that there were stages of design that addressed different issues; thus I created different views for the various stages.

Table 14.2 shows the various views.

Method Notation:

```
nameOfMethod (parameter1PassedIn, parameter2PassedIn) : valuePassedBack
methodWithNoParametersPassedIn ( ) : valuePassedBack
methodWithNoReturnValue ( )
```

References

1. N. Kerth. "A Structured Approach to Object-Oriented Design." Addendum to the OOPSLA Proceedings, 1991.

Table 14.2 MOOD views.	
Model Name	***Purpose***
Object Dictionary	Identify object's name, responsibility, and information hidden or managed.
Concurrent Tasks Model	Shows concurrent threads of execution as well as communication and synchronization between threads.
Critical Region Review	Identifies the objects that may be accessed by two or more separate threads of execution.
Object Interaction Diagram	Shows objects invoking what methods in which other objects.
Object Structure Diagram	Shows the internal structure of an object.
Inheritance Table	For each object, show what methods are inherited, overridden, and created unique.
Creation Diagram	Shows how the object interaction diagram is created — responsibility, order of creation, initialization, and installation.
Removal Diagram	Shows how objects are discarded — responsibility, order of discard, notification, and memory reclamation.
Pseudo Code	Shows the algorithm used for each method.

2. N. Kerth, R. Rhodes, and J. Burley. "How to Deliver 20,000 Lines of Code with only Four Defects for under $2.00 Per Line of Code." Pacific Northwest Software Quality Conference, Fall 1990; Invited Paper.

3. C. Alexander. *The Timeless Way of Building.* Oxford University Press, 1979.

4. C. Alexander et al. *A Pattern Language.* Oxford University Press, 1977.

Figure 14.10

An Object Structure Diagram:

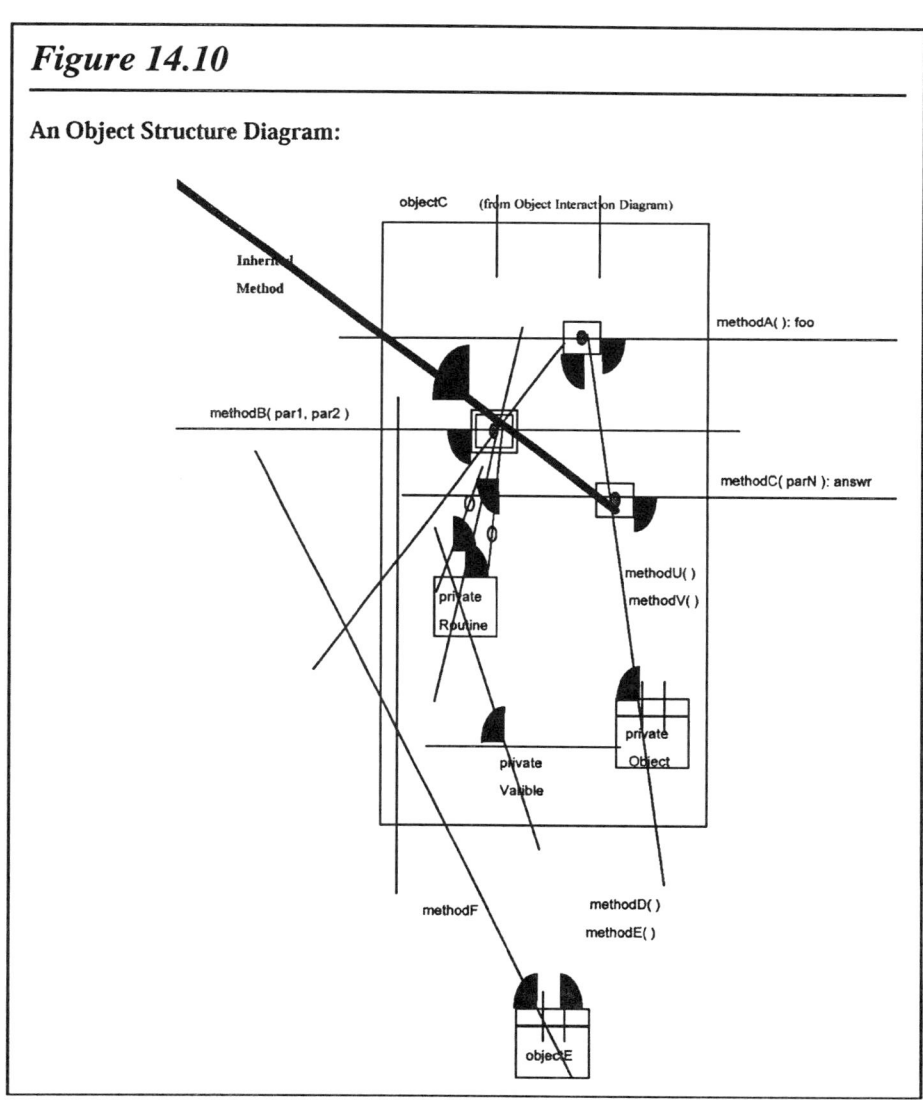

Chapter 15

Object-Oriented Tools for Building Database Applications

David S. Linthicum

Twenty-five years ago, object-oriented development was an interesting concept. Today it's an all-out software development phenomenon. Every development tool on the shelf promotes itself as object-oriented. During the last few years, most development organizations have taken a head-first dive into object-oriented development and spent millions on people, tools, and technology. Objects are a software-development success story, and they are here to stay.

If present trends continue, the object-oriented tools industry will do $2 billion in sales in 1997, up from just $379 million in 1993. The catalyst that drives this massive movement toward object technology is the fundamental belief that the object-oriented development paradigm provides a superior method of building applications. The basic concept is that developers build applications out of standard, reusable components as much as possible, and thus avoid the time-consuming process of developing applications from scratch. Moreover, developers can build applications from the general to the specific, and reuse generalized code whenever possible.

Despite the tremendous success of objects, developers and development organizations still find themselves in the object-oriented learning curve. The use of objects requires a different way of thinking, and it will take time before our neurons are object-oriented. In many cases, the tools are far more advanced than the expertise of the developers who use them.

This article examines state-of-the-art technology in object-oriented database application development, which includes object-oriented fundamentals, emerging object standards, and leveraging objects for client/server. The wide array of existing object-oriented tools and languages, as well as their ability to adhere to the object-oriented model will also be discussed. If you are responsible for developing applications, your competency in objects determines your ability to develop database applications. As object-oriented technology moves forward, make sure that it does not leave you behind.

Basic Building Blocks

Object technology uses three basic building blocks for systems development: objects, messages, and classes. Classes are the templates that define objects (a blueprint for an object), objects are instances or run-time versions of a class that contain related data and methods, and messages are the means by which objects communicate. An object in a class can inherit attributes (data) and procedures (methods) from a higher class. All objects are members of a class, and an object's class membership determines the operations it can perform.

What object technology promotes is the ability to build applications in the same way that Ford assembles Mustangs. Instead of handcrafting every program from scratch, developers assemble software out of standard objects that already exist. For example, most client/server development tools come complete with object libraries. Developers create applications by selecting and assembling preexisting objects from these libraries. If a developer must create a missing object to meet the requirements of the application, that new object may be placed in a library for reuse in future applications. For many simple systems, the developer may not write any code at all but use the available objects to form the entire application. More complex development efforts require the developer to modify the objects to meet the specific requirements. In addition, object-oriented systems are conceptually closer to reality. Therefore, developers and end-users alike find objects much easier to understand.

Developers reuse existing objects through the inheritance mechanism that most object-oriented tools provide. Inheritance is the "money concept" of object-orientation because it allows developers to inherit the capabilities (methods and data) of existing objects. This lets developers "program through plagiarism," or maximize the use of application objects, which is especially effective in a graphical user interface (GUI) development environment. For example, developers no longer write Windows file dialogs from scratch. Instead they inherit the file dialog functionality from an existing file dialog object, usually found in the object library of the tool. Developers can accept the file dialog object as-is, or modify it by adding, changing, or deleting methods and data. The same goes for data windows, buttons, reports, and other application objects.

Developers can utilize inheritance in two modes — single and multiple inheritance. Single inheritance allows the inheritance of information from a single object; multiple inheritance allows objects to inherit information from two objects simultaneously. Most object-oriented tools (such as Smalltalk) do not support multiple inheritance.

In addition to inheritance, the object-oriented development model provides for the encapsulation of data and methods inside an object that make them private within an object. Developers can modify encapsulated data and methods without disturbing other portions of the application. Moreover, the object-oriented model supports polymorphism, meaning that developers can generalize a message to produce different results depending on the target object. This is similar to overloading.

Object orientation is much more than a "way-to" program. It can apply across every system development activity including requirements analysis, design, testing, and business process reengineering. Developing an object-oriented application requires even more thought about the design than developing in the traditional structured programming environment. Many experienced object-oriented developers know that their application is only as good as its design. Object-oriented analysis and design methodologies and the use of computer-aided software engineering (CASE) technology are extensive in the object-oriented world.

Object Purity

Object-oriented development tools do not support the object-oriented model in a consistent manner. Each tool and language has its own way of providing the developer with object-oriented features. It is useful to divide the object-oriented languages (and tools that use the languages) into a few descriptive categories: pure, hybrid, and specialized.

Pure object-oriented languages are object-oriented from the ground up. Everything in the language environment exists as an object, method, or class, and developers have to use the object-oriented model to build applications. The best example of a pure object-oriented language is Smalltalk. Although more than 20 years old, Smalltalk is the base language for many modern client/server development tools including IBM's Visual Age, Digitalk's PARTS, Object Studio from Easel Corporation, and Visual Works from ParcPlace.

When developing applications using a Smalltalk tool, everything is an object and developers accomplish all work using messages. If you're not accustomed to doing things this way, it can be confusing. For example, because everything is an object in Smalltalk, so are classes. Therefore, every object is a member of a class. Objects also define classes. In theory, this could lead to an infinite regression. The designers of Smalltalk solved this problem by declaring that metaclasses define all classes, and all metaclasses are children of a single metaclass. If your Smalltalk application needs to access an external data source, such as a relational database server, Smalltalk must treat those sources as Smalltalk objects. This topic will be discussed later in the article.

Once developers learn to use Smalltalk, they find that developing an application is a relatively quick process. Smalltalk developers mix and match objects from the object library that comes with the Smalltalk tool, and developers can extend the capabilities of those objects using Smalltalk's 4GL-like programming language. Smalltalk compiles code incrementally, and new classes and objects become effective within the environment when the developer creates them. Smalltalk tools also use an interpreter, which means there is no lengthy compile-and-link process. This makes Smalltalk the environment of choice for visual development tools such as Visual Age, Visual Works, and PARTS. However, Smalltalk, like other interpreted languages, does not run as fast as compiled code.

The power of objects is the process of reusing existing objects. When you buy a Smalltalk environment, you're also buying an existing object library; and the objects that come with your Smalltalk tool define its capabilities. For example, while Visual Age and Visual Works both use the Smalltalk language, both provide different sets of application development objects that make the tools very different. When buying Smalltalk tools, consider the number and types of objects that come with them. If the vendor does not give you the objects you need, you'll have to build them yourself.

Developers new to Smalltalk or any other object-oriented tools will spend as much time learning the object library as they will learning how to use the tool itself. Once developers know the object library, they'll find that most of the programming is already done for them. If they do need to program, the Smalltalk language is easy to use, with English-like command statements. In fact, many educational organizations use Smalltalk as the preferred object-oriented language to teach object technology. Smalltalk is rapidly becoming an acceptable language for corporate development, and it's an easy way to break into pure object-oriented development.

Object-Oriented Hybrids

Hybrid languages are built on an existing programming language. They support features of the existing language such as structured programming, as well as an overlay of the object-oriented features. Examples of hybrid languages include Object COBOL and Object Pascal. Both contain traditional features plus support for the object model. The most successful of all the hybrid languages is C++.

The success of C++ is a result of the success of C, the native programming language for UNIX, and the most popular programming language for the PC. Shortly after its release, C++ became an instant success for two major reasons. First, because C was an existing standard in many organizations, C++ was viewed as an upgrade. Second, C++ was available from many vendors. Today, C++ compilers and development environments can be purchased for most platforms. Some of the most popular for client/server development include Borland C++, Watcom C++, and Microsoft Visual C++.

C++ provides a convenient migration path to object-oriented programming, and it supports both the structured and object-oriented paradigm. This convenience, however, can lead to trouble. It's a bit too easy for developers to mix C and C++ code in an application, and not take full advantage of object-oriented programming features. Most new C++ programmers admit to dropping back to structured C code until they fully understand the new object-oriented way of doing things. C++ applications that mix code are difficult to maintain.

The upside is that C++ uses a true compiler. It's a fast, compact language even with the object-oriented extensions. The excellent execution speed has made C++ the language of choice for many commercial software development organizations, even in today's world of rapid application development "wonder" tools.

The popularity of C++ and its ability to support single and multiple inheritance has led to a number of commercial class libraries. The idea is that you can buy objects rather than writing your own. Rouge Wave Software, for example, sells DBTools.h++, a C++ class library that allows C++ applications to link to database servers and manipulate data. Borland ships its Object Windows Library (OWL) with Borland C++. OWL provides all the objects developers need to build Windows applications, including file dialog objects, button objects, and graphic objects. Developers can even deploy portable applications using available portable class libraries such as Zinc from Zinc Software. These class libraries place the operating system and GUI-specific functionality in objects. To port an application, all that is required is swapping in the appropriate objects to support a particular operating system and GUI.

Developers do take the good with the bad. C++ is a complex language with an extensive learning curve. Developers must first learn C, then learn the object-oriented extensions of C++, which is a low-level language that operates very close to the metal. Developers must learn how to perform tasks such as managing memory directly, accessing physical disk storage, and using cryptic Application Programming Interfaces (APIs). The potential for problems is enormous, and it takes about twice as long to develop a client/server application using C++ than it does using other 4GL-driven client/server development environments.

Specialized Object-Oriented Tools

Specialized development tools and languages make up the last object tools category. These are tools built to serve a specific need, such as client/server development for GUI environments. Examples of specialized development tools include PowerSoft's PowerBuilder, Gupta's SQL Windows, Uniface Corporation's Uniface, Unify's Vision, Object Pro from Trinsic, and Enterprise Developer from Symantic, to name only a few. This is the biggest growth area in the object-oriented tools market. These tools support only portions of object modeling in their own proprietary ways. The trick is to select a tool with the key object-oriented features that provide a productive application development environment.

Unlike pure and hybrid object-oriented tools, these specialized tools are all over the object-oriented model. For example, most object-oriented tools support single inheritance, but a few tools such as Gupta's SQL Windows support multiple inheritance. Unify Vision, on the other hand, only supports encapsulation. Regardless of the object-oriented features offered, all tools sell themselves as "object-oriented."

PowerSoft's PowerBuilder ranks as the most popular of the specialized object-oriented development tools. PowerBuilder does not, however, support all aspects of the object-oriented model. Developers need to understand the object-oriented aspects of the tools before they build an application. For example, using PowerBuilder, developers can create a generic data window that contains all the columns they would like to include throughout the application. The data window could also include color, size, fonts, and behavior. After this is complete, developers can reuse or inherit from that generic data windows object anywhere in the application. Although the child object resembles the parent object exactly, controls can be added, deleted, or modified to meet the application's needs. As with other object-oriented development environments, a change such as color or font to the parent object will automatically change every object as well. This time-saving feature only requires that a change be made in just one place. Pure and hybrid object-oriented tools also provide this feature.

The debate raging between the object purists and specialized object tool developers and vendors is the lack of support for the formal object model. Object purists argue that these tools should consistently support all aspects of object-oriented development using nonproprietary mechanisms. However, the tool vendors contend that sticking too close to the object-oriented model makes the tools difficult to learn and use. Vendors continue to promote their tools as having GEOS, or Good Enough Object Support.

Some of these tools are moving toward the best of object-oriented worlds. PowerBuilder, like other specialized object-oriented tools, is becoming more object-oriented as time passes. PowerBuilder Version 3.0a did not support nonvisual objects, but Version 4.0 does. Gupta's SQL Windows also added significant object capabilities with the new Version 5.0. However, if you're only in the market for "all object" development for your next client/server project, your best bet is still a Smalltalk tool.

Looking at Data

A distinguishing factor between the pure object-oriented tools (such as Smalltalk) and the nonpure object-oriented tools (such as hybrid and specialized) is the way they interface with the data. When using a pure object-oriented tool, such as a Smalltalk tool, it treats the data as persistent objects even if the data exists in a relational database. Pure object-oriented tools can translate the relational database model into objects, just to meet the needs of the "all object" development environment.

Smalltalk tools such as VisualWorks provide mechanisms such as ObjectLens and Visual Data Modeler to remap relational databases such as Sybase, ORACLE, or INFORMIX to make them appear as persistent objects. The Visual Data Modeler allows developers to manipulate relationships between relational tables and Smalltalk objects. ObjectLens is a set of Smalltalk classes that provides the capability to access tables that exist on a relational database server as native Smalltalk objects. Other Smalltalk tools use similar mechanisms and will continue to do so as long as relational database management systems (RDBMSs) dominate the marketplace. If you're using an object-oriented database with a Smalltalk tool, there's no remapping required.

Since C++ is a hybrid language that supports both the structured and object-oriented programming models, developers have their choice of ways to access data. For example, developers can access a relational database server using structured native database API calls, or through an open database connectivity (ODBC) API. The drawback is that the developer has to leave the object-oriented paradigm to access the relational database. However, there are several C++ class libraries available commercially (such as Rouge Wave Software's DBTools.h++) that allow developers to use objects to access relational database information for a C++ application. In addition, many database vendors are redeveloping their native database API as C++ objects.

Another example of the marriage of objects and relational databases is NeXT Computer's Enterprise Object Framework (EOF) product. EOF allows developers who use Objective C (NeXT Computer's object-oriented C product) to create and access relational databases as objects, complete with methods (business rules, integrity checking, and so forth) and data. As developers create methods for the database object, EOF translates the methods into the appropriate stored procedure or trigger native to the relational database.

If this sounds like we're going through a lot of trouble to use relational databases as objects, you're right. It's still a relational world, and the paradigms need to get along.

The easiest way to access relational database information is through a specialized tool. These tools have built-in mechanisms to access the database for use within an application, but they don't remap relational databases into objects. Therefore, developers access application objects as objects, and the database as tables, columns, and rows. Although many object-oriented purists believe this is a sacrilege, many developers believe that it's easier to deal with relational databases as relational databases, and not translate them into something they're not — objects. At least for now, these tools may be the quickest road to client/server database development.

Object Standards

Although most object-oriented development tools do promote object reuse, no standard reusable object exists among tools (for example, C++ objects under Smalltalk). To solve this problem, the Object Management Group (OMG) came up with the Common Object Request Broker Architecture (Corba Version 1.1) to define the building of binary objects that are shareable among object-oriented tools. However, the specification was so vague that OMG developed an upgrade to the standard, Version 2.0, which provides more details for developers who want to build a standard binary object.

To date, only a few vendors are offering standard binary object architectures. However, as the object market expands, as Corba 2.0 becomes a reality, and as component development takes off, more object vendors will find interest in standard objects. IBM, for example, bases its object development on its System Object Model (SOM). SOM and its distributed version, DSOM, are language-independent binary objects that developers can use as an object in several diverse application development tools. For instance, C++ DSOM objects can be used in Smalltalk applications. Other examples of distributed objects include NeXT Computer's Portable Distributed Objects (PDO), and Sun's Distributed Objects Everywhere (DOE).

Microsoft is pushing OLE 2.0 and its Component Object Model (COM) as its standard object development strategy. Although not object-oriented, OLE 2.0 objects do work with a number of application development tools that know how to use them, and they are the basis of the new Windows 95 operating system. The sheer power of the Microsoft marketing force may push OLE 2.0 toward being the binary object of choice for component-based development, but further away from the object-oriented model.

Object-Oriented Future

The question is not whether object-oriented development will remain popular, but rather how objects can best be used in application development. More choices of object-oriented tools exist than ever before. To confuse the issue, they all implement objects in their own special way. In addition, the industry is on a long learning curve, and it's going to take a few more years before the optimal payback from object-oriented development is finally realized.

The business argument for object technology remains a compelling one. By using object technology, the cost and time required to build new applications should decrease over time as the reuse library grows and developers leave the learning curve. The quality of applications should also improve as the use of pretested objects continues to increase.

The new drive for client/server application development and the use of rapid application development (RAD) is fueling the movement toward objects, and will continue to do so. Conceptually, it's possible to build applications without programming, by simply assembling and integrating various applications objects. However, most applications still require programming in substantial quantities to bring most complex object-based applications to life. The advent of object standards has the potential to make objects interchangeable commodity products. For now, most objects are only good for the tool that created them. They don't work or play well with others.

Database application development shops are clearly dependent on object-oriented development tools for their future development needs. That is, until someone has a better idea.

References

D. Linthicum. "The Object Revolution." *DBMS,* October 1995, pp. 46–52.

Chapter 16

Full Lifecycle Object-Oriented Testing (FLOOT)

Scott W. Ambler

Testing an object-oriented (OO) application is both very similar and very different as compared to testing a procedural application. The good news, if you can call it that, is that you still need to formulate test cases, you still need to document them, you still need to run and verify them, you still need both black-and-white box tests, you still need regression testing, and you still need stress testing. The bad news, however, is that the new development concepts provided by the OO paradigm require new approaches to testing. In this paper we will discover several key concepts required for testing object-oriented applications.

I'm a strong believer in something called full lifecycle object-oriented testing (FLOOT) (Ambler, 1997), which involves testing your object-oriented applications throughout the entire system development lifecycle (SDLC). We'll see that there are many reasons why you want to test throughout the entire SDLC, not the least of which is if you leave testing to the end of a project it typically doesn't get done properly. In this paper we will discuss a number of testing techniques that together form a FLOOT process (there has to be a music joke in here somewhere).

Before we begin, let's first define some common testing terms that I will use throughout this paper. The central document in testing is called the master test plan, which prescribes the testing approach for your application. You need to create a master test plan for every release of your application. A test-procedure script is the description of the steps that must be carried out to perform all or part of the master test plan. An object-oriented test case, referred to simply as a test case, is a collection of objects that are put into states that are appropriate to what is being tested, message sends to those objects, and the expected results of those message sends. Test cases are used to verify that a specific feature within your application works as you expected. A test log is a chronological recording of your testing activities.

Overview of FLOOT

In this paper we discuss a wide range of testing techniques, summarized below in Figure 16.1. The first thing that needs to be pointed out is the fact that regression testing and quality assurance (QA) need to be considered at all stages of testing. The second point is that we need to distinguish between testing in the small and testing in the large. Testing in the small is a term we use to refer to testing components of our system — the application prototype, portions of the design, some methods, or some classes. For the most part, analysis testing, design reviews, and code-testing techniques are all approaches to testing in the small. Testing in the large refers to testing techniques that are used to test the entire system, or at least very large components of it, at once. System testing and user-acceptance testing are considered to be testing-in-the-large techniques.

Figure 16.1

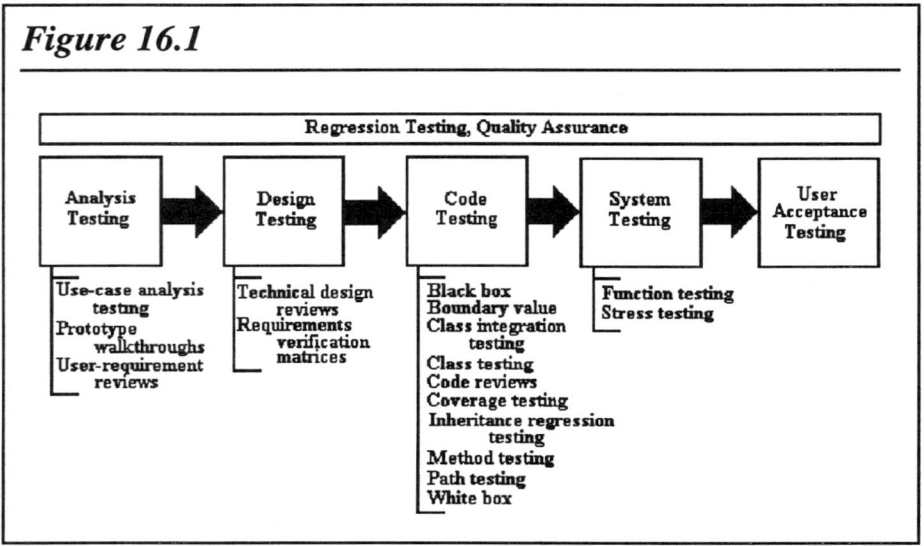

Although I have drawn the FLOOT process in a linear manner, the fact is that testing in the small for the most part can be an iterative process. After you've done some analysis you can test it, after you've done some design you can walk through it, after you've written some code you can test it. The bottom line is that testing is one of several iterative steps of OO development. Testing in the large, however, becomes serial. You have to do it just before you release your application to your users. Testing in the large is often the largest step of your implementation effort, so looking at it like that you could easily say that implementation is one of the iterative steps of OO development, it's just that this step is done in a serial manner. The end result is that OO testing is both a serial and an iterative process.

Why FLOOT?

Why do we need to test throughout the entire development lifecycle? We've always left testing to the end, isn't that the way it works? How can we test unless all the code is written, or at least a portion of the code? Valid questions. Here are some valid points that address these questions:

1. The cost of fixing errors increases the later they are detected in the development lifecycle. The cost of fixing an error, as shown in Figure 16.2, snowballs the longer that it takes to detect it (McConnell, 1993). If you make an analysis error, a missed or

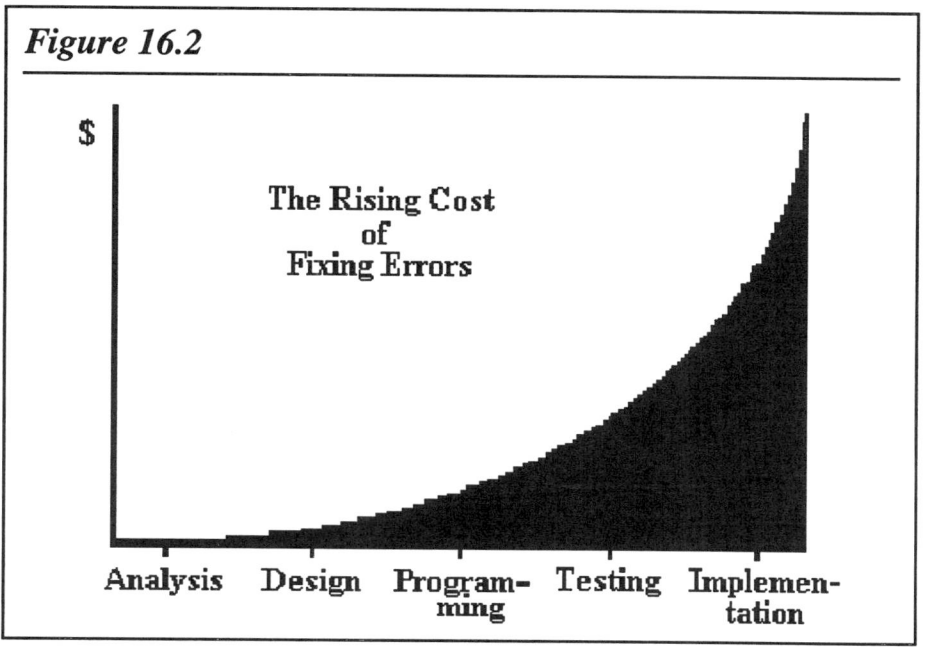

Figure 16.2

The Rising Cost
of
Fixing Errors

Analysis   Design   Program-   Testing   Implemen-
                        ming   tation

misunderstood user requirement, and find it during the analysis process it is very inexpensive to fix. You merely change a portion of your analysis document. A change of this scope is on the order of $1 (you do a little bit of retyping/remodeling). If you don't find it until the design stage it is more expensive to fix. Not only do you have to change your analysis, you also have to reevaluate and potentially modify the sections of your design based on the faulty analysis. This change is on the order of $10 (you do a little more retyping/remodeling). If you don't find the problem until programming you'll need to update your analysis, design, and potentially even scrap portions of your code, all because of a missed or misunderstood user requirement. This error is on the order of $100, because of all the wasted development time based on the faulty requirement. Furthermore, if you find the error during testing, where we typically start looking for errors, the error is on the order of $1,000 to fix (you need to update your documentation, scrap/rewrite large portions of code, and so on). Finally, if the error gets past you into production, you're looking at a repair cost on the order of $10,000 plus to fix (you need to send out update disks, fix the database, restore old data, rewrite/reprint manuals, and so on). It is clear that we want to find and fix errors as early on in the development process as possible.

2. Developers don't like to test their systems. Most developers are programmers at heart, not testers. They want to write code, not test it. To put it bluntly, many programmers simply aren't interested in testing, they'd rather be coding.

3. When left to the end of the lifecycle, testing is often left out. Projects are almost always late, and project managers are often desperate to get the project back on schedule. As a result, they start looking for places to cut corners, and because testing and documentation are often the only things that need to be worked on, they are often cut back or discarded completely. We can't afford to leave testing to the end of the development process anymore, instead we must integrate it into the entire development process.

4. We test systems the way we think they're supposed to work, not in the way they actually get used. Users have a tendency to use systems in completely different ways from those originally intended. The problem with this is that we didn't think they'd try some of the things that they do, and as a result they put the system through situations that it simply can't handle. The end result is that users must be involved as much as possible in the testing process.

One of the most important lessons that you can learn about object-oriented testing is that although many of the techniques are similar to those of structured testing, there are some very significant differences that you need to be aware of. When you consider the fact that the OO and structured/procedural paradigms share some common design principles, and that OO has taken them further and added several new ones, it is only reasonable to expect that we'd have to change our approach to testing OO applications. In this paper we will cover several new OO testing techniques as well as several tried-and-true structured testing methods that are still applicable in the OO world.

Testing Your Previous Efforts — Regression Testing

The first thing that you need to do is ensure that the functionality your application previously supported still works. Regression testing is the act of ensuring that changes to an application haven't been adversely affected. We've all had experiences where we made a small change to a program, we then successfully tested the change that we made thinking that everything was fine, and then we put the program into production only to see it fail because our small change affected another part of the program that we had completely forgotten about. Regression testing is all about avoiding problems like this.

The reason we're talking about regression testing first is because it's the very first thing that you should be thinking about when you begin testing your application. Users really get ticked off when functionality in an application that they are used to having no longer works. They get a lot more ticked off if new functionality doesn't work properly. How angry would you get if you took your car into a garage to have a new stereo system installed just to discover afterward that the new stereo works but that the windshield wipers don't? Pretty mad. How angry do you think your users would get when a new release of an application no longer allows them to fax information to other people because the new e-mail feature that you just added has affected it somehow? Pretty mad.

It is important to recognize that incremental development, a favorite approach in the object world, makes regression testing critical. Whenever you release an application you have to ensure that its previous functionality still works, and because you release applications more often when taking the incremental approach it means that regression testing becomes that much more important.

Testing Your Analysis

In *The Object Primer* (Ambler, 1995) we saw that the most significant mistakes are those that are made during analysis. If you miss or misunderstand a user requirement, you automatically ensure that the system will not completely meet the needs of your users. Either it is missing a feature or a feature is implemented wrong. Analysis errors such as this often result in project failure, or at least in serious cost overruns to fix the problem.

There are three techniques that you may employ to test your analysis:

- use-case scenario testing
- prototype walkthroughs
- user-requirements reviews

Use-Case Scenario Testing

Use-case scenario testing (Ambler, 1995) is a testing process in which users are actively involved with ensuring that user requirements are accurate. The basic idea is that a group of users, with the aid of a facilitator, step through a series of defined use cases to verify that the analysis model, typically a CRC (class responsibility collaborator) or class diagram, accurately reflects their requirements.

The main point that needs to be made is that you need to verify that your model accurately reflects the problem domain. If it doesn't, then your project is in serious jeopardy. I would prefer to find this out early on in the project when I'm still in a position to do something about it rather than later when I probably can't. Wouldn't you?

Prototype Walkthroughs

During analysis it is quite common to create a prototype, a mock-up of the user interface, for your application. Prototyping is an iterative process in which you work closely with your users to design the user interface for the application that you are developing. Although you will eventually create an interface design that your users like (one hopes), the question of whether or not the interface actually works still remains. This is why you need to do a prototype walkthrough.

A prototype walkthrough is an analysis-testing process in which your users work through a collection of use cases to verify that the design of a prototype meets their needs. The basic idea is that they pretend that the prototype is the real application and they try to use it to solve real business problems. Granted, they'll need to use their imaginations to fill in the functionality that the application is missing (such as reading and writing objects from/to permanent storage) but for the most part this is a fairly straightforward process. Your users simply sit down at the computer and begin to work through the use cases. Although they do this, it's your job to sit there and observe them, looking for places where the system is difficult to use or is just plain missing some features. In a lot of ways prototype walkthroughs are a lot like user acceptance tests, the only difference being that you're working with the prototype instead of the real system.

User-Requirement Reviews

After you have gathered user requirements you need to document and present them to your users to both verify that they are accurate and to prioritize them. A user-requirement review is a formal process in which a facilitator puts together a group of users with the authority to confirm and prioritize the user requirements gathered by a development team. This process could take from several hours to several days depending on the size of the project.

It is important to document, review, and prioritize user requirements so as to verify that what you are building will meet the needs of your users and to define the scope of your project. Part of the prioritization process should be to provide an indication as to which release of the application a specific feature will appear in. User-requirement reviews are run in a manner similar to technical-design reviews, discussed in the next section, with the exception that business experts instead of technical experts review the work of the development team. User-requirement reviews are often used in addition to use-case analysis testing and prototype walkthroughs.

Testing Your Design

Just like you need to verify that your analysis is right you also need to verify that your design is correct too. Remember, the sooner in the development lifecycle you discover errors the less expensive they are to fix. There are two techniques for testing your design that we will discuss in this section: (a) technical-design reviews and (b) requirement-verification matrices.

Technical-Design Reviews

It isn't enough to test just your analysis efforts, you also need to test your design. Technical-design reviews, also called design walkthroughs, are a testing technique in which your design efforts are examined critically by a group of your peers. The basic idea is that a group of qualified people, both technical staff and sometimes users, get together in a room and evaluate the design of the application that you are currently developing. The purpose of this evaluation is to determine if the design not only fulfills the demands of the user community but is also of sufficient quality to be easy to develop, maintain, and enhance. When they are done properly, technical-design reviews can have a big payoff because they often identify deficiencies when they are still reasonably inexpensive to address.

Requirement-Verification Matrices

Requirement-verification matrices (Ince, 1994) are used to relate user requirements to the portion(s) of your application that implement those requirements. For OO applications the names of classes are listed across the top of the matrix, the use cases for your application are listed along the left-hand axis of the matrix, and in the squares are listed the main method(s) in each class that are involved in fulfilling each use-case. The advantage of requirement-verification matrices is that they provide a mechanism to trace your design efforts back to your use-case definitions that actually describe the user requirements for your application. This enables you to both verify that your design meets the needs of your users and to determine what classes might be affected by a maintenance change for regression-testing purposes.

Testing Your Program Code

Testing object-oriented programming code in many ways is similar to testing structured/procedural code, although in many ways it is also different. In this section we will discuss many "traditional" testing concepts and even more new OO testing concepts. Don't worry, many of the new testing techniques that we'll discuss are actually extensions of structured testing techniques that have been modified to meet the needs of OO developers.

Code Reviews

Technical reviews, discussed above, are used to determine the quality of your code as well as the quality of your design. Code reviews often reveal problems that normal testing techniques don't, in particular poor coding practices that make your application difficult to extend and maintain. I am a firm believer that code reviews should be done before formal testing because once code has been formally tested and approved developers are rarely motivated to then have their code inspected. Their attitude is that the code works so why bother looking at it again. The end result is that you should first review your code, act on the recommendations from that review, then test it.

Code reviews should concentrate on quality issues such as:

* Naming conventions for your classes, methods, and attributes.
* Code documentation standards and conventions.
  * Have you documented what a method does?
  * Have you documented what parameters must be passed?
  * Have you documented what values are returned by a method?
  * Have you documented both what and why a piece of code does what it does?
* Writing small methods that do one thing and one thing well.
* Can the code be simplified?

Traditional Testing Methods

Many traditional testing techniques are still applicable to object-oriented testing, whereas others aren't. Well, now it's time to put my money where my mouth is and discuss what traditional testing techniques are still viable in the world of OO development. In this section we will discuss black-box testing, white/clear box testing, boundary-value testing, coverage testing, and path testing.

Black-Box Testing

Black-box testing is a technique in which you create test cases based only on the expected functionality of a method, class, or application without any knowledge of its internal workings. One way to define black-box testing, is that given defined input A we should get the expected results B. The goal of black-box testing is to make sure the system can do what it should be able to do, but not how it does it. For example, a black-box test for a word processor would be to verify that it is able to read a file in from disk and then write it back exactly as it was originally. It's a black-box test because we can run it without having any knowledge of how the word processor reads and writes files.

The creation of black-box tests are often driven by the user requirements, typically documented by use cases, for the application. The basic idea is that we look at the user requirement and ask ourselves what needs to be done to show that the user requirement is met. The advantage of black-box tests is that they allow you to prove that your application fulfills the user requirements defined for it. Unfortunately black-box testing doesn't allow you to show that extra, often technical, features not defined by your users also work. For this you need to create white/clear-box test cases.

White/Clear-Box Testing

White-box testing, also called clear-box testing, is based on the concept that your program code can drive the development of test cases. The basic idea is that you look at your code and then create test cases that exercise it. With white-box testing we are able to see the internal workings of an application, and that with this knowledge we create test cases that will run specific sections of code.

The main advantage of white-box testing is that it allows you to create tests that will exercise specific lines of code that may not have been tested by simple black box-test cases. Unfortunately, it does not allow you to confirm that all the user requirements have been met as it only enables you to test the specific code that you have written.

Boundary-Value Testing

Boundary-value testing is based on the fact that you need to test your code to ensure that it can handle unusual and extreme situations. The basic idea is that you want to look for limits defined either by your business rules or by common sense, and create test cases that test attribute values in and around those values. The main advantage of boundary-value testing is that it allows you to confirm that your program code is able to handle unusual or extreme cases.

Coverage and Path Testing

Coverage testing is a technique in which you create a series of test cases designed to test all the code paths in your code. In a lot of ways coverage testing is simply a collection of white-box test cases that together exercise every line of code in your application at least once. Path testing is a superset of coverage testing that ensures that not only have all lines of code been tested, but all paths of logic have been tested as well. The main difference occurs when you have a method with more than one set of case statements or nested IF statements: To determine the number of test cases with coverage testing you would count the maximum number of paths between the sets of case/nested IF statements and with path testing you would multiply the number of logic paths.

Although I am a strong believer in both coverage and path testing I'm a little leery about their use for object-oriented applications. Without a doubt there is value in exercising all of your code at least once. My experience, however, is that this often lulls programmers into a false sense of security that their code actually works. Sure, every line of code was run successfully but does that mean the code actually works? Absolutely NOT in an OO environment.

For the most part the problem has to do with polymorphism, the ability of objects to change their type. You might test some code that works fine when a specific object is customer, but later that same object might become an employee and your code crashes. The ability of objects to change type means that the ground is constantly shifting beneath you, the end result being that just because you have coverage tested and/or path tested successfully it doesn't mean that your code is guaranteed to run perfectly in production. All that it means is that your source was exercised thoroughly.

Coverage and path testing are both good techniques in theory, but in object-oriented practice they often fall short of their ideal. Use these techniques, just don't rely on them.

The Need for a New Testing Paradigm

We need to change our view of how to test applications. First of all the concept of test data sets, a collection of data representing test cases that exercises a program, needs to be thrown out the window. Unlike structured applications that are built from a series of programs that work with data, object-oriented applications are built from interacting objects. We don't use data to exercise our programs anymore, we use objects. Therefore instead of test data sets we need to create test object sets.

Related to this is the need to rethink the concept of a test case. Instead of defining a test case as some data and some code to run against the data, we now have object-oriented test cases that are a collection of objects that have been put into a specified state and a series of messages sent to those objects to exercise them.

New Testing Techniques for OO Program Code

There are three main categories of object-oriented testing techniques: method testing, class testing, and class-integration testing. Although we will explore each of these categories in greater detail, I want to first point out that the traditional testing techniques described in the previous section (black-box, white-box, boundary-value, coverage, and path testing) are all applicable approaches to help you define test cases for method, class, and class-integration testing. Object-oriented code testing is a collection of new and old techniques. The trick is to know which ones to use and which ones not to.

Method Testing

Method testing is the act of ensuring that your methods, called member functions in C++, perform as defined. The closest comparison to method testing in the structured world is the unit testing of functions and procedures. Although some people argue that class testing, discussed below, is really the object-oriented version of unit testing, my experience has been that the creation of test cases for specific methods often proves useful and should not be ignored. Hence the need for method testing.

Class Testing

Class testing is both unit testing and traditional integration testing at the same time. It is unit testing because you are testing the class and its instances as single units in isolation, but at the same time it is integration testing because you need to verify that the methods and attributes of the class work together. The main purpose of class testing is to test classes in isolation, which is difficult to do if you don't assume everything else works.

Inheritance-Regression Testing

Without a doubt the most important part of class testing is inheritance-regression testing — the running of the class and method test cases for all of the superclasses of the class being tested. The motivation behind inheritance-regression testing is simple. It is incredibly naive to expect that errors haven't been introduced by a new subclass. New methods are added and existing methods are often redefined by subclasses, and these methods access and often change the value of the attributes defined in the superclass. It is very possible that a subclass may change the value of the attributes in a way that was never intended in the superclass, or at least was never expected. I can't stress enough that inheritance-regression testing is critical to the success of your project. Just because it works in the superclass doesn't mean it'll work in your subclass. It's as simple as that.

Class-Integration Testing

Class-integration testing addresses the issue of whether or not the classes in your system work together properly. Because we know that the only way classes, or to be more accurate the instances of classes, can work together is via sending each other messages, and that there must be some sort of relationship between those objects before they can send the message, then it is clear that the relationships between classes can be used to drive the development of integration test cases. In other words, our strategy should be to look at the association, aggregation, and inheritance relationships that appear on our class diagram to help us to formulate class-integration test cases.

In the long run, class-integration testing is affected the most by the quality of your code. The better the encapsulation within your system and the looser the coupling between classes then the easier it is to test. Bad coding practices result in your having to spend more time testing, and then fixing, your application.

Testing Your Application As a Whole

Although testing your analysis, your design, and your program code are all very important, they aren't enough. You also have to ensure that the complete application works. All of the components of the application work as they have been defined and the application must meet the needs of its users. To do this, there are several different approaches that we can employ:

- system testing
  - function testing
  - stress testing
  - installation testing
  - operations testing
- user-acceptance testing
- alpha and beta testing

System Testing

System testing is a testing process in which you aim to determine the system's capabilities and then fix any known problems so that the development team can assure themselves that the application is ready for user-acceptance testing. System testing cannot be performed until after code testing is complete. You can't successfully test your application as a whole until you are reasonably confident that your code works. Development teams that try to do so quickly find that their application blows up in their faces. The following are the most common components of system testing: function testing, stress testing, installation testing, and operations testing.

Function Testing

Function testing is a systems-testing process in which development staff verify that their application meets the needs of their users. The main idea is that they run through the main functionality that the system should exhibit to assure themselves that their application is ready for user-acceptance testing (UAT). It is during UAT that the users will confirm for themselves that the system meets their needs. In many ways the only difference between function testing and user-acceptance testing is who does it: testers and users, respectively.

Because system functionality was captured during analysis by use cases, use cases can be used to drive the development of your function test plan because they lay out the exact logic of how the system operates. You'll find that changes in the design of your application will force you to revisit your use cases to verify that they are still applicable. Once that's done you'll find that your use cases are often perfect input to defining the steps for testing each major function in your system.

In addition to verifying that your system supports the functionality that your users require, you must also confirm that it can do so under harsh and unusual conditions. That's what stress testing is all about.

Stress Testing

Stress testing is a systems-testing process in which you determine how well your application performs under high numbers of users, high numbers of transactions (testing of high numbers of transactions is also called volume testing), high numbers of data transmissions, high numbers of printed reports, and so on. The goal is to find the stress points of your application under which it no longer operates so that you can gain insights into how it will perform in unusual and/or stressful situations.

Although stress testing must be performed during the system-testing process, it is also commonly done at the start of a project to verify whether or not a technical alternative works or simply to test the validity of your software. For example, many database administrators will set up a sample database and "pound it" with high numbers of transactions, access requests, and concurrent users to determine its strengths and weaknesses. At the end of a project the real database will be stress tested again to verify that it will meet the needs of peak demand periods.

Stress testing for the most part is a very technical process that should be performed by developers experienced in both the application and the aspect of it that they intend to stress. Stress testing will often take anywhere from several days to several months, depending for the most part on the complexity of what is being stressed and the number of environments that it must be stressed in. For example, one form of stress testing involves using the application on what is considered the minimal computer/network hardware/software configuration(s) to verify that it can be run in the environments that you say it can run in.

Installation Testing

Installation testing is a form of system testing in which the focus is on whether or not your application can be installed successfully. There are several important issues to be considered here:

- Can you successfully install the application into an environment that it hasn't been installed into before?

- Can you successfully install the application into an environment that it has been installed into before?
- Does configuration information get defined correctly?
- Does previous configuration information get taken into account?
- Are there replacements for existing user documentation?
- Is there a distribution plan for these documents?
- Is there a training plan for the application?
- Are any other applications affected by the installation of this one?
- Is there enough disk space/memory available on the machines of users for the application and does the application detect this?

Operations Testing

Operations testing is a type of systems testing that verifies that the needs of operations personnel who have to support and keep the application up and running are met. Examples of the issues that must be addressed by operations testing includes the following:

- Is there operations documentation?
- Does it meet the documentation standards required by your operations department?
- Are there technical manuals available for every component (database, operating system, language, and so on) of the system?
- Is there an error-handling facility in place?
- Is someone available on call to answer questions if something goes wrong?

Without operations testing how can you be assured that your application will be supported properly once it is installed?

User-Acceptance Testing

After your system testing proves successful, your users must perform user-acceptance testing, a process in which they determine whether or not your application truly meets their needs. This means that you have to let your users work with the software that you produced. Because the only person who truly knows your own needs is you, the people involved in the user-acceptance test should be the actual users of the system. Not their managers and not the vice presidents of the division that they work for, but the people who will work day in and day out with the application. Although you may have to give them some training to gain the testing skills that they will need, these are the only people who are qualified to do USER-acceptance testing.

The UAT process should take only a few days to a week at most. UAT is similar in concept to function testing, the main difference being that users do the testing and not developers. Your first step is to get your users working with the system so that they get a feel for what it is all about. Pay careful attention to their initial reactions. Initial reactions will reveal either deficiencies in your system or they will reveal areas in which your user community may need training. For example, many users when presented with a graphical user interface (GUI) for the first time may have difficulties working with it. You may have put together a perfectly good application, but because they didn't have an understanding of how GUIs work they may not have liked it.

Once the initial UAT period is over you want to get your users working through some of your simpler use cases and get them using the system to perform everyday tasks. You then have them slowly build up to more complex or esoteric functions in the application, giving them time to learn how to use the application on their job.

Alpha, Beta, and Pilot Testing

One of the major problems with testing is that you can only test for the things that you know about. As we have discussed before, unless you do the job of your users day in and day out you can never know it as well as they do. The implication of this is that you'll never be able to come up with as many real-life testing scenarios as they can. Furthermore, because your users typically outnumber you (so don't tick them off, or else), and as they say two heads are better than one, they can usually come up with better live tests than you can. Therefore it makes sense to get your users to test for you.

Two common approaches to this are alpha testing and beta testing (this is referred to as pilot testing for applications being developed for use by internal users). Alpha testing is a process in which you send out software that isn't quite ready for prime time to your users to let them work with it and report back to you the problems that they encounter. Although it is typically buggy and may not meet all of their needs, they get a heads-up on what you are doing a lot earlier than if they waited for you to release the software. Beta testing is basically the same process except the software has a lot of the bugs that were found during alpha testing (beta testing follows alpha testing) ironed out of it.

Alpha and beta testing are an important part of the testing process for professional software development houses whose products need to run on many diverse computing environments. These companies typically can't afford to, or simply don't have the time to set up test environments for every possible combination of hardware and operating systems that their software will be running on.

Software Quality Assurance and ISO 9000

Software quality assurance (SQA) is a set of processes and techniques that an organization uses to verify, test, and assure the excellence of the software that they develop. ISO (International Standards Organization) 9003 is the component of the ISO 9000 collection of quality standards that deals specifically with how organizations should manage their software quality-assurance programs. In a lot of ways ISO 9003 is seen as a subset of the ISO 9001 standard, as it defines how organizations should manage their entire quality-assurance programs, and not just software quality assurance.

A simplistic view of ISO 9000 is that it is a definition of how your organization produces the products and services that it sells to its customers, as well as the definition of how the customers can complain about what they have received. In a nutshell, ISO 9000 defines quality standards for the PROCESS by which your company operates. I believe that there is a lot of value in the ISO 9000 standards, and ISO 9003 in particular, for software developers. If you are serious about improving the software-testing process in your organization I highly suggest you look into both of them.

It is important for organizations to have an SQA program in place, as they can truly aid in improving the quality and excellence of internally developed software. SQA departments are typically responsible for aiding in, and often being responsible for, the testing process within a software development project. I've seen organizations in which SQA staff act as consultants on projects, helping staff to put together test plans, technical reviews, and even aiding in the testing itself. I've also seen organizations where the SQA department is directly responsible for testing software, not allowing deficient software to go into production until it meets the standards that they have set. In addition, I've unfortunately seen organizations in which the SQA department is all but ignored, with nobody taking advantage of their advice of their own free will and at the same time nobody being forced to either. Regardless of how the SQA department is being managed in your organization, I highly suggest that if you have access to one that you start working with them closely to help you with testing your OO applications. Although you may need to help them get up to speed on object-oriented development so they can understand your testing needs, there's always value in taking advice from experts. Go have a talk with them.

SQA departments are often the driving force behind bringing ISO 9003, and sometimes even the entire ISO 9000 quality standard, into your organization. Often the reverse is the case. In many organizations you'll see that SQA departments have been created as the direct result of bringing ISO 9000 in. SQA and ISO 9003 go hand in hand.

Testing Tips and Techniques

I'd like to leave you with a few tips that I have discovered over the years to be really helpful when testing object-oriented applications.

1. Successful tests find errors.
2. Learn from your mistakes by analyzing the errors that get past you.
3. Test throughout the lifecycle.
4. Get trained in OO testing techniques, there's a lot to it.

5. A new development paradigm implies a new testing paradigm.
6. The better your design/code, the easier it is to test.
7. Create a Software Quality Assurance department.
8. Create a master test plan
9. Test to the importance of the system.

Conclusion

In this paper we saw that full lifecycle object-oriented testing encompasses a collection of techniques for verifying your analysis, design, and program code. Furthermore we discussed techniques for ensuring that your application as a whole works properly. If there is one message that I want to leave you with it's that testing object-oriented applications is similar yet different from structured testing of the past. Although many of the fundamentals are the same, we've seen that concepts such as inheritance and encapsulation require changes in the approach that you take to testing applications. Although some developers look on testing as a necessary evil that should at best be tolerated, I look at testing as an opportunity to show to the world that my applications work just as I said they would. Which view do you think is better?

By the way, except for now, did you notice how I didn't use the word "bug" anywhere in this paper? If that's not impressive, I don't know what is.

About Building Object Applications

This paper is a summary of Chapter 12 of my second book, *Building Object Applications* (Ambler, 1997). The book is divided into the following five parts:

- Part 1. Introduction
    - Chapter 1: Where We've Been — Object-Oriented Concepts and Techniques
- Part 2. Object-Oriented Analysis, Design, and Architecture
    - Chapter 2: Bubbles and Lines — Useful Diagrams for Object-Oriented Analysis and Design
    - Chapter 3: Improving Your Design — A Class-Type Architecture
    - Chapter 4: Reusing Your Development Efforts — Object-Oriented Patterns
    - Chapter 5: Development in the 90s and Beyond — Distributed Object-Oriented Applications
- Part 3. Object-Oriented Construction
    - Chapter 6: Measuring and Improving the Quality of Your Work — Object-Oriented Metrics

- Chapter 7: Choosing an Object-Oriented Language — Comparing the Leading Languages
- Chapter 8: Building Your Application — Effective Object-Oriented Construction Techniques
- Chapter 9: Making Your Applications Usable — Object-Oriented User Interface Design
- Chapter 10: Making Your Objects Persistent — Object-Orientation and Databases
- Chapter 11: Integrating Legacy Code — Wrapping
- Part 4. Object-Oriented Testing
  - Chapter 12: Making Sure Your Applications Work — Full lifecycle Object-Oriented Testing
- Part 5. Conclusion
  - Chapter 13: Where to Go From Here — Personal Success Strategies

Drop by my personal web site, WWW.Ambysoft.com, if you're interested in learning more about my two books, *The Object Primer* and *Building Object Applications*. At the site you'll also find some more of my writings about OO development, so check it out.

References

S.W. Ambler. *The Object Primer — The Application Developer's Guide to Object Orientation*. New York: SIGS Books, 1995.

S.W. Ambler. *Building Object Applications — Patterns, Architecture, Design, Construction, and Testing*. New York: SIGS Books, 1997.

B. Hetzel. *The Complete Guide to Software Testing*, 2nd ed. New York: Wiley-QED, 1988.

D. Ince. *ISO 9001 and Software Quality Assurance*. London: McGraw-Hill Book Company, 1994.

S. McConnell. *Code Complete*. Redmond, WA: Microsoft Press, 1993.

Chapter 17

A Practical Approach to Object-Oriented UI Design

From User Tasks to Software Objects

Dick Berry, Dave Roberts, Scott Isensee, and John Mullaly

Abstract

Several methods, such as those developed by Booch or Shlaer and Mellor, are available for object-oriented program design. However, these methods do not deal with user interface design. Object View Interaction Design (OVID) is a systematic method for user interface design that complements the program design methods. It is intended for use by user interface professionals. OVID is a major step in changing user interface design from art to science. OVID emphasizes the production of a complete, accurate model of the objects and relationships perceived by users that can be used as input to program design methodologies.

Developing software with a user interface can be thought of in four phases: discovering what is needed, designing a solution, implementing the solution, and deploying it for the users to learn. These phases are shown in Figure 17.1. Usability methods provide means for discovering what users need; and software design methods provide means of implementing solutions. But few methods deal with design — with the conversion of user needs into a solution. At IBM we have developed Object View Interaction Design (OVID) to design solutions and in particular the user interface of these solutions.

OVID is a structured design methodology which leads the design team toward creating a good, object-oriented user interface design. Through the use of a structured process and appropriate tools, the design progresses more quickly with fewer cycles of iteration. There are checks for design completeness and correctness. The output of OVID documents the interface design and feeds directly into tools and methods commonly used for code design, reducing the risk of introducing interface errors later in development. Because of the tools being used in IBM we chose the Booch notation and Rational Rose™ to accomplish this. Other tools that support the formalisms we seek will suffice as well.

Figure 17.1   Phases in designing a user interface.

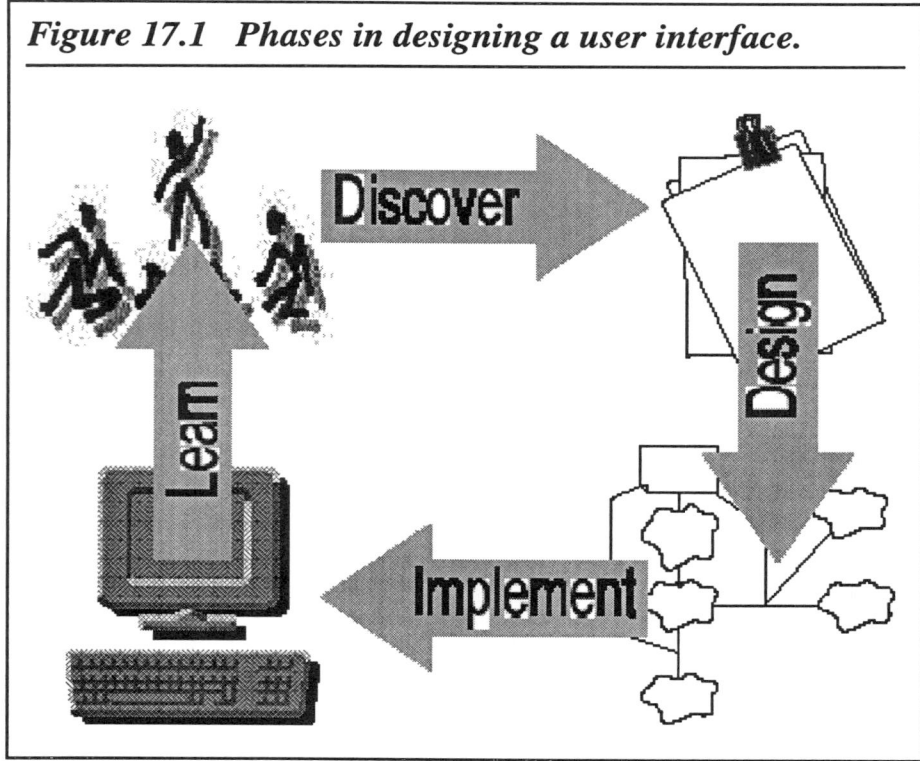

How Users Think

Human beings all go around with a model of the world in their heads. It is a model that describes the objects they meet and the relationships between them. Whenever users deal with something in the world they subconsciously refer to their model. When the object is already part of that model they know how to interact with it. When they meet a new object the model cannot help them directly. So they try to classify that object by matching it with others, noting the differences and updating their model. If the differences are small then they find the new thing easy to learn, or "intuitive"; if the differences are large they may find it hard to learn.

In interface design we call the model in the user's head the "user's model." We try to take advantage of how users employ this model in our designs.

Three Models

There are two other models involved in product design: the designer's model and the implementation model. The designer's model is what users are supposed to perceive when they use the product. The implementation model describes the product in terms of the programming elements used to build it.

We can sum up the design process in terms of these three models:

- In the discovery phase the designers try to understand the users' models of the targeted audience;

- In the design phase the design team develops a designer's model that is intended to complement the users' models and hence be easy to learn;

- In the implementation phase the programmers try to develop a product that matches the designer's model;

In the learning phase the users look at the application on the computer, try to learn what the designer's model is and adapt their user's model to accommodate what they have discovered.

As you can see, this is a process that can easily break down. Using OVID, we have developed our system designs, interface styles, and methods to avoid this breakdown.

A Change

When we developed the Common User Access™ , an interface style widely used by Windows™ and OS/2™ applications, we studied the literature and our own design experiences to determine the aspects most responsible for creating good usability. We concluded that only a small proportion of the usability of a product comes from what you see — we think around 10 percent. More important than look is the feel of the product, for example, does it use standard interaction mechanisms? We believe that this accounts for around 30 percent of the usability. But the majority of the usability comes from the designer's model: the way each part (object) works and how all the parts work together. This accounts for the remaining 60 percent of overall usability. So getting the designer's model right is of critical importance. But as the user cannot see the designer's model (except perhaps as diagrams or explanations in the Help) it is also critical that the look and feel reinforce the model to allow the user to easily understand it.

Figure 17.2   The iceberg analogy of usability.

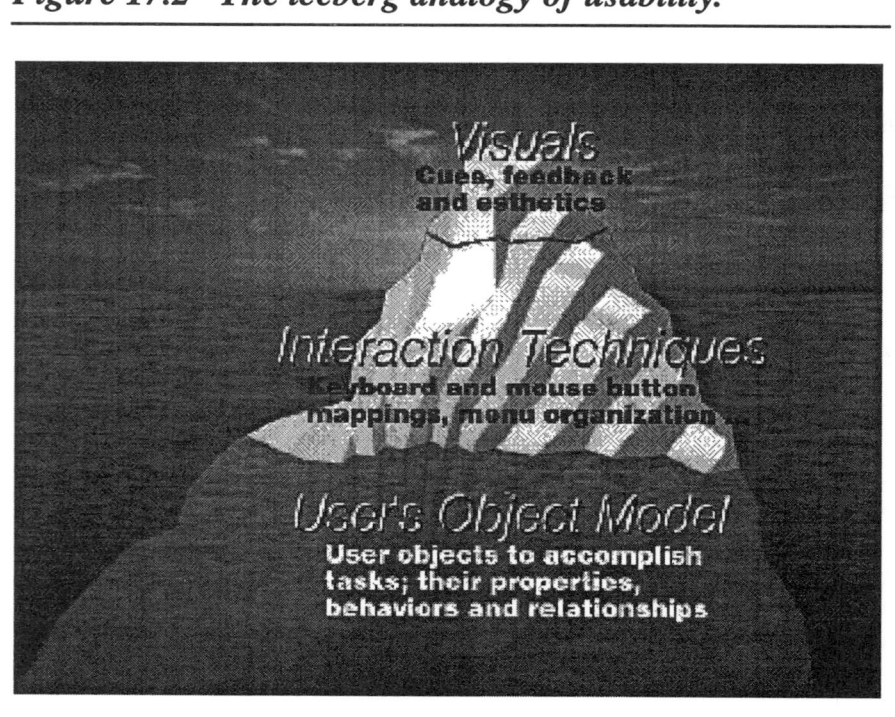

To help designers grasp this concept, around 1990 we began to use an "iceberg" analogy, depicted in Figure 17.2. As with an iceberg, it is not only what you see that you have to worry about (the look and feel), but the larger part, out of sight below the waves (the designer's model), often matters the most.

It was the recognition of what contributes to usability in these terms, and the persuasiveness of the iceberg analogy that persuaded CUA (and OS/2®) to change to an object-oriented user interface (OOUI) in 1991. Thinking about users' tasks, the objects they use and the methods they employ, becomes more natural while designing an OOUI. And having a clearly defined designer's model makes it easier to design the look and feel elements to convey the model to the user. The reference section of the CUA style guide consisted of standard elements of look and feel. Each was designed so that, when combined, it was possible to clearly understand the underlying model.

The Changing GUI

Now all graphical user interfaces are changing. With the advent of the Windows 95™ interface three out of the four major user-interface styles are object-oriented. The Macintosh™ has always been that way inclined, OS/2 changed in 1992, and now Windows has joined the camp. Only OSF/Motif® and CDE remain essentially program-oriented.

Object-oriented user interfaces allow for a more explicit mapping between the designer's model and the implementation. OVID was developed to allow designers to use tools to do just that.

Standard Notation

OVID specifies a notation that we believe designers and implementors, with appropriate training, can understand. Some team members will need to understand just enough of OVID and its notations to do their own job. Others will need to be well practiced in OVID and take on the role of helping others to understand.

The Role of Users

How users form part of the team will vary according to the context in which the team works. OVID can be adapted to each of these situations. For example, in some cases there will be representative users who are full members of the team. This is often called participatory design. In other cases there will be experts who, although not users themselves, have an understanding of the tasks involved and the users who perform them. In yet other cases the information about the users will be gathered by market analysis, surveys, or other studies, and then the experts who performed the studies represent the users.

Overview of Ovid

Object View Interaction Design is a systematic, iterative method for designing user interfaces. It focuses on the second and third phases of the design process — the designer's model and communicating it through the implementation. It takes information about the users' tasks, uses this information to produce a designer's model, and conveys the designers model to the implementors on the team.

OVID takes as input the information obtained from some form of task analysis. It does not really matter which form of task analysis is used to provide the input to OVID. However, as with most methods, the better the input the better the output. So a more complete and rigorous task analysis will give a better application.

Object View Interaction Design, as its name suggests, focuses on three elements of the design:

* the objects users use to accomplish their tasks,

* views of objects presented to users by the implementation,

* and how users interact with the objects through the views.

Figure 17.3   Iterating activities in the design cycle.

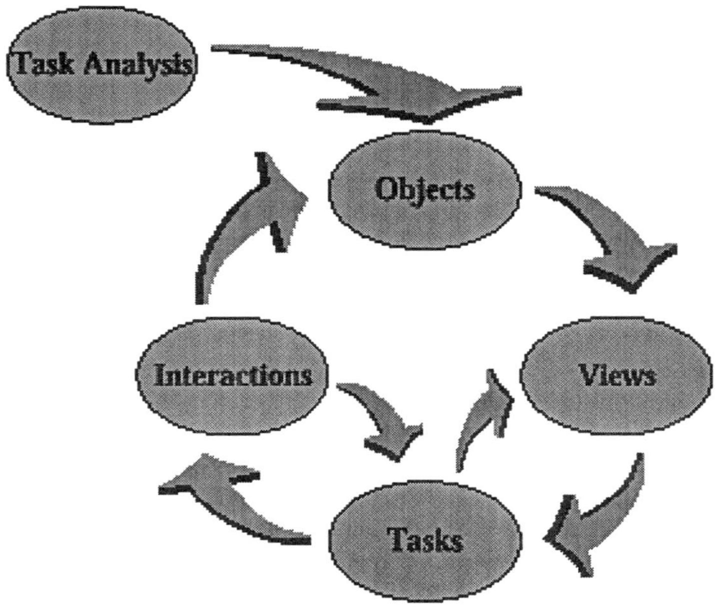

The process is as follows:

- An initial set of objects is generated by examining the users' task analysis;
- views are defined which allow users to see aspects of each object necessary to accomplish certain tasks;
- the users' tasks are described in terms of the OVID objects and views;
- the user interactions provided to accomplish each task within each view are specified.

As shown in Figure 17.3, there is a cycle of these activities which iterates until the design is complete.

Objects

Objects are recorded in OVID using class diagrams. These diagrams show the objects and the relationships between them. An initial set of objects is identified from the task analysis material. This can be done by examining all the nouns that occur in the task descriptions. The most frequently occurring objects form the basis of the initial diagram.

In the early stages it is important to avoid recording all the objects found in the analysis because the class diagram can become too cluttered. It is best to focus on the things that have real world counterparts and add other objects during subsequent iterations.

In this article we have used examples from a hotel management system. The tasks are mainly those of the desk clerk. Figure 17.4 shows a small fragment from an OVID class diagram. Each "cloud" in the diagram represents an object. The lines between objects represent relationships between those objects. Annotations near the lines provide additional information. Figure 17.4 specifies that:

- a hotel has several rooms — there is a line between hotel and room with 1..n written at the end near the room;
- each guest stays in a room — there is a line between guest and room with the 'Stays in' relationship written beside it;
- guests have attributes which include name, address, and telephone — the names of key attributes appear in the cloud.

Views

In order for the user to employ an object in a task, they must be able to see it in one or more views. So, once an initial set of objects has been extracted from the task analysis, the attention switches to the views of those objects. Each view of an object can show some of the properties and/or some of the relationships for that object.

Task priority is used again to guide the work. Starting with the most significant tasks, a view is created showing the objects required to perform the tasks. Each view is represented as an object on the object diagram. The view object is connected to the associations between the viewed object and other objects.

In Figure 17.4 you can see that there are views of Hotel, Room, and Guest available. They are called Hotel View 1, Room View, and Guest View. The diagram also shows that Hotel View 1 shows the rooms in the hotel and Room View shows information about the Guest staying in the room. Using Rose, we have chosen to show a rectangle beside a cloud to represent a view. The rectangle can be used to list key aspects of the view, such as the tasks enabled by the view, for example. Additional detail, not shown in the Rose diagrams, should be recorded to precisely identify the objects, properties, and relationships that need to be presented in each view to enable the intended tasks.

Tasks

The tasks documented during a task analysis are those found in the application as it is done currently, and may include new tasks to be added. The next step is to show how

Figure 17.4   Views in the hotel example.

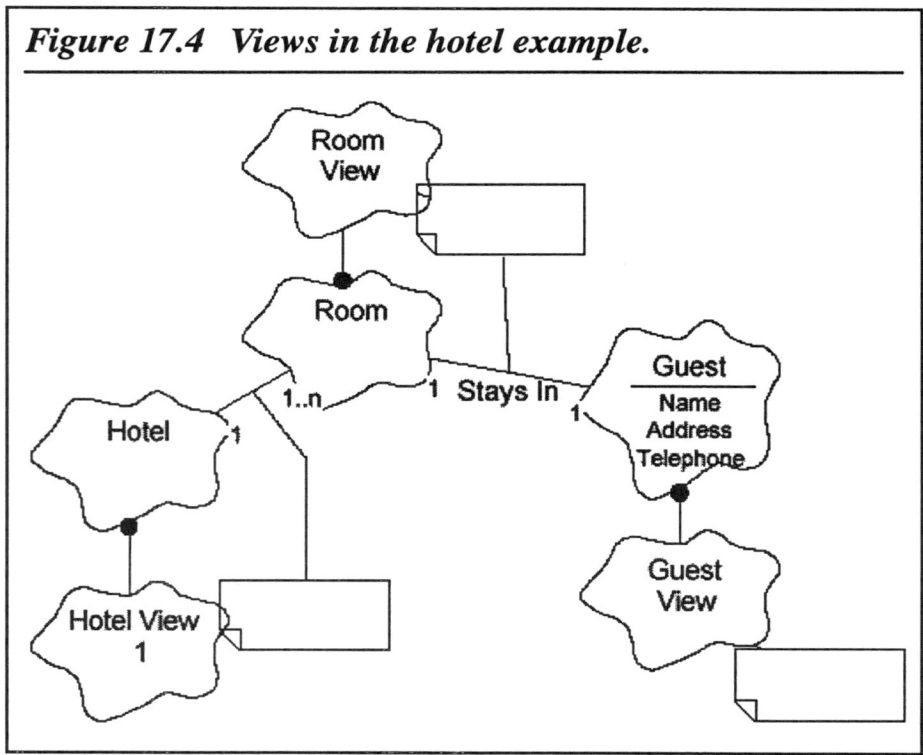

the tasks will be performed in the new design. This is again done with one of the diagrams from the Booch technique.

At this stage we introduce objects to represent the users of the system. This allows the actions of the users to be documented in the same way as any other action. In most cases the user objects are not implemented in the system. However, if any of these objects are found to be the subject of a verb they should be implemented. This may happen if, for example, the user is to be sent a message or request.

Figure 17.5 shows the flow involved in checking in a guest. Each vertical line in the diagram represents an object used in the task. An arrow represents an action caused by the object at the start of the arrow on the object at the tip of the arrow. The example starts with the desk clerk creating some information about a guest and a view being opened to display the information.

Interactions

The interactions for each object are recorded using a state diagram. We show the states of an object in two different notations: the state table and a Harel diagram.

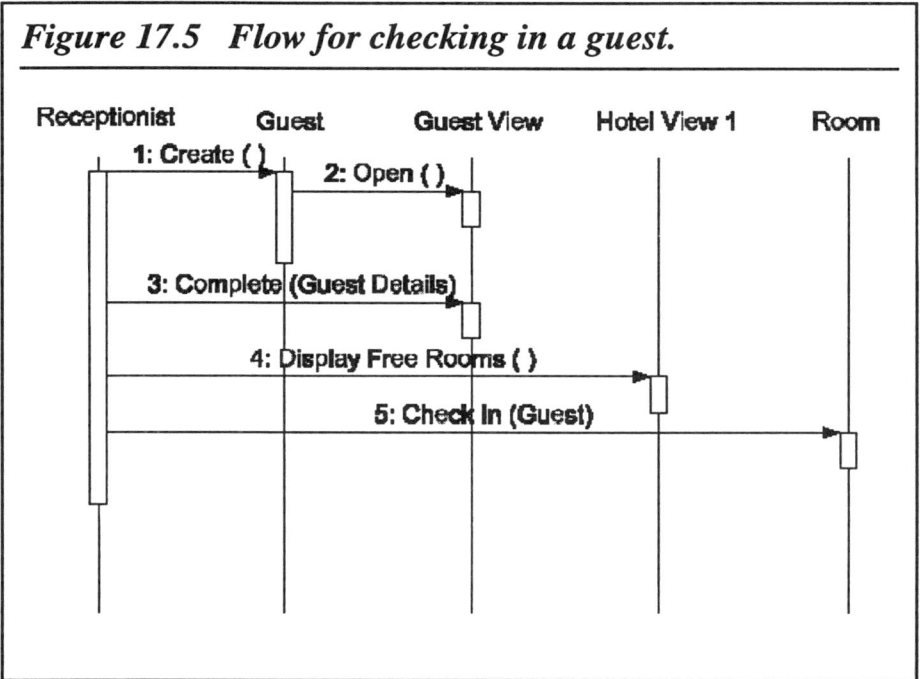

Figure 17.5   Flow for checking in a guest.

In the Harel diagram the rectangles represent the states of the object. The transitions between states are shown as arrows between the rectangles. Each diagram is normally started by showing a base state for the object. Then, taking the tasks one at a time, new states and transitions are added to the diagram.

In Figure 17.6 you can see the Harel diagram for a room. We started with a base state called "Ready" and added the "Occupied" and "Needs Cleaning" states as we considered guests being checked in and out, and rooms being cleaned. Notice that only the normal transitions found in the tasks are shown. If all the interactions were to be documented the diagram would become far too crowded.

It is often difficult to show all possible state transitions in a state diagram, but it is essential in interface design to consider all potential interactions with an object. So we chose to use state tables in addition. In state tables a column corresponds to a rectangle on the diagram: a state. A row in the table corresponds to an arrow on the diagram: an event that causes a state transition.

Table 17.1 shows the same states and transitions as the diagram in Figure 17.6. You may notice that the table has several empty cells. These empty cells are events that do not normally happen. But they are conditions that may occur and must be dealt with in the implementation. So, if the designer leaves these cases undocumented then the programmers may have to decide the result later. And in making that choice they might introduce a usability problem. To avoid these problems the interface designer must complete the descriptions for all the cells in the table.

Table 17.2 shows a more complete version of the same table. In some cases the action shown in the table is 'can't happen'. This is an indication for the designer to prevent the user from even attempting the action. For example, any control that ini-

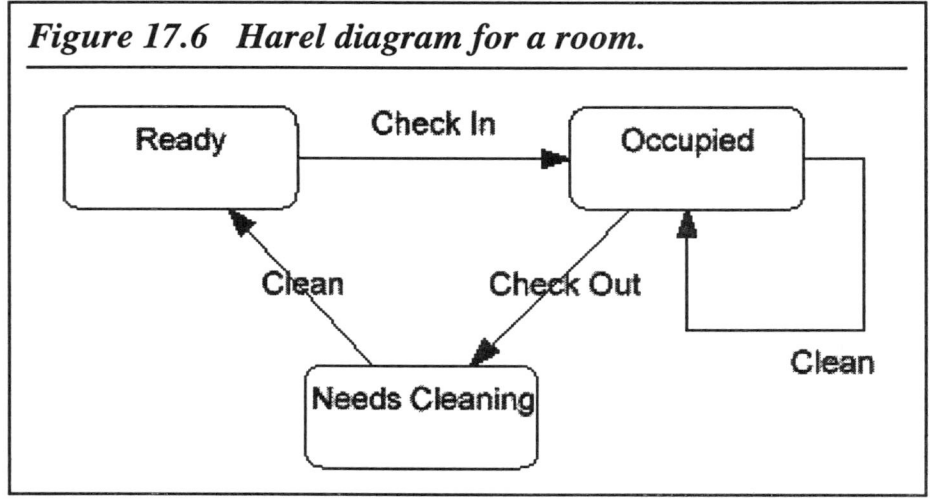

Figure 17.6   Harel diagram for a room.

tiates the action should be disabled in that state. In our hotel example, when the room is in the state called Ready, the control for Check Out is disabled.

In our example we have left one case incomplete. There is a question in the cell where a check-in is attempted for a room that needs cleaning. This indicates an oversight in earlier design sessions. To complete the design an action must be decided that will fit the users' models and requirements. This can be done in the next iteration.

Interaction design sometimes reveals other objects, ones that were not previously obvious. The OVID process relies on iteration to achieve completeness in documenting the objects, relationships, views, and interactions.

Realizing Views

So far we have only described the views of objects in abstract terms. For example, we have indicated in Figure 17.4 that Hotel View 1 shows the Rooms in the hotel. But the

Table 17.1   Room states.

States events	Ready	Occupied	Needs cleaning
Clean		Normal cleaning, no change	Change to ready
Check in	Change to occupied		
Check out		Change to needs cleaning	

Table 17.2   Complete room states.

States event	Ready	Occupied	Needs cleaning
Clean	Should not normally happen	Normal cleaning, no change	Change to ready
Check in	Change to occupied	Not allowed	Do we need to allow this?
Check out	Can't happen	Change to needs cleaning	Can't happen

diagram does not indicate how the list should be shown. We now need to design the views in detail.

Two types of information are passed to the graphics designer. One is the object diagram which indicates what information is to be shown. The other is the state information which shows how the information may vary.

The first stage of the visual design is to produce sketches of each view in each of its states. Sketches can be shared by the design team, and they can be used during evaluations by users. Once the team is happy with these designs the more detailed processes of visual design can be started.

Verification

User interface design is an iterative process. It is hard work to design a usable interface and you can't expect to get it right the first time. You should plan to prototype[1] the interface or at least significant portions of it and conduct usability tests.[2,3] These tests will help you to identify functionality needed to support tasks that may have been missed in the initial task analysis, to identify mismatches between the user and designer models, and find other usability problems resulting in errors or dissatisfaction.

Programs from Ovid

The next phase of product development is implementation. Because the product specification produced by OVID is in a design language used by programmers it requires little translation in this phase. The programmers on the team can derive the implementation classes based on the model that has already been captured.

A further advantage is revealed when some part of the design proves difficult to implement. Because the rest of the team understand the OVID notations, these problems can be discussed by everyone. The difficulties can be expressed in such a way that the impact on the users can be quickly assessed, alternatives can be explored, and optimal solutions found.

Choice of Tools

Most of the work that the authors have done with OVID has been based around the Booch notation[4] and has been captured using Rational Rose.[5] But OVID itself is not tied to any one notation or tool set. It can be easily adapted to create models in whichever notation and tool set the programming team uses.

In some areas the authors have had to work around deficiencies in both the Booch notation and Rational Rose, neither of which were intended specifically for user interface design. Some of these problem areas have been helped recently by the incorporation of notions from OMT[6] into Rose, and by Booch and Rumbaugh's recent work on the Unified Method.[7] But one area has proven more difficult — state diagrams.

As described earlier we adapted the state charts we found in Shlaer and Mellor's work[8] to our need. These charts show all states as columns and all events as rows, avoiding the clutter of the Harel diagrams. To aid in review and avoid duplication, the authors developed a program to create such a diagram (in HTML for online browsing) from the Rose file.

Conclusions

OVID is a design method that focuses team development of products on a common design language. It is a rigorous method that applies engineering disciplines to an area hitherto treated more as art than science. It is a method that is ideally suited to modern user interface styles and component based development — a growing trend in the computer industry.

OVID makes use of models to build software which is easy to learn and to use. Input from task analysis is used to create class and state diagrams. From these diagrams, the interface and visual designers produce designs of the views while the programming team designs the implementation code.

A short article such as this can only give an overview of the methodology. Much more detail is given in *Object Oriented User Interface Design Methodology.*[9] OVID tutorials are scheduled at several major conferences in the fields of software engineering and human-computer interaction.

References

1. Scott Isensee and James Rudd. *The Art of Rapid Prototyping.* International Thompson Computer Press, 1996.
2. J. Nielsen. *Usability Engineering.* John Wiley and Sons, 1993.
3. J. Nielsen and R. Mack.*Usability Inspection Methods.* Ap Professional, 1994.
4. Grady Booch. *Object-Oriented Analysis and Design with Applications.* Benjamin/Cummins, 1993.
5. Rational Rose/C++. Rational Software Corporation.
6. James Rumbaugh et al. *Object-Oriented Modelling and Design.* Prentice Hall International, 1991.

7. Grady Booch and James Rumbaugh. *The Unified Method*, v0.8. Rational Software Corporation, 1995.
8. Sally Shlaer and Stephen Mellor. *Object-Oriented Systems Analysis: Modeling the World in Data.* Yourden Press, 1988.
9. Scott Isensee, Dick Berry, Dave Roberts, and Didier Mullaly. *Object Oriented User Interface Design Methodology.* International Thompson Computer Press, 1997.

Chapter 18

Building a Highly Scalable
Data Warehouse

Ken Rudin

The Market Need for Scalable Solutions

As the information processing needs of modern corporations continue to rapidly grow and change, organizations are finding that it is becoming increasingly difficult to address these dynamic needs using traditional information technology solutions and traditional application design techniques. Customers are becoming more demanding, competition is more fierce, and markets are evolving rapidly. Additionally, strategic applications, such as data warehouses, data mining applications, and high-volume OLTP applications, are growing exponentially. These factors all combine to create requirements that traditional solutions cannot effectively address. A new breed of solution is needed which can handle the rapid increases in the amount of data that enterprises need to collect and analyze, and which can handle the growth in the numbers of users both internal and external to an organization that need access to these applications. These new solutions must be able to grow as quickly as an enterprise's needs grow, and must be able to provide new functionality as quickly as user's needs change. In essence, these solutions must be scalable.

Scalable solutions are strategic business applications that have the ability to grow (or "scale up") very quickly, and which can easily adapt to absorb additional functionality. They are also capable of delivering very high levels of performance and good price/performance, but what makes them unique is their focus on being able to quickly grow and adapt. It is because of this focus that organizations are looking towards scalable solutions as the optimal way to address their constantly growing and changing data processing needs. Any organization that builds a strategic application without focusing on scalability risks being stuck with an application that runs into limits once it begins to grow and therefore needs to be rewritten after only a short amount of time.

As with most strategic applications, scalable solutions must be built, not bought. This means that these solutions require a combination of enabling scalable technologies as well as a set of scalable application design and implementation techniques. Organizations need both the technologies and the techniques to ensure that their applications truly deliver the advantages of scalability. Fortunately, the technologies are largely already in place. Therefore, what the market most needs now are the techniques for using scalable technologies that ensures that an application delivers the unique benefits that scalable solutions offer.

The Enabling Technologies

Let's start by first looking at the technologies that are available. Hardware vendors have already delivered the scalable platforms that are the foundation of a scalable solution. These technologies are based on leveraging the power of commercial parallel processing and distributed processing. Parallel processing is the straightforward notion that by grouping together multiple copies of a resource (for example, multiple CPUs), users can achieve higher performance than is possible with a single copy of that resource. One type of parallel hardware is the symmetric multiprocessor (SMP), which incorporates a few CPUs into a single computer. For some applications, this is still not enough power, so vendors have created ways to tie multiple SMP machines together into a "cluster" architecture. Finally, even clusters aren't able to handle certain classes of applications, so hardware vendors have developed massively parallel processors (MPPs) which allow hundreds of processors to be used together in a single computer.

Distributed computing is another enabling scalable technology that is in fact conceptually very similar to parallel processing. Just as with commercial parallel processing, distributed computing recognizes that multiple combined resources can address bigger applications than can a single resource. The most prominent example of distributed technology is the World Wide Web, which combines the resources of hundreds of thousands of web servers around the world and has proven its ability to grow rapidly and adapt quickly.

Software vendors have also recognized the advantages of scalable solutions, and all major database vendors have delivered parallel versions of their database software to take advantage of scalable hardware architectures. When combined with such hardware, users have all the technological components they need to build scalable applications. If developed correctly, applications that use the technologies described above are optimal solutions for addressing an enterprise's dynamic needs.

The Need for Scalable Application Development Techniques

But, this raises an important issue: How does one develop applications that will effectively take advantage of the underlying scalable hardware and database software? First, as a rule, it is important to remember that for an application to scale, all layers must be designed to scale: the hardware, the database software, and the application itself. Similar to a chain only being as strong as its weakest link, a system is only as scalable as its least scalable component. A poorly designed application can easily destroy all the potential benefits of the underlying scalable platforms on which it is built.

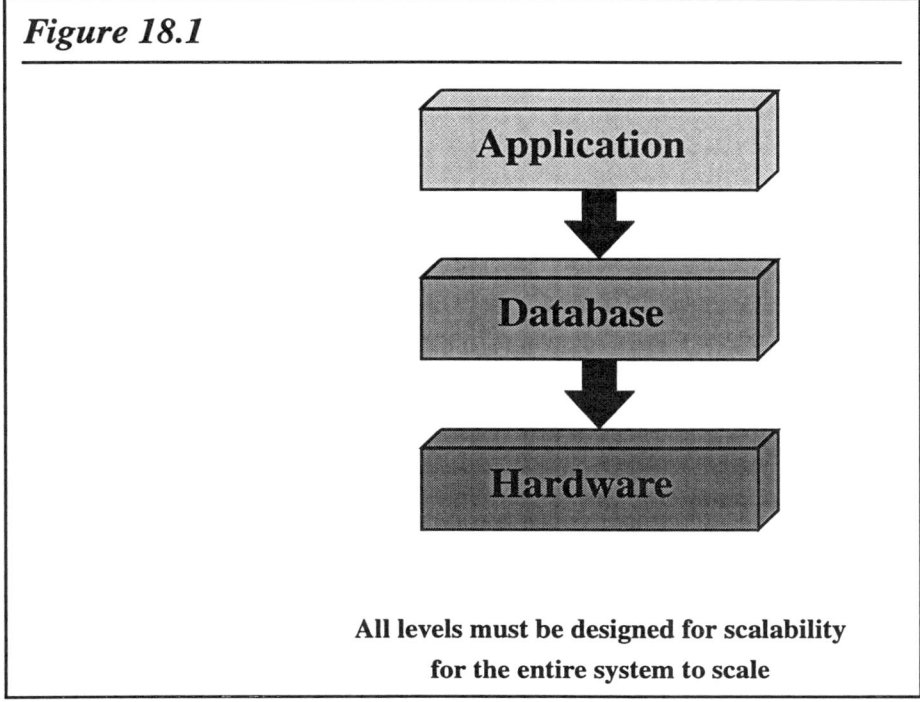

Figure 18.1

**All levels must be designed for scalability
for the entire system to scale**

So, what are the guidelines for building a scalable application? Given that building these applications will involve substantial development efforts, an organized approach must be followed. But, all of the existing application development approaches (a.k.a. "methodologies" or "frameworks") are inadequate for scalable application design, primarily because many of the fundamental assumptions are no longer valid. For example, traditional approaches assumed that all system requirements could be identified in advance, and they would not change during the development cycle. With scalable applications and scalable systems, this is no longer true. As mentioned earlier, strategic applications often grow exponentially, and their functionality needs to adapt and change fairly quickly. These changes do not wait until the development cycle is completed. Therefore, the traditional notion of "freezing the specification" of the application doesn't apply to a scalable environment, where everything is dynamic. A scalable methodology needs to embrace and manage that change, rather than suppress it.

Also, traditional approaches define a point where you're "done," and the application is completed. But, scalable systems are organic. They constantly grow. Like anything else that's organic, the application is never "done." It is dynamic, and therefore the traditional notion of the development cycle needs to be rethought. In addition, historically, organizations would build the entire system, and then cut over to it quickly (possibly running the new system and the old system simultaneously for a while). This isn't feasible with scalable applications for two reasons. First, these systems are often simply too big. Cutting over all at once is far too risky. Second, the concept of "building the entire system" doesn't fit into the scalable model, because the notion of "the entire system" is constantly changing as the application scales up in size and in functionality.

It should come as no surprise that a new technique is needed. Looking at the recent past, we see that the introduction of new technologies always required a different application design approach to make effective use of these technologies. For example, when relational databases were introduced, people had to learn the relational approach to database design. When client/server architectures were popularized, organizations needed to rethink the traditional notion of building monolithic applications. And those who adopted GUI technologies had to rethink the whole concept of the application's front-end. As with these technologies, scalable technologies need new design and development approaches to maximize their value to the enterprise.

Scalable Program Management Philosophy

The Emergent Scalable Program Management application development framework fills that need. It is the first methodology specifically designed for building highly scalable strategic applications, and it focuses on leveraging the business benefits of scalable technologies.

The philosophy behind Scalable Program Management is based on the concepts of incremental design and development. To build scalable applications, an IT department must think incrementally, design incrementally, and implement incrementally. This results in applications which can therefore incrementally scale up in performance and in functionality, allowing them to more easily adapt to changing requirements.

This is in stark contrast to mainframe application design, which focuses on building large, monolithic applications. Given the monolithic nature of the mainframe platform itself, a monolithic development approach is optimally suited to those platforms. However, applications designed in this fashion are poorly suited to the scalable systems environment. In the scalable environment, the platform is comprised of multiple smaller resources all pooled together. A monolithic application cannot be easily divided into smaller components in order to be spread across these multiple resources, and therefore cannot take advantage of the scalable platform. In concrete terms, if a system can have no more than a single CPU, then it is often optimal to write the majority of the application as one large piece of code so the hardware will not have to spend resources switching between various components of the application. However, on a scalable platform with multiple CPUs, this single monolithic application can only run on one processor at a time. To take advantage of the multiple processors, the application must instead be written as a collection of smaller functional components that can incrementally be added and which can be spread across the multiple processors. (Note: Parallel database vendors follow this philosophy in their approach to executing SQL statements. For example, rather than executing an entire query on one processor, the database divides the query processing into a number of subtasks, and runs these subtasks on different processors.)

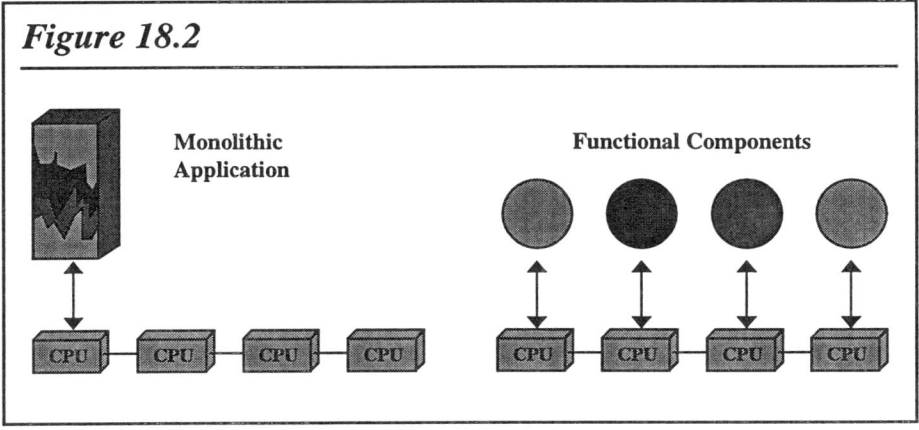

Figure 18.2

Monolithic Application

Functional Components

Overview of the Phases of the Scalable Program Management Framework

The most useful organized development approaches come not from academia, but from the real world. Such was the genesis of the Scalable Program Management approach, which came from the combined experiences of dozens of expert practitioners in the field of scalable application development and commercial parallel processing. As mentioned above, the essence of Emergent's Scalable Program Management is that for an application to be incremental, scalable, and dynamic, it must be designed incrementally, and the development approach itself must also be incremental, scalable, and dynamic. Tangibly, this means that the implementation phases must be iterative, and the scope of the application is scaled up for each iteration.

An outline of the Scalable Program Management implementation phases is as follows:

- Part I: Strategy

  - Step 1: Define the initial functionality required by the application. This is referred to as the "initial application."

  - Step 2: Brainstorm functionality users might want the application to contain in the future. What direction might the company be taking down the road? What are some interesting ways in which users might want to eventually use the application?

- Part II: Architectural Design

  - Step 1: Design the application, and focus on identifying and removing any potential bottlenecks. (There are numerous ways to remove different types of bottlenecks. These include techniques such as partitioning, replication, chunking, and scalable flow analysis, but a discussion of these is outside the scope of this paper.)

- Part III: Iterative Implementation

  - Step 1: Start small. Define the scope of what is going to be built during the first iteration as something that's small enough to be manageable. This scope may very well be significantly smaller than the scope of what was previously defined as the initial application, but the result should be an application that is still useful to the organization, even though it is not yet the full initial application.

  - Step 2: Scale up the scope. Go through additional iterations, each time broadening the scope of the application, but keeping the change in scope small enough that it can be easily managed. At the end of each iteration, the application should be progressively more valuable to the organization. Continue with further iterations until the application reaches what was defined to be the initial application.

- Step 3: Continue scaling beyond the initial goal. Remember that there is no concept of the application being "done." It will continue to scale up organically, and the development effort will continually expand the application's scope.

Tangible Differences Between Scalable Program Management and Traditional Approaches

To truly understand the concepts embodied in this approach, it is helpful to look at each of these phases and highlight some specific differences between the scalable approach and the traditional approach.

Strategy Phase

The goal of this phase is to identify the needs of the organization and to define requirements for the application. This is done via a series of discussions or interviews with senior management, developers, DBAs, end-users, etc. Typically, the focus of these discussions is on the current environment. The questions include, "What information do you need to take advantage of various market opportunities?" and "How do you measure progress against specified goals?" In Scalable Program Management,

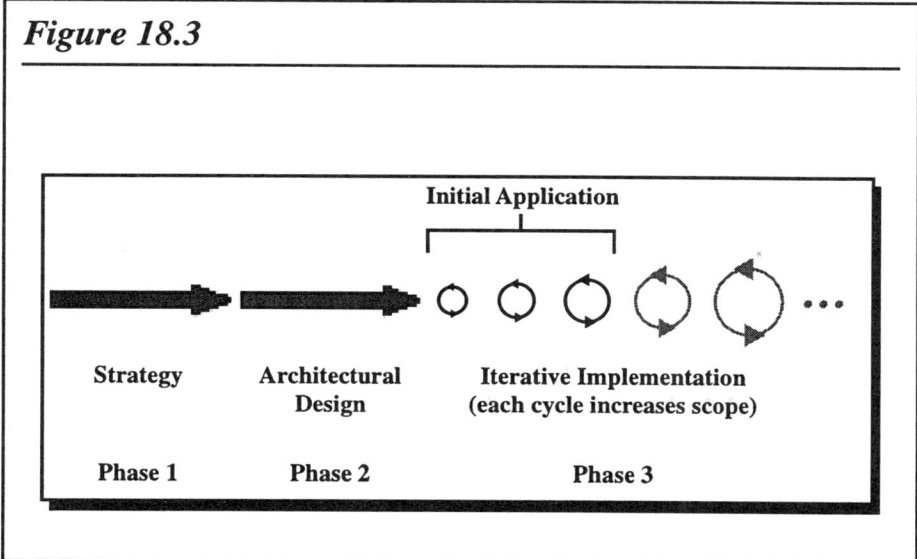

Figure 18.3

Strategy — Phase 1

Architectural Design — Phase 2

Initial Application

Iterative Implementation (each cycle increases scope) — Phase 3 the focus is not solely on the current environment but also includes where the company will be going in the future. Additional questions asked include, "How might your organization's role be changing over time?" and "What other types of information might eventually be useful to add to your database?" The point of this is to brainstorm about how the warehouse might change and grow over time and to be aware of that information during the design phase.

Additionally, in the strategy phase, typical methodologies will result in the building of an in-depth entity relationship diagram for the chosen subject area for the data warehouse. Unfortunately, if designers don't consider what other subject areas might eventually be included in the application, then they can make design decisions that inadvertently preclude easily including other subject areas in the future. Scalable application design calls for a high-level model of a much larger portion of the enterprise, in addition to the in-depth modeling of a particular subject area. This high-level model should not be a major undertaking — at most, a few weeks should be spent on it. The idea is not to have a detailed model of the entire enterprise, but rather to have a high-level feel for how the different organizations interact. Once it is understood how the current subject area fits into the rest of the enterprise, then the application can be designed to easily accommodate growth into those areas.

Architectural Design Phase

There are also tangible differences in the architectural design phase. In existing methodologies, the application specification (the "spec") focuses on the functionality of the application. Prototypes were designed to ensure that the functionality provided by the application met with the end-users' approval. However, many scalable systems are built to handle enormous amounts of processing and data. With these high-end applications, performance is certainly as important as functionality. In addition, in many instances, scalable platforms are chosen as the application foundation primarily because of the potential performance improvements that can be gained from the use of parallelism. For these reasons, the spec must also include performance requirements, not just functionality requirements. That is, a set of benchmark tests must be a part of the prototype of a scalable application. These benchmark tests are used in an ongoing fashion as part of what is called Performance Assurance.

In older approaches, designers were largely unconcerned about application partitioning, particularly if the target platform was a mainframe. As discussed above, on that platform, the entire application could run as one large application. However, the premise behind parallel systems is that the platform has multiple processors, each of which works on a part of the application simultaneously. To make this "divide and conquer" approach work in a scalable fashion, careful consideration needs to be paid to dividing up the work into smaller pieces that are fairly self-contained. If the pieces are divided up incorrectly, then the application will incur excessive overhead as all the processors spend valuable system resources communicating amongst each other in order to coordinate their actions. However, by looking at how the data is used, designers can determine clean ways to partition the functions of an application, thereby minimizing the amount of coordination that needs to be carried out.

Iterative Implementation Phase

This phase shows the most significant differences from older implementation approaches. First, as mentioned above, it is far too difficult (and risky) to build a very large system all at once. It would be similar to attempting to build a large office complex all at once. In the construction industry, the layout of the complex is done up front, and then the first few buildings are constructed. When those are finished, people can move in to those buildings (because those buildings are useful even if the whole complex is not yet complete), and then construction begins on subsequent buildings as the scope of the complex is increased. Applying some of this knowledge to building large, scalable applications, the Scalable Program Management method is to build an application that is first smaller in scope, but which is still useful to the organization. If this means that the new application is not yet ready to replace an old application, then the two must coexist via gateways between the new and old systems. When the first implementation cycle is completed, the scope is expanded and the next iterative implementation cycle begins. This process continually repeats.

Within each cycle of incremental implementation, the process is straightforward. First, define the steps that need to be taken for the development of the phase. Then, rather than proceeding with what is the traditional logical development order, it is instead imperative that the most challenging steps be identified and tested up front. Since the application, the database, and the hardware are all dynamic, it is critical to perform prototyping for each phase to ensure that both functional and performance specifications can be met. Essentially, think of each cycle as a scaled-down development project, and it therefore has its associated prototyping/testing step (also scaled down accordingly, of course).

After the prototyping/testing is completed for a cycle, the implementation occurs. But, what happens when end-users' needs change during the implementation? This is where Performance Assurance plays a critical role by enabling developers to reuse previously defined benchmarks to test whether or not a change will place the application outside its performance requirements. If it does, then either the change can be rejected, or the system (including one or more of either the application, the database, and the hardware) can be modified so that it will be within the required performance constraints. In the meantime, users can still use the previously completed cycle. Note that Performance Assurance certainly doesn't imply that all changes will fall within performance requirements; instead, its goal is to prevent developers from delivering the next cycle to end-users and then discovering that it falls outside of performance specifications.

Conclusion

Large strategic applications have requirements that make them well-suited to scalable hardware and database platforms. An organized approach such as Scalable Program Management recognizes that taking advantage of these platforms requires a different perspective on application development. If an application is intended to be able to continually adapt and grow, then the development process needs to implicitly focus on change and growth. The approach presented here mimics the applications it builds by also being able to incrementally scale up in scope. Finally, again like the applications it builds, the entire Scalable Program Management framework is dynamic. As the IT industry gains more experience in building applications that achieve unprecedented levels of scalability, the approach itself will grow, adapt, and become increasingly robust.

Chapter 19

Oracle vs. Sybase vs. Informix

David S. Linthicum

So what's it going to be? Oracle, Sybase, or Informix? At 35,000 feet, DBMSs look very much the same. However, on closer examination they offer different features, capabilities, and performance. Selecting the proper DBMS can make or break client/server development projects. This presentation introduces the attendee to the world of relational DBMSs, revealing the secrets of major DBMS vendors and how to select the right database for your next client/server project.

Database servers are the unsung heroes of client/server systems. They do most of the work, but end-users don't really know they are there. Data appears on the desktop as if by magic.

Developers know that database servers are the heart of most client/server systems. The database server provides secure access to shared data for client applications and allows client/server developers to split the processing load between the client and the database server.

Basic Idea

The idea of client/server is to do all the database processing on the server using its native operating system, processor, and storage resources. The client sends a request to the server, and the server responds with just the requested data. The client and the server are usually (but not always) separate and distinct, running on different machines connected via a network.

This architecture reduces the load on the network and frees the clients to do more important interface and application processing. Database servers can even take on some of the application processing load through the use of stored procedures and triggers, bounce back from system crashes using roll-back/roll-forward recovery, and guard data through the use of rules and two phase commit. Database servers also provide locking mechanisms and multi-user access controls that protect data from the dangers of concurrent access such as "deadlock" and "deadly embrace." Additionally, the database server secures the data, optimizes database queries, provides caching, and provides a location for the data dictionary.

Most database servers look pretty much the same at 35,000 feet, which makes selecting the right database server for your client/server project risky business. The database server and the operating system where it runs determine the number of clients that your system can support and the processing capacity of your client/server system. Selecting the wrong server (and platform) could mean that your system cannot scale, will fall down under the strain of the processing load, or provide substandard performance. Any of these problems results in project failure.

Truth be told, there is no foolproof way to select the right database server for your client/server project. You must consider the power of the platform that hosts the database server software, SQL standards, features such as stored procedures and triggers, and database administrative and monitoring tools. Let's see if we can shed some light on the features and functions of database servers, as well as what to look for when you select a database server for your client/server development project.

Key Players

In the world of relational database servers there are three major players: Informix Software's Informix, Sybase's Sybase SQL Server, and Oracle's Oracle Server. Each of these database servers can support various platforms including many Unix flavors running on the x86, RISC, and CICS processors, as well as Windows NT in both single processing and multiprocessing incarnations.

Platforms and Processors

In many respects, the platform where the database server runs determines the overall performance of the database server. For instance, Oracle on a 386 will not run as fast as it would on a RISC or Pentium-based computer. Moreover, database servers also depend on the services' host operating system, and the OS's ability to provide disk services, caching services, and network services efficiently. Therefore, selecting the right platform for your database server is as important as selecting the database server itself.

Although many exceptions exist, x86-, RISC-, and Sparc-based servers dominate the market, with many flavors of Unix and Windows NT providing the host operating system services in both uni- and multiprocessing versions. Unix is the old guard of the database server operating systems due to its ability to provide true preemptive multitasking and multithreading to its native applications, including the database server. Unix is sold under many names for many processors and includes SCO Unix, UnixWare, and Solaris for the x86, as well as Solaris for the Sparc, and HP/UX and AIX for RISC processors.

To exploit the best features of Unix, database server vendors such as Oracle, Informix, and Sybase mastered Unix's ability to support many simultaneous client connections as stand-alone processes, or threads (light-weight processes). The also capitalized on Unix's excellent I/O performance, memory management, and task management capabilities. All of this comes at the cost of having to manage the complexities of the Unix operating system. In addition, high-end Unix servers (such as IBM's RS/6000 and HP's HP/9000) can cost upwards of $50,000, depending on the number of processors and configuration.

Despite the continued popularity of Unix as a host operating system for database servers, Windows NT continues its fast popularity gain. Windows NT also provides all the features of Unix, but wraps it in a user-friendly, easily manageable package. Although Windows NT does not have the database server vendor following of Unix, the trend is clearly on its side. Products like Sybase SQL Server can exploit the capabilities of Windows NT, such as the ability to support many client connections in a single thread, and thus increase the server's ability to handle a large connection load.

SQL Standards

The problem with database servers is that they all speak different languages and dialects. As of yet, there is no surefire method to communicate with various database server products using a common SQL. There are several standard versions of the language that servers adhere to as set by a joint agreement with the American National Standard Institute (ANSI) and the International Standards Organization (ISO). It's important that you understand these standards before you select a database server. Currently there are three SQL standards that you should concern yourself with: SQL-89, SQL-92, and SQL3.

SQL-89 is the oldest and most useless of all ANSI SQL standards. SQL-89 is simply the least common denominator of SQL capabilities supported by existing products at the time the standard was adopted. Thus, existing products conformed to SQL-89 at the time of its release, but the label "SQL-89 compliant" is in a large part meaningless. SQL-89 did not move the database server world any closer to a unified SQL. Moreover, to make their products stand out from other database server vendors, most vendors began to add proprietary features that moved them further away from the concept of a database server standard.

The ISO SQL-92 standard adds much more detail to the SQL-89 standard, and standardizes many features that database server vendors practice differently among themselves. As a result, most database servers don't comply with SQL-92, but a few innovative vendors were early to the market with an SQL-92 compliant database server.

SQL-92 compliance is desirable because of the many features it adds to your database server. For example, SQL-92 adds support for SQL agents, which are programs or interactive users that generate SQL. SQL-92 also supports SQL client/server connections, meaning that SQL agents must ask the SQL client code to CONNECT to an available SQL server. In addition, SQL-92 provides embedded SQL support for modern languages, support for dynamic SQL, support for advanced data types such as BLOBS, and standardized error codes and diagnostics, to name only a few of the new features.

Although most database server vendors are not yet SQL-92 compliant, there is another standard on the horizon. SQL3 will add even more features, such as Object SQL capabilities that include encapsulation, methods, user-defined data types, and inheritance. For now, this remains in the future of client/server database servers.

Working Around The OS

Performance is everything in the database server market. In most client/server development projects, the fastest database wins the business. To maintain and improve performance, database server vendors learned to bypass the operating system to get at system resources directly. This trick has some trade-offs.

For example, most database servers (including Informix, Sybase, and Oracle) can bypass the file system that is native to the operating system, and go directly to a physical disk partition called a raw disk partition. Thus, the database server does not have to absorb the overhead required to go through operating system calls to get at the disk. The result is faster disk I/O performance and a faster database server.

You can use a raw disk partition as an option, or use the native file system of your host operating system (e.g., Windows NT, Unix, etc.). Although the raw disk partition usually provides the best performance, you'll need special utilities provided by the database server vendor to back up your database. Also, since the database server does not go through operating system calls to get at the disk, other processes that require disk I/O may be pushed aside by the database server. Generally, it's a good idea to place a database on its own physical disk drive to avoid this problem.

Other tricks that database servers use to gain performance include running the database server as a kernel level process, sometimes as Ring 0. A few Unix-based database servers do this, but the best example is database servers running on NetWare file servers as NetWare Loadable Modules (NLMs). Since NetWare does not have Ring 0 protection (although you can turn it on), the database server can run in Ring 0. While this does increase database server performance, one false move by the server software could crash the server. Most NLM-based database servers (including Oracle and Sybase) run well and fast on NetWare. NLM-based database servers are usually a better fit for organizations that already have a relatively idle NetWare server.

Managing Client Connections

The ability for a server to scale is directly related to how well the database server can handle client connections. A database server that requires a high number of resources (e.g., memory and processor capacity) for each connection can only handle as many users as there are resources available. Sooner or later you hit a wall, and the operating system breaks (usually by running out of physical memory and crashing). For example, a database server that uses 5 percent of a server's capacity for each connection can only handle around 20 users. Of course, this ratio depends largely on what the clients are actually doing.

Database servers handle client connections in three basic ways: processes-per-client, threading, and/or a combination of approaches. The process-per-client approach gives each client connection its own process. Thus, 20 clients would require 20 separate processes. The advantage of this approach is that the connections which operate in their own process address space are protected from other ill-behaved processes. Additionally, the process-per-client approach makes it easy for multiprocessing operating systems to allocate the connection processes to one or more processors to spread the load. The disadvantage of the process-per-client approach is that it eats up a tremendous amount of resources since each client requires a heavyweight process (sometimes two or three). What's more, using this approach, there is context switching and interprocess communications overhead as well. Database servers that use this approach include DB2/2, Oracle 6, and Informix.

The threading approach runs all users connections and the database in the same address space as threads. Threads are simply lightweight processes that run faster and require less resources than true processes since there is not as much context switching. In addition, this approach provides its own internal scheduler, with no dependence on the operating system's process protection mechanisms. This approach is also more portable from platform to platform, since there are usually few dependencies on native operating system services. The drawback of this approach is the ability for a single ill-behaved process or thread to crash the database server. Also, threading does not dole out the operating system resources as evenly as we would like. A single thread can saturate a processor and make the other threads wait in line. Database servers that use this approach include Sybase System 11.

The new Sybase System 11 database server, using threading, only requires about 60Kb of RAM per connection (50Kb for System 10). Other servers that use process-per-client can require as much as 2Mb of RAM per client. Sybase System 11 uses an SQL Server process (known as the dataserver) to create a thread for each client connection, as well as a thread for each logical database device and a thread for an error log.

There are a few database servers that use a combination of the features of threading and process-per-client to create a database server architecture that provides the best of all worlds. Oracle 7, for instance, uses a multithreaded network listener that makes the initial connections by assigning the client to a component called a dispatcher. The dispatcher in turn places messages from the client on an internal queue. A shared server process takes the message off of the queue, executes the request inside the database server engine, and returns the response back to the client, again using the internal queue. Although this is a complex architecture, it does provide several advantages. For instance, it can maintain a protected processing environment without having to dedicate a process for each user connection. On the downside, there are some latency issues with the use of the queue.

Parallel Query Processing

The battle cry of scalable database servers is parallel processing, or the allocation of the operating system's processing load (operating system processes and application processes such as database servers) across several processors. Most hardware and server operating system platforms (including the x86, RISC, and CICS) support multiprocessing. However, they do so in many different ways.

Database servers approach multiprocessing by either letting the operating system allocate the database query processing across available processors (shared memory) or by allowing the database server to allocate the query processing (shared nothing). If you select the latter, you must invest in a special version of a database server built specifically for parallel query processing. These servers break up a database query into smaller subqueries that execute concurrently on different processors. A query manager receives the request and allocates its processing among available database engines. Usually, there is one database engine per processor, and they are functionally equivalent to independent database servers. After the query processing is complete, the query manager reassembles the answer sets into a single set that is returned to the client.

Allocating query processing like this was expensive and experimental just a few years ago. Today there are several database server vendors that provide such features (including Oracle's Parallel Query Option, Sybase's Sybase MPP [formally known as Navigation Server], and Informix Dynamic Server). Some of these servers still have high per-user price tags, but prices are dropping quickly. Parallel database servers work best in database warehousing systems, or other applications where database response time is critical.

Stored Procedures, Triggers, and Rules

In an attempt to provide additional features for developers, Database server vendors began to offer stored procedures, triggers, and rules. These features provide the developer with the ability to program the database server itself, and therefore provide another partition for application processing. Stored procedures and triggers also reduce traffic on the network.

Developers have the option to run portions of a client/server application on the database server and thus balance the processing load in a two-tier client/server application. Client/server tools continue to learn how to exploit the stored procedure capabilities of database servers. For example, Oracle's Developer 2000 client/server development tool allows developers to move Oracle's SQL procedures from the client to the server, and back again, using a drag and drop mechanism on the client side.

Simply put, stored procedures are just a collection of SQL statements and procedural logic that client/server developers can compile and store on the database server as database objects. Client applications execute stored procedures, as well as stored procedures or triggers themselves, by sending a message to the database server where the stored procedures reside.

Triggers, in contrast, are stored procedures activated automatically by data-related events that the database server runs across in the normal course of database processing. For example, deleting a row in one table means automatically deleting a row in another table.

Rules are a special type of trigger that can verify the data before inserting it in the database. Rules generally assure that the data adheres to certain business rules or other criteria before existing in the database. For instance, a tax rate is never a zero.

Although stored procedures, triggers, and rules provide client/server developers with a lot of power, they are proprietary in nature. What's more, the capabilities vary greatly between server vendors. SQL Server, for example, can only fire a single trigger for an INSERT operation, where other database servers (such as Ingres's Ask Ingres database server) can fire multiple triggers. Moreover, stored procedures and triggers are not portable from database server to database server.

Despite a server's ability to support advanced features such as stored procedures, triggers, and rules, any database server should support referential integrity and two-phase commit. Referential integrity is a database server's ability to ensure that all foreign keys match their primary keys. Two-phase commit assures that server crashes won't result in a loss of data, since storing data is a redundant and recoverable process.

Other Features

Other features you should look for include database administration tools and database monitoring tools that come bundled with a database server.

Database administration tools include any software that can backup and restore a database, as well as perform user administration, security administration, and performance tuning. Remember, if they don't provide the tools required, you need to purchase them from a third party vendor (which can be expensive).

In addition to database administration tools, it's desirable for a database server to provide tools for database performance monitoring. These tools allow you to watch all aspects of the database server including cache, disk, processors utilization, etc. A few database server vendors (such as Oracle, Informix, and Sybase) do bundle a complimentary performance monitoring tool. However, if you need additional capabilities, such as a customizable reporting mechanism, you'll find what you need in the third-party marketplace.

Security

Security in the world of client/server is often an afterthought. If you need to run a secure client/server system, you'll need a secure database server to lock the bad people out of your data. In addition, a database server needs to provide security to the database, table, column, and sometimes the row level, to assure that only authorized users can view or update data.

Although most database servers do come with basic security (e.g., database and table-level security), they aren't hack proof by default. There are, however, secure versions of database servers that make the database server comply with government security standards such as C2 and B1. This means they will keep a close watch on user activity, age passwords, detect intruders, and do other "database police" services. Informix On-Line Secure 7.X, for instance, provides such features. There are secure versions of Oracle and Sybase as well. Although enhanced security is usually a good idea, these databases cost more and don't perform as well due to the overhead of the additional security processing.

Selecting A Database Server

As you can see, there is a lot to consider when you select a database server. Developers and architects should consider the following step-by-step procedures:

1. Understand your requirements, including the business problem you're trying to solve. Know what the client/server application will do, what processing load it will place on the database server, and the number of clients the server needs to support now and in the future.

2. List the features that are important to you. For instance, do you need security? What about stored procedures and triggers? What about administration and database monitoring? It's usually a good idea to make a list and provide rankings from 1 to 5, 1 being not important, 5 being most important.

3. Consider your clients. What applications will they run that connect into the database? Also, what type of middleware layer is in use?

4. Using the information above, create a set of at least three database server product candidates.

5. Using your database server candidates, select operating systems and hardware platforms that best meet your requirements. Sometimes this is a given. For instance, many shops only support Unix servers, while others only support Windows NT.

6. Make sure you consider administrative costs, along with hardware and software costs. You should consider cost on a per-user basis.

7. Create a pilot test bed using the database server candidates. Test each product's ability to meet the requirements of the application.

8. May the best server win.

Chapter 20

Nonrelational Databases

Joe Celko

Most of the data in the world is not in a record format that fits nicely into relational databases. Data takes a lot of forms — text, pictures, maps, charts, music, video, still images, etc. This usually get put into blobs in an SQL database and it is up to the host language to handle them when the SQL retrieves them.

Text

Some of the most important data in a business is not kept in records and therefore cannot be put into a database. The data is in text documents such as letters, contracts, manuals, regulations, policies, and procedures. The textbase market is growing at the rate of 50 percent per year, according to a 1991 study by IDC and Delphi Consulting Group. Most of that growth is in centralized data centers.

There are two basic terms used in this field, textbases and document base, which are gradually being grouped under the term textbase. Strictly speaking, a textbase is just text without any structure to it and are treated as blocks of text with a name.

A document base is text which comes arranged in a structured format whose parts have some relationship to each other. Usually the documents have a header record which gives some information about the document and the body or actual text. Most documents are hierarchies of this header-body structure. Books break into chapters,

chapters into paragraphs, paragraphs into sentences, and finally sentences into words. Manuals break into sections, subsections and sub-subsections.

There are two basic kinds of searches — on the headers or in the body of the documents. Much of the initial searching is done on the headers, so it is important that they all have the same format. A body or text search depends on pattern matching within the text itself.

A search has to return a result at a certain level of granularity within the body of the document. This level is usually adjustable. Obviously, searches which return all occurrences of a particular letter or word are useless. The smallest practical unit is a sentence (or enough characters that you will most likely see all of a sentence). The largest practical unit is the document — simply because the next level of this hierarchy is the whole document base itself.

The header is a record with fixed fields that apply to all the documents under consideration. It can be searched like a relational database, which is much faster than searching the text. The header information can include almost anything, but most common fields are the title, author(s), publication date, classification codes, an abstract, or a keyword list.

An abstract is a short summary of the contents of the document to which it is attached. This has to be made by a skilled reader, but there are attempts to automate this process.

A keyword list is a list of words or phrases drawn from a predefined set of words or phrases which have meaning to the searcher. For example, this article might have a keyword with "textbase", "text retrieval", and "document retrieval" in it. A keyword does not have to appear in the body of the document itself. For example, not too many satires would include the word "satire" in themselves. This is a powerful search tool, but it also requires a human being with knowledge of the field to design the vocabulary and make the choice of keywords. The vocabulary will have to be updated on a regular basis, adding and dropping terms.

Notice that the keyword list approach works for a single document, not for a collection of documents. Another version of this approach are the keyword in context (KWIC) systems. They use a set of keywords and locate the words within phrases from the document. Usually the phrases are titles, but they can be short descriptive sentences from the original document. The old printed versions of KWIC indexes would print the phrases around a gutter to highlight the keyword, thus you might look up the keyword "domino" and see a listing like this.

```
                        DOMINO Games for Children
                        DOMINOES and Other Stories
              Fats      DOMINO
           Chinese      DOMINO Games
     Derek and the      DOMINOES
Internal queues in the  DOMINO Operating System
```

Another approach is to give each document a general classification code to narrow a search as soon as possible. The Dewey Decimal System and Library of Congress (LOC) classification schemes are ways of doing that for library books. There is at least one web site using LOC, but most of the services have their own hierarchical schemes with the option to do a full search.

The subheaders become simpler in structure. For example novels have chapters which have only titles (or titles and synopsis if it is a 19th century novel), and paragraphs have no headers. However, a technical manual might break this down further in sections and subsection titles.

Semantic searching is more difficult because it has to understand the meaning of the documents and the search question. For example, an ideal semantic text search engine would have taken my query about "dominoes" and asked if I meant the Domino operating system or the game. When I said "the game", it would then look at the documents available and determine which ones deal with games.

Even better, the engine would have some machine intelligence to associate things that are not normally indexed together and tell someone looking at surgical techniques for damaged livers to consider a magazine article on underwater basket weaving because they use the same methods. Obviously, there are not many working semantic search systems and they are expensive.

Indexing Text

Before text is searched, most systems usually index it. An index is a file of the location of each significant word in the document. The first step in the process is to determine which words are significant and which are noise words.

Noise words are words which are so common in English (or whatever language) that people would not search on them because every document will have them. These are usually linguistic structuring words such as articles, conjunctions, pronouns, and auxiliary verbs. But the noise word list can also include numerals, punctuation marks, numbers, single letters, and words which are so common to a particular discipline that all documents would include them.

Once the noise words are pulled out, the index can be built. The index can point to the whole document, the relevant section, paragraph or sentence, or to an abstract of the document (once you have read the abstracts, you have the option of getting the whole document in hardcopy off-line, or downloaded online. Once indexed, a document is ready for searching. All text query languages are based on matching character string patterns. Complex queries are from the operators using operators such as AND, OR, and NOT to create expressions. The AND operator means that both patterns were found in the document, OR means that one or both patterns were found, and NOT means the term was absent. They are usually called Boolean operators, but they are actually set-oriented membership tests, not logical predicates.

The simplest pattern matching operator is an equality test, where the search string has to match exactly. The next most complicated operator is a pattern matcher which uses wildcards, like the "?" in DOS command lines or "_" in SQL's LIKE predicate, and a multicharacter wildcard, like the "*" in DOS command lines or "%" in SQL's LIKE predicate.

There are three major types of synonyms. A grammatical synonym is a different form of the same word. For example, "be" has grammatical synonyms "am, is, are, been, was, were." Most textbases will have irregular plural forms in their thesaurus. Many automatically recognize grammatical postfixes, such as "-s", "-es", "-ing," and "-ily," and can store information about double the final consonant or dropping the final "e" in the index. This feature is also found in spelling checkers in word processors.

The grammatical forms are often automatic and generated by a parsing program. User controlled synonyms are keep in a thesaurus file, which again will differ from product to product. Most systems keep a list of plural forms and perform an automatic replacement of the original by a list separated by ORs. For example, "wife" might expand out ("wife" OR "wives").

True synonyms have a semantic equality to the word, such as "boat" has the true synonyms "ship," "craft," and "vessel," and they can all be swapped around in place of each other.

Narrow synonyms are specific cases of the concept, such as "Europe" narrowing down to countries such as "France," "Germany," and "Italy."

Synonyms for dates and numbers are a special problem. They are true synonyms, but their forms are very different and can be homonyms for other concepts. For example, "one," "1" and "I" are the English word, Hindu-Arabic numeral, and Roman numeral for the same concept. The Roman numeral is also a homonym for the first person pronoun. But this list does not show 1.0, 1.00, 1.000, and so forth.

Proximity operators look for words within a certain distance of each other, where distance is measured by a word count, sentence count, paragraph count, or other structural unit. At least one version allows the user to set up the borders of his search to the text between a start word and a finish word (as in find the name "Heathcliff" between "Dear" and "Sincerely" in a textbase of love letters).

The quorum operator looks for documents with k out of a list of n words or patterns, as in 2 OF [German, French, Spanish, Czech] for example. The quorum operator is often used to restrict a list of synonyms, but it is a shorthand for a Boolean expression.

Weighted searches assign a score that attempts to measure how well a document fits the query. This can be very useful when searching a large textbase. It can also be disaster if the weighting function is flawed.

There are several types of word scoring schemes. The simplest method is a tally of the presence in or absence of query words from a document. No special weight is assigned to one term over another.

The second method is to report the number of occurrences of each word or pattern. It is assumed that the documents with the most hits are the best ones.

In a mixed strategy, each word or pattern gets a weight which is multiplied by the number of occurrences, to give a score. This a little harder to do, because you must assign weights somehow. The second method is really a special case of this, with a weight of one for each search term.

The fourth method is to have a semantic tree structure that assigns heavier weight to more specific synonyms. This means that the thesaurus has to know the difference between broader and narrower terms. A search for `"Southwest* Indian?"` would give more points to documents containing names of particular tribes ("Hopi," "Zuni," or "Navaho"). A document with "Amerind" or "Native American" would get a few points while a document on Slavic peoples would score nothing. Again, these term weights can be multiplied by the number of occurrences to give a final score.

More elaborate weighting schemes will give points for proximity, order of the search terms in the document, and statistical distribution within the document.

The ANSI Z39.58 "Common Command Language for Online Interactive Information Retrieval" was developed by the National Information Standards Organization (NISO) (Box #1056; Bethesda, MD 20817) and ISO Standard 8777 describes a similar simple text search language. Only a few products actually implement either the ANSI or ISO search languages which are both minimal. The good news is that most products resemble them, so you do not have much trouble moving from one product to another, and they are generally stronger search tools.

Images

If you have become a web-surfing addict, you know that a major part of the "web experience" is downloading all those cool pictures. How do you search a still picture? Human beings do it without any thought at all. A human will simply "just see it right there!" when someone asks him to pick an object from an image. Small children can find Waldo in the most crowded and confused images.

Traditional search engines have relied upon the laborious and time-intensive method of creating and searching a separate text or numeric database describing images. This is not too bad when the class of images is specialized, say houses, and can be described with a limited specialized vocabulary (two-story, Cape Cod, three-bath). But this is impossible given an image database the size of the Internet.

Image queries are done by providing a search image and returning records which score high matches with that image. Some of the attributes, such as color, are adjustable in the scoring system.

Excalibur Technologies Corporation has Excalibur Visual RetrievalWare which they are providing through Yahoo!, a leading guide to the Internet, via a partnership between Excalibur and Interpix. IBM has its Query by Image Content (QBIC) technology, which ships as a DB2 Extender. Virage Inc. (San Mateo, CA) has its Visual Information Retrieval system, which Object Design Inc. (Burlington, MA), an object database vendor, has licensed for its forthcoming Image Object Manager. Virage has also licensed its engine to Informix as a DataBlade.

These technologies work in a similar fashion. The image information is reduced to a searchable index typically less than 10 percent of the size of the original file. The user starts with an image or rough sketch and ask for similar images by assigning weights to major visual attributes (shapes, colors, and textures) in the search criteria. For example, if you are searching a clothing catalog for a blue shirt, you might weight color heavier than texture. The engines process the search images, putting the results of the analysis into a 1- to 2-Kb vector. When performing queries, the search engine uses the vectors to develop a similarity rating for each image. Using the vectors makes the search very fast; the longest part of any query will be drawing the found images on the screen.

These systems can be used across the Web to make an image database available to customers. In fact, the vendors have set up demos on the Web: Virage is at `http://www.virage.com` and IBM is at `http://wwwqbic.almaden.ibm.com`.

Although these search engines are a big step forward, you could get some unexpected answers. For example, with Virage's engine, asking for a match of an image of two roses at a trade show turned up a number of flower images. But it also got a pair of rhinoceros heads because the shapes of the two images were similar.

You also can not ask for objects by name. A child can recognize a "dog" from a cartoon or a photograph, regardless of the species of the particular dog in the image. Semantic analysis is still an unfinished job for the artificial intelligence researchers.

There are other specialized image applications, such as face recognition, fingerprint matching, and video scene change detection. Law enforcement is the first market you might think of for this technology, but as the cost has started to go down, it is being used in other areas, too.

Modeling and talent agencies are using face recognition to match people to search criteria ("Send me a Marilyn Monroe type!"). Experimental ATM machines confirm the identity of their users by matching the face on the video camera to their records or by scanning fingerprints.

Scene change data is used to monitor traffic flow. Before now, traffic engineers had to look at still photographs and count cars and note their positions. Now that information is automatically collected and analyzed.

Geographic Data

GIS (Geographic Information System) stores maps, usually as two dimensional objects, and answers queries based on spatial and traversal relationships. An example of a spatial query would be "How many people live within a one-kilometer radius of my store location?" and the result would be a number. An example of a traversal query would be "Where does the number 42 bus line cross Peachtree Street?" and the answer would be a point on a map. Geobases are used in the utilities industry, for logistics, in marketing, and for traffic control.

There are two fundamental ways to represent maps: vectors or rasters. A raster map divides the map into small uniform squares and each square holds a value for the attribute being mapped. The advantage of this approach is that it is easy to represent in a database; the disadvantage is that the map is a bit unnatural unless the squares are very fine.

For example, if a square has a river and some shore in it, should it count as water or land?

In the vector approach, the objects on the map are made up of points, lines, arcs, or polygons. This requires a lot of machine power to maintain, operate, and store. These maps are usually built by scanning photographs or older maps rather than by programming.

The long time players in this field are Mapinfo Corporation (http://www.mapinfo.com) and Environmental Systems Research Institute (http://www.esri.com). However, they are working with more traditional database companies to add GIS capabilities to SQL databases. This is not just the ability to display a tabular result on a map, but to accept geographical queries along with standard SQL. Oracle, Informix, and Ingres all have GIS units now.

Queries can be submitted in a language, usually an extended SQL, but that is not always the best way. It is often better to use a graphical interface tool to draw or point directly on the map in an interactive session. This means that the geobase is likely to be a client-side tool which loads its data from a server.

Temporal Databases

Temporal databases are now a separate academic area, with most of the research being done at the University of Arizona by Rick Snodgrass and his group. Their TSQL2 (Temporal SQL version 2) is the basis for the current temporal extensions in the ANSI/ISO SQL3 project.

A temporal database is concerned with the history of the world it models, while a traditional relational DBMS is a snapshot of the state of the world it models.

These databases start with temporal logic as their foundation, just as the relational database started with set theory and relations as its formal basis. Let me hit a few major points, without going into any details, to give you a taste of what temporal databases look like.

An event is a point in time ("The train arrives at 15:00 Hours."). A duration is a floating period of time ("The trip takes three hours."). An interval is a fixing period of time ("St. Fred's Festival is March 10 through March 16."). The model for intervals and durations is an open-ended time interval because open-ended intervals can be added or subtracted from each other to produce open-ended interval results.

Queries vary as their time frame changes. Assume that Charlotte was born on 1980 December 31 and that today is 1997 Jan 01. The day before yesterday, she was 17 years old. Next year, she will be 20 years old. She was 18 years old yesterday and will be 19 years old during all of 1997.

If you did a report on the age of your employees a few days apart, you would have had a jump in the age groups which would be noticeable because Charlotte went from being a minor (under 18) to being a legal adult (21 and over) in this period.

Temporal queries ask questions with terms like "before," "after," and "during" or "while," as well as the usual Boolean expressions. The formal definitions of such terms is pretty much what you would expect from English usage, but not always.

Questions about time series and rates are analogs to the GROUP BY clauses and aggregate functions in SQL. Calculating with time to get rates is also troublesome. Try this old puzzle: if a hen-and-a-half can lay an egg-and-a-half in a day-and-a-half, then how many hens does it take to lay six eggs in six days? The answer is a-hen-and-a-half; I leave the algebra to the reader.

People tend to get tripped up on the rate (eggs per hen per day) because they handle time wrong. For example if a cookbook has a recipe that serves one and you want to serve one hundred guests, you increase the amount of ingredients by one hundred, but you don't cook it one hundred times longer.

Conclusions

There are other types of nonrelational databases which have not been covered in this short article. When you read this, someone will have a new nonrelational database on the market or in his laboratory. What the nonrelational databases got from the relational databases is a metamodel of what a database should be.

A database needs to have objects, operators, and logic. The objects can be virtually anything that is of interest to a user. Given the objects, there is an implied set of meaningful operations on them which also have to be part of the database. The logic determines the query system. We have already talked about the use of temporal logic for temporal databases, but it is only one of many choices. For example, an extended fuzzy logic could replace the three-valued logic of SQL.

Chapter 21

Selecting Distributed Objects

David S. Linthicum

Everyone agrees that distributed object standards are a good idea, but no one seems to know how to go about selecting distributed object standards and products. Developers need to consider many factors. These factors include platform support, object communication mechanisms, call level interfaces, and integration with available development tools. This presentation walks the attendee through the world of distributed objects, including emerging standards such as OMG's CORBA (Common Object Request Broker Architecture) specification and Microsoft's Component Object Model.

Slowly but surely, distributed objects continue to make their way into the world of client/server. In the early 90s, what was supposed to be a revolution turned out to be an evolution of specifications and trial balloons. Today, however, we could be on the verge of moving mainstream client/server development into the world of distributed objects, and the Web could be the way to get there.

Other issues that could move developers toward distributed objects include Microsoft's Distributed Component Object Model and its ActiveX (formally OCX) component incarnation. With NT 4.0 already DCOM-ready, and Windows 95 heading there quickly, developers may find that their object request broker (ORB) infrastructure is part of the operating system. Existing OLE-enabled tools are ready to take advantage of the Microsoft giveaway ORB.

Components are part of the game as well. Since OpenDoc did not appear on the desktop as predicted with the poor sales of Macs and OS/2, ActiveX wants to be your component of choice for both client/server and the Web. OpenDoc is a component of IBM's Distributed System Object Model (DSOM), which adheres to the Common Object Request Broker Architecture (CORBA).

There are tough decisions in your future, so let's start from the beginning. In this presentation we'll look at the concept behind distributed objects, as well as the standards that now compete for the hearts and minds of developers and tool vendors. Finally we'll look at components and their links to distributed object standards, then wrap things up with a look at how distributed objects are changing the web.

Defining an ORB

ORBs are the concept of using standard objects that communicate with other standard objects through a well-defined interface. Like objects of C++ or Smalltalk, ORBs invoke each other's methods, as well as send and receive data. ORBs are typically multiplatform, and run on any number of platforms, which lets developers create distributed heterogeneous applications. ORBs are naturally distributed, and communicate within the same server, or with many servers over a network (distributed ORBs or distributed objects).

The concept of an ORB really grew out of the early days of object-oriented development. As developers learned to leverage objects within applications, they looked to mix and match objects with other applications as well. Since objects are tool-dependent (C++, Smalltalk, PowerBuilder, etc.), they don't work and play well with others. Developers needed a binary object standard which would allow them to mix and match language-independent objects.

What ORBs do in their spare time is pass requests from clients to object implementations on which they are invoked. The client makes the request using the ORB Core through the IDL stub, or through the Dynamic Invocation interface. The stub provides the mapping between the language of choice (e.g., C++ or Smalltalk). The ORB has to support the mapping. The ORB Core can then transfer the request to the object implementation that receives the message through an up-call using an IDL skeleton or dynamic skeleton.

In 1989, the Object Management Group, a consortium of technology vendors that include IBM, Apple, Sun, and many others, mobilized to create a cross-compatible distributed object standard. The promise was clear — object reuse regardless of the platform or programming language. The goal was a common binary object with methods and data that work using all types of development environments on all types of platforms.

OMG was not, and is not, a product company. They are in the specification business. Using a committee of organizations, each with their own agenda, OMG set out to create the first Common Object Request Broker Architecture (CORBA) standard which appeared around 1991. CORBA is a specification document that describes a messaging facility for distributed object environments to provide a standard mechanism for objects to invoke each other's services.

The original CORBA specification (Corba 1.1) included two parts: the Interface Definition Language (IDL) and the Dynamic Invocation Interface (DII). Each service exists inside the ORB and the base services form to enable messaging between objects inside a local or distributed system.

The IDL is really just an object structure that provides the developer with an API to access the object services while the objects are up-and-running. The IDL lets developers build applications, while at the same time understanding the types of objects that they can communicate with when an ORB-based application is up-and-running. DDI is also an API that provides developers with dynamic construction of object invocations. You don't have to call a routine to invoke an operation inside a particular object. The client can setup the objects and operations, including any parameters. With DDI, developers can make decisions while the objects are running. IDL requires you to set things up beforehand.

Many commercial ORBs came out of CORBA 1.1, including IBM's Distributed System Object Model (DSOM), Post Modern Computing's (now Visigenic) Orbaline, and Iona's (now a part of IBM) Orbix, to name just a few. Although CORBA 1.1 was a step in the right direction, it did not provide enough detail for tool vendors and developers to create objects that work together. For example, DSOM could not work with Orbix out-of-the-box. So, the OMG began work on another CORBA specification, CORBA 2.0. As Chris Stone, the president of the OMG put it to me a few years ago, "CORBA 1.1 solved the problem of portability. CORBA 2.0 adds interoperability." CORBA 2.0 was released in 1994.

The basic difference between CORBA 1.1 and 2.0 is the addition of specific syntax for a network protocol. The IDL remains largely the same. CORBA 2.0 also provides mapping to C++ and Smalltalk, which rose in popularity after the original specification's release. In addition, CORBA 2.0 defines a TCP/IP-based Inter-ORB backbone, and an Inter-ORB communication service that allows components to generate universal global IDs for their interface.

Anatomy of an ORB

The CORBA ORB provides four main components: the object request broker (ORB), object services, common facilities, and application objects. Although these are related to CORBA, you'll find similar features in Microsoft's COM (more on that later in the article).

As I alluded to above, an ORB is an engine that can communicate with other local or remote objects using a well-defined common interface and line protocol. ORBs make requests to other ORBs (using the same standards, like DCOM and CORBA), and process responses.

The power of ORBs is that all these communications and method invocations take place away from the eye of the user. There is an application built on top of the ORB, and the ORBs carry on business in the background automatically. The concept is to assure the application of portability and interoperability, locally or across a network. The CORBA specification simply defines how these ORBs work together.

Object Services are groups of services that use an object interface to communicate from one service to the next. Object services provide base services such as security, transaction management, and data exchange. Using this base set of services, developers can build other services on top of them. Object Services are mandated by CORBA.

Common Facilities are collections of services as well, but they relate more to a client than a server. You'll see what Common Facilities can do by looking at component document facilities such as OpenDoc. Common Facilities are optional CORBA services.

Application Objects are objects that support the application directly. These are defined by the developer, and are the portions of CORBA that actually solve the business problem at hand. These are the facilities that are built using the IDL. The IDL assures that they can communicate with other CORBA-compliant ORBs.

Microsoft Makes a Move

Although there are many architectural benefits to using CORBA, they are not the only game in town. A few years ago, Microsoft announced their own ORB standard known as the Component Object Model (COM). COM is in every sense an ORB in that it provides an object standard and a common method of inter-ORB communication using OLE.

As OLE automation became a standard on Windows desktops (which almost all of us run), client/server tools such as Delphi, Visual Basic, Visual C++, and Power-Builder began to support COM by providing developers with the ability to create OLE automation servers.

OLE Automation servers come in two flavors: in-process and out-of-process. In-process OLE automation services are really just .DLLs that are loaded directly into the memory space of the application to provide all sorts of application functionality. ActiveX controls are examples of in-process OLE automation servers that act like components.

Out-of-process OLE automation servers are ORBs that function outside the memory space of the application. Out-of-process OLE automation servers are .EXEs, and run in the multitasking environments of Windows 95 and Windows NT. Out-of-process servers communicate with other OLE-enabled ORBs or applications using an RPC (remote procedure call) mechanism, and the standard OLE interface.

The problem with COM was that it could not leverage the power of distributed objects until just a few months ago. With the release of Windows NT 4.0, the Distributed Component Object Model (DCOM) is now a reality for Windows-oriented client/server developers.

DCOM allows COM-enabled (meaning OLE-enabled) application development tools and even office automation applications to access out-of-process OLE automation servers that physically exist on the local machine or on a machine connected by a network. The application simply checks with the registry of Windows NT to locate the remote ORB and invokes its services. For example, you could create a COM ORB using any number of tools that automatically generate a sales report if a certain method in the ORB is invoked. Other COM-enabled applications existing on the network can access that object by locating and invoking its methods through the DCOM mechanism built into the Windows operating system.

DCOM is very different than CORBA because it's built into the infrastructure of the operating system and network and is not delivered by an ORB vendor. That means for existing Windows 95 (where it's soon to be included) and Windows NT shops, it's already there. What's more, where CORBA has yet to attract the mainstream tool market, COM is already a part of most development tools you purchase for Windows. However, DCOM is a Windows-only phenomenon, and those of you who run a hodgepodge of operating systems and processors won't find any value in DCOM.

So What Do DOs Do?

So now that we know what distributed objects are, the question is: What do they do? The real benefit of distributed objects is the ability to take a "divide and conquer" approach to client/server development which allows applications to scale through distribution. This is the same problem that application partitioning products such as Forte and Dynasty solve. However, they do it through the use of proprietary ORBs.

For instance, say you need to create an application to support a banking system. The application needs to include a loan processing system, an investment system, and a system to support new accounts. Rather than create stand-alone applications to solve each problem using any number of client/server development tools, developers can take an open ORB approach.

Leveraging ORBs, developers can create each application by building them as ORBs (or usually a group of ORBs; but for our example, let's not make things more complicated). Creating the Loan Processing System as an ORB is just a matter of defining the application logic inside the ORB using the IDL in the case of CORBA, or the ODL (object definition language) in the case of COM. You can even connect the ORB up to a database server if you need data (and you usually do).

Once created, the ORB can run anywhere on the network, accessible by any application interface that's ORB-aware, for instance, IBM's VisualAge or even PowerBuilder 5.0. The power of such an architecture is that the ORB is accessible by any application running on the network, similar to an application server. Therefore, the logic is centrally located, and developers can change the ORB at any time for any reason, automatically changing the functionality of the applications that use it. ORBs are tool-independent as well, and all sorts of applications can access the services of the banking ORBs. This allows the application services of the ORBs to be reused throughout the application.

Since the ORBs run remotely, the client does not get loaded down with the application processing, as is the case with traditional two-tier "fat client" client/server development. ORBs become an application service layer comparable to TP monitors. Moreover, since the ORBs are portable, developers can move them from platform to platform without having to worry about interoperability with other platforms (all except the Windows-bound COM).

Considering Components

Another issue to consider is the availability of application components that comply to ORB architecture. Here you'll have to pick religions as well. There are two flavors of application components — the CORBA-based OpenDoc from a consortium including Apple and IBM, and the Web-enabled ActiveX from Microsoft.

OpenDoc was supposed to be the de facto component standard. Developed just a few years ago, OpenDoc is really a component-enabled version of IBM's SOM. OpenDoc provided developers with the ability to plug components into applications or documents as needed, mixing and matching components for what ever reason. Today, OpenDoc has not captured hearts and minds, nor market share, despite the fact that its architecture is superior to COM and ActiveX, and OpenDoc is multiplatform as well. OpenDoc is still a factor on non-Windows workstations, as part of the MacOS and OS/2.

ActiveX is COM's answer to components, as well as COM's answer to Java. ActiveX is really just a warmed-over version of OCX, revamped for use inside of web browsers such as Microsoft's Internet Explorer which provides an alternative to Java. You'll also find ActiveX components in ActiveX Documents, running on ActiveX-enabled servers such as Microsoft Internet Information Server and Microsoft's upcoming Viper TP monitor. ActiveX components can also encapsulate Java applets.

Client/server developers embed ActiveX components inside ActiveX-enabled client/server development tools such as Visual Basic, PowerBuilder, and Delphi. The power of ActiveX is not its architecture and its links to COM, but the wide array of tools that support ActiveX. For example, you can create ActiveX components with any number of tools for any number of tools and applications. Tool support is the key to the acceptance of any standard.

The downside of ActiveX is its proprietary links to Microsoft and the Windows operating systems. Microsoft will address the industry's claim that ActiveX is a Microsoft proprietary standard by giving the standard away to an independent organization which will comprise member organizations, including Microsoft, to direct the future of ActiveX. Microsoft also plans to port ActiveX to other platforms. Microsoft is working with Metrowerks to support ActiveX on the Macintosh, and with Bristol and Mainsoft to support ActiveX on Unix platforms. The goal is clearly to provide a multiplatform component standard that competes directly with OpenDoc and Java.

Web-Enabled World

Distributed objects did not set the world on fire until the recent interest in the Web and Web applications. Fueling the fire is an announcement by Netscape that they would base their Internet infrastructure on CORBA's Internet Inter-ORB Protocol (IIOP). IIOP is the plumbing and wiring of CORBA 2.0.

If you listen to Netscape, IIOP is the new protocol for the Web, replacing HTTP as the standard method of Web communications. With over 20 million Netscape browsers in use today, Netscape brings life to an almost nonexistent distributed objects marketplace. IIOP allows ORBs that reside on a client running inside a browser to communicate with any other CORBA-compliant object running on the intranet or Internet.

ORB vendors such as Visigenic are creating CORBA-compliant ORBs specifically for the Web. Visigenic licensed their VisiBroker Java-enabled ORB to Netscape. With the release of Netscape Communicator (formally Navigator) 4.0, millions of Web users will finally understand the power of distributed objects. Or, it could be so much computerized snake oil.

DCOM and Microsoft are taking the same route, but are a bit behind CORBA and Netscape. In May 1996, Microsoft announced the publication of a document that describes ActiveX's answer to IIOP. Using a DCOM-based binary network protocol, Microsoft hopes to link all ActiveX objects up through the Internet and the intranet using a DCE-RPC-enabled communication protocol. This is all just talk for now, but by the end of 1997 we could see DCOM extend itself to the Web by riding on top of the popularity of ActiveX.

Ready for Prime Time?

The question on everyone's mind is: Are distributed objects ready for prime time client/server? The correct answer is "almost."

While distributed objects do provide an advanced architecture for distributed computing, there are limitations which make them not yet read for mission-critical applications. For example, most commercial ORBs are slow and inefficient, meaning you won't be able to pump the number of transactions through them that you need for high-end applications, and there are few recovery mechanisms built into the ORBs. Most of today's ORBs don't perform garbage collection functions, load-balancing, or concurrency control. They do not scale well.

In addition, ORBs are still largely tied to synchronous communications middleware. Missing is support for message-oriented middleware that can operate asynchronously. What's more, the server code is not as portable as it should be. These issues are true for both DCOM and CORBA-based ORBs.

The new generation of distributed objects are supposed to fix all these problems. But products that use these products are slow to appear. The best hope for distributed objects is the Web. As hype drives legions to the Web, they are demanding new, more advanced means to deploy applications. Distributed objects will shine on the Web, and that could be the break we're waiting for.

Appendix

Author Bibliographies

Scott Ambler   is a Senior Object Consultant with Mark Winter & Associates (WWW. MarkWinter.Com) based in Toronto, Canada. He has worked with OO technology since 1990 in various roles: Business Architect, System Analyst, System Designer, Smalltalk programmer, and C++ programmer. He has also been active in education and training as both a formal trainer and as an object mentor. Scott has a Master of Information Science and a Bachelor of Computer Science from the University of Toronto. He is a contributing editor with *Software Development*, writes a column for *Computing Canada*, and has had feature articles appear in *Object Magazine, Micro-Focus Visual Object COBOL Developer's Journal*, and *Client/Server Computing*. He can be reached via e-mail at: ambler@hookup.net and you can visit his personal web site: http://WWW.AmbySoft.Com.

Dick Berry   is a Senior Technical Staff Member in the HCI Architecture and Design group at IBM's Austin, Texas, development lab. He was the lead architect for three generations of IBM's Common User Access, a user interface style widely used by Windows and OS/2 applications. He was also a lead designer of the Workplace UI model, an object-oriented user interface implemented in IBM's OS/2 Workplace Shell. He was recently a guest author in the book *Objects for OS/2*.

Gregory Bumgardner is a senior software developer at Rogue Wave Software. He is the technical lead for Rogue Wave's Threads.h++ library. Prior to joining Rogue Wave in 1994, Greg spent 10 years in the aerospace industry and two years in the computer gaming industry where he has gained extensive experience building high-performance and concurrent applications for command and control, simulation, 3-D graphics, and radar signal processing.

Marco Cantù is a freelance writer and consultant, based in Italy. He has written programming books on both C++ (*Borland C++ 4*, Random House) and Delphi (*Mastering Delphi 3*, Sybex). He contributes to several magazines, enjoys speaking at conferences, and teaches Delphi seminars worldwide. You can reach him at 100273.2610@compuserve.com or http://ourworld.compuserve.com/homepages/marcocantu

David Carter serves as the deputy chief of the Collaborative Engineering Management office. He assists the chief in the day-to-day operations of the center which includes the conducting of various process improvements, planning sessions, training, baseline, activity based cost, alternative, simulation, and economic analysis workshops. He is regarded as a leading expert in the functional and business process engineering field.

William Dodson is a manager in the Software Quality Service practice of Boston, Massachusetts, office of Coopers and Lybrand, L.L.P., an international consultancy. Since 1988 Mr. Dodson has facilitated the success of IS enterprise projects across a variety of industries.

Jocelyn Garner is a software design engineer for the Microsoft Foundation Class Library that ships with Microsoft's Visual C++ product. Her specialty is database technology. Ms. Garner has presented Visual C++ and MFC to audiences throughout the USA and a dozen other countries. Jocelyn is also an experienced instructor and writer, and is committed to helping developers become more productive by explaining the principles of software development in plain language.

Ellen Gottesdiener is President of EBG Consulting, Inc., a facilitation, training, and consulting company. She provides facilitation services to business and technology customers and conducts training workshops on modeling techniques. Ellen has authored numerous articles and contributed to several books. You can e-mail Ellen at 73201.3153@compuserve.com or visit her web site at http://ourworld.compuserve.com/homepages/EBG_Ellen_Gottesdiener.

Cecilia Haskins is vice president of Reich Technologies, Corporation. Her career spans over two decades and includes programming, design, and analysis work for the Fortune 100. She currently specializes in the challenge of creating precise requirements specifications.

Cay Horstmann is associate professor for computer science at San Jose State University. He is author of six books on object-oriented design, C++, and Java, published by John Wiley & Sons. He is a contributor to C++ Report and Java Report, and frequently speaks at conferences such as Software Development, JavaWorld, and the Borland Developers Conference. His consulting company, Horstmann Software, advises clients on internet programming and electronic commerce.

Scott Isensee is a user interface architect with IBM in Austin, Texas where he works on advanced user interface design architecture, guidelines, and methodologies. He was user interface team leader for the Common Desktop Environment (CDE). Scott is a member of ANSI and ISO committees writing software user interface and usability standards. He holds master's degrees in computer science and industrial psychology. He is also a Certified Professional Ergonomist (CPE). Scott is an author of the recent book *The Art of Rapid Prototyping*.

Normal Kerth is a recognized expert in object-oriented methodologies. He is a leader in the new field of extending object-oriented development through patterns. He is the author of Caterpillar's Fate, and was coeditor of Pattern Languages on Program design, Vol. 2. He has a decade of engineering experience with Tektronix, and has over 25 years of experience in front of students and computer professionals. He is a member of the Weinberg & Weinberg faculty, and has taught PSL for over five years.

David Linthicum is a senior manager with AT&T Solution's System Integration Practice in Vienna, VA. Dave has consulted for dozens of major corporations engaged in systems analysis, design, and development, concentrating on complex distributed systems. In addition, Dave is the author of over 200 articles that have appeared in major computer related publications. Dave has also authored or coauthored six books on software development, and is working on his seventh book forthcoming from John Wiley and Sons. Dave writes the "Application Architect" column that appears monthly in Miller Freeman's DBMS magazine and he speaks at technical conferences throughout the United States.

Stephen Mellor   us best known for his contribution to the development of object-oriented analysis and to the Ward-Mellor modeling technique. He is currently vice president of Project Technology, Inc., where he serves as instructor for Project Technology's courses on information modeling, object-oriented analysis, and system design. He is the coauthor, with Sally Schlaer of Object-Oriented Systems Analysis: Modeling the World in Data, Object Lifecycles: Modeling the World in States, and with Paul Ward of Structured Development for Real-Time Systems.

John Mullaly   is a user interface architect and designer with IBM's advanced human-computer interaction group in Austin, Texas. He joined IBM in 1987 as a computer graphics specialist, and has been working in the field of HCI since 1992. He holds a bachelor of science degree from the New York Institute of Technology, where he studied math, art, and computer science.

Dave Roberts   is a Senior Software Designer working in IBM's HCI Strategy and Design group in Warwick, UK. Dave has been with IBM since 1974. He has worked in many areas of computer development and support, including hardware design, systems support, and the design of OS/2 Presentation Manager. Since 1986 he has worked on user interface architecture topics including all versions of CUA. He was a principal architect of the 1992 version of CUA.

Ken Rudin   is a managing director of Emergent Corporation, an independent consulting firm dedicated to helping business design and implement scalable IT solutions. Ken's involvement with scalable systems began in 1988 when he became director of Oracle Corporation's Parallel Systems Division. Ken has helped implement numerous commercial parallel processing systems, and has published numerous articles on designing and implementing scalable solutions.

George Shepherd   currently splits his time between three jobs. He develops mapping and terrain software for Orbital Sciences Corporation, teaches DevelopMentor's MFC/OLE and Holistic OLE classes, and writes the "Pointers and Persiflage" column for Windows Tech Journal. He also coauthors Dr. Dobb's Journal's "Undocumented MFC" column with Scot Wingo. He and Scot wrote MFC Internals.

Karl Wiegers   is a software process engineer in a large product software division at Eastman Kodak Company in Rochester, New York. During his 17 hears at Kodak, he has also held assignments as a photographic research scientist, software applications developer, software manager, and software quality engineer. Karl holds a Ph.D. degree in organic chemistry from the University of Illinois. Karl is the author of Creating a Software Engineering Culture (Dorset House, 1996) and over 100 articles on many aspects of computing, chemistry, and military history. He is a frequent speaker at software conferences and professional society meetings.